STEPS MATHEMATICS

TEACHER'S HANDBOOK

4a

Series Editor
ANNE WOODMAN

Co-Editor
PAUL HARLING

Consultant Editor
ERIC ALBANY

STEPS Teacher's Handbook 4a

ISBN 0 00 313837 2

Published 1994 by Collins Educational
(an imprint of HarperCollins*Publishers*)
77-85 Fulham Palace Road
Hammersmith
London W6 8JB

© HarperCollins Publishers 1994
The authors assert the moral right to be identified as authors of this work.

All rights reserved. No part of this publication may be reproduced, stored in a retrieval system, or transmitted in any form by any means – electronic, mechanical, photocopying, recording or otherwise – without the prior permission of the publisher.

Illustrations: Kathy Baxendale, Jean de Lemos, Jenny Mumford, Julia Osorno, Archie Plumb and Jane Taylor
Photographs: Martyn Chillmaid
Design and setting: Eric Drewery

Printed in Great Britain by Scotprint, Musselburgh

Acknowledgement
We should like to thank NES Arnold for lending equipment for photographs and artists' reference.

CONTENTS

STEPS Structure 8
The STEPS Team 10
Developing STEPS 11

■ SECTION ONE   How to use STEPS
STEPS 4a Materials 14
Looking at a Step 16
Assessment 20

■ SECTION TWO   The STEPS

Step No. & Title	Objectives	
1. Place value (1)	a Read, write and order numbers to 10 000 at least b Understand the effect of multiplying whole numbers by ten c Recognise whole numbers > 1000 divisible by ten d Approximate numbers > 1000 to the nearest 10 or 100	27
2. Angles	a Recognise and make acute, obtuse and reflex angles b Recognise perpendicular lines and planes	39
3. Multiplication patterns (1)	a Know and apply facts in the x 8 and 8 x tables b Understand the relationships between multiples of two, four and eight c Test simple related statements or generalisations	47
4. Time	a Relate times shown on the 24-hour clock to everyday events b Convert 24-hour times to and from 12-hour times	55
5. Addition (1)	a Add mentally at least three one-digit numbers b Add mentally a one-digit number to a two-digit number c Apply knowledge of these facts to solve problems	63
6. Bar-line graphs	a Construct bar-line graphs b Read and interpret bar-line graphs using different scales to represent frequencies	69
7. Subtraction (1)	a Subtract mentally at least two single-digit numbers from 20 b Subtract mentally a one-digit number from a two-digit number c Solve problems or describe situations from which such subtractions might have arisen	77

Step No. & Title	Objectives	
8. 2-D shape (1)	a Know and use properties associated with triangles b Know and use language associated with triangles c Construct triangles from given information d Make generalisations or test statements about triangles	83
9. Percentages	a Understand and use simple percentages to describe situations b Know that a half, a quarter, three-quarters and multiples of a tenth can be expressed in different ways	91
10. Length	a Measure in millimetres with reasonable accuracy b Estimate or approximate to the nearest centimetre c Solve problems involving kilometres d Appreciate the relationships between metric units of length and know when it is sensible to use these units e Record lengths using numbers with up to one decimal place	99
11. Addition (2)	a Add a one-, two- or three-digit number to a three-digit number without a calculator or apparatus (totals ≤ 999) b Choose methods to solve problems methodically c Estimate or approximate answers d Start to add numbers with totals > 1000	107
12. 3-D shape	a Construct tetrahedra, cuboids or cubes at least from given information or from provided nets b Use or interpret language relating to 3-D shapes c Revise the properties of other familiar 3-D shapes	117
13. Subtraction (2)	a Subtract a one-, two- or three-digit number from a three-digit number without a calculator or apparatus b Choose methods to solve problems methodically c Estimate or approximate answers	125
14. Co-ordinates	a Read and interpret co-ordinates in the first quadrant b Join co-ordinates in order to draw simple shapes	135
15. Area & Perimeter	a Construct simple 2-D shapes using data related to area or perimeter b Measure, compare and order areas using the square centimetre or other appropriate units of area c Test statements about areas or perimeters d Compare the square millimetre, centimetre, decimetre and metre	143
16. Weight	a Make sensible estimates in relation to weight b Solve practical and written problems involving weight c Record weights appropriately	151
17. Decimal fractions	a Understand and use decimal fractions to two decimal places in numbers up to ten b Interpret a calculator display to two decimal places c Start to add or subtract numbers to two places of decimals	159

Step No. & Title	Objectives	
18. Volume & Capacity (1)	**a** Estimate, measure and record volumes of 3-D shapes by counting centimetre cubes **b** Estimate, measure and record approximate capacities of small boxes by counting centimetre cubes	169
19. Multiplication patterns (2)	**a** Know and apply facts in the × 6 or 6 × tables **b** Know and apply facts in the × 9 or 9 × tables **c** Understand simple relationships between multiples of 3, 6 and 9 **d** Test simple related statements or make generalisations	177
20. Rotation	**a** Create patterns with rotational symmetry or rotate shapes systematically from given information **b** Choose the materials and mathematics to test polygons for rotational symmetry **c** Use or interpret language related to rotation	185
21. Place value (2)	**a** Read, write and order numbers to 100 000 at least **b** Understand the positional relationship between the digits **c** Relate numbers of this magnitude to some real-life examples	193
22. Probability	**a** Use a probability scale marked 0, $\frac{1}{2}$, 1 to estimate and compare likelihood **b** Make and test predictions or statements related to simple experiments **c** Start to give and justify estimates of probability	203
23. Division (1)	**a** Solve division problems related to facts within the multiplication tables or suggest a situation from which a division expression might have arisen **b** Know division facts related to the × 6, × 8 or × 9 tables by quick recall **c** Start to interpret remainders shown on the calculator	211
24. Money	**a** Extend experience of reading, writing and ordering amounts of money **b** Develop written methods to solve simple problems related to money, using all four operations **c** Use and interpret a calculator in the context of money	219
25. Translation	**a** Translate points or shapes a specified distance or in a given direction **b** Select the materials and mathematics to create simple patterns by translation and plan work methodically **c** Use or interpret language associated with translation	229
26. Time (2)	**a** Read and interpret 12- and 24-hour timetables **b** Estimate and measure duration in seconds **c** Extend awareness of the use and interpretation of calendars	235

Step No. & Title	Objectives	
27. Multiplication	a Know facts in the x 7 or 7 x tables b Multiply two-digit numbers by a one-digit number with products not exceeding 300 c Solve multiplication problems without or with a calculator and consider the reasonableness of the answer	243
28. 2-D shape (2)	a Know and use properties associated with quadrilaterals b Construct quadrilaterals from given information c Make simple generalisations or test statements	253
29. Functions	a Interpret function machines with more than one operation b Use function machines to investigate multiplication as the inverse of division c Explain how function machines operate, using associated terms, or how input and output numbers are related	263
30. Division (2)	a Know and apply division facts related to the x 7 table b Use pencil-and-paper methods to solve division problems related to tables facts, without and with remainders c Develop pencil-and-paper methods to divide two-digit numbers by one-digit numbers with answers > 10 d Estimate or consider the reasonableness of answers, calculated without or with a calculator	271
31. Reflection	a Create and analyse shapes and patterns with two (or more) axes of reflective symmetry b Use axes of symmetry as an aid to classification of 2-D shapes	279
32. Logic	a Use decision trees or Venn diagrams to represent the results of classification, using three criteria b Identify the attributes of objects within the regions of sorting diagrams	287
33. Tessellation	a Continue or construct tessellations from given information b Test statements, hypothesise or make simple generalisations about the tessellating properties of triangles c Select the materials or mathematics to create a tessellation	295
34. Scale	a Revise measurement in millimetres and centimetres and co-ordinates in the first quadrant b Use halving and doubling to explore scale c Make simple hypotheses or generalisations	303
35. Volume & Capacity (2)	a Make sensible estimates in relation to capacity b Solve problems related to capacity c Record appropriately	311

Step No. & Title	Objectives	
36. Common fractions	**a** Explore practically the ordering and equivalence of fractions **b** Estimate and calculate simple fractions **c** Add and subtract simple fractions related to practical situations	317
37. Line graphs	**a** Start to construct line graphs **b** Read and interpret line graphs	327
38. Location	**a** Use and interpret instructions related to angle (direction) and distance	333

■ SECTION THREE Supporting information

Calculators 340
Summary of Equipment and Suppliers' Details 342

Particular thanks to the children and teachers of Chadsway Junior School where the photographs in this handbook were taken.

STEPS STRUCTURE

The structure of STEPS is simple and is shown in the diagram opposite. At the heart of the scheme is a series of **Teacher's Handbooks** with a consistent format. Each Handbook contains about 40 Steps (teaching units), which are cross-referenced to the Programmes of Study.

Each Step focuses on specific elements of the Programme of Study and can be organised to suit the needs of individual teachers and their classes.

Care has been taken to ensure that the Programme of Study for Using and Applying Mathematics is integrated throughout.

The seven Handbooks provide guidance on classroom management and the choice of learning activities, and suggest appropriate methods of assessment as an integral part of each Step.

There are four Handbooks to support the Programme of Study for Key Stage 1 (appropriate for pupils working at levels 1 to 3): STEPS 1, 2, 3a and 3b. There are six Handbooks to support the Programme of Study for Key Stage 2 (appropriate for pupils working at levels 2 to 5): STEPS 2, 3a, 3b, 4a, 4b and 5.

A variety of **pupils' materials** accompany the Teacher's Handbook at each Level. These are fully keyed and cross-referenced to the Steps in the Handbook to which they relate. The language level in these materials has been carefully monitored and care has been taken to ensure that pages are not overcrowded.

There are **Activity Cards** and **Activity Books** (expendable) or **Activity Masters** (photocopiable) to support STEPS 1 and STEPS 2. **Extra Activity Books** are also available for those who want additional practice materials. **Textbooks** are introduced from STEPS 3a.

For all Handbooks, photocopiable **Resource Masters** provide forecasting, planning and record sheets for the teacher, and activity pages and practice materials for the children.

FOR TEACHERS

Teacher's Handbooks
A4 loose-leaf files of approximately 350 full colour pages each.

FOR PUPILS

Activity Cards
(*STEPS 1 and 2*) each box contains 120 laminated, large (A4), full colour cards.

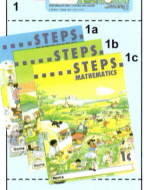

FOR PUPILS

Activity Books
(*STEPS 1 and 2*) and **Textbooks** (*STEPS 3a onwards*) in full colour throughout. Activity Books are available in packs of 10.

FOR PUPILS

Activity Masters
A4 photocopy masters as an alternative to the Activity Books. Use of colour identifies master copies.

FOR PUPILS & TEACHERS

Resource Masters
A4 photocopy masters. Use of colour identifies master copies.
Answer Books
Facsimile pages of pupils' books. Answers to questions are shown in colour.

SECTION TWO
THE STEPS

1. PLACE VALUE (1)

LEARNING CONTEXT

Contribution made by this Step

Children explore numbers up to 10 000 and just beyond, using structural apparatus and calculators to develop images of large numbers. They refine their ability to read, write and order such numbers, and practise the skills of approximation and rounding. Knowledge of the positional relationship between digits is refined through studying the effects of multiplying numbers by ten. Further activities in this area are included in Step 21.

Objectives

To enable children to:
a   Read, write and order numbers to 10 000 at least.
b   Understand the effect of multiplying whole numbers by ten.
c   Recognise whole numbers greater than 1000 divisible by ten.
d   Approximate numbers > 1000 to the nearest ten or 100.

Background

Everyday life seems to be full of large numbers and, if only for this reason, it is important that children develop accurate images of large numbers so that they can interpret them correctly. Such images can be introduced and strengthened by the use of structural apparatus, but regular oral, written and calculator-based exploration of four- and five- figure numbers also greatly enhances the children's ability to make sense of large numbers in a variety of contexts, such as measurement and money.

> **Mathematics in the National Curriculum**
>
> **Programme of Study: KS2**
> Pupils should be taught to:
> ■ read, write and order whole numbers, understanding that the position of a digit signifies its value; use their understanding of place value to develop methods of computation, to approximate numbers to the nearest 10 or 100, and to multiply and divide by powers of 10 when there are whole-number answers. (N 2.a)
> ■ understand and use the relationships between the four operations, including inverses. (N 3.f)
> ■ check results by different methods, including repeating the operations in a different order or using inverse operations; gain a sense of the size of a solution, and estimate and approximate solutions to problems. (N 4.c)
> ■ search for patterns in their results. (UA 4.b)
> ■ make general statements of their own, based on evidence they have produced. (UA 4.c)

THINKING AND TALKING MATHEMATICALLY

Starting points for discussion

Discuss the sizes of the populations of selected local communities.

Attendance at sports events, e.g. football matches, listed in national or local newspapers. *Which game had the highest/lowest attendance?*

> **Key language**
>
> units, longs, flats, squares, blocks, 'long-block', digit, value, column, exchange, larger, smaller, greater than, less than, roughly, approximately, round up (down), zero, place holder, ascending order, descending order, multiple, product

STEPS 4a

ACTIVITIES IN DETAIL

A   More thousands   C G P

Resources

School
Base 10 materials; place value boards; four-spike abacus

Scheme
Resource Master 1; Book 4a, pages 1 and 2

*In advance, make enough copies of RM 1 on card for each pair.

1 Talk about the everyday observation and use of numbers larger than 1000, such as distance running events (e.g. 5000 metres), dates (e.g. A.D. 1999), and measurement of weight in grams or capacity in millilitres.

2 The children make their own four-column place value boards. Show base 10 materials. Discuss previous activities (Handbook 3b:10) and give the children the opportunity to revise the images of numbers shown by the materials, and to build larger pieces, using combinations of smaller pieces.

 block 1000
 flat 100
 long 10   unit 1

3 Extend previous activities by asking children to represent, read and write several larger numbers (between 5000 and 9999), using base 10 materials placed on the boards. Include examples which need a zero to be used as a place-holder.

thousands (blocks)	hundreds (flats)	tens (longs)	ones (units)
5 blocks		2 longs	5 units
5	0	2	5

five thousand and twenty-five

4 Repeat, using a four-spike abacus to emphasise that the position of a digit indicates its value.

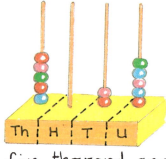

5 0 2 5
→ 5 units
→ 2 tens
→ 0 hundreds
→ 5 thousands

five thousand and twenty-five

5 Ask children, working in pairs, to cut up RM 1 to make the cards. They use the two sets of cards to generate pairs of four-digit numbers. They decide which number is the larger and produce a number sentence to match:

Encourage the children to show the two numbers on a place value board or an abacus, if necessary.

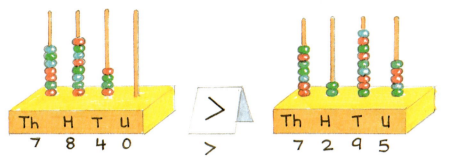

Book 4a, pages 1 and 2, provides further practice.

EXTENSION

- Use reference material (e.g. the *Guinness Book of Records*) to find and list examples of numbers between 1000 and 9999.

B Introducing 10 000   C G

1 Ask the children to use base 10 materials to illustrate 9990 on their place value boards. Ensure that everyone can read and write the number.

thousands (blocks)	hundreds (flats)	tens (longs)	ones (units)
9	9	9	0

Resources

School
Base 10 materials; place value boards; five-spike abacus

Scheme
Book 4a, page 3

2 Ask them to add units one at a time, saying and writing 9991, 9992 … 9999. Ask, *What happens if we add one more unit?*

3 The children do so, then exchange the ten units for a long, the resulting ten longs for another flat, the ten flats for another block, to give ten blocks in the fourth column.

4 Remind them that empty columns are marked with a zero as a place-holder, and that only single digits are allowed in a column. Therefore a new (fifth) column has to be created to hold the ten blocks (thousands). This is the 10 000 (ten thousands) column.

ten thousands ('long-block')	thousands (blocks)	hundreds (flats)	tens (longs)	ones (units)
1	0	0	0	0

5 Repeat using a five-spike abacus.

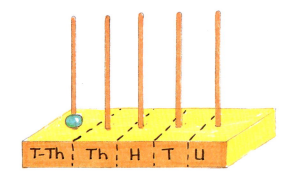

10 000

ten thousand

There is no piece for 10 000, but it can be thought of as a 'long-block' to emphasise its size relative to the other pieces.

6 Ensure that the children can read, write and say 10 000.

7 The process can also be shown on a calculator, using either:

(a) [9][9][9][0][+][1][+][1][+][1][+][1][+][1][+][1][+][1][+][1][+][1][+][1][=], or

(b) the constant for addition of one, i.e. [1][+][+][=][0],
followed by [9][9][9][0], then .

8 Encourage the children to carry on adding one, recording and saying aloud numbers beyond 10 000.

Further practice in reading, writing and ordering numbers to about 10 000 can be found on Book 4a, page 3.

C Patterns of hundreds   C G

Part 1: Counting on and back in hundreds

1 Ask the children to 'count on' orally in hundreds, from zero and then from other starting numbers, e.g. 800, 900, 1000, 1100.

2 Discuss the fact that, say, 1100 can be said as 'one thousand one hundred', or as 'eleven hundred'.

3 Choose various starting numbers and ask the children to 'count back' in hundreds, e.g. 2300, 2200, 2100, 2000, 1900.

Resources

School calculators

Scheme
Resource Masters 2 and 3

4 Explain how to use the constant function of the calculator to count on (or back) in hundreds (1 0 0 + + = 0, or 1 0 0 − − = 0, followed by the starting number, followed by = = = ...).

Part 2: Patterns and sequences of hundreds

1 Provide each pair with a copy of RM 2.

2 Ask the children to enter 100 and 1000 in the first and last squares on the top row and 9100 and 10 000 in the first and last squares in the bottom row.

3 Using pencil (to make changes if necessary), the children decide which numbers go in the empty cells.

4 Afterwards, discuss:
(a) how the four number clues helped them;
(b) patterns in the rows and columns;
(c) what number is, say, in the fourth row and fifth column (initially with the grid face up, then face down).

RM 3 provides individual practice.

100	200	300	400	500	600	700	800	900	1000
1100	1200	1300	1400	1500	1600	1700	1800	1900	2000
2100	2200	2300							
3100									
4100									
9100									10 000

D Rounding larger numbers   C G

Part 1: To the nearest ten

1 Revise rounding of small four-digit numbers to the nearest ten (Handbook 3b:10). Remind the children that this requires concentration on the tens column and adjustment of the number of units.

2 Use a four- or five-spike abacus and sections of a number line to demonstrate that the rules also apply to larger numbers.

Resources

School
Four- or five-spike abacus; number lines marked on the board

Scheme
Resource Master 4

Note that in the text 'units' and 'ones' are used interchangeably, but *in abbreviations* in pupils' materials 'U' is used in preference to 'O', to avoid confusion with zero.

Remind the children of the convention that numbers ending in five are rounded up.

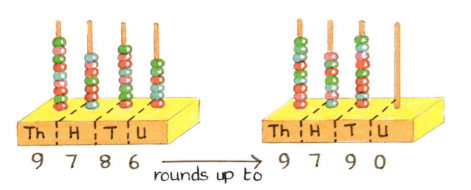

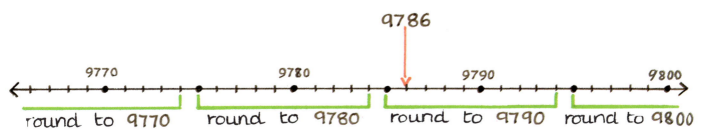

STEPS 4a

3 Say a selection of large four-digit numbers, including some just over 10 000. Ask the children to round up or down to the nearest ten, using apparatus or a number line if required.

Part 2: To the nearest 100

1 Again, revise rounding of small four-digit numbers to the nearest 100 (Handbook 3b:10). Explain that this requires concentration on the hundreds column with a rounding down if the tens and units columns contain 49 or less, and rounding up if they contain 50 or more.

2 Use a four- or five-spike abacus and sections of a number line to show that the rules apply to larger numbers.

> It is important that children begin to round numbers mentally as an aid to calculation, particularly as they start to operate without apparatus.

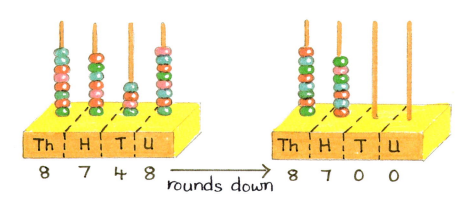

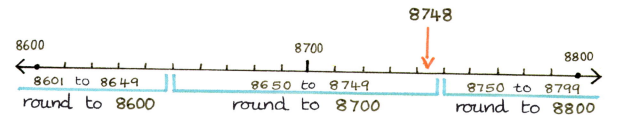

6 Give children the opportunity to practise rounding large four-digit numbers, including some just over 10 000, using apparatus or a number line if required.

Further practice can be found on RM 4.

E Multiplying and dividing by ten   C G

Part 1: Practising exchange

1 Revise orally the ten times (× 10) table and the sequence of counting in tens.

2 Use base 10 materials. Ask the children to choose either a unit (one), a long (ten) or a flat (100), then to collect ten of the chosen pieces and place them on the place value boards.

3 Remind them that ten of a piece requires:
– their exchange for one larger piece;
– its transfer into the next column to the left;
– the empty place being 'held' with a zero.

Resources

School
Base 10 materials; place value boards; four-spike abacus; calculators

Scheme
Resource Master 5

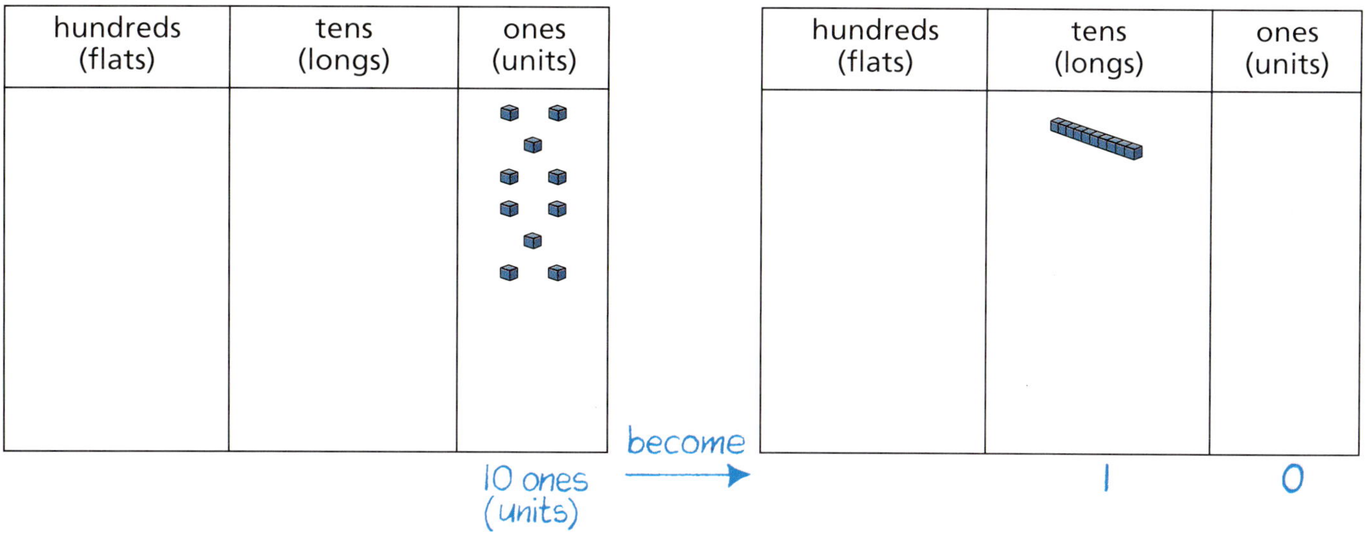

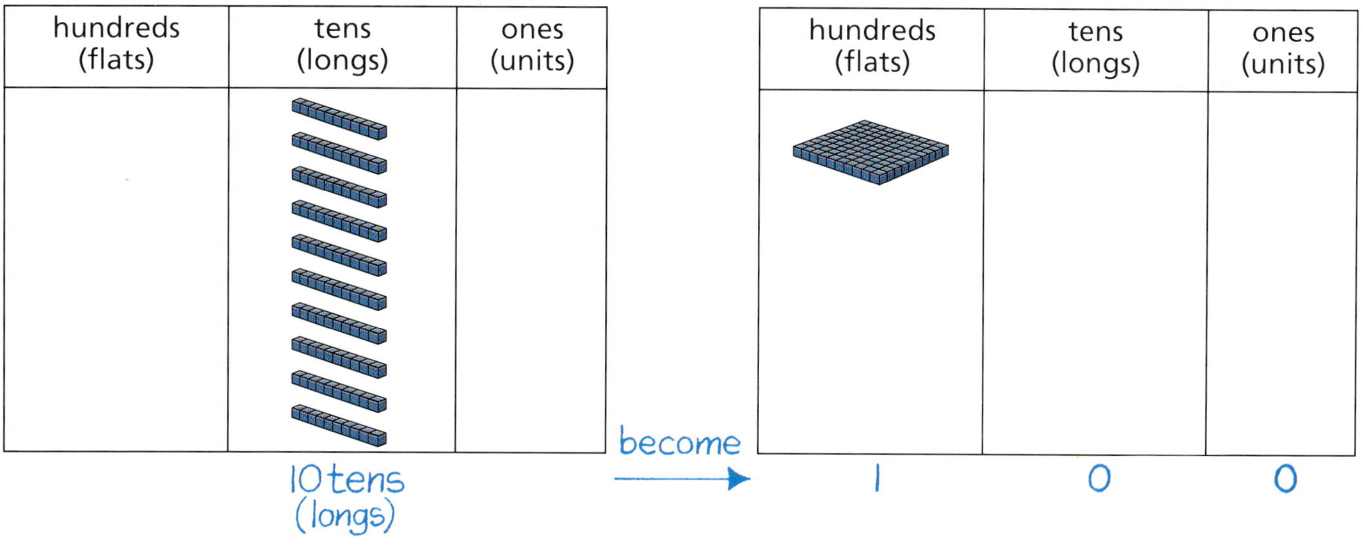

hundreds (flats)	tens (longs)	ones (units)
		(10 cubes shown)

become →

hundreds (flats)	tens (longs)	ones (units)
	1	0

10 ones (units)

hundreds (flats)	tens (longs)	ones (units)
	(10 longs shown)	

become →

hundreds (flats)	tens (longs)	ones (units)
1	0	0

10 tens (longs)

4 Show the exchange also on an abacus, and give children the opportunity to practise this, using various small starting numbers (limited by the number of units available).

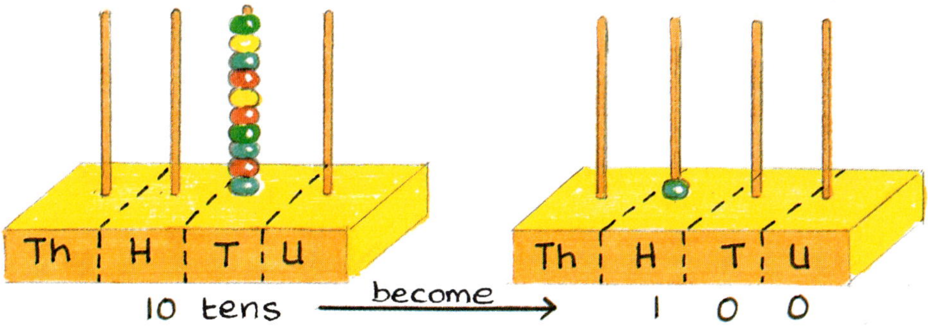

10 tens → become → 1 0 0

Part 2: Multiplying by ten

1 On the board write several simple ×10 multiplication calculations. For example:

```
    3         6         8        10
  ×10       ×10       ×10       ×10
  ───       ───       ───       ───
   30        60        80       100
```

STEPS 4a

2 Discuss the pattern of the answers, encouraging them to see that:
- each answer has a zero in the units position;
- each number being multiplied by ten is moved one column to the left, into a column with a value ten times larger.

3 Ask the children to use calculators to explore, and record, the results of multiplying various two- and three-digit numbers by ten. This can be done by asking them to enter the constant for multiplication by ten, then any starting number followed by = will multiply it by ten.

Press:	Display:
1 0 × × = 0	0.
3 5	35.
=	350.
1 2 4	124.
=	1240.

4 Discuss the results which emerge. Emphasise that the numbers being multiplied move one place (or column) to the left.

It is important to avoid such statements as 'When we multiply by ten we write the number and then add a zero at the end'.

Part 3: Divisible by ten?

1 Use the calculations already recorded in Part 2. Ask, *How can we tell if a number is exactly divisible by ten?*

2 Encourage the children to see, by looking at calculations, and using a calculator if desired, that any whole number which has a zero in the units column is exactly divisible by ten.

3 Ask them to check a further selection of numbers, recording them in two sets to emphasise the patterns.

Further practice is found on RM 5.

Exactly divisible by 10	Not exactly divisible by 10
50 210 160	25 2481
500 4880	637 4112

EXTENSION

■ The children use calculators to explore and record the results of multiplying any large number by ten.

F Assessment activity

*In advance, prepare about 20 cards showing random four-digit numbers (including some ending in 0, 5 and 50) and one card showing 10 000.

Part 1: Reading, writing and ordering numbers

1 Ask the child to choose one of the cards and to illustrate the number, using base 10 materials or an abacus.

2 Ask her/him to choose another card showing a larger/smaller number, and to explain why it is larger/smaller.

3 Ask the child to write the two numbers in digits and write > or < between them to make a true sentence, reading it aloud.

I Resources

School
Base 10 materials; five-spike abacus; about 20 number cards*

4 Ask the child to pick out the card showing 10 000.

Part 2: Nearest ten and 100

1 Pick three of the cards. Ask the child to round the numbers to the nearest ten and to explain why it was rounded up or down.

2 Repeat with a different set of cards, asking the child to round to the nearest 100.

Part 3: Multiples of ten

1 Tell the child to write a two-digit number. Ask him/her to write and say the number which is ten times larger.

2 Show about five of the cards, including one or more with a zero in the units column. Ask, *Which numbers can be divided exactly by ten?*

Assessment notes

Oral response	✔
Practical response	✔
Pictorial response	
Written response	✔

The child has:
correctly illustrated four-digit numbers using apparatus;
AND
correctly interpreted, read, written and rounded some numbers to 10 000;
AND
correctly multiplied a number by ten, using the 'quick' method;
AND
correctly recognised a number exactly divisible by ten.

STRENGTHENING ACTIVITIES

Place invaders

Try playing the game on Book 4a, page 1, to establish if the child knows the value of each digit in a four-digit number. Enter any four-digit number on the calculator and ask the child to 'knock out' the digits until zero is reached. For example:

3767 −   7 = 3760
3760 −   60 = 3700
3700 − 700 = 3000
3000 − 3000 =   0

Dominoes

Using a normal set of dominoes, how many different four-digit numbers can be made, read, said and recorded?

Note that placing a blank or zero on the left does not count as a four-digit number!

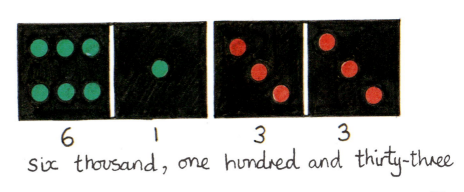

6   1   3   3
six thousand, one hundred and thirty-three

STEPS 4a

Evens to win

In this game for two players, the children use RM 2 as the board, and need a dice and two counters.

- ❏ Take turns to roll the dice. If an even number is rolled, move the counter on five hundreds.
- ❏ If an odd number is rolled, move the counter back one hundred.
- ❏ The first to pass 10 000 is the winner.

CHALLENGING ACTIVITIES

Palindromic numbers

Investigate how many palindromic four-digit numbers there are between 1001 and 9999. Can they be recorded in a pattern?

1001	2002	3003	...	9009
1111	2112	3113	...	9119
1221	2222	3223	...	9229

....

| 1991 | 2992 | 3993 | ... | 9999 |

Cross-numbers

Design a cross-number puzzle in which the clues are word forms of four-digit numbers, and the answers are in digits placed appropriately on the grid.

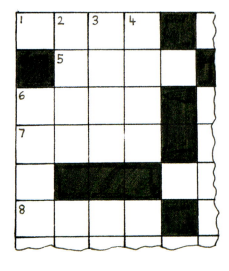

Clues

Across
1. Three thousand, eight hundred and twenty-four
5. Six thousand and one
6. ......
7. ......
8. ......

Down
2. Eight thousand, six hundred
3. Two thousand and ten
4. Four thousand and ninety-nine
5. ......

HOME/SCHOOL PROJECTS

Ask the children to collect, and bring to school, examples of four- and five-digit numbers found on everyday documents or packages. The numbers should then be grouped and ordered in a variety of ways and the results displayed.

IDEAS BOARD

■ Grid games

These games can be played by the whole class, a group or pair of children. They use a pack of playing cards with the tens and picture cards removed.

❏ By shuffling the pack and turning over cards, a sequence of four 'random' digits is made.
❏ The random digits are read out one at a time and the children record them, as they are turned over and read, in the cells of a grid of four squares in a row.
❏ Once the number has been written, it cannot be repositioned.
❏ Variations include:
  (a) Winners make the largest/smallest (odd, even) number to fit in the grid:

  | 1 | 5 | 6 | 2 |

  (b) Winners make true sentences of these kinds:

  ▢▢▢▢ > ▢▢▢▢

  or ▢▢▢▢ < ▢▢▢▢

  (c) Winners make true sentences of these kinds:

  ▢▢▢▢ > ▢▢▢▢ > ▢▢▢▢

  or ▢▢▢▢ < ▢▢▢▢ < ▢▢▢▢

  (d) Winners make true sentences of this kind:

  ▢▢▢▢ < ▢▢▢▢ > ▢▢▢▢

■ Adders

Key a four-digit number into the calculator. Add to each column in turn to make the number up to 10 000. For example:

6 5 8 2 + 8 = 6590.
6 5 9 0 + 1 0 = 6600.
6 6 0 0 + 4 0 0 = 7000.
7 0 0 0 + 3 0 0 0 = 10 000.

SUPPORT MATERIALS

Teaching aids
100-Square Stamp (Taskmaster)
Place Value Rubber Stamps (Taskmaster)
Multibase System (Hope Education, NES Arnold)
100 Number Board (Hope Education)
Four-Spike Abacus (Hope Education)
5-Hooped Abacus (NES Arnold)
5-Row Abacus (NES Arnold)

Teachers' reference materials
Lines of Development in Primary Mathematics, Mary Deboys and Eunice Pitt (Blackstaff Press)
Maths Plus: Adding and Subtracting, 1 and 2, Paul Harling (Ward Lock Educational)
Calculated To Please: Calculator Activities for the National Curriculum, Paul Harling (Collins Educational)

Software
Boxes from *MicroSMILE 1* (ILECC)
Find Me and *Size Game* (MEP Primary Maths)
Counters from *Micros in the Primary Classroom* (Longman)
Line Up, *Spots* and *Make 37* from *Number Games*, Anita Straker (ESM)
Cranky (ESM)
Ergo (MEP Microprimer)
Monty (ATM)
Target from *Games Activities and Investigations in the Primary Classroom*, Anita Straker (Capital Media)

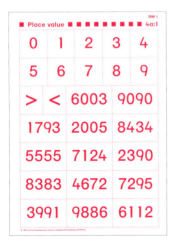

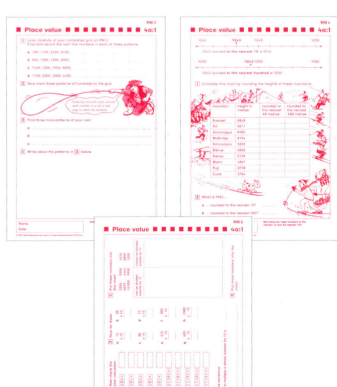

2. ANGLES

LEARNING CONTEXT

Contribution made by this Step

Children make, recognise and name different types of angle and recognise perpendicular lines and planes.

Objectives

To enable children to:
a Recognise and make acute, obtuse and reflex angles.
b Recognise perpendicular lines and planes.

Background

From earlier activities, children will be familiar with right angles, half right angles and straight angles and how they are related to fractions of a whole turn and to compass points. This Step provides revision of right angles leading to recognition of perpendicular lines and planes in 2-D and 3-D shapes and in the environment.

Other activities include ordering, comparing and matching angles by size, and using the terms acute, obtuse and reflex.

As in STEPS 3a and 3b it is recommended that children experience both the dynamic and static aspects of angles. This will help to provide the foundation of understanding necessary before measurement in degrees introduced in STEPS 4b.

> **Mathematics in the National Curriculum**
>
> **Programme of Study: KS2**
> Pupils should be taught to:
> ■ use right angles, fractions of a turn and, later, degrees, to measure rotation, and use the associated language. (SSM 3.c)
> ■ select and use the appropriate mathematics and materials. (UA 2.a)

THINKING AND TALKING MATHEMATICALLY

Starting points for discussion

Display Geostrips (or similar) with fasteners. Loosely join two strips. Move them to show different sharp and blunt angles to show rotation and static angles.

Display folded paper and cut-out right angles, and a (commercial or homemade) rotagram. Encourage experimentation, testing angles in the classroom.

Show 2-D and 3-D shapes. *Can you show me sharp/blunt angles?*

> **Key language**
>
> turn, angle, rotate, rotation, right angle, acute, obtuse, straight angle, reflex, horizontal, vertical, perpendicular, parallel, arms of an angle, sectors of a circle

STEPS 4a

ACTIVITIES IN DETAIL

A Perpendicular lines and planes C G

Resources

School
Scrap paper for making right-angle measures; rulers; sets of 2-D and 3-D shapes; card for word cards*

Scheme
Book 4a, page 4

*In advance prepare three word cards showing: right angle, perpendicular and parallel.

1 Remind the children how to make a right-angle measure by folding a scrap or circle of paper twice. An 'angle eater' can also be made to check convex or external angles.

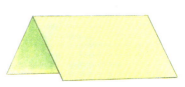 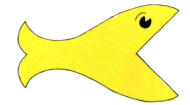

2 Ask the children to find examples of convex and concave right angles in the classroom, including both 2-D and 3-D shapes.

3 Using the word card, explain that 'perpendicular' means 'at right angles to' and discuss examples the children have found. Make sure that you include perpendicular lines and planes which are not horizontal and/or vertical.

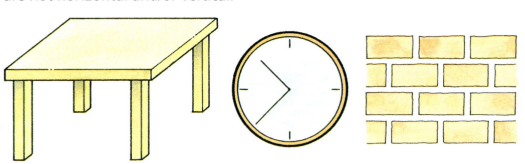 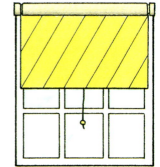

4 Revise the recognition of parallel lines before discussing Book 4a, page 4 where the children are asked to find perpendicular and parallel lines.

EXTENSION

■ The children can draw different shapes or patterns with perpendicular lines on squared paper or using set squares.

B Acute and obtuse angles C I

Resources

School
Geostrips (or similar) with fasteners or card strips and fasteners; right-angle measures (made in Activity A); card for word cards*

Scheme
Book 4a, page 5

*For this activity each child needs two strips loosely joined by a fastener. Use Geostrips or strips from construction material such as Meccano or BrioMec. Alternatively cut card strips, approximately 2 cm wide and of different lengths (say 5 cm to 20 cm) with holes punched near each end. Prepare a set of word cards, showing: sharp/acute angle, right angle, blunt/obtuse angle.

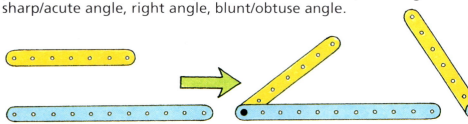

STEPS 4a

1 Ask each child to use two connected strips to show a right angle. Use the folded paper right-angle measure to check the angle.

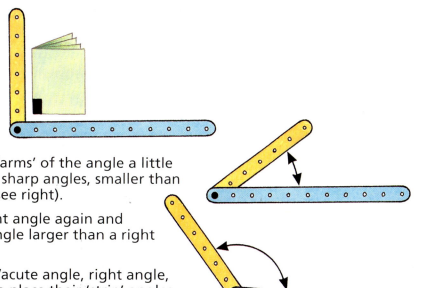

2 Suggest that the children close the 'arms' of the angle a little to make a sharp angle. Explain that all sharp angles, smaller than a right angle, are called acute angles (see right).

3 Next ask the children to make a right angle again and then open the arms to make a blunt angle larger than a right angle – an obtuse angle (see right).

4 Display the set of word cards: sharp/acute angle, right angle, blunt/obtuse angle. Ask the children to place their 'strip' angles in the appropriate set.

5 Discuss Book 4a, page 5 where the children need to recognise acute, right and obtuse angles in circle sectors and in familiar 2-D shapes. You may wish to demonstrate and revise drawing shapes using a pencil and ruler before the children attempt task 3.

EXTENSION

■ Cut several circles into four sectors of different sizes. Arrange the sectors in angle sets: acute, right and obtuse. Challenge the children to re-make whole circles.

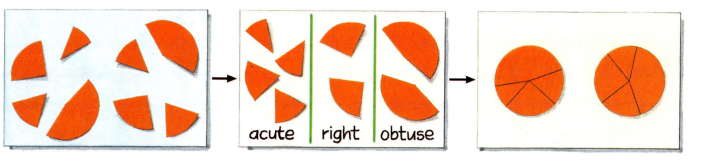

C Comparing angles   C G P I

Part 1: Ordering angles

1 Introduce the angle ordering activity on RMs 6 and 7. Make sure the children can compare two angles to decide which is larger.

2 Afterwards, discuss which angles are acute and which obtuse.

Part 2: Turns as angles

1 Using a clockface, demonstrate a $\frac{1}{4}$ turn, $\frac{1}{2}$ turn and whole turn. Ask different children to make these turns clockwise and anticlockwise. Can they recognise that acute angles are all less than a $\frac{1}{4}$ turn? … that obtuse angles are larger than a $\frac{1}{4}$ turn but less than a $\frac{1}{2}$ turn?

Resources

School
Scissors; glue; clockface

Scheme
Resource Masters 6 and 7

Encourage careful cutting and sticking.

STEPS 4a

D Introducing reflex angles   C G P

1 Introduce the term 'reflex' for angles between a $\frac{1}{2}$ turn and a whole turn, i.e. larger than two right angles or a straight angle. Show examples of reflex angles. On the clockface practise turning through reflex angles, e.g. $\frac{3}{4}$ turn.

2 Ask pairs or small groups of children to use the cards on RMs 8 and 9 to make sentences about angles. For example:

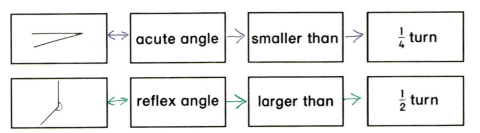

Resources

School
Clockface

Scheme
Resource Masters 8 and 9

EXTENSION

■ Using the eight points of the compass, describe examples of acute, right, obtuse and reflex angles. For example:

  from N to SE clockwise   – obtuse angle
  from SW to NW clockwise – right angle
  from S to NE clockwise   – reflex angle.

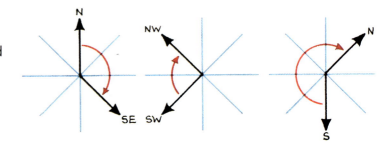

E Matching angles   G P I

*In this activity, children need some means to compare sizes of angles without cutting out. To make angle 'gauges' and home-made rotagrams, provide either tracing paper or small acetate sheets and suitable pens.

1 Discuss RM 10. Ask the children how angles could be compared without cutting them out.

2 Demonstrate how to make an angle gauge to place on other angles for comparison (**a**); or a home-made rotagram (**b**) (see opposite).

Resources

School
Materials for making an angle 'gauges' and rotagrams*; commercial rotagrams

Scheme
Resource Master 10

a

42   STEPS 4a

b

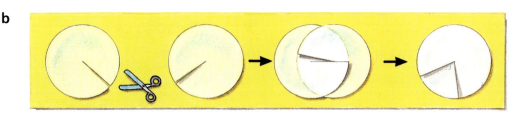

3 Make sure the children appreciate which angles are to be compared on the Resource Master. Can they, for example, recognise the reflex angles?

4 When the matching pairs have been identified, ask the children to check their sheet with a friend's.

EXTENSION

■ Draw round different shapes from a 2-D shape set. Using an angle gauge, can the children find and mark angles of the same size?

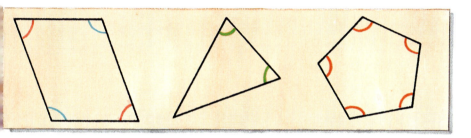

F Angle card games

Resources
Scheme
Resource Masters 8 and 9*

*If possible, copy or mount RMs 8 and 9 onto card and cut up. You may need multiple copies of these RMs, depending on the size of the groups playing together. These angle cards can be used in different games:

1 *Sorting* The children practise sorting the angle cards into acute, right, obtuse and reflex angles.

2 *Matching* Angle cards are spread face down and children take turns to reveal two cards. If they have a pair of angles from the same 'family' (e.g. acute) they keep the cards. Later you can specify that pairs of cards must have angles of exactly the same size. Any dispute must be resolved by comparing angles by the techniques used in Activity **E**.

3 *Snap* (in threes) Each child is dealt the same number of angle cards and places one face up in turn. When any two cards are of the same angle family the child calls *Snap* and says the family name. If correct she/he keeps the cards. One variation would be to include the cards with angle family names.

4 *Angle rummy* Children play a rummy-type game aiming to collect three-card sets of angle families.

5 *Find a shape* A child takes an angle card and has to find a shape from a set of 2-D shapes which has an angle of approximately the same size. Later the children could take two angle cards and find one shape containing both angles.

G Assessment activity · I

1 Show the angles on RM 8 and RM 9. Ask the child to point to:
- an acute angle;
- a right angle;
- an obtuse angle;
- a reflex angle.

2 Ask the child to say why the example was chosen.

3 Repeat, using 2-D shapes.

4 Show the 3-D shapes. Ask the child to show examples of each of the types of angle.

5 Ask the child to show you a few classroom examples of perpendicular lines and perpendicular planes.

Resources

School
Selection of 2-D and 3-D shapes; a folded paper right angle; an angle measure

Scheme
Resource Masters 8 and 9

Assessment notes

Oral response	✔
Practical response	✔
Pictorial response	
Written response	

The child has:
recognised and made examples of acute, obtuse and reflex angles;
AND
recognised some examples of perpendicular lines and planes.

STRENGTHENING ACTIVITIES

Perpendicular

Place a Geostrip (or similar) on the table. Ask a child to place other strips at right angles to your strip so that they are perpendicular. Revise recognition of parallel lines in the same way.

Ordering

Using some angle cards on RMs 8 and 9, ask the child to order the angles in size by sight and then check them using an angle gauge (see Activity **E**).

Circles

Ask the child to fold a circle into quarters, then to cut along the diameter and rule and cut a radius not along the right angle fold line. This makes a sector with an acute angle and a sector with an obtuse angle.

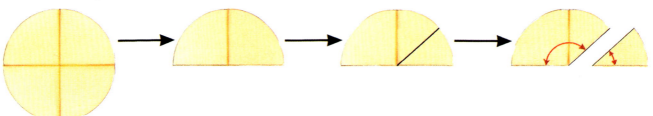

Discuss why you always have an obtuse angle if you cut an acute angle from a semicircle.

CHALLENGING ACTIVITIES

Growing

On squared paper, the children draw simple shapes where the lengths of sides increase but the angle sizes remain the same.

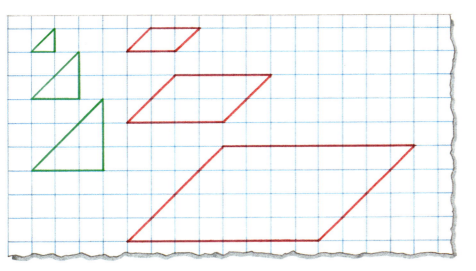

Distortions

The children make shapes with four Geostrips (or similar) and investigate what happens to sides and angle sizes when the shapes are distorted. For example:

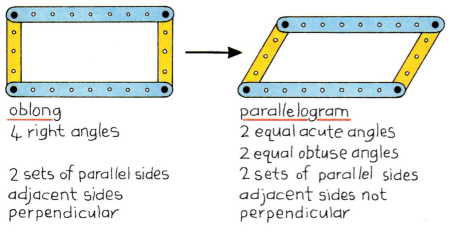

oblong
4 right angles

2 sets of parallel sides
adjacent sides
perpendicular

parallelogram
2 equal acute angles
2 equal obtuse angles
2 sets of parallel sides
adjacent sides not
perpendicular

HOME/SCHOOL PROJECTS

- At home, find pictures or objects which show different angle sizes. If possible, bring them to school to add to the display.
- List five objects in your home which would not work if certain parts were not perpendicular, e.g. a door would not close.

STEPS 4a

IDEAS BOARD

- **Typical projects**
  Structures, Shape, Pattern

- **Geography**
  Link work on compass directions in the National Curriculum for geography.

- **Science**
  Investigate friction at different gradients.

- **Technology**
  Use a spirit-level to check for horizontals and verticals. Make constructions with perpendicular parts.

- **P.E.**
  Link work on turning and angles in dance/movement/games.

- **Geoboards**
  Investigate different angles on a 3 by 3 Geoboard. Record on lattice paper.

- **Angles around us**
  Build up a display of pictures and objects in which different sizes of angles can be seen. Make sets of acute, obtuse and reflex angles.

- **Angle of vision**
  Investigate the eyesight of different creatures. Why do some animals have eyes on either side of the head? How far can an owl turn its head to see? How can you measure your own angle of vision?

- **LOGO**
  Investigate the numbers which are required when turning to produce acute, obtuse and reflex angles of turn.

SUPPORT MATERIALS

Teaching aids
Geostrips (NES Arnold)
Rotagrams (NES Arnold)
Rotagrams Project Pack (Dime) (NES Arnold)
Solid Shapes (NES Arnold)
3 x 3 Matrix Geoboard (NES Arnold)
Angle Race (NES Arnold)

Teachers' reference materials
Maths Plus: Angles 1, Paul Harling (Ward Lock Educational)
Primary Mathematics Today, 3rd edn, chapters 5 and 20, Elizabeth Williams and Hilary Shuard

Radio and TV
Turning and *Bounce* from *Videomaths* (ITV Schools)

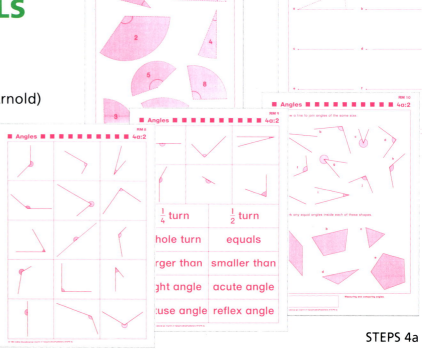

3. MULTIPLICATION PATTERNS (1)

LEARNING CONTEXT

Contribution made by this Step

The children learn the remaining 'new' facts in the x 8 and 8 x tables, i.e. 6 x 8, 7 x 8, 8 x 8, 9 x 8 (and their reversals), and go on to explore the relationships between the x 2, x 4 and x 8 tables.

Objectives

To enable children to:
a Know and apply facts in the x 8 and 8 x tables.
b Understand the relationships between multiples of two, four and eight.
c Test simple related statements or generalisations.

Background

In previous Steps, the children had opportunities to memorise the facts shown in this diagram in green. The seven new facts to be learned are shown in red, but, allowing for commutativity, these might be regarded as only four new facts to learn.

The further study of the x 2, x 4 and x 8 tables as a family and other multiples of 2, 4 and 8 can assist the long-term memorisation of the facts as well as being of interest in their own right because of the patterns and relationships.

> **Mathematics in the National Curriculum**
>
> **Programme of Study: KS2**
> Pupils should be taught to:
> - explore number sequences, *e.g. counting in different sizes of step, doubling and halving, using a multiplication square, explaining patterns and using simple relationships.* (N 3.a)
> - know the multiplication facts to 10 x 10; develop a range of mental methods for finding quickly from known facts those that they cannot recall; use some properties of numbers, including multiples, factors and squares, extending to primes, cubes and square roots. (N 3.c)
> - understand and investigate general statements, *e.g. 'wrist size is half neck size', 'there are four prime numbers less than 10'.* (UA 4.a)
> - search for patterns in their results. (UA 4.b)

10	10	20	30	40	50	60	70	80	90	100
9	9	18	27	36	45	54	63	72	81	90
8	8	16	24	32	40	48	56	64	72	80
7	7	14	21	28	35	42	49	56	63	70
6	6	12	18	24	30	36	42	48	54	60
5	5	10	15	20	25	30	35	40	45	50
4	4	8	12	16	20	24	28	32	36	40
3	3	6	9	12	15	18	21	24	27	30
2	2	4	6	8	10	12	14	16	18	20
1	1	2	3	4	5	6	7	8	9	10
X	1	2	3	4	5	6	7	8	9	10

THINKING AND TALKING MATHEMATICALLY

Starting points for discussion

Revision: *Tell me an answer which is in both the x 2 and x 5 tables ... x 2 and x 10 tables ... x 2, x 5 and x 10 tables ... not in the x 2, x 5 and x 10 tables.*

How do you recognise an even/odd number straight away?

How far can the multiplication tables continue?

What does 'having something in common' mean?

What is the difference between the x 2 and the 2 x tables? How are they the same? How do you read '4 x 2 = 8' and '2 x 4 = 8'?

> **Key language**
>
> multiple, common, product, multiplied by, times, groups, sets, pattern, link, relationship

ACTIVITIES IN DETAIL

A Memorising the x 8 and 8 x tables

Resources

School
Cuisenaire Rods; metre rules calibrated in centimetres; calculators

Scheme
Resource Master 11; Resource Master 12, one copy between two children

Part 1: Working with Cuisenaire Rods

1 Working in pairs or small groups, get the children to build up the 8 x table with 8-rods and metre rules, asking them to predict each time where the next rod will reach before it is positioned.

Eight four times makes thirty-two. Eight five times will make …?

8 × 4 = 32

2 Record the table as the model develops:

8 × 1 = 8
8 × 2 = 16
8 × 3 = 24
8 × 4 = 32…

3 Compare this with the pattern made by modelling the x 8 table:

Four multiplied by eight equals thirty-two. What will five multiplied by eight equal?

4 × 8 = 32

4 Record the table as the pattern develops:

1 × 8 = 8
2 × 8 = 16
3 × 8 = 24
4 × 8 = 32…

Part 2: Multiplication bingo

1 The children space out on paper any nine of these:
0, 8, 16, 24, 32, 40, 48, 56, 64, 72, 80.

2 Call out (or display) the multiplication expressions for these, e.g. 8 x 7, in random order, keeping a note of those called.

3 The children put a ring around the answers until at least one child calls 'House', when all his/her numbers are ringed.

4 You can repeat this by getting the children to put a ring of a different colour around the multiples on the next round.

Variations

1 The children write the options on their card from either:
- the multiplication expressions, e.g. 6 x 8, and you call the answers;
- numerals 1 – 10 as the answers to divisions, e.g. 56 ÷ 8, called by you;
- the division expressions, e.g. 80 ÷ 8, and you call the answers;
- answers to problems related to money or measures called out by you, e.g. the cost of eight stamps at 8p each.

RM 11 provides individual practice. RM 12 provides a calculator game for two players to practise the x 2, x 4 and x 8 tables.

B Common multiples of two, four and eight

Resources
Scheme
Book 4a, page 6; Resource Master 13

1 Revise the meaning of multiples – the answer when whole numbers are multiplied together – by displaying the multiples of 3 up to 30, in order.

2 Ask questions like, *What is the third/fifth multiple of three? Which multiple is twenty-four? Why do you recognise these multiples? How might the table continue? What is the twentieth multiple of three? How do you know?*

3 Extend by asking the children to calculate mentally, for example, *What is the third multiple of two, seventh multiple of four? etc. How did you decide? Can you tell me any multiples which are in both the two times and five times tables? What about four ... fifteen ... twenty?*

4 Afterwards, introduce the investigation in Book 4a, page 6, asking the children to decide on their own way to find and show their results. RM 13 provides optional reinforcement for children who will benefit from a more structured approach.

5 Afterwards, compare results. Can the children explain any links between say, the x 2 and x 4 tables or the x 4 and x 8 tables?

6 Explain that multiples found in more than one table are called 'common multiples'.

The children should appreciate that the answers in the multiplication tables which they try to memorise are the first ten multiples only for those tables, and that these can continue infinitely. Note that zero is not regarded as a multiple since it is not a whole number.

EXTENSION
- The children might choose three other multiplication tables and try to find and record common multiples in these.

C Sorting diagrams

Resources

School
Large sheets of paper;
numeral cards 0 – 20*;
scissors

Scheme
Resource Masters 14 and 15

*In advance, prepare a large sorting diagram and labels like the one shown in the following illustration. Prepare a set of numeral cards 1 – 20. (RM 14, with the zero card removed, can be used.)

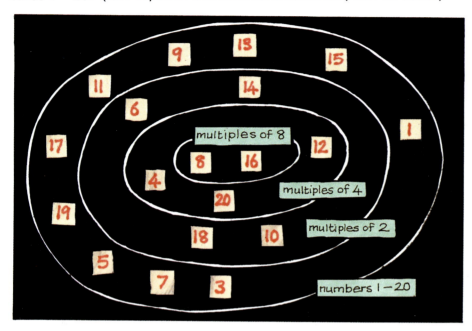

In this sorting diagram, the children are considering which numbers from 1 – 20 form the subset of multiples of two. Then they consider which of these form a further subset of multiples of four, and, finally, which of these form a subset of multiples of eight, i.e. subsets within subsets.

Part 1: Circle diagram

1 Ask the children to explain what they think the diagram means and why. *Where do you think this number twelve should go? Why?*

2 Position all the numeral cards in the outer region and ask, *Can you see any numbers which you think should go into the next circle? Why?*

3 Ask for volunteers to move cards into the adjacent region.

4 Repeat for the two remaining inner circles until all the numerals are used up.

5 To see if the children can interpret the diagram, ask questions like:
(a) *Which numbers are multiples of two?*
(b) *Which numbers are multiples of two and four?*
(c) *What can you tell me about the numbers in the centre region?*
(d) *Why are the odd numbers in the outside region?*
(e) *In which regions can you see multiples of two?*

Part 2: Group work

1 Organise the children to work in small groups. Each one needs to make a sorting diagram like the one above on a large sheet of paper.

2 Using the numeral cards cut from RM 15, each group tries to position as many of these as they can (which include numbers extending beyond tables facts) on their sorting diagram.

3 If permanent recording is required, the children can glue down the numerals and present the group's results or record individually in their own way.

D Common multiples C G I

Part 1: Patterns and relationships on the 100-square

1 Introduce the tasks on Book 4a, page 7, which use RM 16.

2 It may help to point out that, in task 4b, the three multiplications should include an eight, four and two each time.

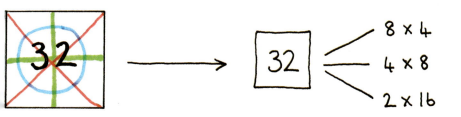

3 Afterwards, ask the children to describe any patterns or relationships they have spotted within multiples of two, four and eight up to 100.

Part 2: Investigating general statements

1 Provide a supply of 'True and False' statements from RM 17, which you might prefer to cut into strips so that children can choose one at a time.

2 Suggest that:
(a) the children might prefer to work with one or two friends to do this;
(b) they should choose the best way to 'test' the sentence and not ask you how to solve the problem;
(c) they should write down what they did and found out, to show you afterwards.

3 Afterwards, children can explain and compare their conclusions with each other.

EXTENSION

■ Make up more examples like this: 32 is the fourth multiple of eight, the eighth multiple of four and the sixteenth multiple of two.

Resources
Scheme
Book 4a, page 7; Resource Masters 16 and 17

This activity extends the patterns in the ×2, ×4 and ×8 tables to include multiples up to 100. The children will, it is hoped, start to realise that:
– every second multiple of two is a multiple of four;
– every second multiple of four is a multiple of eight; and
– every fourth multiple of two is a multiple of eight.

E Assessment activity I

*In advance, make a set of cards like this:

1 Place the cards face downwards and ask the child to turn them over one at a time and to tell you the answer as quickly as possible. (Ten seconds is a reasonable time limit for each response.)

2 Ask the child to choose any card and to tell you a situation or story from which that multiplication might have arisen.

Resources
School
Tables cards*

Scheme
Resource Master 17 (see stage 3)

STEPS 4a

3 Either ask the child to explain and justify his/her results from a task undertaken on RM 17 or ask the child to choose one of these and to explain and justify his/her conclusions afterwards.

Assessment notes

Oral response	✔
Practical response	(will depend on strategy chosen for stage 3)
Pictorial response	(will depend on strategy chosen for stage 3)
Written response	(will depend on strategy chosen for stage 3)

The child has:
given correctly at least eight correct answers for the x 8 or 8 x table facts in a reasonable time;
AND
given an application for a multiplication expression;
AND
has justified his/her solution to a 'true or false' statement involving relationships between multiples of two, four and eight by testing examples or by reasoning.

STRENGTHENING ACTIVITIES

x 8 table

If the child is having difficulty with memorising the table facts, he/she may need more experience of building up the tables with materials which highlight the patterns.

Patterns and relationships

If the child cannot see the relationship between the x 2, x 4 and x 8 tables, concentrate initially on relationships between the x 2 and x 4 tables, then the x 4 and the x 8 tables. A 100 number track might assist, on which the child places the same colour cube, say, blue, on all the multiples of two, then a second colour, say, yellow, on the multiples of four. The yellow cubes are positioned on top of the appropriate blue ones to create towers so that the relationship is clearly visible.

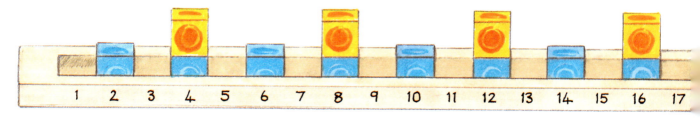

Eventually, the child can position a third colour of cubes on top of the multiples of eight and be encouraged to describe the repeating pattern of cubes.

CHALLENGING ACTIVITIES

Halving and doubling

Provide an example of a sequence like this in which halving and doubling feature.

What similar examples can the child create? (This may lead to multiplication of decimal or common fractions, e.g. the next element of the example featured is 2.5 x 16.) A calculator will be useful for trialling such examples.

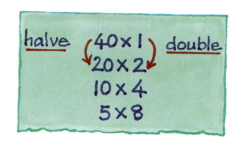

IDEAS BOARD

■ English
– Dictate story 'problems' which require the children to multiply by eight to find the answer.
– By choosing a multiplication expression, e.g. 7 x 8 or 8 x 6, the children tell or write about and illustrate a suitable story.

■ Art
Design a spider frieze to illustrate the x 8 table.

■ Button game
Play the game in the *Home/school projects* so the children can teach others at home.

■ Cuisenaire Rods
The children place Cuisenaire 2-, 4- and 8-rods along the edge of a metre rule, calibrated in centimetres. They record in their own way the numbers where ends of two or more rods are in line.

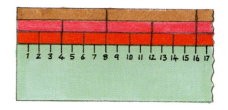

(With less able children, you might use a 25 or 30 cm ruler.)

■ Fizz...buzz...hiss

Put cards numbered in twos, say from 2 to 62 in a bag, one card for each child. Each child withdraws a card in random order. In order from 2 – 62, the children stand up and have to say 'Fizz' if they are a multiple of two, 'Fizz buzz' if they are a multiple of two and four, and 'Fizz, buzz, hiss' if they are a multiple of two, four and eight. Listen for the repeating word patterns. Try starting at 62 and working backwards. Alternatively, give group commands, *All the children who have 'Fizz, buzz, hiss' cards come to the front and put yourselves in order.*

Invent new trios of words to represent the multiples when you play again.

TEPS 4a

HOME/SCHOOL PROJECTS

The child takes home a set of numeral cards 1 – 20. A supply of buttons (or similar) is needed. The cards are shuffled, placed face downwards and the two or four players take turns to turn over the top card. A multiple of eight wins the player three buttons, a multiple of four wins two buttons, a multiple of two wins one button. The player with most buttons at the end wins.

SUPPORT MATERIALS

Teaching aids
Cuisenaire Rods (NES Arnold)
TI 1103, 1104 and *Galaxy 9x calculators* (Texas Instruments)
Multilink 100 Track and Cubes (NES Arnold)

Children's books
Anno's Mysterious Multiplying Jar, Mitsumasa and Masaichiro Anno (Bodley Head)

Software
Dots and Pattern 1 from *Mathematical Investigations*, Anita Straker (ILECC)
Multiple from *MicroSMILE The first 31* (ILECC)
Gusinter from *Number Games*, Anita Straker (ILECC)

Radio and TV
Doubling from *Videomaths* (ITV Schools)

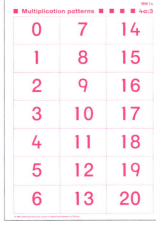

4. TIME (1)

LEARNING CONTEXT

Contribution made by this Step

Telling the time, using the 24-hour clock and relating times to events in the children's lives.

Objectives

To enable children to:
a Relate times shown on the 24-hour clock to everyday events.
b Convert 24-hour times to and from 12-hour times.

Background

In everyday situations, we employ a wide range of expressions to indicate approximate times – 'just before four', 'at sunset', 'around midday', 'nine-ish'. When it is necessary to give a precise time, a range of timing devices is available. Many now use the 24-hour convention and almost all timetables use the formal four-digit 24-hour times. Children, therefore, need to understand and use am and pm and to recognise and use their equivalents on the 24-hour clock.

It is recommended that children use and interpret timing devices on different appliances. While we probably cannot teach every child to set a timer on a cooker or video, we can provide opportunities for them to become familiar with digital 24-hour notation, and at the same time to recognise analogue and 12-hour equivalents.

> **Mathematics in the National Curriculum**
>
> **Programme of Study: KS2**
> Pupils should be taught to:
> ■ choose appropriate standard units of length, mass, capacity and time, and make sensible estimates with them in everyday situations; extend their understanding of the relationship between units. (SSM 4.a)
> ■ choose and use appropriate measuring instruments; interpret numbers and read scales to an increasing degree of accuracy. (SSM 4.b)

THINKING AND TALKING MATHEMATICALLY

Starting points for discussion

Provide analogue clockfaces. *Show these times: 4:15, 7:50. Show me the time five minutes before (after)...*

Display a range of bus and train timetables or TV programme listings. *Who uses these? Why?*

Show pictures or examples of timing devices (e.g. cooker, clock/radio, video).

> **Key language**
>
> hour (h, hr, hrs), minute (min, mins), o'clock, to, past, am (ante meridiem), pm (post meridiem), hands, 12-hour clock, 24-hour clock, digits, digital, display, timer, equivalent

STEPS 4a

ACTIVITIES IN DETAIL

A Using am and pm

1 Revise oral time-telling with groups of children, using a geared clockface. For example, a quarter past seven, twenty to ten, three minutes to four (Handbook 3b:5).

2 Remind the children how to write 12-hour digital times, e.g. 9:10, 2:45. If necessary, provide digital and analogue outlines for each child to write the hours and also the minutes past.

Resources

School
Geared clockface; real clocks and watches – digital and analogue, if possible; 12-hour clockfaces; clockface rubber stamps (optional)

Scheme
Resource Master 18

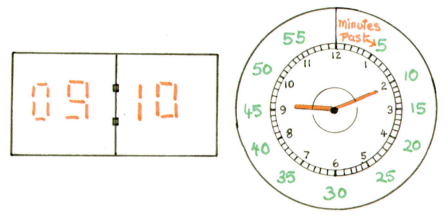

3 Make sure the children are aware of the number of minutes in an hour, a half-hour and a quarter of an hour and the number of hours in a day. Ask, *When does a new day start? If the date today is _____ , at what precise time will it change to _____ (next date)?*

4 Can the children explain when to use am and pm? Show a time on the clockface and invite the children to say what they might be doing at that time for am and then for pm. For example:

5 Provide clockfaces for pairs of children to practise saying times and what might happen at am and pm for each time. Use RM 18 for this type of practice.

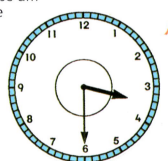

At 3:30 a m I am asleep in bed.

At 3:30 p m I finish school and walk home.

EXTENSION

- Make and order a collection of words and phrases for different times, e.g. morn, forenoon, dawn, noon, twilight, dusk, sunset.

B The 24-hour clock

1 Ask the children if they know how times can be described without using am and pm. They may already be familiar with some examples of four-digit times.

2 Explain that in the 24-hour clock, am times remain the same, except that there are always four digits, an extra zero being added if necessary. For example:

Resources

School
Geared clockface; 24-hour clockfaces; digital clockface or digital clock rubber stamps (optional)

Scheme
Resource Master 19

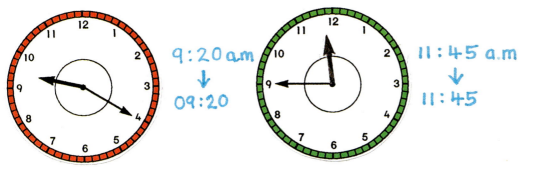

3 Can the children tell you what happens to pm times? Explain that by midday, 12 hours of any day have already passed, so 12 hours are added on to the am times.

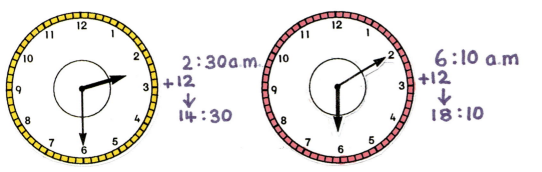

4 Show the children that in this way we need just one four-digit time for any time of day – known as the 24-hour clock.

5 The children practise adding 12 to pm times, (and subtracting 12 from times between 13 and 24):
– using round hours, e.g. 4:00 + 12 hours is 16:00;
– using hours and minutes, e.g. 1:15 + 12 hours is 13:15.

6 Explain that, with the 24-hour clock, o'clock times are sometimes spoken as '___ hundred hours', for example, 15:00 is the same as 'fifteen hundred hours'.

Emphasise that this does not mean that there are now one hundred minutes in the hour!

7 Also remind the children that midnight usually appears as 00:00 – the start of the new day. However, occasionally they may see this time written as 24:00.

RM 19 provides practice in recognising and writing equivalent 24-hour times.

EXTENSION

- Play games using 24-hour domino or *Snap* cards. Some good domino games are available from educational suppliers (see *Support Materials*) or they can be homemade.

STEPS 4a

C Times in your day   C G I

1 The children work in groups. Ask a child to show a time on a geared clockface, e.g. a quarter past six in the evening, to the others and say whether it is to be am or pm. They all write down am/pm time and the corresponding 24-hour time. For example:

Resources

School
Geared clockface

Scheme
Book 4a, page 8; Resource Master 20

12-hour	24-hour
6:15 pm	18:15

It's the evening – so it's pm.

2 Also practise recognition of am/pm times from 24-hour digital time by displaying different four-digit times. The children write or say the corresponding am/pm time.

3 Encourage them to suggest what they might be doing at each time. For example: 04:05/4:05 am – 'I hope I'd be asleep at five past four.'

4 Discuss the dual timeline on Book 4a, page 8. Point out the correspondence between am/pm and 24-hour times.

On RM 20, the children complete their own timeline and devise questions.

Try to include examples of the everyday variations in writing 24-hour times, e.g. 1455 hours, 14.55, 14:55.

EXTENSION

- The children make a timeline for some imaginary/fictitious character in a story. For example:
    09:30 Arrived at haunted house
    09:40 Entered secret room
    09:45 Drank magic potion …

D How long?   G

*In advance, prepare 'How long?' question cards, on which the hands of the clock can be moved, and cards for the activities and for digital times are attached with Blu-Tack:

Resources

School
Geared clockfaces; stopwatch or timer; analogue clockface rubber stamp (optional); A5 paper or thin card*

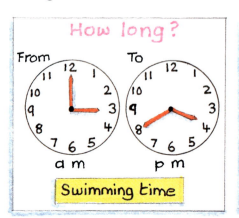

1 Provide groups of children with geared clockfaces, if possible, and ask them to practise counting on to find how much time has elapsed between certain times in the school day, for example, between start of school and morning break.

2 Show the children your examples of 'How long?' questions. Ask them to make up their own questions, using analogue clockface rubber stamps or giving digital times. You may want them to write the answer on the back.

3 Children can exchange 'How long?' questions and calculate the answers.

Remind children that calculations involving hours and minutes cannot be made using a calculator. Ask them to explain why not.

EXTENSION

■ Research into times for various sport and games. Make 'How long?' questions for those of a set duration, e.g. netball/football. What are record times – shortest and longest – for 'open-ended' sports events, e.g. tennis/marathon?

E Timing devices

*Collect and display different timers, e.g. sand/egg timers, kitchen timers, wind-up clock, digital watch, stop watch, chess clock, metronome.

Resources

School
Examples of timers*; pictures of appliances with timers

Scheme
Book 4a, page 9

1 Discuss the accuracy of different timers. Use one to check another.

2 Ask the children to suggest the different levels of accuracy required in measuring time, for example:
- dating pottery discovered on an archaeological dig – to the nearest century;
- a train departure – to the nearest minute;
- cooking in a microwave oven – to the nearest second;
- recording a 100 m sprint in a competition – to the nearest one-hundredth of a second.

3 Ask the children to make lists, with pictures if possible, of timing devices they have seen or used, for example, a clock-radio, delay timer on a camera, microwave oven, video.

4 Discuss the information needed to use different timers.

5 Show Book 4a, page 9 where the children have to decide which programmes to record on a 180-minute video. Encourage them to try out different programme combinations.

Most devices have a book of instructions.

EXTENSION

■ Invent and draw a new appliance for use in school or at home which would require a timer – for example, a shoe-cleaning machine could need five seconds for a quick polish, or 45 seconds for a more drastic clean!

F Assessment activity

1 Show three or four times (to one-minute intervals) on the geared analogue clockface. Ask the child to tell you the time shown.

2 If the time is a 'morning' time, that is, an am time, ask the child to show it on a digital clockface.

3 If the time is an 'afternoon' time, that is, a pm time, ask the child to tell you the time, saying it in the 24-hour clock style.

4 Say some afternoon times, using the 24-hour clock style. Ask the child to show these on a geared analogue clockface and on a 24-hour digital clockface, to say whether it is an am or a pm time and to tell you what he/she is likely to be doing then.

Resources

School
Geared analogue clockface; 24-hour digital clockface

Assessment notes

Oral response	✔
Practical response	✔
Pictorial response	
Written response	

The child has:
read and told the time to one-minute intervals on analogue and digital clockfaces, using appropriate and correct verbal forms to describe the 24-hour style;
AND
shown given 24-hour clock times to one-minute intervals on analogue and digital clockfaces, recognising equivalent forms.

STRENGTHENING ACTIVITIES

Match the time

Show different times, using a geared clockface. Can the child tell the time? Ask the child to select, from a set of digital time cards, a time to match the clockface time when you say 'am' or 'pm'.

Set a video

The children use a set of digit cards to show start and finish times of a particular TV programme.

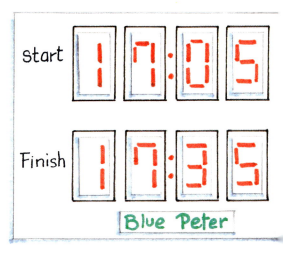

Light or dark

Use selected digital time cards. The child says whether it is light or dark at that time. For example:

CHALLENGING ACTIVITIES

Bus times

The children find out the frequency of buses at different times of the day from a local bus timetable. They investigate the possibility of making identical journeys at different times of day. Can the children explain the variations in the number of buses available?

Up, up and away

From holiday brochures, the children find how long it takes to fly to different destinations. They work out a timetable for day one of a holiday, to allow for booking-in time at the airport of, say, 90 minutes.

Example:
Leave home   11:50
Arrive airport   13:40
Flight leaves   15:10
Flight arrives   17:35

Lighting-up times

The children carry out research into lighting-up times throughout a year for your area (local library or newspaper). They compare earliest/latest times. If possible, they compare times for different parts of the country, e.g. Inverness and Plymouth.

IDEAS BOARD

■ Typical projects

Journeys; Communications; Time Machines

■ Phone charges

Display a leaflet listing telephone charges. *Which are the most and least expensive times for making calls? Are there differences for local, long distance or international calls?* Questions can be made up: 'What is the cost of a five-minute call to _____ at 19:00 on a Tuesday?'

■ How many hours?

If there are 24 hours in a day, calculate the number of hours in a week … a month (which month?) … a year.

■ High noon

A game for two or three players, using a normal dice and a geared clockface.
- Players take turns to roll the dice. The numbers represent multiples of ten minutes.
- The number rolled is added to a starting time (e.g. 9:00) until a player reaches 12:00 exactly.
- Players record the progress of their games, for example:

Dice Throw	Minutes	Time
		09:00
2	20	09:20
6	60	10:20
4	40	11:00
1	10	11:10

■ Science

– Compare the accuracy of different timing devices.
– Calculate finishing times for cooking/firing pottery.

HOME/SCHOOL PROJECTS

The children make three lists of where they see examples of different timing devices: 12-hour analogue, 12-hour digital, 24-hour digital.

SUPPORT MATERIALS

Teaching aids
Card Clock Faces (12- and 24-hour) (NES Arnold)
Digital Clock Face (NES Arnold)
12 Hour Clock Rubber Stamp (NES Arnold)
24 Hour Clock Rubber Stamp (NES Arnold)
Digital Time Rubber Stamps (NES Arnold)
Time Dominoes – Set 2 (NES Arnold)
Train Journeys (NES Arnold)
It's About Time – Clocks and Calendars Kit (Taskmaster)

Teachers' reference materials
Primary Mathematics Today, 3rd edn, chapter 16, Elizabeth Williams and Hilary Shuard (Longman)
Maths Plus: Time 1 and *Time 2,* Paul Harling (Ward Lock Educational)
Lines of Development in Primary Mathematics, Mary Deboys and Eunice Pitt (Blackstaff Press)

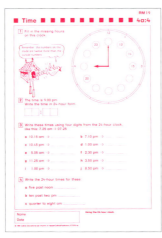

5. ADDITION (1)

LEARNING CONTEXT

Contribution made by this Step

The emphasis is on mental calculations. After revision of addition bonds to 20, the children consider strategies for adding mentally several one-digit numbers and a one-digit number to a two-digit number.

Objectives

To enable children to:
a Add mentally at least three one-digit numbers.
b Add mentally a one-digit number to a two-digit number.
c Apply knowledge of these facts to solve problems.

Background

In Step 3a:25, the activities focused on children memorising number bonds to 20 at least, by adding pairs of numbers then trios of numbers. Strategies to make this easier were considered: e.g. finding pairs of numbers which total ten, using brackets or rearranging the order to make the numbers easier to add. They applied this knowledge to adding mentally multiples of 10 – 200 at least. Now these skills are extended.

When adding mentally a one-digit number to a two-digit number, pattern-building can help, e.g. if 5 + 4 = 9 then 15 + 4 = 19, 45 + 4 = 49, etc.

When adding several one-digit numbers mentally, the children need to be able to 'hold' the first total in their mind before adding the next number. Often this can be made easier by deciding the order in which to add the numbers. They also need to be able to total two or more numbers for pencil/paper calculations in the absence of practical apparatus. As stressed previously, it is important that the children think in advance, *What will my answer be about?* and think afterwards, *Is my answer sensible?*

> **Mathematics in the National Curriculum**
>
> **Programme of Study: KS2**
> Pupils should be taught to:
> ■ develop a variety of mental methods of computation with whole numbers up to 100, and explain patterns used; extend mental methods to develop a range of non-calculator methods of computation that involve addition and subtraction of whole numbers, progressing to methods for multiplication and division of up to three-digit by two-digit whole numbers. (N 3.d)

THINKING AND TALKING MATHEMATICALLY

Starting points for discussion

Show (or say) an example of a one-digit (or two-digit) number.

What single-digit numbers can you add together in your head?

Why is it useful to be able to add numbers in your head?

Number posters for totals 10 – 20 (or beyond) to which the children contribute as confidence grows (see above).

> **Key language**
>
> total, combine, plus, add, running total, altogether, order of addition, one- (single-) digit/two-digit numbers

STEPS 4a

ACTIVITIES IN DETAIL

A Revision: mental addition to 20

Part 1: Number pairs to 20

1 Revise number bonds to 20 by asking the children to add two numbers on the calculator which will give a display of, say, 18, as the total.

2 Compare the results, using terms like *total, plus, combined with*, etc.

3 Extend the rules, e.g.:

(a) Add a one-digit number and a two-digit number together to get a total of 20.

(b) Add two one-digit numbers together to get a total of 13, record these, then loop those made by combining one-digit numbers.

Resources

School
Calculators

Scheme
Book 4a, pages 10 and 11;
Resource Master 21

Part 2: Number trios

1 Display some one-digit numbers, say, 2, 3, 5, 8, 9.

2 Ask the children to find and record, in their own way, different totals up to 20 when any three of these are combined. (They can use the same number more than once if they want to.)

3 Afterwards, compare the range of results and strategies used to make the addition easier.

Book 4a, pages 10 and 11 and Resource Master 21 provide further practice.

EXTENSION

- The children can try to find:
  - totals greater than 20 by combining any three one-digit numbers.
  - totals greater than 20 by combining four or more given numbers.

- After completing RM 21, groups of children might collate their results by listing all the totals made and putting these in order. Can they find number trios to combine to make any missing totals?

To make adding easier, some children may have used brackets, some may have set out the numbers in the order they consider easiest to add and others may have found number pairs which total ten.

Children who need extra practice may benefit from redoing Book 3b, page 62 and RM 3b: 105.

B Adding several single-digit numbers   C P I

Resources

School
Calculators; scissors; scrap paper for score sheets

Scheme
Resource Masters 22 and 23*, one copy of each between two children; Resource Master 24

*If possible, copy RM 23 on to card before cutting up.

1 If necessary, organise the children to work in pairs and introduce the games on RM 22.

2 Introduce the term 'running total' to explain a number added to a previous total.

3 Afterwards, discuss:

(a) any methods the children used to make the mental addition easier, e.g. finding number pairs which total ten or adding the larger numbers first, doubling or trebling;

(b) which strategy for addition they prefer – adding a number to a previously calculated total (a running total) as in Game A or being able to see all the numbers to be combined in one go as in Game B – and why.

RM 24 provides individual practice.

If copies of RM 23 are produced on paper and the numerals show through to the back, the pack can be placed in an envelope and the cards withdrawn from there. Playing cards might be used instead of RM 23 with any picture card having a value of zero.

EXTENSION

■ The children might play Game B again but now choose four cards at a time, with the winner of each go having the total closer to 30.

C Combining one- and two-digit numbers   C I

Resources

Scheme
Resource Master 25; Book 4a, page 12

Part 1: Pattern building

1 Display the start of patterns like these:

2 Ask, *What comes next? Why?* and continue the sequences.

Part 2: Combinations

1 Extend by displaying some two- and one-digit numbers like these:

2 Ask the children to combine pairs of numbers, one from each set, and to write these down with their totals.

3 Afterwards, the children can compare the range of answers with each other and how they decided on the answer.

4 If necessary, explain that it often helps to go back to an easier example, e.g. 8 + 3 = 11 might help with 48 + 3 = …

RM 25 and Book 4a, page 12 provide individual practice.

In stage 1 of Part 2, there are 25 possible combinations, if all are found, with totals ranging from 17 to 90.

D **Assessment activity**

*In advance, make ten addition cards like these:

7+3+6	8+5+2	6+8+6	4+2+9	8+9+3
26+3	37+5	56+8	75+8	91+9

I **Resources**

School
Addition cards*

1 Using the first set of cards, ask the child to choose one at a time and to tell you the total.

2 Repeat with the second set of cards.

3 Ask the child to choose one of these cards and either to tell you or write a story to illustrate what this might mean.

Since you are assessing mental ability in stages 1 and 2, you may wish to decide on a reasonable time-limit for the child to respond, e.g. ten seconds for each response.

Assessment notes

Oral response	✔
Practical response	
Pictorial response	
Written response	✔ (depending on method chosen for stage 3)

The child has:
correctly added by mental recall several one-digit numbers on at least four out of five occasions;
AND
correctly added by mental recall a one-digit number to a two-digit number on at least four out of five occasions;
AND
applied knowlege of these facts to suggest a situation from which one of these additions might have arisen.

STRENGTHENING ACTIVITIES

Single-digit numbers

If the child is having difficulty adding mentally more than two numbers up to 20, he/she may benefit from more pattern-building or going back to using practical or pictorial aids. For example,

(a) The child might combine pairs of dominoes and write the total number of spots for each pair as an addition;

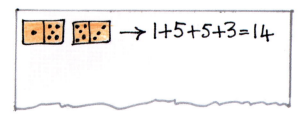

66　　　　　　　　　　　　　　　　　　　　　　　　　　　STEPS 4a

b) She/he might use three Cuisenaire Rods each time but keep one as a constant to find different ways of making, say, 15;

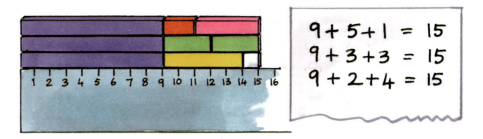

c) She/he might find numbers which total, say, 20, of which one is ten.

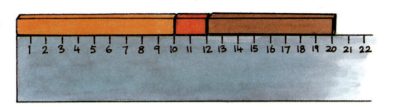

Two-digit and one-digit addition

If the child finds this difficult, it may help to use, as an intermediate step, pairs of numbers written on cards which combine to give a multiple of ten. An example could be 26 + 4, with the answer written on the reverse side. The child can put together cards showing numbers which have the same total, then check the answers on the back.

CHALLENGING ACTIVITIES

Different orders

Prepare workcards of this type.

HOME/SCHOOL PROJECTS

Children play a card game for up to four players. All the tens and picture cards are removed from a pack of playing cards. The remaining cards are shuffled and placed face downwards. Each player takes three cards from the top of the pack, turns them over and totals them. The player with the highest total wins that round. The first player to win three rounds wins that game. In another game, the players might choose four or more cards at a time.

STEPS 4a

IDEAS BOARD

■ Addition snake

In pairs or small groups, the children use the cards on RM 23 without the zero cards, shuffle them and lay them out to form a chain or snake of numbers. By studying the numbers, the children have to decide which adjacent two, three, four, five … numbers will give the largest, then smallest, totals. Reshuffle the cards and try to get higher totals. A calculator will be useful to trial examples.

■ Bean bag addition

Make a target area outdoors with chalk. By throwing three (or four or five) beanbags from an agreed starting position, the children have to see who can score the highest total each time to win that round. The person with the highest score after five rounds wins the game.

■ Corner totals

The children construct or draw around the outlines of 2-D geometric shapes, and write on numbers so that the numbers at the corners total the number inside.

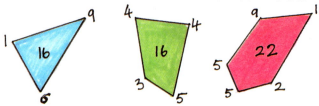

■ Dice numbers

The children, working in pairs, number two blank dice, one with one-digit numbers, the other with two-digit numbers. They take it in turn to roll both dice, and to give the answer by mental addition. A calculator can be used to confirm the answers. How many different combinations of numbers are possible?

SUPPORT MATERIALS

Teaching aids
Dominoes (NES Arnold/Hope Education)
Cuisenaire Rods (NES Arnold)
0 – 100 Wall and Table-top Number Lines (Taskmaster)
TI 1103, 1104 and Galaxy 9x calculators (Texas Instruments)
Blank dice (Hope Education)

Teachers' reference materials
Primary Mathematics Today, 3rd edn, chapter 9, Elizabeth Williams and Hilary Shuard (Longman)

Software
Chains, Counters, Make 37 and Make 57 from Number Games, Anita Straker (ILECC)

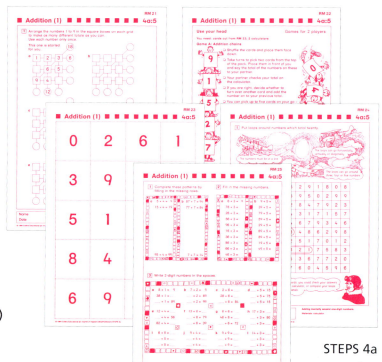

6. BAR-LINE GRAPHS

LEARNING CONTEXT

Contribution made by this Step

The children build on their previous experience of simple bar charts and pictograms to construct, read and interpret bar-line graphs of discrete data. An understanding of the use of a variety of scales to represent frequencies is also developed.

Objectives

To enable children to:
a Construct bar-line graphs.
b Read and interpret bar-line graphs using different scales to represent frequencies.

Background

Experience of constructing and interpreting graphs is a useful foundation skill for many areas of the curriculum, especially those in which clarification of relationships and clear communication of information are important. In this Step activities encourage children to represent data for others to understand, and to make sense of other people's representations.

Bar-line graphs (sometimes known as stick graphs) are, fundamentally, a stylised version of bar charts. This link can be reinforced by using the data from Handbook 3a: 4 and 3b: 1, for instance, to construct bar-line graphs. More topics are suggested in the Ideas Board.

> **Mathematics in the National Curriculum**
>
> **Programme of Study: KS2**
> Pupils should be taught to:
> ■ interpret tables used in everyday life; interpret and create frequency tables, including those for grouped discrete data. (HD 2.a)
> ■ collect and represent discrete data appropriately using graphs and diagrams, including block graphs, pictograms and line graphs; interpret a wider range of graphs and diagrams that represent data, including pie charts, using a computer where appropriate. (HD 2.b)
> ■ draw conclusions from statistics and graphs, and recognise why some conclusions can be uncertain or misleading. (HD 2.d)
> ■ use diagrams, graphs and simple algebraic symbols. (UA 3.b)
> ■ present information and results clearly, and explain the reasons for their choice of presentation. (UA 3.c)

THINKING AND TALKING MATHEMATICALLY

Starting points for discussion

Show a collection of number rods (e.g. Cuisenaire or Colour Factor), standing on end. *Which is the longest ... shortest? Which pairs of shorter rods are the same length as the longest?*

Display a collection of simple graphs and charts from magazines. *What can we 'read' from them?*

> **Key language**
>
> Data, bar graph, bar-line graph, bar chart, horizontal, vertical, axis, axes, most (least) popular, frequency, total, scale, represent, different, amounts, table, tabulate

STEPS 4a

ACTIVITIES IN DETAIL

A Revising simple block graphs and bar charts   C G

1 Remind the children of their previous experience of constructing and interpreting of 1:1 block graphs and 1:1 bar charts. Show an example of identical information presented in the two ways. For example:

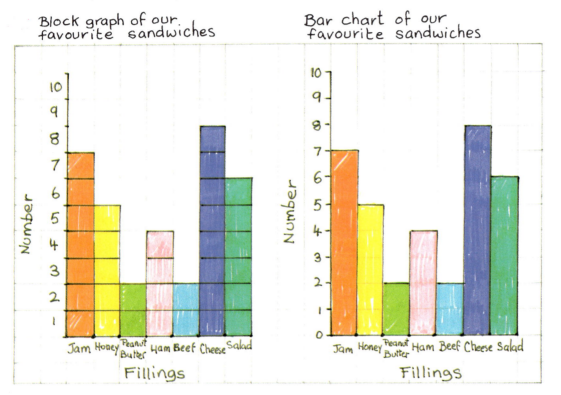

Resources

Scheme
Resource Master 26 (optional); Resource Masters A–C (squared and graph papers)

2 Discuss the similarities and differences between the two forms. For example:

Similarities
- Each graph has been given a title.
- The horizontal and vertical axes are labelled.
- The categories are evenly spaced so that each column or bar has the same width.

Differences
- Each occurrence is shown as a separate unit only on the block graph.
- The numbers of occurrences are written 'in the spaces' on the vertical axis of a block graph, but 'on the lines' on the vertical axis of a bar chart.
- On a block graph the number of occurrences in each category can be found by counting the blocks and/or reading the appropriate number on the vertical axis, but on the bar chart it is measured by reference to the scale which defines the length (or height) of the bar.

3 Ask the children to collaborate in choosing a topic for which they can collect data and draw graphs and charts. Remind them about the design and use of a 'tallying' chart and the need to draw up a frequency table. For example:

Introduce the terms 'tabulate' and 'tabulation' if you wish.

Favourite Sandwiches		
Filling	Tally	Total/Frequency
Jam	ℍℍ ll	7
Honey	ℍℍ	5
Peanut Butter	ll	2
Ham	llll	4
Beef	ll	2
Cheese	ℍℍ lll	8
Salad	ℍℍ l	6

4 Get each group to carry out the collection and tabulation of data and to draw both a block graph *and* a bar chart with a scale of 1:1.

5 Display the pairs of graphs and ask the children to describe to you the process of data collection, recording and graph construction, highlighting the similarities and differences of the two forms.

The children can choose a single size and design of squared or graph paper on which to construct the graphs, or they could use RM 26 if appropriate.

EXTENSION

■ The children can investigate other ways they know of representing data – for example pictograms, Venn diagrams, Carroll diagrams, arrow diagrams. (See Steps 3a:4 and 3b:1 and 38.)

B Bar-line graphs (1:1)

Part 1: vertical form

1 Use the example of a bar chart from Activity **A**. Demonstrate how it can be re-drawn on squared paper as a bar-line graph. Emphasise that the bar-lines (and therefore the categories) are now drawn on the lines of the paper, not in the spaces. Discuss the fact that the general rules about titles, labels and so on still apply.

Resources

Scheme
Resource Masters 26 and 27 (optional); Resource Masters A–C (squared and graph papers)

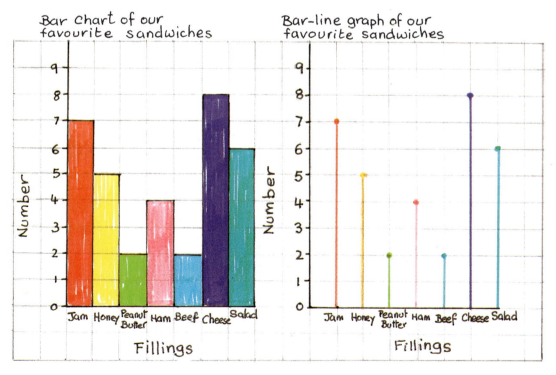

STEPS 4a

2 Ask the children to work together using the data collected and tabulated in Activity **A**, and to represent it in the form of a bar-line graph, using squared paper or RM 26.

Part 2: horizontal form

1 Demonstrate that the bar-line graph (and indeed the block graph and the bar chart) can be shown in a horizontal form, perhaps using RM 27. Point out that the labels have changed places but that the information is unchanged.

2 Check that the children can read and interpret the bar-line graph in this form.

At this stage it is recommended that a variety of squared or graph papers (Resource Masters A–C) is made available. Encourage the children to choose an appropriate paper on which to draw a graph.

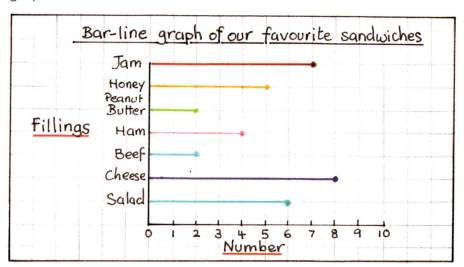

C Bar-line graphs and scale   C G

Part 1: scale of 1:2

1 Ask the children to choose a subject for data collection which will produce larger frequencies and/or a wider range of frequencies than a class survey. For example:

Numbers playing tennis each day at the leisure centre.

Day	Number
Monday	14
Tuesday	20
Wednesday	5
Thursday	16
Friday	24
Saturday	29
Sunday	36

2 Discuss the fact that recording this information would produce either a very tall graph, or a vertical axis with very small calibrations.

Resources

Scheme
Resource Masters 26 and 27 (optional); Book 4a, pages 13 and 14; Resource Masters A–C (squared and graph papers)

Perhaps the whole school could be surveyed, or an outside organisation like a leisure centre.

3 Remind the children of their previous experience of scale and bar charts (Handbook 3b:1). Demonstrate how to draw a vertical or horizontal bar-line graph with a scale of 1:2 on squared paper, or on RM 26 or RM 27 (see right). Children who are able to should be encouraged to draw bar-line graphs on plain paper.

4 Discuss ways to read and interpret the graph, emphasising the importance of careful reading of frequencies which are odd numbers and therefore lie between the calibrations.

Part 2: Other scales

1 Ask the children: *What size of numbers would we have if we asked, say, the leisure centre about total attendances in a week for all activities?* Discuss the likely numbers.

2 Point out that a graph is a way of illustrating *patterns* of information. Talk about rounding attendances, perhaps to the nearest ten (see Step 1), and using a different scale so that the pattern is clear, and the drawing of the graph easier (see right).

3 Discuss different scales which could be used. If they do not raise it as an option, lead the children towards using a scale of, for example, 1:10.

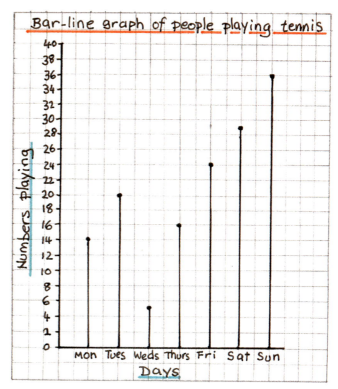

Total attendance at the leisure centre		
Day	Actual attendance	Rounded to nearest 10
Monday	74	70
Tuesday	86	90
Wednesday	49	50
Thursday	54	50
Friday	103	100
Saturday	123	120
Sunday	117	120

4 Ask the children to work in groups to select a suitable squared paper (or use RM 26 or RM 27) and to draw a bar-line graph of the data collected (see right).

5 Display the graphs. Ask some children to describe their work and the reasons why they chose a particular type of paper.

6 Discuss the need to produce graphs which:
(a) show the information accurately and clearly;
(b) can be understood and interpreted by other people.

Further practice in drawing bar-line graphs with scales other than 1:1 can be found on Book 4a, pages 13 and 14.

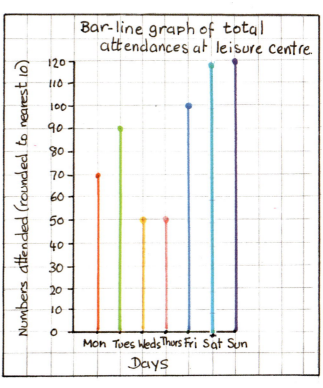

STEPS 4a

EXTENSION

■ Ask the children to represent some or all of the information used in Activity **C** in another way, perhaps using an arrow diagram, a Venn diagram, a Carroll diagram, a block graph, a bar chart or a pictogram.

D Changing scales

1 Introduce the children to the fact that sometimes they may need to interpret several different scales at the same time, or change the scale of a bar-line graph as additional information becomes available.

C Resources

Scheme
Resource Masters A–C (squared and graph papers)

2 Show about three bar-line graphs which contain the same kind of information, but which have been drawn on different scales. For example:

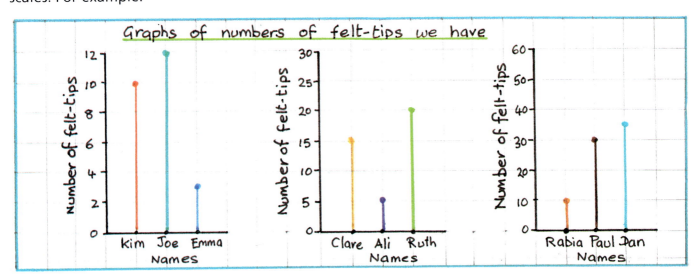

3 Ask questions such as:
How many felt-tips does each child have? Who has most/least? Which two children have the same number? Who has twice as many/half as many as...?

E Assessment notes

An individual assessment activity is not provided for this Step. Since data handling of this kind can be applied to a wide range of data, we recommend that you make use of this informal checklist of relevant skills as they are used in general mathematical work as well as in the activities in this Step.

Oral response	✔
Practical response	✔
Pictorial response	✔
Written response	✔

The child has:
selected and used a tallying system and frequency table for systematic collection of data;
AND
specified an issue for which data are needed;
AND
used the results of a survey, or some given data, to construct a bar-line graph, following the conventional rules of structure, and various simple scales;
AND
read and interpreted a bar-line graph, showing ability to reflect upon, and make deductions from, the patterns of data illustrated.

STRENGTHENING ACTIVITIES

Practising scales

Children who have difficulty choosing and using an appropriate scale can be encouraged to use squared paper, or blank number lines to try out possible scales in areas other than graph work.

Blocks, bars and lines

Some children benefit from further use of earlier, more familiar forms of pictorial representation (block graphs and bar charts) to help them recognise that the same information can be represented in different, but similar, ways.

Mapping

Ask the children to transfer information like this on to a simple bar-line graph.

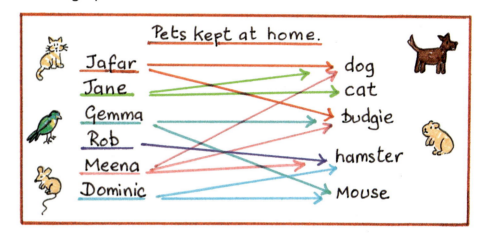

CHALLENGING ACTIVITIES

Ups and downs

Ask the children to write, or talk about, the week in which a graph such as this was drawn (see right).

Open-ended data handling

Capable children should be encouraged to carry out data collection, tabulation, pictorial representation and written or oral interpretation on subjects of their own choice. Encourage them to use a variety of approaches and to use different scales. Afterwards, they can present their findings to the class or a group.

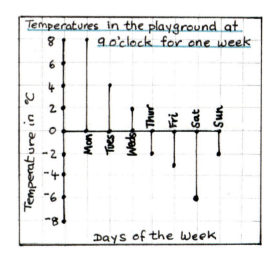

HOME/SCHOOL PROJECTS

Survey the different sorts of breakfasts eaten by members of families within a week. Discuss appropriate means of recording the data, especially the categories (and their subdivisions) which are to be investigated.

Ask the children to bring the data into school. Examine different ways to illustrate the information, and perhaps discuss differences between families, and age and gender groups.

STEPS 4a

IDEAS BOARD

■ Typical projects
Any in which surveys and data collection can be illustrated on bar-line graphs:

(a) Data collected by children

- Times
  birthday months and days of the week;
  times of leaving home for school.
- Numbers
  attendances at school during a week;
  numbers in each class of the school;
  numbers of children in families;
  numbers of letters in last name;
  heights, weights, reach, span, cubit.
- Choices
  colours of socks, shoes, bags, pencil cases;
  pets kept by families;
  soap powders/detergents used at home;
  favourite drinks, cereals, television programmes, comics, hobbies, sports, sports teams, bands/singers, board/computer games.

(b) Data collected from other investigations

- Environment
  readings of temperature, rainfall, wind speed;
  wildlife visiting the school grounds;
  numbers of vehicles passing the school gate;
  amount and type of litter dropped;
  types of local shops;
  building styles nearby.
- Probability
  numbers of each coin in a random handful;
  results of dice-rolling experiments.

(c) Information from reference materials

- Distances from home town to others.
- Lengths of rivers.
- Heights of mountains.
- Frequency of word lengths in books.
- Numbers of advertisements on each page of newspapers.

SUPPORT MATERIALS

Teaching aids
Block Graph Kit (NES Arnold/Hope Education/LDA-Invicta)

Teachers' reference materials
Maths Plus: Graphs 1, Paul Harling (Ward Lock Educational)
Spectrum Maths: Data Handling, Dave Kirkby (Collins Educational)
Lines of Development in Primary Mathematics, Mary Deboys and Eunice Pitt (Blackstaff Press)
Practical Handling Data, Book 4, Glyn Davies (Hodder & Stoughton)

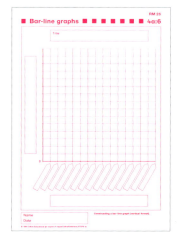
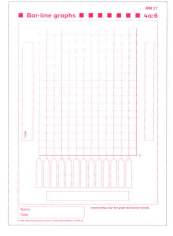

7. SUBTRACTION (1)

LEARNING CONTEXT

Contribution made by this Step

The children consider methods for subtracting mentally more than one number from 20. Also, as preparation for subtracting mentally a two-digit number from a two-digit number, the children develop strategies for subtracting a one-digit number from a two-digit number. Finally, mental addition and subtraction are combined to investigate number loops.

Objectives

To enable children to:
a Subtract mentally at least two single-digit numbers from 20.
b Subtract mentally a one-digit number from a two-digit number.
c Solve problems or describe situations from which such subtractions might have arisen.

Background

In conventional pencil and paper subtraction, an important skill is to be able to subtract a single-digit number from any number up to nineteen. (See Step 3b:28.) However, we are sometimes faced with situations, for example when shopping, where we have to subtract mentally more than one number or amount, and we need to have strategies for tackling this.

Because many of us find mental addition easier than mental subtraction, we often convert a problem so that it can be solved by addition. So a problem such as working out the change from £20, when two items costing £7 and £6 are purchased, might be tackled by subtracting £13 from £20 (20 − (7 + 6)) rather than by successive subtraction, i.e. subtracting £7 from £20 then a further £6 (20 − 7 = 13; 13 − 6 = 7).

Another useful mental skill is to be able to subtract a single-digit number from a two-digit number. The development of these skills is the focus in this Step.

> **Mathematics in the National Curriculum**
>
> **Programme of Study: KS2**
> Pupils should be taught to:
> - develop a variety of mental methods of computation with whole numbers up to 100, and explain patterns used; extend mental methods to develop a range of non-calculator methods of computation that involve addition and subtraction of whole numbers. (N 3.d)
> - choose sequences of methods of computation appropriate to a problem, adapt them and apply them accurately. (N 4.b)

THINKING AND TALKING MATHEMATICALLY

Starting points for discussion

Given an expression such as 20 − 5 − 3, can the children suggest 'stories' from which this subtraction might have arisen and provide the answer. Tell subtraction stories which include terms such as 'difference', 'count back', 'take away', etc. for the children to solve and to compare how they worked out the answers.

> **Key language**
>
> subtract, take away, difference, count back, order, remaining, left over

STEPS 4a

ACTIVITIES IN DETAIL

A   Revision: subtraction facts to 20   C G I

Part 1: Revising equations

1 Revise the meaning of equations such as 17 – 4 = 13 to include these situations:

2 Ask the children to suggest stories or situations which might have given rise to these subtractions.

Part 2: Methods of subtraction

1 Organise the children to try the collaborative activities on RM 28.

2 Afterwards, compare how the children worked out the answers using:
(a) pencil and paper calculations in Activity 1 on RM 28;
(b) mental calculations only in Activity 2.

Book 4a, page 15 provides individual practice.

Resources

School
Calculators; blank dice or dice numbered 1 to 6; good supply of small blank cards

Scheme
Resource Master 28; Book 4a, page 15

The most likely methods of calculation to be used here are either subtracting one number then the other, e.g. 15 – 2 = 13, 13 – 6 = 7 or adding together the two numbers to be subtracted then subtracting this total from the third number, e.g. 15 – (2 + 6) = 15 – 8 = 7.

B   Subtracting one- from two-digit numbers   C I

Part 1: Pattern building

1 Display the start of patterns like these:

17 – 11 =   14 – 8 =
27 – 11 =   24 – 8 =
37 – 11 =   34 – 8 =

2 Ask, *What comes next? Why?* and continue the sequences.

3 If helpful, the operation can be demonstrated by counting back on a number line.

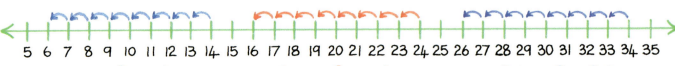

Resources

School
Wall number line 0 to 100; water-based marker pen

Scheme
Resource Master 29; Book 4a, page 16

78   STEPS 4a

Part 2: Subtraction pairs

1 Extend by displaying some two- and one-digit numbers like these:

In stage 1 of Part 2, there are 25 possible subtractions with answers ranging from 17 to 69.

2 Ask the children to work out and record in their own way subtractions by subtracting a number in the second set from one in the first.

3 Afterwards, the children can compare the range of answers with each other and how they worked these out.

4 If necessary, explain that it often helps to go back to an easier example either to find or check the answer, e.g. 17 – 8 = 9 might help to calculate 67 – 8 = 59.

RM 29 and Book 4a, page 16 provide individual practice.

 Assessment activity

*In advance, make ten cards like these:

Resources

School
Subtraction cards*

| 14-1-2 | 11-4-3 | 16-8-4 | 15-5-5 | 20-8-4 |
| 28-4 | 36-6 | 45-6 | 71-7 | 84-9 |

1 Using the first set of cards, ask the child to choose one at a time and to tell you the answer.

2 Repeat for the second set of cards.

3 Ask the child to choose one of the cards and to either tell you or write a story to show how this subtraction might have arisen.

Assessment notes

Oral response	✔
Practical response	
Pictorial response	
Written response	✔ (depending on method chosen for stage 3)

The child has:
correctly subtracted by mental recall two single-digit numbers from a number up to 20 at least four out of five times;
AND
correctly subtracted by mental recall a single-digit number from a two-digit number at least four out of five times;
AND
has applied knowledge of these facts to suggest a situation from which one of these subtractions might have arisen.

D Mixed operations   C G

1 Introduce the tasks on RM 30 which combine the mental skills developed in Steps 5 and 7.

2 Afterwards, the range of results can be compared within groups or by the class.

EXTENSION

■ Using either number loops **2c** or **2d** on RM 30, the children find as many correct solutions as they can.

Resources

School
Calculators

Scheme
Resource Master 30

Less able children may be able to attempt the tasks on RM 30 with the help of a calculator or apparatus. Since the tasks have different correct solutions, the children might afterwards check each other's or their own solutions with a calculator.

STRENGTHENING ACTIVITIES

Children who cannot subtract mentally more than one single-digit number from 20, may require more practical work with apparatus and recording the intermediate operation.

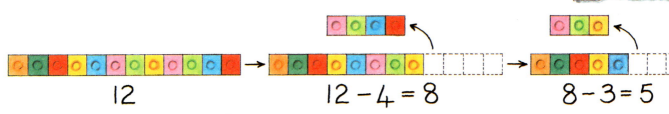

Subtracting one-digit from two-digit numbers

If the child is having problems with this mental skill, he/she may benefit from going through:

(a) patterns involving subtracting a single-digit number from a two-digit number where no 'bridging the ten' is required, e.g. 8 – 5, 18 – 5, 28 – 5, etc.;

(b) subtracting a one-digit number from a multiple of ten, e.g. 10 – 4, 20 – 4, 30 – 4, etc.

CHALLENGING ACTIVITIES

Number pyramids

Provide a workcard of this type:

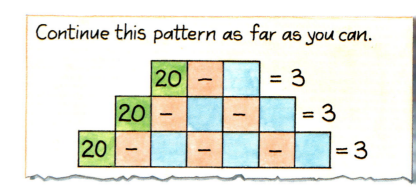

STEPS 4a

IDEAS BOARD

■ Spinner subtraction
❏ Up to four children share a spinner 1 to 10.
❏ They agree on a two-digit number greater than 20 and write it down on a card.
❏ They take it in turns to spin the spinner.
❏ They each subtract mentally the number spun from the number on the card and write down the answer.
❏ They compare results after each go.
❏ After five goes, a new starting number is chosen and the activity repeated.

■ Beat the calculator
❏ Using cards displaying additions such as 67 – 5, 42 – 8, etc., the children play in pairs.
❏ One works out the answer on the calculator, the other by mental recall, to see who is quicker.
❏ If you wish to make it competitive, whoever is quicker each time wins the card.
❏ Whoever wins more cards wins the game.
❏ On the next round, roles are reversed.

■ Team games

Provide half the children with a large card each on which they display a two-digit number in colour A. The other half of the group should each have a large card showing a one-digit number in colour B. The children walk around in a large space and, at a given signal, respond to your instructions. For example,

(a) Stand with one person with a different colour of card so that the difference between you is an odd (even) number;

(b) Stand with the person nearest to you. Which pair has the largest (smallest) difference between them? Which pairs have the same difference between them?

HOME/SCHOOL PROJECTS

The children take home four cards showing two-digit numbers and four showing one-digit numbers. By pairing any two cards together, the family find and record as many differences as they can. (Sixteen solutions are possible.)

SUPPORT MATERIALS

Teaching aids
TI 1103, 1104 and *Galaxy 9x calculators* (Texas Instruments)
Wall Number Line 0 – 100 (Taskmaster)
Blank dice (Hope Education)
Multilink Cubes (NES Arnold)

Teachers' reference materials
Primary Mathematics Today, 3rd edn, chapter 9, Elizabeth Williams and Hilary Shuard (Longman)

 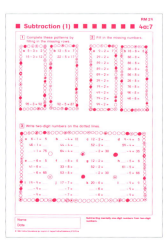 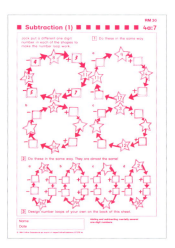

8. 2-D SHAPE (1)

LEARNING CONTEXT

Contribution made by this Step

The children focus on triangles and find out about:
- classifying triangles using terms like 'equilateral', 'isosceles', 'scalene';
- constructing angles from given information about sides or angles using different techniques;
- generalising about the interior angles of triangles;
- investigating the triangle as a rigid shape and as a means of constructing other polygons.

Objectives

To enable children to:
a Know and use properties associated with triangles.
b Know and use language associated with triangles.
c Construct triangles from given information.
d Make generalisations or test statements about triangles.

Background

In Step 3b:29, the children sorted 2-D shapes into families: triangles, quadrilaterals, pentagons and hexagons, etc., and sorted one collection of shapes in different ways using criteria such as 'regular', 'equal sides or angles', 'right-angled corners', etc. Now there is a specific focus on the construction and classification of triangles, using the properties of their sides and angles. Further exploration of triangles will continue in work in Steps 4a:28 and 4a:34. In Steps 4b, work on the interior angles of triangles will be extended when measurement in degrees is introduced.

Mathematics in the National Curriculum

Programme of Study: KS2
Pupils should be taught to:
- visualise and describe shapes and movements, developing precision in using related geometrical language. (SSM 2.a)
- make 2-D and 3-D shapes and patterns with increasing accuracy, recognise their geometrical features and properties, and use these to classify shapes and solve problems. (SSM 2.b)
- use right angles, fractions of a turn and, later, degrees, to measure rotation, and use the associated language. (SSM 3.c)
- select and use the appropriate mathematics and materials. (UA 2.a)
- understand and investigate general statements, *e.g. 'wrist size is half neck size', 'there are four prime numbers less than 10'*. (UA 4.a)
- make general statements of their own, based on evidence they have produced. (UA 4.c)

THINKING AND TALKING MATHEMATICALLY

Starting points for discussion

Road signs: *Which are shown in triangles? Why?*

What can you tell me about a triangle?

2-D geometric shapes: *How many different kinds of triangles can you find?*

3-D geometric shapes: *Find and name shapes with triangular faces.*

Key language

construct, angle, acute, obtuse, interior, opposite, adjacent, rigid, deformed, equal; triangles: equilateral, isosceles, scalene, right-angled, triangular, framework, diagonal

STEPS 4a

ACTIVITIES IN DETAIL

A Family of triangles

Resources

School
Geostrips (or similar) and fasteners for each group; name cards for triangles*

Scheme
Resource Master 31

*In advance, make three name cards: equilateral triangles – three equal sides; isosceles triangles – two equal sides; scalene triangles – no equal sides.

1 Ask each child to join sets of three strips to make different triangles.

2 Compare the different types of triangles with the focus on sides and angles.

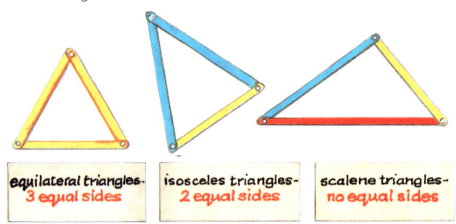

In this Step, if commercial strips are in short supply, they can be supplemented with strips of strong card (2 to 3 cm wide, of varying lengths, e.g. 8, 12, 16 and 20 cm) and brass fasteners.

3 Use the name cards to introduce the terms 'equilateral', 'isosceles' and 'scalene'.

4 Practise saying the terms by asking children to hold up a triangle and to describe it. *Which triangles are not isosceles and not equilateral? Why?*

5 By using the prepared triangles or remaking them, the children can take turns to sort the triangles into three sets, using the name cards as labels.

6 Retain the triangles for Activity **B**.

RM 31 provides individual practice in classifying triangles according to whether they are equilateral, isosceles or scalene.

An isosceles triangle has two sides of equal length, an equilateral triangle three sides of equal length. (An equilateral triangle is a special kind of isosceles triangle but with the third side also equal.) A scalene triangle has no equal sides.

EXTENSION

- Practise constructing:
  - isosceles triangles of different sizes on squared paper;
  - different triangles which are isosceles and right-angled.

B Angle properties of triangles

Resources

School
Geostrip triangles made for Activity **A**; assorted triangles from geometric shape sets; right-angle testers*

Scheme
Resource Master 32; Book 4a, page 17

*The children will each need to make a right-angled tester.

 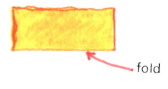

Part 1: Sorting angles

1 Provide each group with some triangles made in Activity **A**.

2 Ask the children how the triangles could be sorted by comparing angles. For example:
- all acute-angled corners;
- one right-angled corner;
- one obtuse-angled corner.

3 Include some impossible constructions! *Who can make a triangle with more than one right angle? Can you make a right-angled equilateral triangle? Why not?*

4 The right-angled testers can be used to confirm the type of angle where this is uncertain.

Part 2: Identifying angles in triangles

1 Introduce the tasks on RM 32, in which the children have to identify acute, right or obtuse angles in triangles.

2 Afterwards, see if the children can generalise about triangles, i.e. that they can either have three acute angles, or one right angle and two acute angles or one obtuse angle and two acute angles.

3 Retain the geostrip triangles for Activity **C**.

Book 4a, page 17, provides practice in constructing and recognising triangles from given information.

EXTENSION

- The children can design a modular structure of triangles on which each new triangle is constructed on one of the sides of one previously drawn. (They might practise with geostrips first.)

C Pinboard triangles   C I

1 Allow time for the children to find out which of the Geostrip triangles can be constructed on the 3 by 3 pinboards.

2 Afterwards, discuss, *What kinds of triangles were you able to construct? Were any impossible? Why?*

Resources

School
3 by 3 pinboards; elastic bands; geostrip triangles from Activity **A**

Scheme
Resource Masters 33, 34, 35

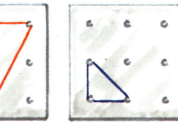

It is impossible to construct equilateral triangles on a pinboard of squares.

3 Introduce the tasks on RM 33 and RM 34 which provide practice in constructing or classifying triangles from given information. Make sure that the children understand what is meant by 'a triangle with no pin in the middle'.

4 Afterwards, the children can compare and discuss their results.

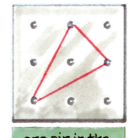

no pin in the middle / one pin in the middle

If 3 by 3 pinboards are not available, you can use larger versions, section off a 3 by 3 array with rubber bands and use only this area.

STEPS 4a

EXTENSION

■ The children might construct, then record on RM 35, different triangles on a 6 by 6 pinboard. Underneath each one, they write what they can about each triangle.

■ *Find triangles with one pin only in the middle.*

D Interior angles of triangles

Part 1: Revising straight angles

1 Get the children to fit together at least two lengths of Geostrip, to stand them upright on their desks and to open them to show straight angles.

2 Ask, *How many angles make up your straight angle?* Point to the angles.

Resources

School
Geostrips and fasteners or similar; assorted gummed paper triangles; shape stencils or templates which include a selection of triangles

Scheme
Book 4a, page 18

Part 1 will provide an ideal opportunity to revise the terms for angles; 'acute', 'obtuse' and 'right'.

Part 2: Interior angles of triangles.

1 Introduce the task on Book 4a, page 18, giving as little help as possible.

2 Make sure that the children tear rather than cut the pieces to ensure a ragged edge.

3 Encourage the children to experiment with triangles they have constructed, as well as provided triangles.

4 Afterwards, compare results and ask, *What can you tell me about the inside or interior angles of triangles? What if you started with a very large (or very small) triangle? Does it matter if it is scalene, isosceles or equilateral?*

5 You might wish to organise a class wall display in which the children cut out pairs of congruent triangles, including larger examples and show what happens when the corners of one are added together.

Here one, two and three angles make up the straight angle. What can you tell someone near you about the angles?

By testing triangles of as many shapes and sizes as possible, the children should be able to generalise/ hypothesise that if the three angles of any triangle are added together (in this case by being arranged to meet at a common point), they form a straight angle (Ma 1/4d).

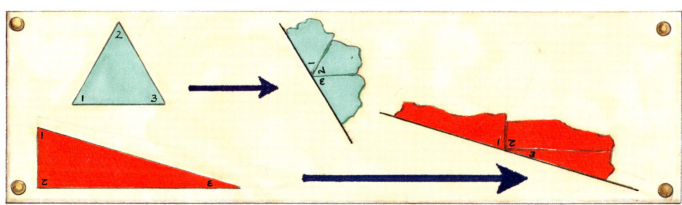

STEPS 4a

EXTENSION

■ *Investigate what happens when you start with quadrilaterals instead of triangles. What about their interior angles? Present your results and conclusions in your own way.*

E   Triangles and rigidity [C] [P] [I]

*In advance, prepare three name cards: rigid, deformed, diagonal.

Part 1: Diagonals

1 Working in pairs, ask the children to join strips to make at least one each of these: triangle, quadrilateral, pentagon, hexagon and octagon. (They do not have to be regular.)

2 Discuss which can be moved (or deformed) and those which cannot, i.e. are rigid.

3 Encourage the children to find the fewest diagonals needed to make all the polygons rigid.

4 As work proceeds, ask the children to explain to you any patterns or relationships they are finding. For example:

Resources

School
Geostrips and fasteners or similar; pictures of roof girders, pylons, metal bridges, etc. to show triangular frameworks (optional); name cards*

If the names of specific polygons are not known, the children might use reference books to find the correct names or classify the shape by its number of sides.

Shape	Number of sides	Number of diagonals
triangle	3	0
quadrilateral	4	1
pentagon	5	2
hexagon	6	3 etc

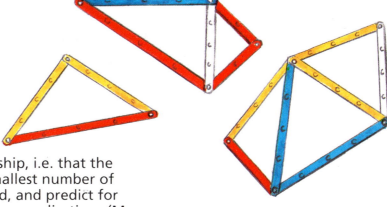

5 Children who can explain the relationship, i.e. that the number of sides minus three gives the smallest number of diagonals needed to make the shape rigid, and predict for polygons not trialled, are making simple generalisations (Ma 1/4d). (Some may also notice that the number of internal triangles created is two less than the number of sides of the polygon.)

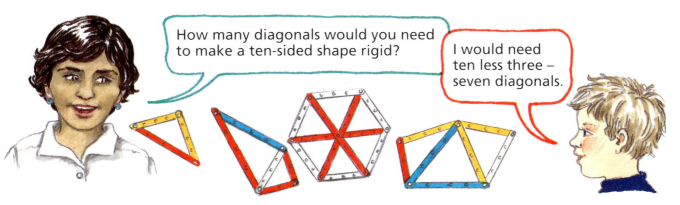

How many diagonals would you need to make a ten-sided shape rigid?

I would need ten less three – seven diagonals.

Part 2: Constructing polygons from triangles

1 Some children may enjoy making pencil/ruler constructions to confirm the relationship in Part 1 by adding a triangle each time with a common vertex and side.

STEPS 4a

2 Other statements/ generalisations which might be explored by simple constructions can be of this type:
(a) All quadrilaterals can be divided into two triangles with one straight line.
(b) You can fit three triangles together to make different pentagons.

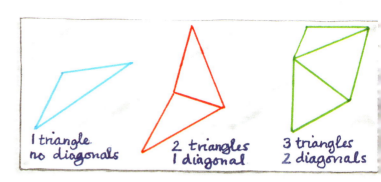

F Assessment activity

1 Ask the child to choose a scalene triangle and tell you about it. If necessary, prompt by asking more direct questions: *What can you tell me about its angles? How do you know it is a scalene triangle?*

2 Repeat stage 1 for equilateral, isosceles and right-angled triangles.

3 Ask the child to construct one each of these four kinds of triangles, using any preferred materials.

4 Afterwards, show how you can make a rectangle with two matching paper right-angled triangles.

5 Ask the child to choose materials to test if you can always make a rectangle with two matching right-angled triangles.

I Resources

School
Assorted paper triangles which include equilateral, isosceles, scalene and right-angled; right-angled triangles with different dimensions; access to construction materials, e.g. grid papers, pinboards, Geostrips, etc.

Allow the child to carry out the tasks described in stages 3 and 5 in his/her own time and to explain to you afterwards what has been done.

Assessment notes

Oral response	✔
Practical response	✔
Pictorial response	✔
Written response	✔

The child has:
identified different triangles by name, e.g. scalene;
AND
described triangles using terms related to angles, sides, etc.;
AND
chosen materials to construct triangles of different types;
AND
used examples to test a generalisation about triangles.

STRENGTHENING ACTIVITIES

Geostrip triangles

Use Geostrips of three lengths only, each length a different colour. Establish the equality of the sides of each colour. Ask the child to make different triangles with these, then to explain to you how the triangles are the same/different and any special names for the triangles. This may help you discover areas of misunderstanding.

Angles

A child struggling with recognising acute, obtuse or right angles in triangles may benefit from repeating some of the work in Step 2.

'I spy …'

Practise recognition of triangles and use of their names, e.g. 'I spy a scalene triangle'. The child finds relevant shapes from a set and says why the triangle is of this type. This may also help you diagnose any areas of misunderstanding.

CHALLENGING ACTIVITIES

Area

On 1 cm squared paper, which triangles can be drawn, using whole and half squares only? Calculate their areas. For example:

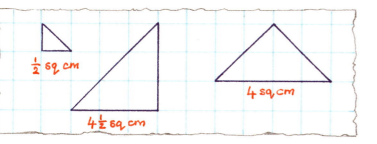

Interior angles

Ask children to decide on the best way to prove and display their results for this statement: 'The interior angles of a quadrilateral, added together, are the same as the interior angles of two triangles.'

IDEAS BOARD

■ Typical projects

Structures; Bridges; Pattern; Shape and Size; Buildings.

■ Technology

The children can:

- measure, mark out and cut out accurately triangles in different materials, e.g. balsa wood, to make modular structures, etc.;
- design fair tests and build models to compare the strength of triangular frameworks with other frameworks, e.g. of squares;
- find examples of pylons, bridges, etc. where triangular frameworks can be seen.

■ Programmed shapes

The children can try to write programs to create triangles, using LOGO, Pip or Roamer.

■ Sorting diagrams

- Sort one collection of triangles in as many ways as possible.
- Take turns to position a triangle in the correct region of this diagram.

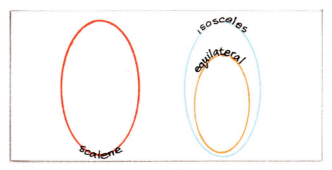

■ Art

- Collect and display examples of artefacts, textiles, etc. from other times and cultures in which triangles feature as a decorative element.
- Make 'cut and stretched' paper triangles.

- Make observational drawings of places in the environment where triangles can be seen.

STEPS 4a

HOME/SCHOOL PROJECTS

Find examples of triangles in advertisements, trademarks, logos, etc. Bring these to school to build up a display.

SUPPORT MATERIALS

Teaching aids
Gummed paper triangles (Playaway)
3 x 3 Pinboard (Hope Education)
Transparent 3 x 3 Matrix Geoboard (NES Arnold)
Geostrips (NES Arnold)
Brass paper fasteners
Geometric Shapes (NES Arnold)
Orbit Material (NES Arnold)
Angle Strips (Philip & Tacey)
Pip (Swallow Systems)
Roamer (Valiant Technology)

Teachers' reference materials
Triangles from *Crosslinks* series (Tarquin Publications)
Making Star Shapes, Marion Hine and Roger Limbrick (Tarquin Publications)
READY, STEADY, LOGO!, Pauline Millward and Eric Albany (Longman)

Children's books
Shapes and *Solids* from *Fun with Maths* series (Wayland)
Shape from *Understanding Maths* series (Wayland)

Software
Picture Builder (Hill McGibbon Software)
Picture Craft (ILECC)

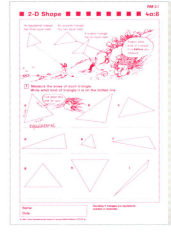

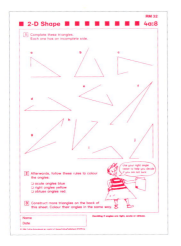

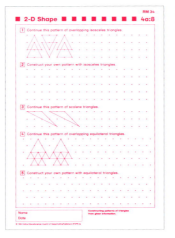

9. PERCENTAGES

LEARNING CONTEXT

Contribution made by this Step

Children are introduced to percentages as a form of notation to indicate a portion of a whole. They begin to recognise the equivalence of some simple percentage forms with decimals and fractions already experienced.

Objectives

To enable children to:
a   Understand and use simple percentages to describe situations.
b   Know that a half, a quarter, three-quarters and multiples of a tenth can be expressed in different ways.

Background

In everyday life percentages are used at least as often as fractions or decimals to describe parts of a whole. They form a convenient and consistent way to compare fractions of amounts. Children will be familiar with such phrases as '… kills 99 per cent of all household germs', and many will have seen posters or leaflets about percentage rates of interest on savings accounts. It is important that the concept is introduced gradually so this Step builds upon approaches used in STEPS 3a and 3b in relation to simple fractions and decimals. Calculations which use the percentage form will be dealt with in STEPS 4b and STEPS 5.

Before introducing the percentage form it is important that the children have a firm grasp of the images and notation of simple fractions up to one whole, and one-place decimals. Similar resources and structures are used to introduce percentages.

> **Mathematics in the National Curriculum**
>
> Programme of Study: KS2
> Pupils should be taught to:
> ■ understand and use, in context, fractions and percentages to estimate, describe and compare proportions of a whole. (N 2.c)
> ■ understand and use the language of number. (UA 3.a)

THINKING AND TALKING MATHEMATICALLY

Starting points for discussion

Display a range of advertisements which include percentages. Ask, for example, *If '99 per cent of all known germs are killed', what do you think this means? If all the germs were killed, what percentage would that be?*

> **Key language**
>
> Percentage, per cent (%), hundredth part, parts out of a hundred

STEPS 4a

ACTIVITIES IN DETAIL

A Introducing the percentage form

Part 1: Multiples of ten expressed as percentages

1 Explain that the children are going to learn about an alternative way to represent parts of a whole, and that this is called percentages.

2 Write *per cent* on the board and ask, *Where have you seen or heard the words before?*

3 Explain that per cent means 'for every hundred' or 'out of one hundred'.

4 Write the symbol %, pointing out that it can be used instead of the words 'per cent'. Give the children a chance to practise writing the symbol.

5 Use RM 68 or similar, drawn on squared paper. Ask them to colour, say, ten of the small squares. Explain that this is ten squares 'out of' 100 and can be written as 10 per cent, or 10%. Ask, *What percentage is not coloured?*

Resources

School
Scissors

Scheme
Resource Masters 36 and 68; Book 4a, page 19

Most children will be familiar with miles per gallon (kilometres per litre), miles/kilometres per hour, so they may know that *per* means 'for every'. Also *cent* will be familiar to some in such currencies as cents and centimes, and words such as century, centenarian, centurian, centenary. Note that the Latin word *centum* means 'one hundred'.

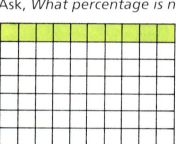

10 squares out of 100 are coloured.
10% are coloured.
90% are not coloured.

6 Ask them to use a second colour to mark other, different, sets of ten squares, pointing out that each set is also ten per cent of the whole.

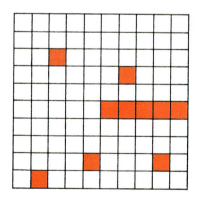

10% are coloured.

7 Repeat for other multiples of ten per cent up to, and including, 100 per cent. Each time ask, *What percentage is not coloured?*

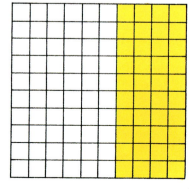

40% are coloured.
60% are not coloured.

Part 2: $\frac{1}{2}$, $\frac{1}{4}$ and $\frac{3}{4}$ expressed as percentages

1 Draw three plain squares on the board. Shade or mark a quarter, a half and three quarters. Discuss how many of the hundred small squares would be shaded to give percentages which match these fractions of the whole squares.

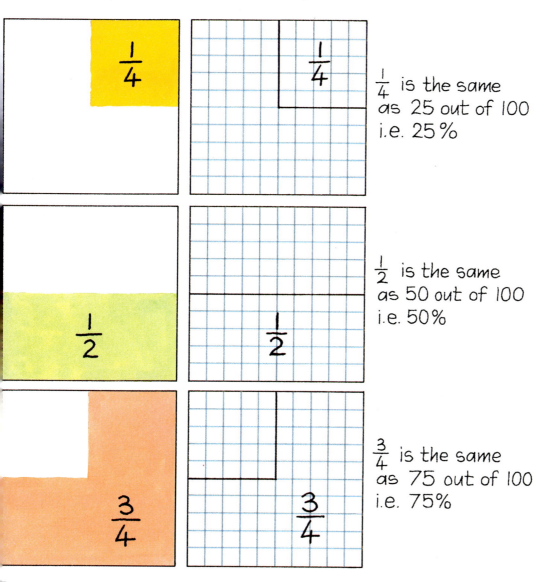

$\frac{1}{4}$ is the same as 25 out of 100 i.e. 25%

$\frac{1}{2}$ is the same as 50 out of 100 i.e. 50%

$\frac{3}{4}$ is the same as 75 out of 100 i.e. 75%

2 Use RM 36. Ask the children to represent some percentages on the grids which have units other than squares.

Further practice at representing percentages can be found in Book 4a, page 19.

It is important that images of percentages are not always associated with squares.

B Matching and ordering percentages   C G P

Part 1: Matching percentages, fractions and one-place decimals

1 Remind the children of their previous experiences of marking fractions and one-place decimals on a number line. Build up a series of lines, of identical length, on which you and the children mark the position of simple fractions and single place decimals, to include some of those on the number lines overleaf.

Resources

School
Number lines drawn on the board or on a large sheet of paper or an OHP transparency

Scheme
Resource Masters 37 and 38

TEPS 4a

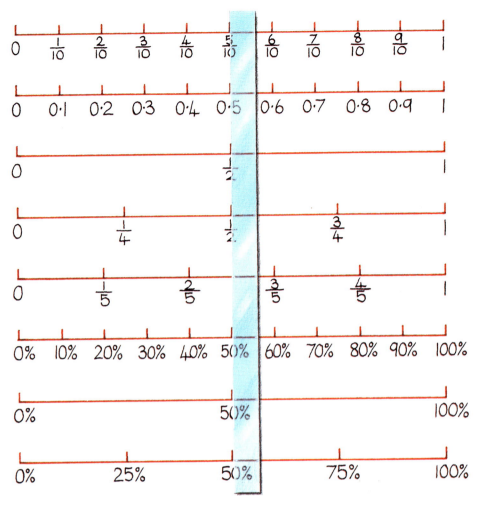

For teaching purposes, use a notional 20 unit line which can be easily divided into two, four, five and ten parts.

2 By placing a thin stick, or transparent ruler, vertically across the lines, various equivalents will be shown and children will be able to observe the relative size of a mixture of fractions, one-place decimals and the percentages already experienced. Discuss and note any interesting patterns.

Use RM 37 to give practice in matching and ordering percentages, one-place decimals and simple fractions.

Part 2: Percentage, fraction and decimal cards

- ❏ The children cut up copies of RM 38 to make the cards.
- ❏ Two players shuffle and share out the cards leaving those marked > and < to one side.
- ❏ Players take turns to choose an inequality card and place it on the table, along with a number card to its right or left.
- ❏ The second player places an appropriate card to complete the number statement.
- ❏ Play continues until one player has used all his or her cards (to win), or a player is unable to place a card (and loses).

EXTENSION

■ Choose a percentage. Make two lists; all the known fractions and decimals larger than the given percentage (up to one whole), and all the known fractions and decimals smaller than the given percentage.

C Describing situations G

Part 1: Percentage statements

1 Remind the children that a whole is 100 per cent. Discuss, for example, possible surveys of 100 children in a school. If 50 per cent are wearing black shoes and 20 per cent are wearing brown shoes, what percentage have footwear of any other colour?

2 Ask them to think about a statement such as 'Fifty per cent of my friends have seen Buckingham Palace, fifty per cent have seen the Tower of London, and fifty per cent have seen the Houses of Parliament. So one hundred and fifty per cent of my friends have visited these places.'

Part 2: Describing the results of sorting

1 Using 100 counters of assorted sizes and colours, organise small groups to:
- sort these in their own way;
- describe the numbers in each subset, using percentages;
- design a pictorial means of representing the data using percentage notation;
- check that the percentages totalled equal 100 per cent to represent the whole set.

2 Remind the children that each counter is a hundredth part of the set, or one per cent.

Book 4a, page 20 and RM 36 provide further practice.

Resources
School
Counters of mixed colours and sizes

Scheme
Book 4a, page 20, Resource Master 36

This activity provides an opportunity to introduce percentages which are not necessarily linked to halves, quarters, tenths, etc. This work is developed more fully in Steps 4b. Other sets of 100 objects can be sorted similarly.

D Assessment activity I

1 Use RM 36. Ask the child to choose a grid and colour 20 per cent of it red. Ask, *What percentage is not coloured red?*

2 Using the same grid, ask the child to colour another 50 per cent of it blue. Ask, *What percentage is still not coloured?*

3 Repeat for other percentages as appropriate on other grids (including 25 per cent and 75 per cent), asking the child to tell you why he/she is colouring the chosen number of units, and how the amount not coloured is being calculated.

Assessment notes

Oral response	✔
Practical response	✔
Pictorial response	✔
Written response	

The child has:
illustrated some simple percentages, including 50 per cent, 25 per cent and 75 per cent and some multiples of 10 per cent;
AND
used the terminology of percentages to describe simple amounts.

Resources
School
Colouring materials

Scheme
Resource Master 36

STRENGTHENING ACTIVITIES

Simple matching

Make a set of cards containing diagrammatic, numerical and word forms of simple fractions, decimals and percentages (multiples of 10 per cent, 25 per cent and 75 per cent). Use the cards to play *Snap* or pairing and matching games. (RM 38 can be used as the basic non-pictorial set.)

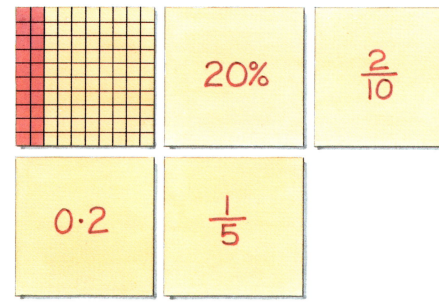

Ten per cent bars

Use number rods such as Cuisenaire or Colour Factor to show the step pattern from 0–100 per cent in multiples of 10 per cent. The step pattern can be copied and coloured on squared paper, using ten squares to represent 100 per cent.

Alternatively, the children can put base 10 longs on a 10 by 10 1 cm squared grid to show 10 per cent, 20 per cent, etc. What they find out can be recorded on cm squared grid paper.

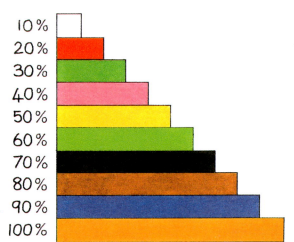

Ten per cent more or less

Use a ten space number line with the two ends labelled 0 per cent and 100 per cent. Point to a calibration. Ask the child to tell you what 'per cent' of the line the point represents, and also the percentage 'name' of the points on either side.

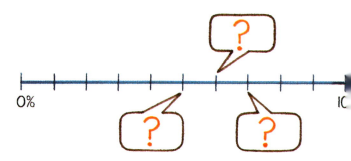

CHALLENGING ACTIVITIES

Survey

The children conduct a survey of 100 people (or 100 cars passing by the school), having decided upon categories within which to tally the information. This can be done on a blank 100 square (e.g. RM 16). The proportions of the sample of 100 are expressed as percentages and then used to draw, label and interpret a bar chart or bar-line graph.

Calculator

Ask children to explore the use of the % key on a calculator.

IDEAS BOARD

■ Base 10 materials

Use base 10 materials. Discuss the percentage relationships of the pieces. For example:
– a unit is 10 per cent of a long;
– a long is 10 per cent of a flat;
– a flat is 10 per cent of a block.
What does 100 per cent of a flat look like?

■ VAT

Discuss current VAT rates and how this affects the pricing of goods, services, etc.

■ Money

Using £1 as the whole, other coins can be expressed as percentages of £1.
50p = 50 per cent of £1
20p = 20 per cent of £1
10p = 10 per cent of £1
So how could 1p and 5p be expressed? What about 27p?

■ Logic blocks

Using selected pieces from a set of Logic Blocks, investigate the percentage which are red … thick … circles …

■ Story of 100 per cent

Show the story of 100 per cent using squared paper.

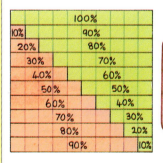

What other patterns could be made?

■ Weather forecasts

Examine some television or newspaper weather forecasts. What is meant by *'a 50 per cent likelihood of rain tomorrow'* or *'Ten per cent possibility of a thunderstorm?'*

■ Science

Each group plants 100 mustard seeds on blotting papers divided into 100 squares. They record and compare the percentage which germinates, for example, in different growing conditions.

■ School survey

Ask the children to comment on statements such as, *About 10 per cent of children in the school will be left-handed*. The class design and agree on fields for a database to be completed for 100 children chosen at random. Each group can interview, say, ten children each.

Name	birthday month	has sisters	has brothers	favourite colour	favourite fruit
Sue Jenkins	March	✓		red	apples
Hardib Raschid	October	✓	✓	yellow	grapes
Craig Smith	June	✓	✓	red	pears

Afterwards, they convert the information on each field into percentage notation and decide the best way to display it.

■ Measurement

Draw lines. Can the children mark a point, say, about 20 per cent of the whole distance from the left hand end? How did they decide where to mark the point?

■ Go for 100 per cent

Use a blank 100 square (RM 2), small counters and percentage cards, several of each, labelled 0%, 10%, 20%, 25%, 30%. The cards are shuffled and placed numbers down. Players take turns to take the top card and place counters on the sheet to match the percentage. The first to fill the sheet is the winner.

HOME/SCHOOL PROJECTS

The children collect from home examples of the use of percentages in newspapers, magazines and television. Make a display of the examples.

SUPPORT MATERIALS

Teaching aids
Fraction Percentage Dominoes (NES Arnold)

Teachers' reference materials
Primary Mathematics Today, 3rd edn, chapter 30, Elizabeth Williams and Hilary Shuard (Longman)
Maths Plus: Decimals and Percentages 2, Paul Harling (Ward Lock Educational)

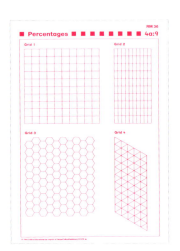

10. LENGTH

LEARNING CONTEXT

Contribution made by this Step

The children carry out activities in which they:
– measure and construct lines in millimetre units;
– estimate and approximate lengths to the nearest centimetre;
– decide the most sensible unit of length for measuring or tool for a specific task;
– explore relationships between millimetres and centimetres then metres and kilometres.

Objectives

To enable children to:
a Measure in millimetres with reasonable accuracy.
b Estimate or approximate to the nearest centimetre.
c Solve problems involving kilometres.
d Appreciate the relationships between metric units of length and know when it is sensible to use these units.
e Record lengths using numbers with up to one decimal place.

Background

In Step 3b:9, the children estimated and measured in centimetres, using equivalent notation such as 1 m 20 cm, 120 cm and 1·2 m. This Step concentrates on units appropriate for measuring very short or long lengths. Further work on length will be included in Step 35.

In Handbook 4b, there will be an emphasis on solving problems, using the four rules of number and the construction of 2-D and 3-D shapes with given dimensions. Measuring in millimetres is a demanding skill so it is reasonable to allow a tolerance of one millimetre either way when checking results.

The importance of children learning to use and recognise the need for instruments like micrometers and callipers is emphasised.

THINKING AND TALKING MATHEMATICALLY

Starting points for discussion

Samples of 1 mm or 2 mm graph paper.

Revision of notation 134 cm or 1 m 34 cm: *What height do you think you are? How can you write it?*

Prefixes for a metre: *milli, centi, kilo*.

Display of equipment, e.g. tapes, expanding rules, micrometers, dressmakers' tapes, trundle wheels. *Who might use these? Why?*

Mathematics in the National Curriculum

Programme of Study: KS2
Pupils should be taught to:
■ extend their understanding of the number system to ... decimals with no more than two decimal places in the context of measurement and money. (N 2.b)
■ develop their use of the four operations to solve problems, including those involving money and measures, using a calculator where appropriate. (N 4.a)
■ choose appropriate standard units of length, mass, capacity and time, and make sensible estimates with them in everyday situations; extend their understanding of the relationship between units; convert one metric unit to another. (SSM 4.a)
■ choose and use appropriate measuring instruments; interpret numbers and read scales to an increasing degree of accuracy. (SSM 4.b)

Key language

estimate, measure, approximate, construct, length, distance, circumference, depth, perimeter, diameter, millimetre (mm), centimetre (cm), metre (m), kilometre (km), calliper, micrometer, gauge

ACTIVITIES IN DETAIL

A Half-centimetre units C I

1 Ask everyone to construct a line which is, say, halfway between 8 cm and 9 cm.

2 Ask the children how this length might be described in words, then in written forms.

3 If necessary, revise recording in fractional notation.

> This line measures eight-and-a-half centimetres.

8·5 cm or $8\tfrac{1}{2}$ cm

(Some children may already know about millimetres but this is not essential here.)

4 Ask questions to encourage mental arithmetic, e.g.
(a) *What length would the line be if you rubbed out 3 cm?*
(b) *What length would it be if you doubled it?*

5 Repeat with other examples if necessary.

RM 39 and Book 4a, page 21 provide further practice in estimating, measuring and constructing lines.

Resources
School
Rulers with whole- and half-centimetre calibrations at least

Scheme
Book 4a, page 21;
Resource Master 39

Remind the children to:
(a) use a well-sharpened pencil;
(b) measure from the zero calibration;
(c) keep the eye directly in front of the calibration being read.

B Introducing the millimetre C G

1 Ask the children to tell you what they think the calibrations marked between the whole centimetres are and why. Do they recognise that the centimetre divisions are divided into ten smaller divisions?

2 Ask the children to rule a straight line between, say, 6 cm and 7 cm long.

3 Get the children within a group to compare their lines. *How are they the same? Different? How can you describe the length of your line as accurately as possible? How might you write it?*

4 Display suggestions for written forms and introduce the millimetre notation.

6·4 cm or $6\tfrac{4}{10}$ cm or 64 mm

5 Repeat for other lengths.

6 In particular, draw attention to:
(a) the relationship between the centimetre and millimetre;
(b) the abbreviation for millimetre or millimetres, mm;
(c) the high degree of accuracy when this unit of length is used (but note that the measurement is still approximate since a line can still be between, say, 15 mm and 16 mm long);
(d) the need for precise measuring skills.

RM 40 and Book 4a, page 22 provide individual practice.

Resources
School
Rulers with mm calibrations

Scheme
Book 4a, page 22;
Resource Masters 40 and 41

> Which of you has drawn a line $6\tfrac{4}{10}$ centimetres or 64 millimetres long?

For RM 40, you may need to revise the fact that, when approximating to the nearest centimetre, half-centimetre lengths such as 4.5 cm are rounded up.

STEPS 4a

RM 41 provides more demanding problems which can be solved individually or collaboratively.

EXTENSION

■ Look in magazines, colour catalogues, etc. for examples of measurements up to 100 mm. Cut out and display examples with their measurements.

RM 41 requires the children to identify and obtain information necessary to solve problems and interpret situations mathematically, so it may be used to provide evidence of these skills (Ma 1/4a, b).

C Measuring real objects

Resources

School
Objects of various lengths up to 10 cm (see Part 1); measuring instruments (see Part 2)

Part 1: Measuring everyday objects

1 With the children's help and suggestions, collect together for each group different objects with well-defined end points up to 10 cm long initially, e.g. paper-clips, staples, short pencils, crayons, short pieces of string, craft sticks, nails, screws, etc.

2 Working in pairs, the children measure the length of these in millimetres. (Remind them to estimate first!)

3 The children might devise their own means of recording, or you can show them a conventional form of recording in which scale drawings are made and dimension lines shown.

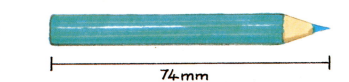

4 Afterwards, children within groups can compare results.

5 Remind the children that since the millimetre is such a small unit of length, results may vary to within one or two millimetres for the same object.

Part 2: Other measuring instruments

1 Make available as many of these as possible: depth gauge, bow callipers, graduated callipers, micrometer, diameter gauge, feeler gauges.

2 After having time to examine the various instruments, get the children to suggest how they might be used and to interpret the calibrations.

All of the resources mentioned here can be found in the Osmiroid Measuring Set. Most of the instruments can also be bought individually.

3 Demonstrate the use of the instruments and clarify the purpose for which they are intended.

STEPS 4a

4 Working in pairs (or small groups), the children can estimate and measure lengths, depths, diameters, widths of narrow openings and cracks, recording in their own way.

EXTENSION

■ Draw dots on paper. Estimate then measure in millimetres the distance between pairs of points.

■ Using several feeler gauges, the children can investigate the different sizes of narrow openings which can be measured with these. For example, with a 3 mm, 4 mm and 5 mm gauge, what measurements can be taken?

D Kilometres   C G

Part 1: How long is a kilometre?

1 What can the children tell you about a kilometre? *What is measured in kilometres?*

2 Establish that 'kilo-' means 'one thousand' and that 'kilometre' means 'one thousand metres', and introduce the abbreviated form.

Resources

School
Metre rule; surveyors' tapes of assorted lengths; trundle wheels, etc.; timers

Scheme
Book 4a, page 23;
Resource Master 42

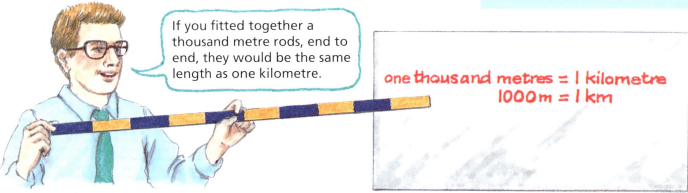

3 Ask questions like, *How many metres in a half-kilometre? What fraction of a kilometre is 200 metres? How far would you have to walk to travel one-tenth of a kilometre?*

4 Give the children experience of walking a kilometre (a sponsored walk for a charity?).

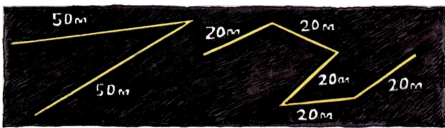

5 Before their walk, get groups of children to choose measuring instruments to mark out a 100 m chalk line.

6 The children should estimate, then check, how long it takes them to walk one 100 m length. They then use this information to predict the time it will take to walk a kilometre.

7 Afterwards, discuss the times taken to walk a kilometre – it is likely to be just over ten minutes.

If trundle wheels are used, make sure the children know what each 'click' represents, i.e. a full rotation of a wheel has a circumference of 1m. This can be demonstrated alongside a 10 m surveyors' tape so that ten clicks can be counted.

The lines might be different shapes, depending on available space.

Part 2: Lengths greater than one kilometre

1 Through questioning and discussion, establish the links between kilometres and metres using initially examples up to 1km based on tenths.

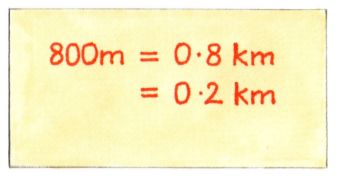

How many metres in two tenths of a kilometre?

2 Extend to distances greater than 1km.

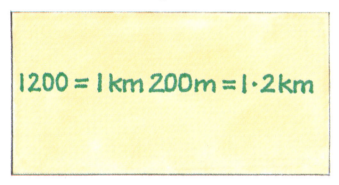

3 Working in pairs, suggest that the children record further examples like this using distances up to 10 km.

4 Afterwards, discuss places about 1km distant from school, i.e. about ten minutes' walk away, or distances from local towns/landmarks.

RM 42 and Book 4a, page 23 provide individual practice. For this book page, you may need to clarify the meaning of 'via' in connection with a journey.

E Most sensible instrument/measure

1 Introduce the task on RM 43 which would be suited to paired work. This RM also revises some of the language of probability.

2 Afterwards, compare results.

3 The children might each contribute an entry and appropriate illustration from task 3 on this RM for a class display of what is best measured in kilometres.

Resources

Scheme
Resource Master 43

F Assessment activity

1 Introduce the tasks on RM 44, giving help with reading or rephrasing instructions if necessary.

2 Afterwards, ask the child to suggest something which would be best measured in millimetres, centimetres, metres and kilometres.

Resources

School
Ruler with mm calibrations

Scheme
Resource Master 44

STEPS 4a

Assessment notes

Oral response	✔
Practical response	✔
Pictorial response	
Written response	✔

The child has:
estimated lengths up to 10 cm to the nearest centimetre with reasonable accuracy;
AND
measured and constructed lines with dimensions given in millimetres;
AND
solved some problems involving kilometres;
AND
completed diagrams showing the relationship between units of length and ways of recording these using numbers with up to one decimal place;
AND
has suggested what might be measured with each metric unit of length.

STRENGTHENING ACTIVITIES

Estimating

Children whose centimetre estimates are 'way out' may need to repeat some of the activities in Step 3a:9.

Measuring

If the child is not measuring in millimetres correctly, observe him or her, as this is carried out, to establish the error, e.g. positioning the zero mark on the ruler or counting the number of millimetre divisions incorrectly.

Constructing lines in millimetres

If the child's manipulative skill is poor, we suggest that this is deferred until the work is revised and extended in STEPS 4b.

Kilometre

At this time, it is more important that the child has an idea of the length of a kilometre, how long this might take to walk and what is measured in kilometres rather than interpret the kind of problems such as those on RM 42.

Relationship patterns

If the child does not appreciate the relationship between centimetres and millimetres, draw lines of 1 cm, 2 cm, …10 cm. Label each line in cm and mm. Draw attention to the way the numbers grow in increments of one in cm, i.e. 1, 2, 3, … 0 and of tens in mm, i.e. 10, 20, … 100. Introduce half-centimetre lengths next in the same way.

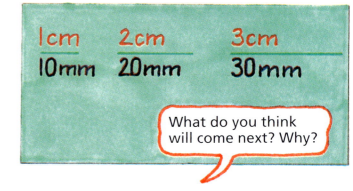

STEPS 4a

CHALLENGING ACTIVITIES

How many steps in a kilometre?

The children measure and record the time it takes them to walk twenty normal walking steps and the distance covered. They then try to work out, perhaps with a calculator, the time it will probably take to walk a kilometre and how many steps they will take.

Lengths in miniature

The children can draw closed shapes or spirals along the lines of 2 mm graph paper or 5 mm squared grid, then calculate the perimeters or lengths. This spiral increases by 4 mm on each new side.

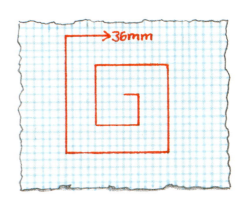

IDEAS BOARD

■ Display

Get the children to build up a display of items which would most sensibly be measured in millimetres, e.g. coins, stamps, buttons, staples, paperclips, etc. These can be used to give practice in estimating, measuring or accurate 1:1 scale drawings. More able children might try to make enlargements using a 1:2, 1:5 or 1:10 scale.

■ Pencil graph

The children can make a bar-line graph of the life of a pencil by recording its new length in millimetres after each sharpening until it is no longer useable.

■ Technology

Think of and examine examples of machines which have distance counters. *How are they used? Why? What do the numbers mean?*

■ Geography

What landmarks can the children suggest are about 1 km distant from the school? Get a large-scale map of the area around the school, draw a circle with the radius set at the length representing a kilometre and the school as the centre. Identify places on the circumference of the circle. Examine and interpret kilometre scales on large-scale maps.

HOME/SCHOOL PROJECTS

On a journey on a bicycle or in a car, predict where you will be when you have travelled 1 km. Record the distance on the distance counter. As your journey progresses, you might like to change your mind as the counter moves on.

STEPS 4a

SUPPORT MATERIALS

Teaching aids
Measuring Set and *Tape Measure* (10 m) (Osmiroid)
Primary Metre Rule and *Tape Measures* (10 m up to 50 m) (NES Arnold)
Vertical and Horizontal Tape Measures (NES Arnold)
30 cm Bevelled Rulers (NES Arnold)
2 m Metal Tape Measure (NES Arnold)
Plastic Trundle Wheel (NES Arnold)
Calliper Pack (NES Arnold)
1 mm Measure (Taskmaster)

Teachers' reference materials
Basic Measurement Activities, Dorothy Diamond (Hulton)

Children's books
Measuring from *Fun with Maths* series (Franklin Watts)
Length from *Knowabout* series, Henry Pluckrose (Franklin Watts)
Measurement from *Understanding Maths* series (Wayland)

Radio and TV
Measuring from *Mathscope* (BBC Television)

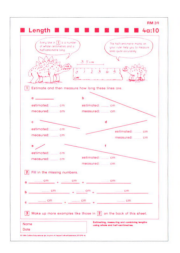
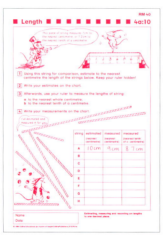
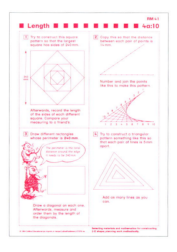
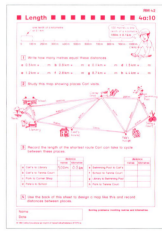

11. ADDITION (2)

LEARNING CONTEXT

Contribution made by this Step

The children develop strategies, using standard and non-standard methods of recording, to add numbers with totals to 999 at least. Although apparatus and calculators are used, the emphasis is on developing reliable pencil-and-paper methods.

Objectives

To enable children to:
a Add a one-, two- or three-digit number to a three-digit number without a calculator or apparatus (totals < 999).
b Choose methods to solve problems methodically.
c Estimate or approximate answers.
d Start to add numbers with totals > 1000.

Background

In this Step, the children put to good use their mental knowledge of addition pairs to 20, adding several single-digit numbers, and place value. As the children make increasing use of pencil-and-paper calculations, either using standard or non-standard methods, they need to build on the mental methods they have previously acquired, particularly for addition without apparatus or the calculator.

When using apparatus, the calculator or written methods, the children should be continually encouraged to ask themselves in advance, *What kind of answer do I expect?* and, afterwards, *Is my answer sensible?*

Although this Step introduces some standard pencil-and-paper methods, the children are also encouraged to develop and practise methods of their own, based on their own understanding of numbers, the processes of addition and knowledge of place value.

Mathematics in the National Curriculum

Programme of Study: KS2
Pupils should be taught to:
■ read, write and order whole numbers, understanding that the position of a digit signifies its value; use their understanding of place value to develop methods of computation, to approximate numbers to the nearest 10 or 100, and to multiply and divide by powers of 10 when there are whole-number answers. (N 2.a)
■ develop a variety of mental methods of computation with whole numbers up to 100, and explain patterns used; extend mental methods to develop a range of non-calculator methods of computation that involve addition and subtraction of whole numbers. (N 3.d)
■ develop their use of the four operations to solve problems, including those involving money and measures, using a calculator where appropriate. (N 4.a)
■ check results by different methods, including repeating the operations in a different order or using inverse operations; gain a sense of the size of a solution, and estimate and approximate solutions to problems. (N 4.c)

THINKING AND TALKING MATHEMATICALLY

Starting points for discussion

Words relating to addition: *Tell me a sentence which uses 'total'* (or *'sum'*, *'plus'*, *'count on'*, *'combine'*, etc.) *in it.*

Given an addition sentence such as 345 + 74 = 419, can the children suggest a situation from which it might have arisen?

Key language

add, sum, total, running total, count on, combine, plus, exchange, value, one- two- and three-digit numbers

ACTIVITIES IN DETAIL

A Revision: mental addition [C] [I]

1 Introduce the tasks on Book 4a, pages 24 and 25 which revise addition bonds to 20, equivalence and adding several one-digit numbers.

2 Although the activities are intended as a mental exercise, it may help some children if base 10 materials are available.

EXTENSION

■ The children can extend the investigation in instruction 1 of Book 4a, page 25 by extending the total beyond 20.

Resources

School
Base 10 materials

Scheme
Book 4a, pages 24 and 25

B Adding pairs of three-digit numbers [C] [P] [I]

*If not already available, get the children to make, on card or paper, place value boards with divisions wide enough to allow base 10 hundreds, tens and ones to be positioned. (See the illustration for stage 6b.)

1 Display two sets of numerals like these:

2 Ask the children, preferably working in pairs, to find as many different totals as they can by adding together pairs of numbers, one from each box.

3 Suggest that they find the totals using any method they like but that they check each total *afterwards* using the base 10 materials.

4 Remind the children to approximate the answer first.

5 Discuss the range of results and how answers were found and recorded.

6 Draw attention to the check with materials where:

(a) no exchange of ten ones for one ten or ten tens for 100 is needed, e.g. 107 + 220;

Resources

School
Base 10 materials: hundreds, tens and ones; 3-column place value boards*; place value rubber stamps; OHP, pens and screen (optional)

Scheme
Book 4a, page 26

Normally, base 10 materials are used to find totals but now, since we are leading the children towards pencil-and-paper calculations without the need for apparatus, the material is being used as a checking device.

An OHP and screen are very useful to demonstrate the use of base 10 materials to the whole class.

b) an exchange of ten ones for one ten is needed, e.g. 338 + 425:

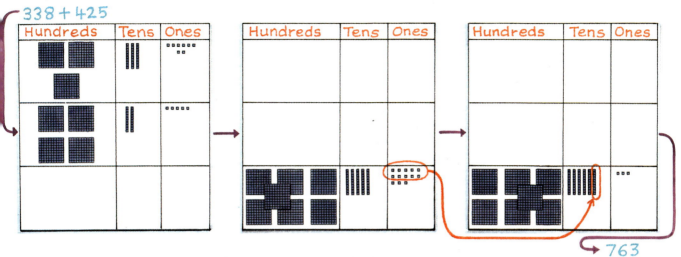

c) an exchange of ten tens for one hundred is needed, e.g. 273 + 355:

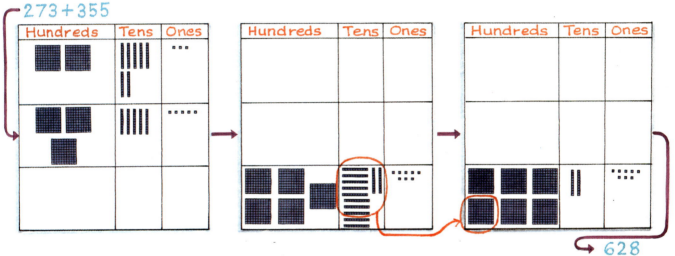

d) a double exchange is needed, e.g. 169 + 273.

7 Can the children suggest situations giving rise to some of the addition sentences?

Book 4a, page 26, provides individual practice.

C Conventional recording C I

1 Display an addition such as 156 + 227. Can the children suggest:
- situations in which this addition might be needed;
- an estimate or approximate answer and justify it?

2 Using base 10 materials, ask the children to find the answer, to record the operation, then compare what they did, i.e. the order in which the pieces were added, the exchanging procedure (see over, left-hand column).

3 Introduce the conventional procedure, explaining that this is another way of adding numbers, starting with the ones and working from right to left (see over, left-hand column).

Resources

School
Base 10 materials; place value boards made for Activity B; OHP, pens and screen (optional)

Scheme
Resource Masters 45 and 46

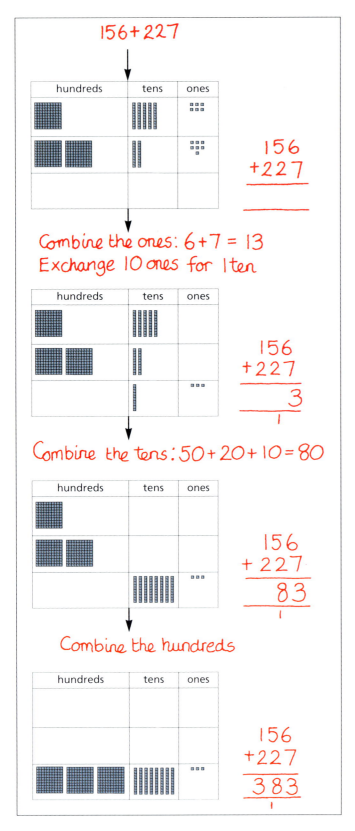

4 Relate this to the method of recording introduced in previous Steps (see above **a**) and to the 'shorthand' method (**b**), so that the relationship between the two is understood.

(Not all teachers will wish to introduce this formal method (**b**). However, it is a reliable, systematic pencil-and-paper method which, if based on understanding, may benefit some children).

5 Repeat if necessary for other examples such as:

(a) 483
    + 274
    ‾‾‾‾‾
     757
      1

Exchange needed in the tens column

(b) 577
    + 185
    ‾‾‾‾‾
     762
      1 1

Exchange needed in both the ones column and the tens column

6 Display other examples (with totals up to 999) for the children to practise this conventional method.

7 Remind the children that their own methods are just as important and can be used in preference to this method.

RM 45 and 46 provide optional practice for children who will benefit from a highly structured approach.

STEPS 4a

D Approximating [C] [P] [I]

Resources
School
Calculators

Scheme
Resource Master 47

1 Revise the convention for rounding off three-digit numbers to the nearest 100, by asking, *Tell me numbers which you would round down (or up) to, say, 700? What are the largest and smallest numbers you would round off to 700?*

2 Extend this to using rounding off to approximate totals.

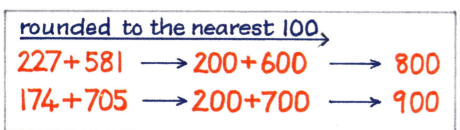

Why is it important to know what the answer will be about?

3 Preferably working in pairs, the children can create similar examples of their own to revise this skill introduced in Step 3a:36.

4 Children who need a more structured approach may benefit from redoing RM 135 from Step 3a.

RM 47 provides further practice, particularly suited to paired work where the children can make and compare predictions with each other.

The convention for rounding off to the nearest hundred is that whole numbers ending in 1 to 49 are rounded down, those ending in 50 to 99 are rounded up; 650 to 699 will be rounded up to 700; 701 to 749 will be rounded down to 700.

EXTENSION

- Children design other examples like those on RM 47, instruction 1 for friends to try. Include totals to 2000.

E Combining numbers [C] [P] [I]

Resources
School
Calculators; base 10 materials; place value boards

Scheme
Book 4a, pages 27 and 28

Part 1: Combining a two- and three-digit number mentally

1 Display two sets of numbers like these:

2 Working individually or in pairs, ask the children to find different totals by combining one number from each set, after estimating or approximating the total first.

3 Although different forms of recording will be chosen, important points to establish are:

(a) combining numbers of the same place value, e.g. units numbers;

(b) the need to exchange ten ones for a ten or ten tens for a hundred where appropriate.

STEPS 4a

4 Totals can be checked with base 10 materials or the calculator. (Less able children might use the materials to find the totals.)

5 Afterwards, compare results, strategies used and any difficulties.

Part 2: Include one-digit numbers

1 Extend Part 1 to include a third set of one-digit numbers.

2 Now the children combine one number from each set, using pencil-and-paper calculations initially before an optional check with apparatus.

3 Afterwards, when comparing results, ask the children to comment on some incorrect examples. *What is wrong with these?*

```
    5        275       609         2
  717         85        85        36
+  50       + 5       +  2      +275
-----      -----     -----      -----
 7612       1625       686        213
```

Book 4a, pages 27 and 28 provide individual practice.

Using the sets of numbers suggested in Part 1, there are nine possible totals ranging from 195 to 938. In Part 2, there are 27 different combinations of three-number additions with totals ranging from 313 to 810.

EXTENSION

■ The children try to find a systematic way of recording all 27 combinations from Part 2, perhaps using a calculator to find the totals.

F Assessment activity

*In advance, make ten cards like these which include one-, two- and three-digit numbers.

1 Set out the number cards and explain that these are used in a game where you have to choose two, three or four cards to make totals up to 999.

2 Set out the number cards and ask the child to sort them into four sets so that the numbers in any of these sets will total less than 1000 if added together.

Resources
School
Number cards*

3 Ask the child to explain his/her selection by giving you an estimated or approximated answer.

4 Leave the child to calculate the four totals using any preferred method of recording.

Assessment notes

Oral response	✔
Practical response	
Pictorial response	
Written response	✔

The child has:
added pairs of three-digit numbers or other combinations of numbers with totals to 999 without a calculator or apparatus;
AND
given reasonable estimates or approximations for totals;
AND
worked methodically in choosing appropriate numbers for a given task and in recording his/her additions.

Since the activity allows for individual choices, several children might be assessed simultaneously provided they each have a set of cards and know that you will be looking for evidence of individual achievement.

G Four-digit totals   C G P

*If blank dice are in short supply, use the spinners on RM 49.

1 Revise by asking the children to describe the relationship between the different pieces of base 10 materials and the various terms to describe these:

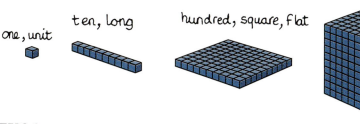

Resources

School
Base 10 materials; place value boards; blank dice

Scheme
Resource Master 48, one copy between two or three children; Resource Master 49 (optional)*

STEPS 4a

2 Introduce the activities on RM 48 and organise pairs or trios to work together. (Activity 1 is collaborative; Activity 2 is competitive.)

3 As the activities get under way, make sure the children are exchanging, positioning and describing the pieces correctly.

4 Afterwards, ask, *Does the order in which you place the hundreds, tens and ones matter? Does the order in which you exchange matter?* As alternatives to using base 10 materials, use a four-spike abacus or store the running totals on a calculator.

Addition using numbers greater than 1000 will be developed more fully in Step 4b, but RM 48 will give children some appreciation of the process of addition with totals > 1000.

STRENGTHENING ACTIVITIES

Base 10 materials

A child who cannot add using numbers to 999 without apparatus, is better succeeding with apparatus than failing without it. However, it is important to observe and question the child as he or she tries to calculate without apparatus to establish areas of difficulty or misunderstanding so that appropriate remedial work can be provided.

Pairs of three-digit numbers

If the child cannot add pairs of three-digit numbers without apparatus, provide some structured additions like these to see at which point the child has problems. When the problem is diagnosed, more work with base 10 apparatus is probably required.

100 + 300 =
213 + 100 =
241 + 536 = (no exchanges needed)
247 + 315 = (one exchange needed: one ten for ten ones)
372 + 180 = (one exchange needed: one hundred for ten tens)
576 + 264 = (double exchange needed)

A progression for adding a two- and three-digit number might be developed similarly.

CHALLENGING ACTIVITIES

Provide a task of this type for individual or paired work:

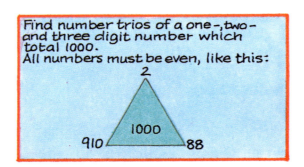
Find number trios of a one-, two- and three digit number which total 1000.
All numbers must be even, like this:
2, 910, 88 (1000)

IDEAS BOARD

■ Six-card additions

The children make a set of cards numbered 1 – 6. They arrange these to make different additions and have to try to make a total between 1 – 99, 100 – 199, 200 – 299, … until they can go no further.

123 + 4 + 56 = 183

The class results might be collated on a frieze subdivided with headings as suggested.

■ Racing for £10

The two activities on RM 48 can be modified by heading the place value boards and numbering the three dice as shown.

£10	£1	10p	1p

Dice 1: 1p, 2p, 3p, 4p, 5p, 6p
Dice 2: 10p, 20p, 30p, 40p, 50p, 60p
Dice 3: £1, £1, £2, £2, £3, £4

Now the children have to exchange ten 1p coins for one 10p coin, etc. until ten £1 coins are exchanged for a £10 note.

■ Technology

The children can design, trial and modify games which give practice in addition, e.g. hoopla, skittles.

HOME/SCHOOL PROJECTS

If the children learn to play *Six-card additions* (see *Ideas Board*), they can try this out with others in the family. Parents or grandparents may be willing to make and laminate place value boards or to supervise children playing the place value games.

SUPPORT MATERIALS

Teaching aids
Texas 1103, 1104 and *Galaxy 9X Calculators* (Texas Instruments)
Rod Abacus and *Multibase Loop Abacus* (Hope Education)
Multibase System (Hope Education)
Place Value Rubber Stamps and *Dominoes* (Taskmaster)
Hoop Abacus and *Abacus Stamps* (Taskmaster)
Blank Dice (Hope Education)

Teachers' reference materials
Calculated to Please: Calculator Activities for the National Curriculum, Paul Harling (Collins Educational)
Primary Mathematics Today, 3rd edn, chapter 13, Elizabeth Williams and Hilary Shuard (Longman)

Software
Abacus (Disk 1) from *Videomaths Computer Software* (Central Software)
Boxes, Make 37 and *Chains* from *Number Games*, Anita Straker (ILECC)
Place Value, Anita Straker (ESM)
Abacus from *Volume 2* of *Games, Activities and Investigations for the Primary School,* Anita Straker (ILECC)

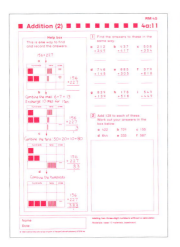
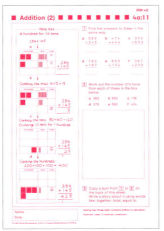

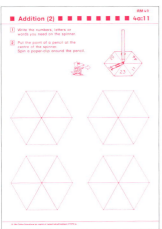

12. 3-D SHAPE

LEARNING CONTEXT

Contribution made by this Step

The children explore the properties and construction of 3-D shapes – in particular, tetrahedra and hexahedra (cubes, cuboids, etc.) through:
- using construction techniques of their own choice and with provided nets;
- constructing skeletal cuboids, leading to some simple generalisations;
- deciding which shapes are/are not nets for cuboids and trialling these;
- revising other common 3-D shapes through consideration of nets.

Objectives

To enable children to:
a Construct tetrahedra, cuboids or cubes at least from given information or from provided nets.
b Use or interpret language relating to 3-D shapes.
c Revise the properties of other familiar 3-D shapes.

Background

In STEPS 3b, activities included sorting 3-D shapes in different ways, making solid and skeletal shapes with apparatus, examining nets of shapes and making cubes and tetrahedra from provided nets. Now the children are encouraged to choose the materials and mathematics to construct shapes and to try to overcome difficulties as well as being shown some conventional construction techniques.

Mathematics in the National Curriculum

Programme of Study: KS2
Pupils should be taught to:
- visualise and describe shapes and movements, developing precision in using related geometrical language. (SSM 2.a)
- make 2-D and 3-D shapes and patterns with increasing accuracy, recognise their geometrical features and properties, and use these to classify shapes and solve problems. (SSM 2.b)
- understand the congruence of simple shapes. (SSM 2.c)
- use right angles, fractions of a turn and, later, degrees, to measure rotation, and use the associated language. (SSM 3.c)
- select and use the appropriate mathematics and materials. (UA 2.a)

THINKING AND TALKING MATHEMATICALLY

Starting points for discussion

Cubes from *Videomaths* (ITV Schools).

Collection of boxes/packages.

Play 'I spy', e.g. *I spy with my little eye a shape with five faces* …

Comparing two 3-D shapes for similarities and differences.

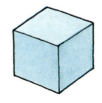 

Key language

3-D, three-dimensional, solid, cube, cuboid, sphere, cone, cylinder, prism, pyramid, tetrahedron/hedra, hexahedron/hedra, triangular, hexagonal, net, skeleton, tab, face, edge, points, vertex/vertices, score, fold up, construct

STEPS 4a

ACTIVITIES IN DETAIL

A Construction of cubes

Part 1: Making a cube

1 Get the children to each make a closed cube from six tiles and revise the properties of the shape. *What can you tell me about a cube ... its faces, vertices (points), edges ...?*

2 By choosing from the available materials, ask the children to try to make an accurate card copy of their cube, using any method they like.

3 Afterwards, compare results and construction techniques chosen.

4 If pieces do not fit together well, discuss how such problems can be overcome, e.g. do the children acknowledge the need for accurate construction/measurements?

Part 2: Creating a net without measuring

1 Depending on the children's output from Part 1, they may benefit from experimenting with this method of designing a net: number the faces of a cube-shaped box (environmental or made from wood or tiles), and show how by rolling it carefully in different directions, you can trace around the outline of each face.

2 The children can try this method which will provide the opportunity to revise that there are different nets for cubes.

3 Discuss these points as work progresses:
(a) You do not have to 'roll' the faces in any particular order.
(b) It is best to hold the pencil upright and flush with the vertical faces of the cube 'template'.
(c) You trace each numbered face once only.
(d) The edges must be scored carefully – this is best demonstrated.

Resources

School
Interlocking square tiles, e.g. Polydron or Clixi; card; scissors; glue; masking tape or similar; small cube-shaped boxes (optional); small adhesive stickers

Some children may be interested to know that a cube is an example of a hexahedron – *hexa*: six, *hedra*: seat (face). A hexahedron is any solid shape with six plane (flat) faces, the most common examples being cubes and cuboids.

One effective way to score the edge of a net is to place it on a pad of newspaper then rule over the fold lines with a ballpoint pen or sharp pencil (see below). Edges should be scored before applying glue!

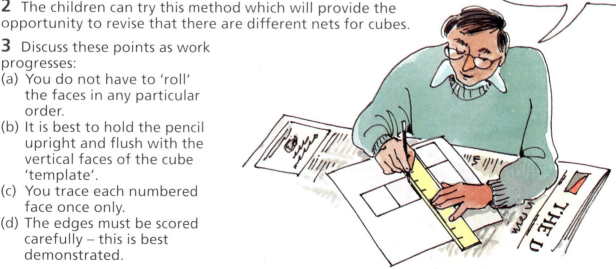

This is one good way to score the edges. Take care to position the ruler carefully.

4 If masking tape has been used, the cubes can be painted over and decorated or simply covered in decorative paper.

EXTENSION

Design a net for a closed cube which fits together without any masking tape.

B Cubes from provided nets   C I

Resources

School
Scissors; neat PVA glue; masking tape; examples of cubes; newspapers; 1cm or 2cm squared card

Scheme
Resource Master 50*; Book 4a, page 29; Resource Master A (1 cm squared grid)

*If commercial card grid is not available, RM 50 can be photocopied on to card. If this is not possible, the children will need to glue a card backing to the reverse side, then leave this to dry before use.

1 Introduce the task on RM 50 which also revises line symmetry.

2 As nets are cut out, revise how to score the edges. *What would happen if you didn't score the edges?*

3 Remind the children that the tabs can be glued inside or outside.

4 Afterwards, you can discuss the length of each edge, area of each face, etc.

5 Children who finish early might try to design on RM A (1cm squared grid) either:
– a matching cube made from a different net; or
– a cube which is a sensible size to hold, say, a small ball or 100 g nuts.

6 Retain the cubes for Activity **C**.

Book 4a, page 29 provides opportunities for problem solving and collaborative work.

C Prepared nets for tetrahedra and related hexahedra   C I

Resources

School
Interlocking equilateral triangles (Polydron, Clixi, etc.); newspapers; scissors; examples of tetrahedra; neat PVA glue

Scheme
Resource Master 51; Resource Master D (1cm isometric grid); Book 4a, pages 30 and 31

1 Introduce the nets on RM 51 and develop in the same way as in Activity **B**. The nets will fold up to form these:

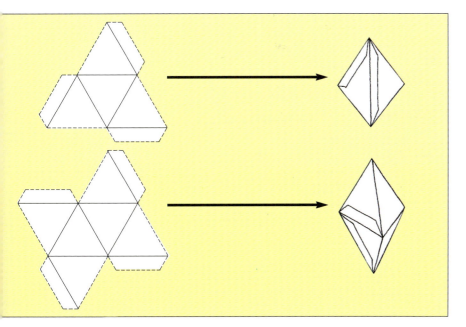

A tetrahedron is any solid shape with four plane faces. By fitting together two card tetrahedra along one common face, the children will be able to see that the 'diamond' hexahedron is an equivalent structure. The dimensions of these nets match those of Clixi tiles.

2 Afterwards, discuss:
(a) the names for these shapes and the meaning of *tetra* (four), *hexa* (six) and *hedron* (seat, face);
(b) the similarities and differences between the three shapes constructed in Activities **B** and **C**.

Book 4a, pages 30 and 31 provide individual practice.

In the Handbooks, the plural forms tetrahedra and hexahedra have been used. However, the forms tetrahedrons and hexahedrons are equally acceptable, according to modern dictionaries. It will make more sense to many children to use the 's' form of the plural.

D Cuboids   C G

*If Kugeli or similar construction apparatus is not available, get each group to cut up a supply of straws in three different lengths, e.g. 4 cm, 7 cm and 10 cm (or so that you can cut three from each straw).

1 Ask each group to make a shared collection of as many different 'skeleton' cuboids (including cubes which also belong to this family) as they can, using one, two or three different lengths to form the edges.

2 If using straws, the edges can be joined at common vertices with Plasticine or Blu-Tack or with pipe cleaner joints, the use of which you may need to demonstrate.

Resources

School
Kugeli or straws, pipe cleaners or Plasticine/Blu-Tack*; examples of cuboids

Skeletal shapes enable the children to focus on edges and vertices rather than the faces which have to be imagined. The children can be reminded that cuboids also belong to the family of hexahedra.

3 Encourage the children to eliminate repetitions: *These two cuboids are the same but in different orientations.*

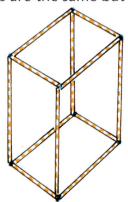 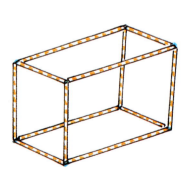

4 Afterwards, groups can compare their results.

5 By questioning and discussion, you can help the children to make some conclusions/generalisations, e.g.:
– there are ten different cuboids (of which three are cubes);
– all the cuboids have twelve edges and eight vertices;
– all the cuboids have four, eight or twelve equal edges;
– each cuboid has three sets of four parallel lines;
– they are all prisms;
– they each have 24 right-angled corners.

(These facts might also be presented as statements on which the children can comment, e.g. *Every cuboid has 24 right-angled corners.*)

6 Encourage the children to find a way to record their results so that the ten different cuboids are distinguishable.

7 If children can't do this, you might suggest a method such as:

	HEIGHT	WIDTH	LENGTH
Cuboid 1	4 long straws	4 short straws	4 medium straws
Cuboid 2	4 medium straws	4 medium straws	4 short straws

EXTENSIONS

- The children can take it in turn to sort the group's collection of cuboids in different ways.
- The children try to make a card net of the same dimensions as one of the skeleton cuboids.

E Nets for cuboids

*In advance, collect examples of environmental cuboids, such as cereal boxes. If possible, some should be identical.

1 Ask the children what they can tell you from memory about a cuboid.

2 By cutting along the edges of the boxes until they can be opened and flattened, the children can then compare the different nets. *What is the same about all nets for a cuboid? What can you tell me about the faces? Why are tabs needed?*

3 Organise small groups (two to four children) to carry out the task on Book 4a, page 32 for which cuboids should be available to handle.

Resources

School
Examples of environmental cuboids*; scissors

Scheme
Book 4a, page 32

F Assessment activity

1 Provide examples of cubes, cuboids and tetrahedra.

2 Ask the child to choose one and to construct one of the same family.

3 Explain that he or she can choose materials or use a prepared net.

4 Afterwards, ask the child to explain what she or he has done and to tell you about the constructed shape.

Resources

School
Card; glue; tape; scissors; prepared net for a tetrahedra and cube

Objective **D** is not assessed here since it is revision of ideas previously introduced. (See Activity **G**.)

Assessment notes

Oral response	✔
Practical response	✔
Pictorial response	✔
Written response	

The child has:
constructed either a tetrahedron, cuboid or cube from given information or from provided nets;
AND
explained his or her construction using language relating to 3-D shapes.

STEPS 4a

G Revision of 3-D shapes   C G P

1 Revise the names and properties of 3-D shapes by listing terms the children suggest are useful when describing these.

> edges   right-angled   equal   2-D
> faces   acute   curved 3-D
> vertices obtuse   straight
> corners

Resources

School
Geometric 3-D shapes; interlocking tiles

Scheme
Book 4a, pages 30 and 31; Resource Master 52

What other words can we use when describing three-dimensional shapes?

2 Extend by organising some of these:
(a) Ask the children to show you a shape with a particular property: *Show me a shape with five faces.*
(b) *Show me some pyramids. Tell me how they are the same (different).*
(c) *Work in pairs, choose a shape then take it in turn to tell each other something about that shape.*

3 Suggest that in pairs or small groups, the children design a poster about a particular shape and discuss the kinds of information which might be included, e.g. examples of nets, the 3-D shape itself, drawings, drawings of environmental examples, etc.

4 Afterwards, groups can comment on each other's display.

Book 4a, pages 30 and 31, and RM 52 provide revision and recognition of nets.

STRENGTHENING ACTIVITY

Nets from interlocking tiles

Some children may lack the manipulative skills to construct with card nets, glue, etc. If this is the case, they may need to concentrate on constructing 3-D shapes from given information, using commercial materials such as Polydron tiles or Kugeli, or to be given extra help with card constructions.

CHALLENGING ACTIVITIES

Pyramids

Use 2 cm squared grid to design nets for different square-based pyramids. Try different sized isosceles triangles, for example:

Will these nets both make pyramids? About what height will they be?

STEPS 4a

Open box

Design and make a container with a separate and well-fitting lid. (See *The Gift Box Book*.)

Heptahedron

Design a box with seven faces. Find out what this shape is called.

IDEAS BOARD

■ Typical projects

Shops; Food; Packaging; Structures; Shape and Size; Growth

■ Art

Mathematics through Art and Design has many ideas for constructing, decorating and displaying hexahedra, etc.

■ Triangular faces

Revise which 3-D shapes have triangular faces. Make skeletal shapes as in these examples, showing less familiar triangular prisms constructed with equilateral (**a**), right-angled (**b**) and isosceles (**c**) triangles as well as the most familiar with end faces of equilateral triangles (extension of ideas in Step 8).

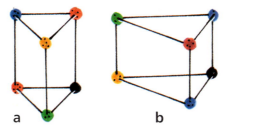

a   b   c

■ Copy a box

Take careful measurements from a small box (e.g. matchbox, fun-size Smarties) without opening it out. Use squared paper to design a net and make a copy of the box. Have a vote for the best copy.

■ Largest cube

Investigate. Ask, *What is the largest cube which can be made from an A4 sheet of squared paper?*

■ Technology

Design and make 3-D models for an identified need.

■ Wrapping

Use sheets of kitchen paper or inexpensive wrapping paper to practise wrapping cube- and cuboid-shaped parcels. Ask, for example, *What is the most economical method of wrapping a cube?*

HOME/SCHOOL PROJECTS

Get the children to bring from home empty, clean boxes and packages, e.g. different tissue boxes, Easter egg boxes. Ask the children, *Could you make a copy of any of these boxes? Try, at school.*

SUPPORT MATERIALS

Teaching aids
Basic Solid Shapes and *Solid Shapes* (NES Arnold)
Clixi squares, triangles and *Rubber Stamps* (NES Arnold)
Kugeli and *Construct O Straws* (NES Arnold)
Solid Shapes Frieze (NES Arnold)
Polydron (Taskmaster and Hope Education)
3-D Geometric Rubber Stamps (Philip & Tacey)
Geometrical Models, Large Solid Shapes and *Solid Shape Stamps* (Taskmaster)
Solid Shape Set (Hope Education)
Square Centimetre Printed Cards, *1 cm and 2 cm grid Ready-Fold Cards* (Philip & Tacey)

Teachers' reference materials
Mathematics through Art and Design, Anne Woodman and Eric Albany (Collins Educational)
Hollows and Solids (BEAM)
The Gift Box Book (Tarquin)

Radio and TV
Cubes from *Videomaths* (ITV Schools)

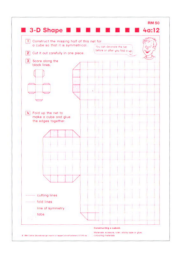
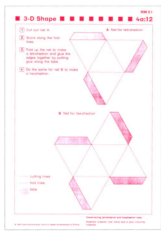
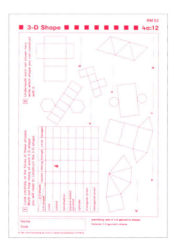

13. SUBTRACTION (2)

LEARNING CONTEXT

Contribution made by this Step

The children develop strategies to subtract, mainly using numbers to 999, using standard and non-standard methods of recording. Although apparatus and calculators are used, the emphasis is on developing reliable pencil-and-paper methods.

Objectives

To enable children to:
a Subtract a one-, two- or three-digit number from a three-digit number without a calculator or apparatus.
b Choose methods to solve problems methodically.
c Estimate or approximate answers.

Background

In this Step, the children put to good use their mental knowledge of subtraction facts to 20 and place value. As the children make increasing use of pencil-and-paper calculations, using either standard or non-standard methods, these need to build on the mental methods previously acquired if they are to operate without apparatus or the calculator.

Whether using apparatus, the calculator or written methods, the children should be encouraged continually to ask themselves in advance, *What kind of answer do I expect?* and, afterwards, *Is my answer sensible?*

Although this Step introduces some standard pencil-and-paper methods, the children are also encouraged to develop and practise methods of their own, based on their own, understanding of numbers and the processes of subtraction.

Mathematics in the National Curriculum

Programme of Study: KS2
Pupils should be taught to:
■ read, write and order whole numbers, understanding that the position of a digit signifies its value; use their understanding of place value to develop methods of computation, to approximate numbers to the nearest 10 or 100, and to multiply and divide by powers of 10 when there are whole-number answers. (N 2.a)
■ develop a variety of mental methods of computation with whole numbers up to 100, and explain patterns used; extend mental methods to develop a range of non-calculator methods of computation that involve addition and subtraction of whole numbers. (N 3.d)
■ develop their use of the four operations to solve problems, including those involving money and measures, using a calculator where appropriate. (N 4.a)
■ check results by different methods, including repeating the operations in a different order or using inverse operations; gain a sense of the size of a solution, and estimate and approximate solutions to problems. (N 4.c)

THINKING AND TALKING MATHEMATICALLY

Starting points for discussion

Revising subtraction facts to 20, e.g. *Tell me two numbers up to twenty which are different by five.*

Given a subtraction expression, e.g. 741 – 125, can the children give:
– an approximate or estimated answer and justify it;
– a difference situation from which it might have arisen;
– a 'take away' situation from which it might have arisen.

Words relating to subtraction: *Tell me a number sentence which uses minus, difference, etc.*

Key language

difference, greater than (>), fewer/less than (<), count on/back, remove, take away, compare, exchange, subtract, minus

ACTIVITIES IN DETAIL

A Revising differences

C I

Part 1: Counting on and counting back

1 Revise the difference aspect of subtraction by using operation arrows to count on from, say, 140 to 230 or 345 to 427. (For the moment, limit the differences to numbers < 100.)

2 Explain that you can count on in different ways and still get the correct answer, using steps you can manage 'in your head'. One way might be:

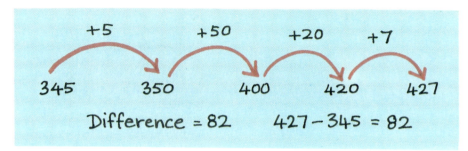

3 This can be compared with counting back to find the difference.

After sufficient examples have been trialled and discussed, Book 4a, page 33 provides individual practice.

Part 2: Comparing methods

1 The children could contribute to a wall display of different ways to count on or back to find the difference between two particular numbers.

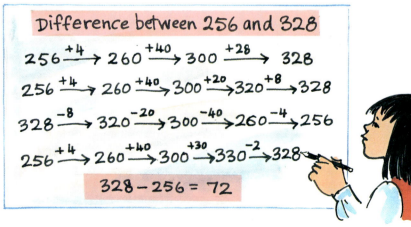

EXTENSION

■ Suggest tasks which might include differences >100. For example, find all the numbers between 300 and 500 with a difference of 141.

Resources

Scheme
Book 4a, page 33

This activity makes use of and extends mental skills acquired in previous Steps, i.e. addition and subtraction of numbers to 20, multiples of ten to 200, and knowledge of place value.

Can anyone think of a different way to count on?

Which do you think is easier – counting on or back – to find the difference?

B Exchanging and equivalences   C I

Resources
School
Base 10 materials
Scheme
Resource Master 53

1 Introduce the tasks on RM 53 which revise equivalence of numbers where one exchange of a ten for ten ones or a hundred for ten tens is carried out.

2 Although the activities are intended as a mental exercise, base 10 materials should be available to model the operation where required.

EXTENSION

■ Using three-digit numbers, the children can try to devise notation to show what happens when exchanges of a hundred for ten tens *and* a ten for ten ones take place.

C Subtracting three-digit numbers   C P

Resources
School
Base 10 materials: 'flats' or squares, longs and ones; three-column place value boards*; place value rubber stamps; OHP, pens and screen (optional)
Scheme
Resource Master 54

*Get the children to make place value boards with rows and columns wide enough to allow base 10 hundreds, tens and ones to be positioned.

1 Display two sets of numerals like these:

2 Ask the children, preferably working in pairs, to find as many different answers as they can by subtracting a number in the second box from one in the first.

3 Suggest that they find and record the answers using any method they like but that they check each answer *afterwards* using the base 10 materials. (Less confident children may need to use the materials before recording.)

4 Remind the children to approximate the answer first.

5 Discuss the range of results and how answers were found and recorded.

6 In particular, draw attention to the check with materials where:
(a) no exchange of one ten for ten ones or one hundred for ten tens is needed, e.g. 457 − 133:

An OHP and screen are very useful to demonstrate the use of base 10 materials to the whole class as shown in stage 6.

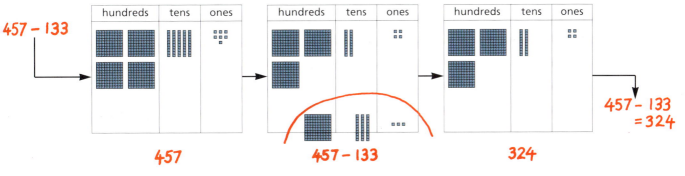

STEPS 4a   127

(b) an exchange of one ten for ten ones is needed,
e.g. 625 – 419:

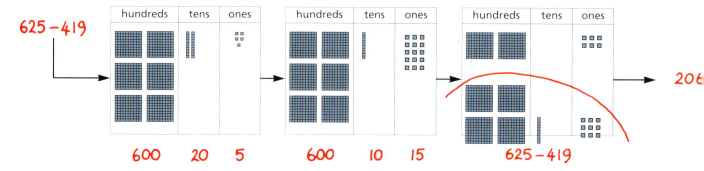

(c) an exchange of one hundred for ten tens is needed,
e.g. 316 – 133:

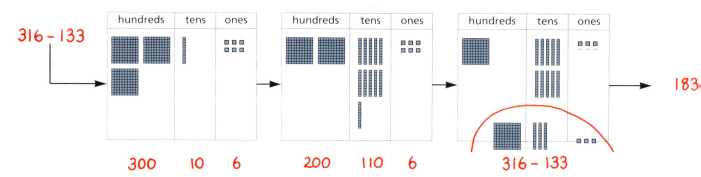

(d) a double exchange is needed, e.g. 625 – 249.

7 Can the children suggest difference and 'take away' situations out of which some of the subtraction problems might have arisen?

RM 54 provides individual practice.

Normally, base 10 materials are used to find answers but now, since we are leading the children towards pencil-and-paper calculations without the need for apparatus, the material is being used as a checking device.

Variation
1 Use hoop abaci and beads instead of the base 10 materials.

D Checking strategies

Part 1: Approximating

1 Ask the children to explain and give examples of the convention for rounding off three-digit numbers to the nearest hundred.

2 Extend this to using rounding off to approximate answers.

Resources
School
Calculators

Scheme
Resource Master 55

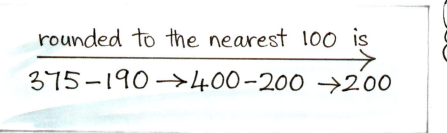

The answer will be about 200. Why is it useful to approximate answers?

3 Preferably working in pairs, the children can create similar examples of their own to revise this skill, introduced in Step 3a:30.

128

STEPS 4a

Part 2: Using addition to check subtraction

1 Display some three-digit subtractions, at least one of which is incorrect.

2 Ask the children, working individually or in pairs, to decide the best way to check the answers and find any errors.

3 Compare strategies, in particular drawing attention to checking subtraction by addition with a calculator.

4 Remind the children of the need to check the reasonableness of answers by:
- estimating or approximating answers;
- checking subtraction by addition, particularly when using a calculator.

Whole numbers ending in 1 to 49 are rounded down; those ending in 50 to 99 are rounded up.

RM 55 provides further practice, particularly suited to paired work where the children can make and compare predictions with each other.

EXTENSION

■ *Design other examples like those on RM 55, stage 1 for friends to try but using numbers up to 2000.*

E Conventional recording of 'take aways'

1 Display a subtraction such as 481 – 157. Can the children suggest:
- situations for which this subtraction might be needed;
- an approximate answer and justify it?

2 Using the base 10 materials, ask the children to find the answer, record the operation and then compare what they did, i.e. the order in which the pieces were subtracted, the exchanging procedure.

3 Introduce the conventional procedure and explain that this is *one* way of subtracting numbers, starting with the ones and working from right to left.

Resources

School
Base 10 materials; place value boards made for Activity **A**; OHP, pens and screen (optional)

Scheme
Resource Masters 56, 57 and 58

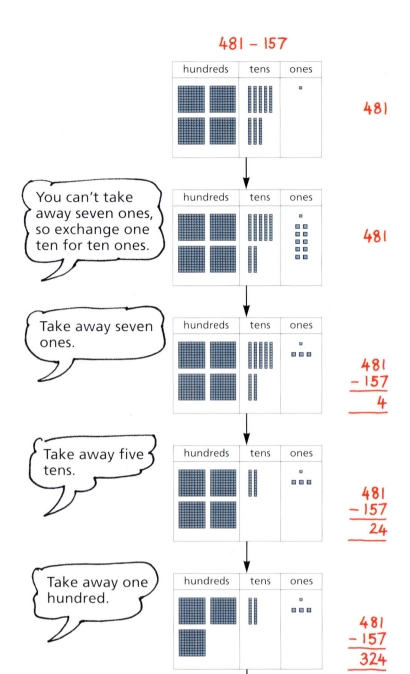

Not all teachers will wish to introduce the formal method shown in stage 4. However, it is a reliable, systematic pencil-and-paper method which, if based on understanding, may benefit some children.

4 Introduce the standard vertical recording, relating it to the operation with the base 10 materials, so that the link between the two is understood.

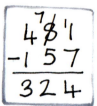

Why has the eight in the tens column been changed to seven tens?

5 Repeat if necessary for other examples such as:

(a)   483
    − 274   (exchange needed in the ones column);

(b)   322
    − 157   (exchange needed in both the ones and tens columns).

6 Display other examples (totals <1000) for the children to practise this conventional method of adding and recording.

7 Remind the children that their own methods are just as important and can be used in preference to this method.

8 Points to discuss as work progresses are:
- estimating or approximating each answer;
- trying to calculate with pencil and paper before checking with apparatus.

RMs 56, 57 and 58 provide optional practice for children who will benefit from a highly structured approach.

F Combining one-, two- and three-digit numbers

1 Provide each group with five cards of both colours, A and B, on which they write:
- five different three-digit numbers in colour A;
- assorted one- and two-digit numbers in colour B.

196	823	507	990	355
9	38	6	45	72

2 They find and record in their own way different subtraction sentences using any pair of cards, one of each colour.

3 Each group's results might be collated on a poster.

Variation

1 Nine cards of the same colour are numbered, three each for one-, two- and three-digit numbers, all different.

2 Individual children create different subtraction sentences using any pair of cards then collaborate in presenting the group's results on a poster.

3 Although different forms of recording will be chosen, important points to establish are:
- subtracting numbers of like values, e.g. units numbers;
- the need to exchange ten ones for a ten or ten tens for a hundred where appropriate.

4 Afterwards, compare results, strategies used and any difficulties.

Book 4a, page 34 provides individual practice using calculators.

EXTENSION

■ Choose a three-digit number between 600 and 999 and record it. Make number trios like this from each number you choose:

$745 - 6 = ?, \quad 745 - 60 = ?, \quad 745 - 600 = ?$

Resources

School
Calculators; good supply of blank cards (postcard size) in two colours; large sheets of paper

Scheme
Book 4a, page 34

Using the set of cards suggested in Part 1, there are 25 possible subtraction sentences. For the variation, there are 36 solutions using the cards suggested.

STEPS 4a

G Assessment activity

*In advance, make cards like these:

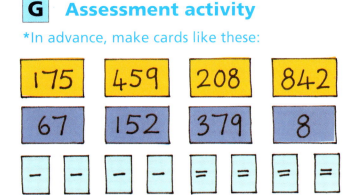

I Resources

School
Number cards*

1 Ask the child to pair the cards in set A and set B and then to arrange them as four subtraction problems.

2 Ask the child to estimate or approximate the answer to each one.

3 Leave the child to work out the answers in his or her own way using pencil-and-paper methods.

Since the Activity allows for individual choices, several children might be assessed simultaneously provided each one has a set of cards and knows that you will be looking for evidence of individual achievement.

Assessment notes

Oral response	✔
Practical response	
Pictorial response	
Written response	✔

The child has:
given reasonable estimates or approximations for four three-digit subtractions using one-, two- and three-digit numbers;
AND
subtracted a one-, two- and three-digit number from a three-digit number, using pencil-and-paper methods at least three times out of four;
AND
planned her/his work methodically.

STRENGTHENING ACTIVITIES

Base 10 materials

If the child cannot subtract using numbers to 999 without apparatus, it is better that he or she succeeds with apparatus rather than fails without it.

However, it is important to observe and question the child while she or he tries to calculate without apparatus to establish areas of difficulty or misunderstanding so that appropriate remedial work can be provided.

Pairs of three-digit numbers

If the child cannot subtract pairs of three-digit numbers without apparatus, you could provide some structured subtractions like the following to see at which point he or she has problems. When the problem is diagnosed, more work with base 10 apparatus is probably required.

600 – 100
347 – 200 (no exchanges needed)
821 – 709 (exchange of one ten for ten ones needed)
528 – 372 (exchange of one hundred for ten tens needed)
413 – 167 (double exchange needed)

A similar progression for subtracting a two- from a three-digit number might be developed.

CHALLENGING ACTIVITIES

True or false?

Provide a statement of this type for individual or paired work: If you subtract a one-, two- or three-digit odd number from an odd number up to 999, the answer will always be an even number. *True or false? Investigate.*

IDEAS BOARD

■ History

Work out the difference in prices (to the nearest pound) of items costing up to £999 today compared with, say, ten years ago.

■ Technology

The children can design, trial and modify games which give practice in subtraction, e.g. hoopla, skittles, safe 'darts'. The children might start with a score of 999, and subtract the numbers displayed on the skittles bowled over. The first player to get her or his score to reach zero wins.

■ Sorting

The children can contribute to a sorting diagram of this type:

Differences using numbers between 750 and 850

odd answers	even answers
801 − 798 = 3	830 − 820 = 10
768 − 751 = 17	800 − 760 = 40
801 − 760 = 41	813 − 791 = 22

What generalisations can the children make from these results?

■ Six-card subtraction

The children use any six cards from a set numbered 1 to 9, and cards for a − and an = sign. They arrange all these to make different subtractions to solve a particular challenge, e.g. answers which are odd numbers only or between 100 and 300.

HOME/SCHOOL PROJECTS

The children play *Six-card subtraction* with a number challenge as described above, at school and then at home, with a number challenge to solve with others in the family.

TEPS 4a

SUPPORT MATERIALS

Teaching aids
TI 1103, 1104 and *Galaxy 9 X calculators* (Texas Instruments)
Rod Abacus and *Multibase Loop Abacus* (Hope Education)
Multibase System (Hope Education)
Place Value Rubber Stamps and *Dominoes* (Taskmaster)
Hoop Abacus and *Abacus Stamps* (Taskmaster)
Blank Dice (Hope Education)

Teachers' reference materials
Calculated to Please: Calculator Activities for the National Curriculum, Paul Harling (Collins Educational)
Primary Mathematics Today, 3rd edn, chapter 13, Elizabeth Williams and Hilary Shuard (Longman)

Software
Abacus (Disk 1) from *Videomaths Computer Software* (Central Software)
Boxes, Make 37 and *Chains* from *Number Games*, Anita Straker (ILECC)
Place Value, Anita Straker (ESM)
Abacus from Volume 2 of *Games, Activities and Investigations for the Primary School*, Anita Straker (ILECC)

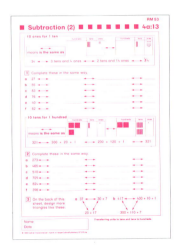
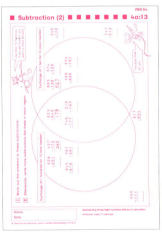
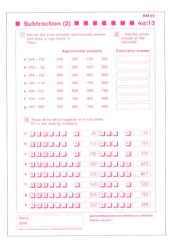
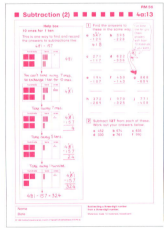
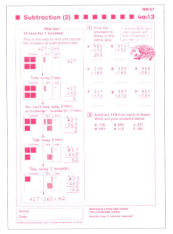
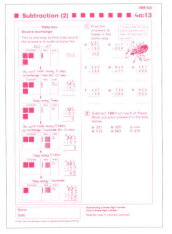

14. CO-ORDINATES

LEARNING CONTEXT

Contribution made by this Step

The children develop their experience of the conventions of co-ordinates in the first quadrant and draw simple shapes by joining points in order.

Objectives

To enable children to:
a Read and interpret co-ordinates in the first quadrant.
b Join co-ordinates in order to draw simple shapes.

Background

In Handbook 3b:14, children used letter and number references, such as B5, to identify regions on a grid, and were introduced to co-ordinates, e.g. (2,3), to locate and define the intersection of two lines.

In this Step, children become more familiar with the conventions of co-ordinate notation, including their use to define and draw simple shapes. At this stage, co-ordinates are confined to the first quadrant.

It is extremely important that the conventional procedure of reading, writing and interpreting an 'ordered pair' of co-ordinates is established from the beginning.

> **Mathematics in the National Curriculum**
>
> **Programme of Study: KS2**
> Pupils should be taught to:
> ■ recognise the number relationship between co-ordinates in the first quadrant of related points on a line or in a shape, *e.g. the vertices of a rectangle, a graph of the multiples of 3.* (N 3.b)
> ■ use co-ordinates to specify location, *e.g. map references, representation of 2-D shapes.* (SSM 3.b)
> ■ understand and use the language of number. (UA 3.a)

THINKING AND TALKING MATHEMATICALLY

Starting points for discussion

Mark a simple grid in the playground. Make cards labelled with the co-ordinates of each intersection. Ask children to stand on the intersections, one child on each. Read out the co-ordinates on the cards, one at a time. The child standing on the given location is 'out'. Continue until only one child remains in place. On each move, encourage the children to say why that child is 'out'.

> **Key language**
>
> co-ordinates, axis/axes, horizontal(ly), vertical(ly), diagonal(ly), point, plot, join, row, column, intersection, origin, grid, lattice

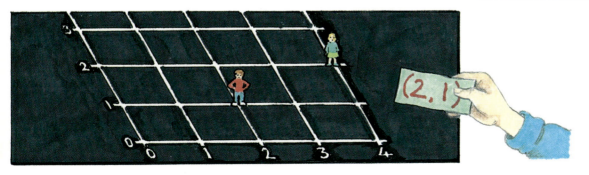

STEPS 4a

ACTIVITIES IN DETAIL

A Points on a lattice   C G

Resources

School
OHP; OHP transparency*;
OHP pens

Scheme
Resource Master 59;
Book 4a, page 35

*In advance, prepare a demonstration OHP grid, based on RM 59, or draw the grid on the board.

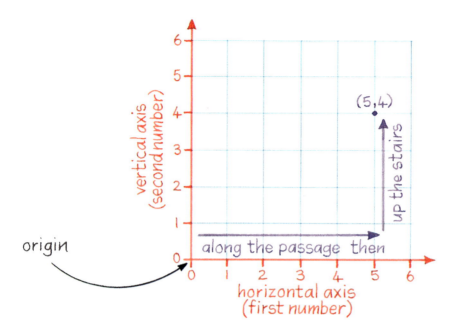

1 Display the demonstration grid. Revise the conventions of co-ordinate notation. Include discussion of the following points:

(a) the use of the lines and intersections to define locations on the grid or lattice;
(b) the naming and appropriate labelling of the horizontal and vertical axes;
(c) the position of the 'special' point (0,0) known as 'the origin';
(d) the possible extension of the axes, denoted by the arrowhead;
(e) the ordering of the pair of numbers (the co-ordinates), the first indicating horizontal movement, the second vertical movement – 'along the passageway, then up the stairs'.

2 Working with copies of RM 59, invite children to:
– mark (plot) points, including some with a zero, e.g. (0,3) or (3,0);
– tell you the co-ordinates for specified points, again including some with a zero.

Book 4a, page 35, provides further individual practice. The children should be encouraged to check each other's results in task 2.

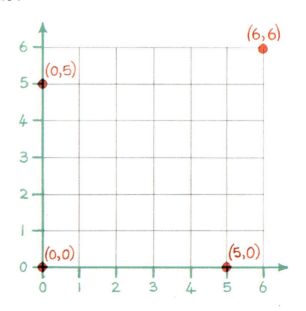

136

STEPS 4a

B Co-ordinates and dice   G P I

Resources

School
Coloured and white standard dice 1–6

Scheme
Book 4a, page 36;
Resource Masters 59, 61 and 62

Part 1: Patterns of co-ordinates

1 Introduce the tasks on Book 4a, page 36.

2 Afterwards, discuss and compare the patterns to be found in the co-ordinates. *How are your results the same (different)? What do you notice about the co-ordinates for points which are in the same vertical (horizontal) line?*

(The first number in co-ordinates, for points on the same vertical line, will be the same, e.g. (1,0), (1,1), (1,2) … Similarly, the second number, for those on the same horizontal line, will be the same, e.g. (0,1), (1,1), (2,1) … Children able to explain this are making a generalisation.)

Part 2: Co-ordinate games

1 RMs 61 and 62 provide a selection of dice games for two to four players which require children to plot and interpret whole-number co-ordinates on a 6 by 6 grid.

If white dice are in short supply, use unit pieces from base 10 materials, numbered.

EXTENSION

1 Ask the children to alter the dice so that co-ordinates which contain zero can be included. *How does this affect the games on RMs 61 and 62?*

2 Present this investigation: *In how many different positions on the grid on RM 59 can you get a row (or column) of four counters? Decide how to present your results.*

C Lines and letters   C P

Resources

School
OHP; OHP transparency*; OHP pens

Scheme
Resource Masters 59 and 60

*In advance, prepare a demonstration OHP grid, based on RM 59, or draw the grid on the board.

Part 1: Plotting letters

1 Ask the children to suggest how to plot and join co-ordinates to draw lines which together form, say, a capital W.

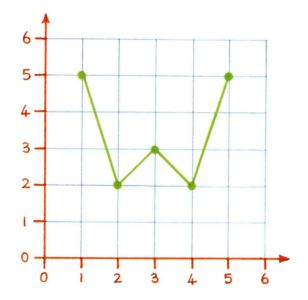

STEPS 4a   137

2 Ask the children, preferably working in pairs, to use RM 60 to plot a given sequence of co-ordinates to draw a letter.

$$(1,1) \rightarrow (1,5) \rightarrow (4,1) \rightarrow (4,5)$$

3 Show a letter on the demonstration grid and ask the children to list its co-ordinates in order.

Part 2: Guessing letters activity

1 Ask the children to work in pairs. Provide each child with a copy of RM 60.

2 Each child takes it in turn to draw three letters on a grid on RM 60, and to write the co-ordinates underneath, concealing the RM from his/her partner.

3 The child tells the co-ordinates for these letters to the partner who has to recreate the letters on a blank grid on his/her copy of the RM.

4 The partners then reverse roles.

5 Afterwards, they compare letters.

EXTENSION

■ Sort into two sets letters which can be drawn in one sequence without having to retrace any lines, and those which cannot.

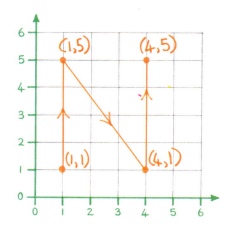

For some letters, e.g. X or Y, it may be necessary to have two parts to the sequence, similar to using 'pen up' in LOGO.

D Drawing geometric shapes   C

*In advance prepare a demonstration grid based on RM 59, or draw the grid on the board.

1 List co-ordinates such as (2,4), (4,1), (0,1), (2,4) which will draw a closed shape (in this case an isosceles triangle). *What do you predict the instructions will draw? Why?*

2 Using the demonstration grid, plot and join the points in order:

$$(2,4) \longrightarrow (4,1) \longrightarrow (0,1) \longrightarrow (2,4)$$

Why is the last co-ordinate the same as the first? How many co-ordinates would you need to draw a hexagon?

Resources

School
OHP and pens; demonstration grid*; squared paper

Scheme
Resource Master 59; Book 4a, page 37

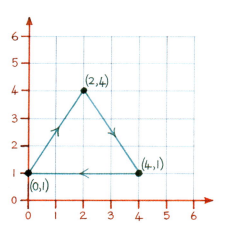

Book 4a, page 37, provides work in plotting and joining points to form simple geometrical shapes.

EXTENSION

- List the co-ordinates of the outline of a simple building (or boat). Ask the children to draw it on squared paper, then to add further details such as windows, doors (sails), drawing the lines and listing the co-ordinates.

- Use the hexagon in task 4 of Book 4a, page 35. Ask the children to predict, then check, what will happen if they:
- double the first number of each co-ordinate;
- double the second number of each co-ordinate;
- double both numbers of the co-ordinates.

E Assessment activity

1 Ask the child to use squared paper to draw a labelled co-ordinate grid with numbers up to six on each axis.

2 Say and/or write four or five pairs of co-ordinates and ask the child to plot them.

3 Mark a point on the grid and ask the child to tell you the co-ordinates of that point.

4 Ask the child to draw a simple geometric shape, using the intersections of the grid and to write the co-ordinates in an appropriate order so that someone else could construct the same shape.

Resources
Scheme
Resource Master A (1 cm squared grid)

Assessment notes

Oral response	✔
Practical response	✔
Pictorial response	✔
Written response	

The child has:
correctly specified locations in terms of whole-number co-ordinates;
AND
correctly interpreted verbal and written co-ordinates in plotting points;
AND
listed in an appropriate order co-ordinates needed to construct a simple geometric shape.

STRENGTHENING ACTIVITIES

Joining points

Create some 'dot-to-dot' type designs on squared paper. The child practises joining dots in order, using a ruler. Next check that the child can plot points accurately from co-ordinates and join them in order.

Geoboards

Give the children some grid paper with axes numbered to correspond to a Geoboard (e.g. 25 pin). They make shapes on the Geoboard, record them on the grid paper and list the co-ordinates. *Are any of the shapes symmetrical?*

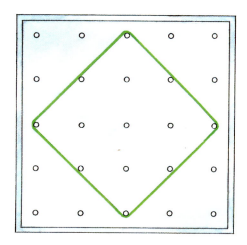
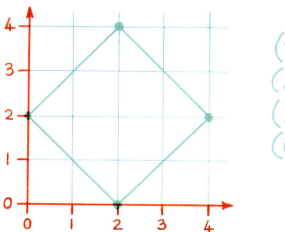

Listing co-ordinates

Provide a simple shape or picture drawn on a grid, together with its co-ordinates, but with some numbers missing. Ask the children to tell you the missing numbers.

Decisions

The children use the grid on RM 59. They place small items on the intersections of the grid (e.g. a drawing pin, a rubber, a paperclip, a counter and so on). They then specify and write the co-ordinates of the intersections they have chosen.

CHALLENGING ACTIVITIES

Diagonal reflection

The children investigate the co-ordinates of a simple shape reflected across a diagonal line of symmetry. They use a mirror to check the symmetry. For example:

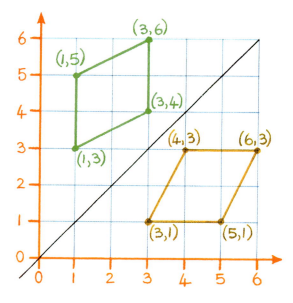

140   STEPS 4a

Quiz

The children work in pairs. One in each pair marks some random points on a grid.

The other then asks questions about the points. For example:

Which point is it if:
- the first number is four?
- the point is on the horizontal (vertical) axis?
- the second number is zero?
- the first number is twice as large as the second number?

IDEAS BOARD

■ Typical projects

Journeys; Our Neighbourhood; Games; Communication; Maps and Plans; Shapes

■ BASIC

Try this BASIC program to draw a square.
```
10    MODE 1
20    MOVE 200, 200
30    DRAW 400, 200
40    DRAW 400, 400
50    DRAW 200, 400
60    DRAW 200, 200
70    END
```

Try this BASIC program to draw a rectangle.
```
10    MODE 4
20    MOVE 300, 100
30    DRAW 300, 500
40    DRAW 800, 500
50    DRAW 800, 100
60    DRAW 300, 100
70    END
```

■ Step patterns

List the co-ordinates for 'step' patterns, for example, (0,0), (2,1), (4,2), (6,3). The children draw them on squared paper and continue the pattern of numbers. *Can anyone recognise intermediate points, e.g. (3, 1.5)?*

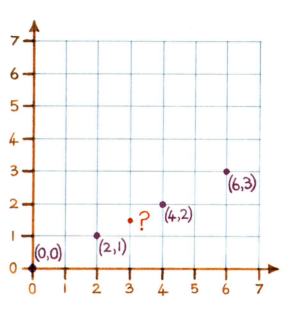

■ Art

Plan simple designs and list the co-ordinates of the vertices. Can the design be reproduced by another child or on a computer screen?

■ Names

Children draw capital letter short names or initials on squared paper, using straight lines only, and label the co-ordinates. Can they transfer the initials to the computer screen, using BASIC?

■ Descartes

Use reference materials to find out about René Descartes who, in the 17th century, developed the idea of using an ordered pair of numbers to define the position of an item.

■ Technology

The children make up a game which uses co-ordinates.

HOME/SCHOOL PROJECTS

The children choose a (rectangular) room at home and sketch the position of some items of furniture or fittings on a piece of A4 plain paper. Ask them to bring the plan into school and try to define the position of some of the items by overlaying on it a transparent acetate grid of 1 cm or 2 cm squares.

SUPPORT MATERIALS

Teaching aids
Pin Board 5 X 5 and 6 X 6 (NES Arnold)
Games: *Connect Four, Space Lines, Othello* (NES Arnold)

Teachers' reference materials
Primary Mathematics Today, 3rd edn, chapter 38, Elizabeth Williams and Hilary Shuard (Longman)
Maths Plus: Graphs 1 and 2, Paul Harling (Ward Lock Educational)
Lines of Development in Primary Mathematics, Mary Deboys and Eunice Pitt (Blackstaff Press)

Software
Pirate Gold from *Maths with a Story 2* (BBC Publications)
Lines from *MicroSMILE 1* (ILECC)
Rhino from *MicroSMILE 1* (ILECC)
Co-ordinate Jigsaw from *Maths With a Story 1* (BBC Publications)

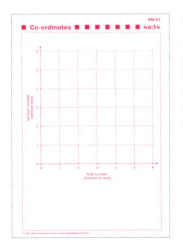
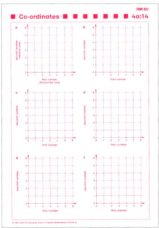

15. AREA & PERIMETER

LEARNING CONTEXT

Contribution made by this Step
The children estimate and find areas by counting centimetre squares and perimeters by counting centimetre lengths.

Objectives
To enable children to:
a Construct simple 2-D shapes using data related to area or perimeter.
b Measure, compare and order areas using the square centimetre or other appropriate units of area.
c Test statements about areas or perimeters.
d Compare the square millimetre, centimetre, decimetre and metre.

Background
In previous Steps, the children have used arbitrary units of different shapes and sizes to estimate, measure and order areas of regular and irregular surfaces. In Step 3a:35, perimeters were introduced. Most recently, in Step 3b:15, the children used the square centimetre to estimate and find areas of simple 2-D and 3-D surfaces and centimetres to estimate and measure perimeters.
   Since the SI unit for area is the square metre, which is often too big for measuring surfaces unless we use decimal fractions, other practical teaching units are needed such as the square decimetre, square centimetre and, as introduced in this Step, the square millimetre.
   Several elements of the PoS for Using and Applying Mathematics feature in this Step and may offer opportunities for assessment.

> **Mathematics in the National Curriculum**
>
> **Programme of Study: KS2**
> Pupils should be taught to:
> ■ make 2-D and 3-D shapes and patterns with increasing accuracy, recognise their geometrical features and properties, and use these to classify shapes and solve problems. (SSM 2.b)
> ■ find perimeters of simple shapes; find areas and volumes by counting methods, leading to the use of other practical methods, *e.g. dissection*. (SSM 4.c)
> ■ select and use the appropriate mathematics and materials. (UA 2.a)
> ■ understand and investigate general statements, *e.g. 'wrist size is half neck size', 'there are four prime numbers less than 10'.* (UA 4.a)

THINKING AND TALKING MATHEMATICALLY

Starting points for discussion
Surfaces from *Videomaths* (ITV Schools).

What is area? A perimeter?

What shapes are best for measuring area? Why?

Revise the terms 'square decimetre' and 'square metre'. Ask, *What can you tell me about these? How can you make a unit of this area? What would you measure with them?*

What is the difference between an open and closed shape? Why can't you find the area of an open shape?

> **Key language**
>
> estimate, measure, compare, order, enclose, cover, area, surface, amount, unit, square millimetre (sq mm), square centimetre (sq cm), square decimetre (sq dm), square metre (sq m), about, approximately, ascending, descending

STEPS 4a

ACTIVITIES IN DETAIL

A Revision: square centimetres C

1 What can the children remember about previous work with area? List some terms likely to be used in connection with area and ask the children to give examples of sentences using them or to explain what the terms mean.

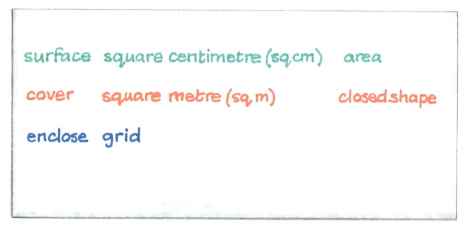

surface square centimetre (sq.cm) area
cover square metre (sq.m) closed shape
enclose grid

2 Introduce the tasks from Book 4a, page 38 which provides individual practice and RM 63 which suggests a collaborative group project and a challenging individual activity. (The latter may help you make individual assessments against Ma1/4a.)

Resources

School
Scissors

Scheme
Book 4a, page 38;
Resource Master 63;
Resource Master A (1cm squared grid)

You may wish to introduce informally the notation 'cm²' as the mathematical shorthand for writing 'square centimetre'. However, until some work is introduced on indices, this notation is not likely to make much sense.

B Rectangles: areas and perimeters C

1 Can the children indicate the perimeters of objects near them? Can they define a perimeter, i.e. the distance around a closed shape? What can they remember about previous work with perimeters?

2 Introduce the tasks from Book 4a, page 39, which revise and extend previous work on perimeters measured in cm. Book 4a, page 40 provides an investigatory task.

EXTENSION

- Provide copies of RM B (1cm squared paper with $\frac{1}{2}$ cm grid). On this, the children find and record different shapes with the same perimeter but with sides which are not whole centimetres long, e.g.:

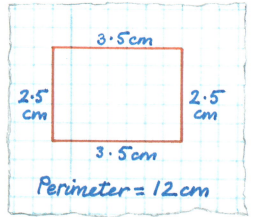

Resources

Scheme
Book 4a, pages 39 and 40;
Resource Master B (1cm squared paper with $\frac{1}{2}$ cm grid)

C Irregular areas `C` `G` `P` `I`

1 Provide each group with a supply of small items with irregular surfaces and square centimetre grid.

2 Ask the children, preferably working in pairs, to choose one item at a time, to draw around its outline, then to estimate and count its area in square centimetres.

3 If necessary, revise the convention for counting part-squares.

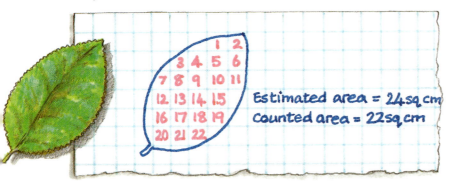

4 Explain that they should record each estimate and count in their own way.

5 As work progresses, discuss why different people might get a slightly different count in squares for the same item, e.g. the approximate nature of area when measuring irregular surfaces.

6 Introduce the terms 'ascending order' and 'descending order'. Can the children order the items by area both ways?

RM 64 provides individual practice.

EXTENSION

This is an activity for a pair or small group. Using a rectangle, cut from a 1cm squared grid, with an area of, say, 20 square cm for reference, the children tear or cut from paper areas they consider to be about the same.

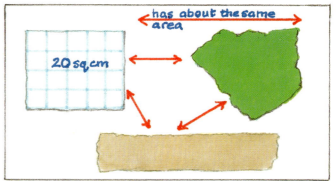

Resources

School
Small flat objects such as leaves, paper geometric shapes (not rectangles) or torn paper shapes

Scheme
Resource Master 64

It is usual to count part-squares of which half or more is included in the area being measured, and to discount part-squares which are less than half a square. This generally gives a good approximation.

D Comparing units: square mm, square cm, square dm and square m `C`

Part 1: Magnifying the grid

1 Allow time to investigate the dimensions of the grid on the Magnispectors and ask, *What can you tell me about the grid on the base?*

2 Points to draw out in discussion are that:
– the smaller squares have an edge length of 1mm, the larger 1cm;
– 100 of the smaller squares equal one larger square;
– the smaller square has an area of one square millimetre and the larger one square centimetre;
– sometimes the centimetre square is too large for measuring areas of very small surfaces.

3 Discuss situations where measuring with square mm might be

Resources

School
Osmiroid Magnispectors or similar; four 1m rules; metric base 10 hundreds; 1mm squared graph paper (optional)

Scheme
Resource Master 65

Magnispectors are magnifying boxes. The base has a transparent mm grid with cm divisions. Can the children suggest why magnification is needed or helpful?

STEPS 4a

appropriate, e.g. scientists measuring the growth of a small insect, surgeons in laser surgery.

4 To give them a 'feel' for this very small unit of area, the children might try estimating and measuring areas of very small objects, e.g. petals of flowers.

5 If available, the children might examine 1mm squared graph paper.

Part 2: Revision: the square decimetre and square metre

1 Fit together four metre rods.

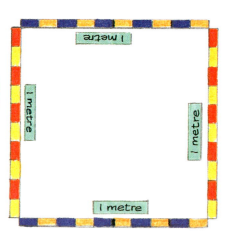

2 Revise similarly the use of the square decimetre using base 10 squares for reference.

RM 65 provides individual practice in choosing appropriate units of area.

E Surface areas of 3-D rods

1 Provide each group with two or three full sets of Cuisenaire Rods.

2 Introduce the task in Book 4a, page 41.

3 Afterwards compare results and how the areas were estimated. For example, did anyone find a quick way to calculate the area of a rod by multiplying the area of a lengthwise face four times and adding 2 square centimetres for the end faces?

4 By referring to the growth pattern listed in question 2 of Book 4a, page 41, can the children predict the area of longer rods, e.g.

Resources

School
Cuisenaire Rods

Scheme
Book 4a, page 41; Resource Master A (1 cm squared grid)

This activity will enable you to remind children that 3-D shapes also have surfaces which can be measured.

What would the area of an 11 centimetre ... 12 centimetre ...
20 centimetre ... 100 centimetre, etc., rod be? How do you know?

5 What other 3-D objects can the children name with an area about the same as, say, a tan rod?

EXTENSION

■ The children could try to design a net for a cube with each face having an area of 16 square centimetres. Ask, *What is the surface area of the cube?*

F Assessment activity   I

*Make a card on which this example and statement are written:

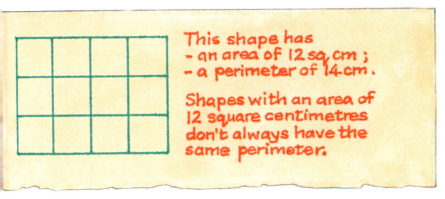

Resources

School
Statement card*

Scheme
Resource Master A (1cm squared grid)

1 Using the centimetre squared grid, ask the child to construct some shapes to show you that the statement on the card is true. (Read this aloud if necessary.)

2 Afterwards, ask the child to explain her or his results and conclusion. (If perimeter lengths have not been recorded, the child can do this now.)

3 Ask, *What other units for measuring area do you know about?* (If necessary, prompt by asking, *What would you use to measure surfaces like ... the footprint of a mouse ... a netball pitch?*)

4 Ask the child to suggest one surface he or she might measure in square mm, square cm, square dm and square m.

Assessment notes

Oral response	✔
Practical response	
Pictorial response	✔
Written response	✔

The child has:
constructed simple shapes using data related to area or perimeter;
AND
found areas by counting square centimetres;
AND
used examples to test a statement and justified it;
AND
made comparisons between mm², cm², dm² and m².

STRENGTHENING ACTIVITIES

Appropriate units

A child who is unable to suggest surfaces which might be measured in the different metric units (square cm, square dm and square m) probably needs further practical experience of using these.

Areas of rods

Children having problems finding the total surface area of rods in Activity **E** might use instead the longs from Multibase equipment. These have the advantage of the whole surface being marked in square centimetres so making counting easier.

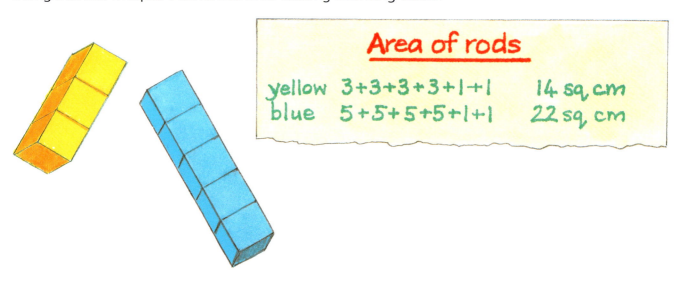

CHALLENGING ACTIVITIES

Area dominoes

Design a set of area dominoes which uses centimetre square grid and the terms 'square centimetre' and 'sq cm'. The last domino should link with the first to form a loop. Try them out on friends.

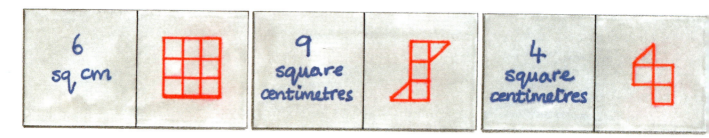

Cube design

Design a cube with a total surface area of 150 square cm.

IDEAS BOARD

■ Typical projects
Ourselves, Shape and Size, Surfaces, Growth, Natural things: Trees, Plants, etc.

■ Display
Using actual objects, drawings, photographs, etc., make a display of objects whose area would most sensibly be measured in square mm, square cm or square m.

■ Science
- A class competition to find the leaf (tree or flower) with the largest area.
- Compare the area of leaves from different parts of one tree.
- Estimate then check how much bigger your footprint is than your handprint. (The ratio of footprint:handprint is likely to be in the region of 1.5:1.)

■ Art and design
- Make a gallery where pictures/patterns on cm squared paper have a constant area or perimeter.
- Everyone explodes or expands a square with an area of 100 sq cm in different ways.

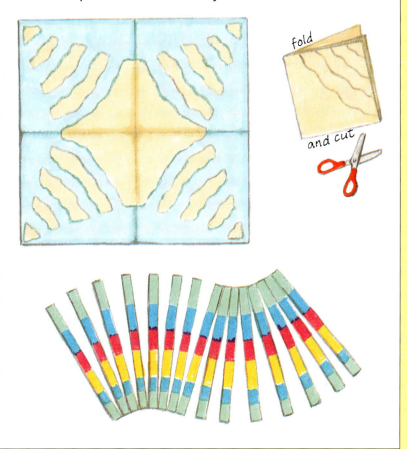

HOME/SCHOOL PROJECTS

Each child brings to school a surface which he or she estimates has an area of about, say, 50 sq cm to generate an instant display at school.

SUPPORT MATERIALS

Teaching aids
Assorted pinboards (NES Arnold, Taskmaster, Hope Education)
New Pinboard (Philip & Tacey)
Transparent Pinboard (NES Arnold)
Centicubes and *Magnispector* (Osmiroid Educational)
Centimetre Grid (Taskmaster)
Area Dominoes (Taskmaster)

STEPS 4a

Teachers' reference materials
Basic Measurement Activities, Dorothy Diamond (Hulton)
Primary Mathematics Today, 3rd edn, chapter 22, Elizabeth Williams and Hilary Shuard (Longman)
Starting from Squares (BEAM Project)
Mathematics through Art and Design, Anne Woodman and Eric Albany (Collins Educational)

Children's books
Area, Joan Jonas Srivastava (A & C Black)

Software
Squares from *Surfaces* (Disk 1) and *Squeeze* (Disk 2), *Videomaths Software* (Central Software)

Radio and TV
Surfaces from *Videomaths* (ITV Schools)

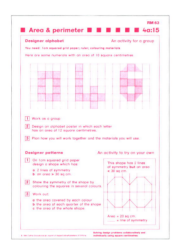

16. WEIGHT

LEARNING CONTEXT

Contribution made by this Step

As the children explore ways of measuring weight with increasing accuracy, their ability to read and interpret the dials on different weighing instruments is strengthened. Simple problems involving weight are investigated, and appropriate forms of recording weight discussed.

Objectives

To enable children to:
a Make sensible estimates in relation to weight.
b Solve practical and written problems involving weight.
c Record weights appropriately.

Background

As children become more proficient in measuring weight, the need for increasing accuracy becomes clear. This is developed in this Step as children develop awareness of the use of precise weights in consumer packaging.

The relationship between units of weight needs to be gradually extended so the children can develop their choice of appropriate units for different situations. For most practical purposes, weighing in units of 10 g is an appropriate level of accuracy; the 100 g weight (hectogram), introduced in Step 3a:34, remains a useful unit to bridge the vast difference between gram and kilogram.

It is important that the children have the opportunity to practise reading and interpreting various dials on different kinds of weighing instruments. Cooking and class shop activities continue to offer excellent informal opportunities to develop weighing skills, and solving practical or written problems.

Although it is important to use good-quality scales (and the maintenance and checking of weighing instruments is encouraged) it is the *process of measurement*, rather than the accuracy of results, which is the focus of these activities.

Mathematics in the National Curriculum

Programme of Study: KS2
Pupils should be taught to:
- choose appropriate standard units of length, mass, capacity and time, and make sensible estimates with them in everyday situations; extend their understanding of the relationship between units. (SSM 4.a)
- choose and use appropriate measuring instruments; interpret numbers and read scales to an increasing degree of accuracy. (SSM 4.b)
- try different mathematical approaches; identify and obtain information needed to carry out their work. (UA 2.b)
- check their results and consider whether they are reasonable. (UA 2.d)

THINKING AND TALKING MATHEMATICALLY

Starting points for discussion

Display a range of weighing instruments including balance- and compression scales, standard weights (1 g to 1 kg), weighing materials (e.g. sand, rice, dried peas/beans) and plastic bags.

Encourage informal estimation, then weighing, of the different materials 'as accurately as you can'.

Ask the children to check the measured weights, using alternative weighing instruments.

Key language

Balance-scales, compression scales, dial, division, calibration, equivalent, spring balance, gram, hectogram, kilogram, to the nearest ...

ACTIVITIES IN DETAIL

A Weighing with Centicubes   C G

Part 1: Investigating Centicubes

1 Revise the use of Centicubes, allowing time for exploratory play. *How many different shapes can you make with ten Centicubes?*

2 Ask the children to suggest methods to check the weight of Centicubes.

3 Provide balance-scales, standard weights and other weighing instruments. Suggest that groups of children check the weights of different numbers of Centicubes, e.g. 100, 50, 20, etc.

4 Discuss the results of weighing the sets of Centicubes. Make sure the children agree that if 50 Centicubes weigh 50 g, then each one must weigh 1 g. Ask them to calculate and then check the weights of different shapes made with Centicubes.

Resources

School
Balance-scales and standard weights (1 g to 100 g); other weighing instruments (spring balances, compression scales, letter balances, etc.); Centicubes

With an accurate weight of 1 g each and a volume of one cubic centimetre, Centicubes can be used in many different activities.

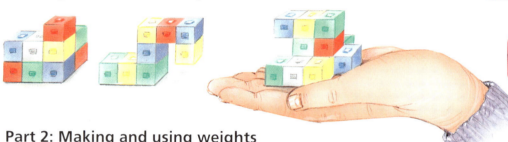

What is the weight of this Centicube model?

Part 2: Making and using weights

1 Provide a selection of items (weighing less than 100 g) and ask the children to estimate their weights using Centicubes. Record the estimates then check and record weights using balance-scales. Ask, *Is it useful to make 'sticks' of Centicubes? What size stick is best?*

2 Ask the groups of children to use Centicubes to make a set of weights from 1 g to 100 g and use them to find the weight of small objects.

3 Discuss the range and type of items which are most appropriately weighed using grams (in contrast to larger items which are weighed in multiples of 1 kg). Ask the children to list and/or display suitable items.

EXTENSION

- If you have a thousand Centicubes, children can make 10 g 'sticks' or 'longs', then join them together to make 100 g 'flats' and eventually a cube. *How much does the large cube weigh? What are its dimensions?*

B Estimating, weighing and recording

Part 1: Estimating and recording weights

1 Use balance-scales to revise standard weights. Ask groups of children to estimate the weights of two or three different items, and to check using the balance-scales. *How can you use the balance-scales to find the lighter of two objects? ... to order three objects by weight?*

2 Remind the children that different small weights can be used to match a larger weight, and revise the relationship between units of weight. For example, ask: *How many 100 g (hectogram) weights are needed to balance half a kilogram? What different weights can you use to make up a quarter of a kilogram?*

3 Explain how to record weights which are larger than 1 kilogram (that is, more than 1000 grams). For example:

One thousand five hundred grams = 1500 grams = 1500 g = 1 kilogram and 500 grams = 1 kg 500 g.

4 Ask the children to work in pairs to find and record the weights of different items (to the nearest 10 g), using grams alone and/or kilograms and grams. Include some items weighing less then 100 g and some weighing more than 1 kg.

Part 2: Comparing weighing instruments

1 Make available the loose weighing materials. Children work in pairs to weigh out some specific amounts (e.g. 220 g of rice) using two or more different weighing instruments. Encourage the children to compare measurements and check the accuracy of the different scales.

2 Discuss the results.

Further practice of estimating, measuring and recording weights can be found on RM 66.

Resources

School
Balance-scales and weights; other weighing instruments (compression scales, spring balances, etc.); items for weighing, including some weighing over 1 kg; weighing materials (e.g. dry sand, rice, pulses, Plasticine, small stones, nuts and bolts, marbles, wood shavings); plastic bags

Scheme
Resource Master 66

C Interpreting readings on weighing instruments

1 Display and compare different weighing instruments. *How does each work? What is it called? Is it accurate? How can you check? What types of things could you weigh on each? What things would be unsuitable? Do you know of any other types of weighing instruments? Where do people use weighing instruments in their jobs* (supermarket, post office, health centre, airport luggage check-in desk)?

2 Use standard weights (e.g. 10 g, 100 g, 200 g, 500 g and 1 kg) to compare readings on different weighing instruments. *Which is most suitable for small weights? Which is most suitable for heavier weights?*

3 Show that the scales differ and explain that to read the weight correctly you must recognise:
- the range of the scale;
- important calibrations which might or might not be labelled, e.g. 5 g, 10 g, 20 g, 50 g, … 1 kg … ;
- the amount represented by single divisions on the scale.

4 Ask the children to find and record the weights of various objects using different weighing instruments. Encourage the children to use, for example, a spring balance to weigh an item previously weighed on balance-scales.

C Resources

School
Selection of weighing instruments (e.g. balance-scales, compression scales, spring balance, bathroom scales, 'add-on' kitchen scales, electronic (digital) scales)

Scheme
Book 4a, page 42;
Resource Master 66

Some older measuring instruments can be inaccurate. Make sure the children know how to adjust a pointer to zero, where appropriate, and to check accuracy using standard weights.

Some scales are labelled, for example, 1 kg × 100 g, meaning that it weighs up to 1 kg and is calibrated in 100 g intervals.

5 Discuss the advantages and disadvantages of the different weighing instruments. Make sure all the children experience reading and interpreting a variety of scales.

Book 4a, page 42, and RM 66, provide further practice in reading scales.

EXTENSION

■ Fix a paper cover on a dial of some compression scales. The children put $\frac{1}{2}$ kg standard weights on the scales and mark the paper to show the position of the calibrations. The activity can be repeated with new covers, and 100 g and 10 g weights.

D Solving problems involving weight   C I

Resources

School
Weights (10 g to 1 kg); bathroom scales; spring balance; sticky tape

Scheme
Book 4a, pages 43 and 44

It is important for children to develop the ability to think logically in grams and kilograms in real situations and in written problems. These topics, among others, will offer opportunities to incorporate problems involving weight.

1 *'Best buy' products.* Children compare a small number of containers and packets of food and household items. For example, *Which biscuits are the least expensive per 100 grams? Is packaging deceptive?*

2 *Strength tests.* Devise and carry out a test to see which type of plastic shopping bag is the strongest. Is it dependent on the plastic used, or the design of the handle, or other factor(s)?

3 *Supporting weights.* Challenge the children to design and make a construction to support a 50 g weight, using one sheet of A4 paper and 10 cm sticky tape only.

Further numerical and puzzle activities which involve weight are found on Book 4a, pages 43 and 44.

One obvious activity would be for the children to measure and record their own weights. As this could be a sensitive topic among children of this age, we recommend that this is done only where the teacher feels confident that it will not cause anxiety in his/her class.

E Assessment activity   I

Resources

School
Selected items (of known weight) from less than 100 g to over 1 kg; weighing instruments (including balance-scales and compression scales); 10 g, 20 g, 50 g, 100 g, 200 g, 500 g and 1 kg weights

1 Ask the child to select three items and, by feel, place them in order of weight.

2 Allow the child to handle the weights and compare them with one of the selected items, telling you an appropriate estimate of its weight.

3 Ask the child to measure the actual weight of the item on the appropriate weighing instrument and write it in a suitable form.

4 Place the weighed item with some others on a compression scale to make up a weight greater than 1 kg. Ask the child to tell you the weight and record it appropriately.

Assessment notes

Oral response	✔
Practical response	✔
Pictorial response	
Written response	✔

The child has:
made a sensible estimate of the weight of an object;
AND
correctly measured the weight of an object using an appropriate technique;
AND
correctly recorded the weight of objects less than and greater than 1 kg.

STEPS 4a

STRENGTHENING ACTIVITIES

Heavier and lighter

If a child is having difficulty comparing and ordering three weights, ask him/her to order two objects first, and then make a comparison with a third.

Weighing out

Ask a child to weigh out a quantity, rounded to the nearest 100 grams, of dry sand (or similar) using different weighing instruments. Can she/he check that the weight is the same on the different scales?

Reading weights

To practise interpreting divisions on dials, ask a child to weigh standard weights on different weighing instruments and read the dials, then progress to weighing unknown amounts.

CHALLENGING ACTIVITIES

Wet and dry

Compare the weights of two identical objects, one of which has been left to soak in water. For example: sponge, brick, J cloth.

Spring balances

Can the children design and make a balance using elastic bands? One example might be:

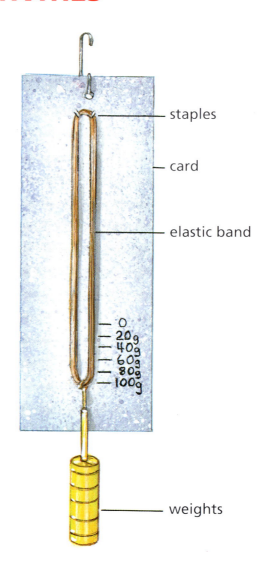

Letters and parcels

Find out the cost of sending letters and parcels in the U.K. Children make up mystery parcels for others to weigh and draw or stick on home-made stamps of the correct value.

How many?

– Estimate, then find by weighing, how many apples you get if you buy 1kg of them.

– Display different fruit and vegetables. Estimate, then check by weighing, how much waste there is. For example, compare the weight of a banana and its peel.

IDEAS BOARD

■ Typical projects
Food; Packaging; Size; Measurement

■ Technology
– Design and construct models to support a certain weight, e.g. arch, bridge, pillar.
– Compare architectural designs to solve weight-bearing requirements.

■ Science
Research into and/or measure animal weights. *Which breed of dog is heaviest/lightest? What is the heaviest mammal?*

■ Weight-lifting
Look at the *Guinness Book of Records* for records in weight-lifting. Compare with weights of cars. For example, can a person lift a car?

■ Cooking
Encourage children to follow simple recipes which use multiples of 10 grams. Make sure they weigh out the ingredients with care, using kitchen scales. If possible, show an add-on kitchen scale – the type of scale which can be reset at zero as each ingredient is added to the pan.

■ Snow shoes
Why do snow shoes shaped like large racquets help prevent someone sinking into snow? Why do stiletto heels make holes in floor surfaces? Investigate.

■ The weight of money
Research the weight of different coins. For each coin, work out how many would weigh 1kg. How do banks check they have certain amounts of money? (See *Support Materials*.)

■ Lifts
Look at lifts in public buildings for maximum weights. Record whether they indicate a maximum number of people or state a weight in kilograms, or both. Investigate their different functions.

STEPS 4a

HOME/SCHOOL PROJECT

Ask the children to look at home for food and household products which have a given weight. *What units are used? Make a list and, if possible, bring clean empty packets and containers to school. Find out why 454 g is such a popular size.*

SUPPORT MATERIALS

Teaching aids
Centicubes (NES Arnold)
Compression Scale with Pan (Taskmaster)
Spring Balance (Taskmaster)
Simple Pan Balance (Hope Education)
Simple Scales (Hope Education)
Osmiroid Super Beamer Balance (NES Arnold)
Basic Adjustable and Counterbalance Scale (Philip and Tacey)
Weights (Yorkshire Purchasing Organisation)
Electronic Scales (NES Arnold)
Waymaster Add-and-Weigh (2 kg) (NES Arnold)

Teachers' reference materials
Primary Mathematics Today, 3rd edn, chapters 7 and 27, Elizabeth Williams and Hilary Shuard (Longman)
Children Learn to Measure, John Glenn (Ed.) (Harper and Row)
Maths Plus: Mass and Weighing 1 and 2, Paul Harling (Ward Lock Educational)
Bank of England Resource Pack for Primary Schools (The Bank of England, Threadneedle Street, London EC2R 8AH)
The Royal Mint, Llantrisant, Pontycwm, Glamorgan, CF7 8YT

17. DECIMAL FRACTIONS

LEARNING CONTEXT

Contribution made by this Step

The children are introduced to the structure of decimals to two places. They experience a variety of resources which illustrate the relationship between whole numbers, tenths and hundredths. They also use decimals in practical contexts and begin to develop computational skills (addition and subtraction), using small numbers, to two places of decimals, with and without the use of a calculator. Work on length and money is included.

Objectives

To enable children to:
a Understand and use decimal fractions to two decimal places in numbers up to ten.
b Interpret a calculator display to two decimal places.
c Start to add or subtract numbers to two places of decimals.

Background

Decimals are an extension of the base ten place value system. It is therefore important for the children to see the decimal point as only an indicator of the position of the units column; so we should refer, for example, to 'one place to the right of the units column' rather than 'one place to the right of the decimal point'. The use of column headings such as H T U · t h can help to remind the children of the value of each digit. There are obvious links with simple fractions and percentages so equivalents can be made clear when appropriate. When possible, activities should be placed in practical contexts, for example, measurement.

THINKING AND TALKING MATHEMATICALLY

Starting points for discussion

Use the results of an international sprint race. List the times in random order, e.g. A – 9·98 seconds, B – 10·02 seconds, C – 9·97 seconds, D – 9·99 seconds, E – 10·00 seconds, F – 10·01 seconds. *Who won the race? How do you know? Who was last?*

Display some numbers such as 3·1, 8·7, etc. *What do these numbers mean? What about 3·17, 8·72? etc.*

Can the children suggest sentences using the terms, 'tenths' and 'hundredths'?

Mathematics in the National Curriculum

Programme of Study: KS2
Pupils should be taught to:
■ extend their understanding of the number system to ... decimals with no more than two decimal places in the context of measurement and money. (N 2.b)
■ extend methods of computation to include ... all four operations with decimals, and calculating fractions and percentages of quantities, using a calculator where appropriate. (N 3.g)
■ check results by different methods, including repeating the operations in a different order or using inverse operations; gain a sense of the size of a solution, and estimate and approximate solutions to problems. (N 4.c)

Key language

tenths, units, separates, hundredths, decimal, decimal point, place(s), decimal form, fraction, column, zero, nought, percentage, metre, decimetre, centimetre, millimetre

ACTIVITIES IN DETAIL

A Hundredths and money

C **I**

Resources

School
Real or facsimile £1, 10p and 1p coins; calculators

Part 1: £1 coins and 10p coins

1 Revise the notation of money. Remind the children that since ten 10p coins make £1, 10p is one tenth of £1. *What is one tenth written as a decimal?*

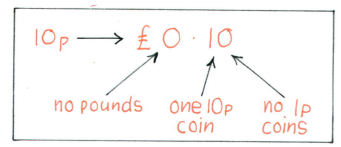

2 Build up a sequence, showing the forms of notation of money to 90p, asking the children to count on, and back, in 10p amounts.

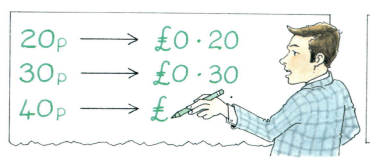

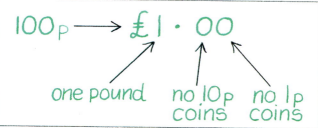

3 Extend the list beyond £1, explaining the notation and again asking children to count on and back in 10p amounts.

Part 2: £1 coins and 1p coins

1 Remind the children that since one hundred 1p coins make £1, 1p is a hundredth of £1. Discuss and show the notation (see right).

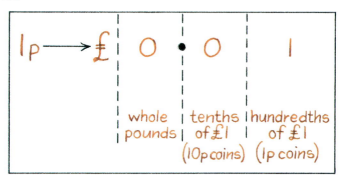

Part 3: £1 coins, 10p coins and 1p coins

1 Take a small number of facsimile mixed £1, 10p and 1p coins. Illustrate the decimal place value relationship of the coins (see right).

2 Ask the children to make money charts with labelled columns and to mark the decimal point. They take small numbers of mixed coins and show and describe them on their charts (see below).

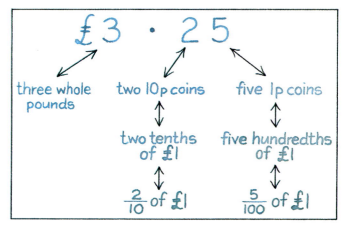

STEPS 4a

3 Ask them to insert a number such as 1·56 into a calculator and ensure that the children can interpret the display in the context of money (£1·56).

4 Next, ask them to insert the number 1·70 into the calculator, then press $\boxed{=}$. The display changes to 1·7. Discuss the fact that £1·7 is the same as £1·70, because 0·7 of a pound is actually seven 10p coins or 70p. Repeat with other amounts, including inserting 1·00 then pressing $\boxed{=}$.

B Base 10 materials and the abacus C G

Part 1: Representing numbers

1 Show the base 10 materials. Can the children give the relative values of the pieces?

2 Tell the children that they are going to 'change the rule' for the pieces, making the flat represent a one. Therefore, each long will be one tenth of the one (flat), each small cube will be one tenth of a long and, since there are one hundred small cubes in a flat, each small cube is one hundredth of a flat.

3 Get the children to make and label place value boards. Can they show how to represent a number with two decimal places? If a class demonstration is preferred, use a transparency of a place value board and base 10 pieces.

Resources

School
Base 10 materials; blank place value boards*; three- or four-spike decimal abacus

Scheme
Resource Master 67

Emphasise the fact that a decimal such as 1·1 can also be written 1·10.

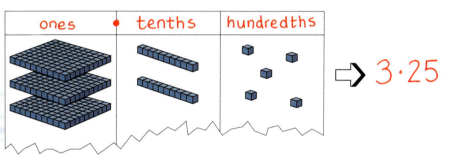

4 Encourage the children to illustrate other numbers, including some which contain a zero, in one or more of the columns.

Part 2: Ordering

1 Discuss the fact that base 10 materials clearly indicate the relative size of the decimals, and that this can be checked by physically comparing pieces.

STEPS 4a

2 The children, working in pairs, can practise putting numbers on the boards and placing the correct sign between them.

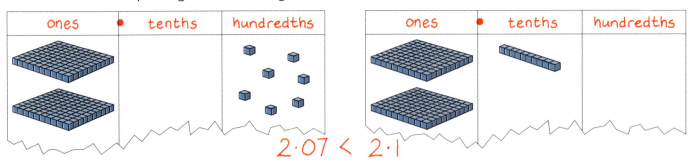

3 At another time, use an appropriately labelled three- or four-spike abaci to represent or compare similar numbers.

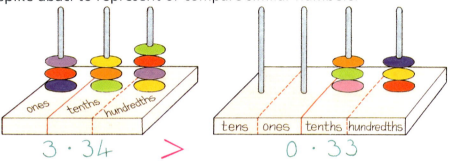

Part 3: Equivalence

1 Ask the children to count in longs (tenths) and in small cubes (hundredths), showing that, for example, ten hundredths are equivalent to one tenth.

RM 67 provides a related game. As play proceeds, ask the children to describe the value of the pieces on their board.

C Hundredths on 100-square grids

*In advance, make a transparency of RM 68, shading the whole of the first square, three vertical strips of the second and six small squares of the third.

Part 1: Representing two decimal places

1 Show the transparency of RM 68 on the OHP. Display written forms of the number shown on the transparency.

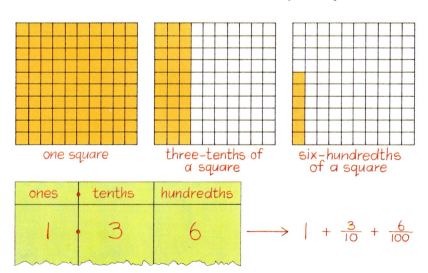

Resources

School
Squared paper; OHP; OHP pens; calculators

Scheme
Resource Master 68*;
Book 4a, page 45

Emphasise that *any* 36 of the squares could be coloured.

2 Discuss the features of this 'model' of two places of decimals which are similar to those using base 10 materials, the abacus and money.

Part 2: Equivalence

1 Show the children, by combining the second and third squares on the transparency, that three tenths of the square and six hundredths of the square are the same as thirty-six hundredths of the square.

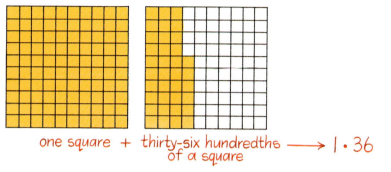

one square + thirty-six hundredths of a square ⟶ 1·36

2 Ask the children to colour representations of several numbers between one and two, to two places of decimals, in the same way, using copies of RM 68 or squared paper.

Make sure that you include some familiar decimals, such as 0·25 ($\frac{1}{4}$, 25%) and 0·75 ($\frac{3}{4}$, 75%).

Book 4a, page 45, provides individual practice in comparing and ordering two-place decimals up to one. Emphasise that, for example, 0·5 can be written 0·50.

EXTENSION

■ The children can investigate ways in which the two-place decimals less than one can be related to the percentage form (Step 9).

D Hundredths on a number line   C   I

Part 1: Representing numbers

1 Show a demonstration number line, labelled 0 to 10.

Resources

School
Demonstration number lines

Scheme
Resource Master 69; Book 4a, pages 46 and 47

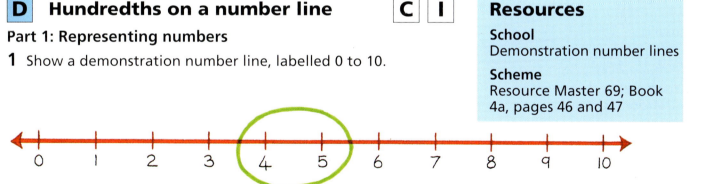

2 Ask a child to choose two consecutive numbers from the line, e.g. 4 and 5. On a second number line, show an expanded version of that space with ten sections. Ask the children to tell you the numbers for each mark.

If necessary refer back to Handbook 3b:23 to revise one-place decimals.

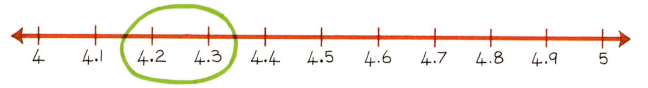

STEPS 4a

163

3 Again ask a child to choose two consecutive numbers, e.g. 4·2 and 4·3 and, on a third number line, show that space expanded to include ten sections. *How can these points be numbered?* If necessary, explain and show that each division is a tenth of a space on the previous line and a hundredth of a space on the first number line. It can be labelled like this:

4 On RM 69, ask the children to:

(a) Mark consecutive numbers on line **1a**, indicate the section they wish to expand, then calibrate this in tenths on line **1b**. They then indicate the section they wish to expand on line **1b** and show this section as hundredths on line **1c**.

(b) Repeat this activity on the other two sets of number lines on RM 69, using different consecutive numbers to start each time.

Use Book 4a, pages 46 and 47, for further individual practice.

EXTENSION

■ Explore ways to illustrate larger numbers such as 385·78 on the number lines on RM 69.

E Hundredths and length   C I

1 Show examples of metre rules and tape measures calibrated in centimetres, decimetres and metres. Discuss the style and meaning of the calibrations.

2 Remind the children how to use the various measuring instruments. Ask them to measure distances in or around the classroom, choosing appropriate equipment and recording the distances in their own way.

3 Display one or two of these measurements. Can the children suggest how to write these as a fraction with two places of decimals?

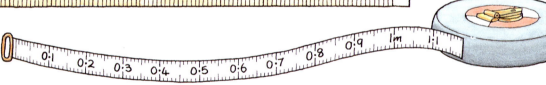

Resources

School
Metre rules, tape measures, trundle wheels, calibrated in centimetres, decimetres and metres

Reference can be made to Step 10 (Length) during this activity.

Make sure that you remind the children that, for example, 1·4 m can also be written 1·40 m because 0·4 m is the same as 40 cm.

STEPS 4a

4 Provide further opportunities for children to measure lengths and record them in the decimal form. For example:

object	length			
	cm	m	cm	m
bookcase	275	2	75	2·75
window	80	0	80	0·80

F Adding and subtracting small decimals C I

1 Discuss the way to add and subtract small numbers to two places of decimals, using base 10 materials and/or a decimal abacus, as appropriate.

2 Show that the process, with and without apparatus, is essentially the same as adding and subtracting three digit numbers but that the decimal points must be carefully aligned.

$$\begin{array}{r} 1 \cdot 46 \\ + \; 2 \cdot 38 \\ \hline 3 \cdot 84 \end{array} \qquad \begin{array}{r} {}^1\!2 \cdot {}^{12}\!3\,{}^1\!5 \\ - \; 0 \cdot 66 \\ \hline 1 \cdot 69 \end{array}$$

3 Ask the children to record two lengths in decimal form, then to find the total length and the difference between them.

RMs 70 and 71 provide individual practice.

Resources

School
Base 10 materials; decimal place value charts from Activity B; three- or four-spike decimal abacus; measuring equipment (see Activity E); calculators

Scheme
Resource Masters 70 and 71

Encourage the children to estimate the answer, and then to check it, using a calculator, making sure that the correct units are used to label the written length.

G Assessment activity I

Ask the child to carry out the following activities:

1 Shade, say, 0·18 of a grid on RM 68.

2 Measure and record, in metres and centimetres, the length and width of, say, a table top.

3 Say and record each length in two-place decimal form.

4 Add the two lengths in writing and check the answer with a calculator.

4 Find the difference between the two lengths, in writing, then using a calculator.

6 Using a calculator, add £0·75 and £1·35 (or 0·75m and 1·35m) and tell you what the display (showing 2·1) means in the context of money or length.

Resources

School
Measuring tape; calculator

Scheme
Resource Master 68

Assessment notes

Oral response	✔
Practical response	✔
Pictorial response	
Written response	✔

The child has:
correctly illustrated a number to two places of decimals;
AND
correctly used two places of decimals in the context of measurement;
AND
correctly added and subtracted a pair of small numbers to two places of decimals;
AND
appropriately interpreted a calculator display of a number to two places of decimals, in the context of measurement or money.

STEPS 4a

STRENGTHENING ACTIVITIES

One place of decimals

Further work on tenths and one-place decimals (preferably in the context of measurement) may be necessary if a child's understanding of the second place (hundredths) is underdeveloped.

Three coin shopping

The children buy and sell items in the class shop, using only £1 coins, 10p coins and 1p coins, to emphasise the place value of columns in the notation of decimal money.

Counting on and back in hundredths

Use base 10 materials and a two-place decimal place value board. Children count on (or back) in hundredths (small cubes) making exchanges as necessary.

CHALLENGING ACTIVITIES

Story of one

Use 100-square grids and/or calculators. The children explore patterns of numbers to two places of decimals which give a total of one, e.g.:

   0.01 + 0.99   0.01 + 0.50 + 0.49
   0.02 + 0.98   0.02 + 0.50 + 0.48

Hundreds of hundredths

If you had seven hundred and sixty-five hundredths, how many ones, tenths and hundredths is it worth? Is there a rule for converting the amount into a decimal form? What if you had a thousand hundredths? ... nine thousand nine hundred and ninety-nine hundredths?

HOME/SCHOOL PROJECTS

The children collect till receipts from a variety of sources. They bring these into school for displaying, comparing and sorting.

IDEAS BOARD

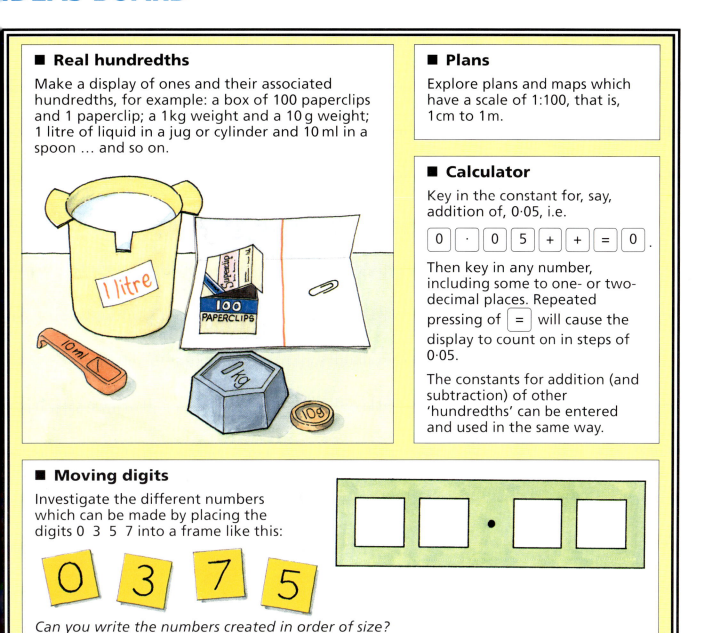

■ Real hundredths
Make a display of ones and their associated hundredths, for example: a box of 100 paperclips and 1 paperclip; a 1kg weight and a 10g weight; 1 litre of liquid in a jug or cylinder and 10 ml in a spoon … and so on.

■ Plans
Explore plans and maps which have a scale of 1:100, that is, 1cm to 1m.

■ Calculator
Key in the constant for, say, addition of, 0·05, i.e.

| 0 | · | 0 | 5 | + | + | = | 0 |

Then key in any number, including some to one- or two-decimal places. Repeated pressing of | = | will cause the display to count on in steps of 0·05.

The constants for addition (and subtraction) of other 'hundredths' can be entered and used in the same way.

■ Moving digits
Investigate the different numbers which can be made by placing the digits 0 3 5 7 into a frame like this:

Can you write the numbers created in order of size?

SUPPORT MATERIALS

Teaching aids
Primary Metre Rule (NES Arnold)
Chunky Metre Stick (NES Arnold)
10 Metre Tape (NES Arnold)
Plastic Trundle Wheel (NES Arnold)
Decimal Place Value Dominoes (Taskmaster)
Equivalence Dominoes (Taskmaster)
Decimal Maze (Hope Education)
Decimal Dominoes (NES Arnold)

Teachers' reference materials

Primary Mathematics Today, 3rd edn, chapters 19 and 20, Elizabeth Williams and Hilary Shuard (Longman)
Calculated to Please: Calculator Activities for the National Curriculum, Paul Harling (Collins Educational)
Maths Plus: Decimals and Percentages 2, Paul Harling (Ward Lock Educational)

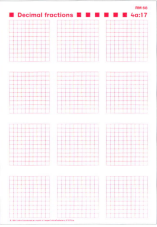

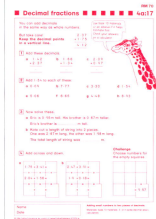

18. VOLUME & CAPACITY (1)

LEARNING CONTEXT

Contribution made by this Step

The children are reminded of the need for a standard unit of measurement of volume, the cubic centimetre. They use cubic centimetres to estimate and measure volumes of 3-D shapes and capacities of simple trays (open cuboids).

Objectives

To enable children to:
a Estimate, measure and record volumes of 3-D shapes by counting centimetre cubes.
b Estimate, measure and record approximate capacities of small boxes by counting centimetre cubes.

Background

The conceptual distinction between volume as the amount of space taken up by a solid, and capacity as the amount of space inside a hollow container is an important one. However, when filling a box with, say, interlocking cubes, the distinction becomes blurred. The block of cubes taking up space inside the box has a 'volume' which is the same as the capacity of the box. It may then be useful to refer to the 'internal volume' of the box.

In this Step, the children begin to investigate links between the dimensions of solids (and boxes) and their volumes, as a prelude to the more formal arithmetical methods developed in Step 4b.

> **Mathematics in the National Curriculum**
>
> **Programme of Study: KS2**
> Pupils should be taught to:
> ■ make 2-D and 3-D shapes and patterns with increasing accuracy, recognise their geometrical features and properties, and use these to classify shapes and solve problems. (SSM 2.b)
> ■ find areas and volumes by counting methods, leading to the use of other practical methods, *e.g. dissection*. (SSM 4.c)
> ■ select and use the appropriate mathematics and materials. (UA 2.a)
> ■ search for patterns in their results. (UA 4.b)
> ■ make general statements of their own, based on evidence they have produced. (UA 4.c)

THINKING AND TALKING MATHEMATICALLY

Starting points for discussion

Collection of empty containers used to hold unit solids, e.g. stock cube packs and tins, biscuit tins, bathcube packs, cereal variety packs. *Can these be ordered according to the amounts they hold? What might we use to fill them to check?*

Discuss the way that in shops small boxes are packed in larger boxes.

> **Key language**
>
> centimetre, centimetre cube, cubic centimetre, capacity, volume, space, length, breadth, width, wide, high, cuboids, prisms, estimate, count, measure, container, layers

STEPS 4a

ACTIVITIES IN DETAIL

A Revision   G

1 Ask the children, working in groups, to fit together ten cubes, each trying to make a shape different from everyone else's. *Are they all different? How much space is taken up by each shape?*

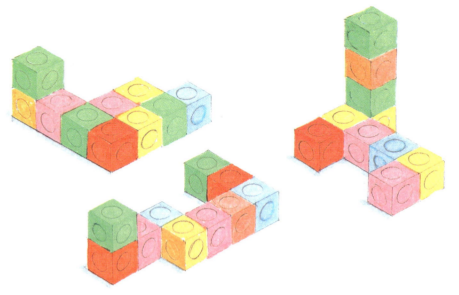
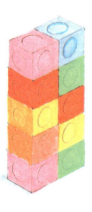

2 Remind them of the term 'volume' – it can be thought of as the amount of space taken up, or the number of cubes used.

3 Ask them to make shapes using other numbers of cubes (up to 20). *Working together, can you arrange all the shapes in order of volume? How could we show clearly that several have the same volume?* (Ringing them with a hoop? … labelling? …)

Resources

School
Interlocking cubes (Multilink, Clicubes, Maths Cubes)

B Choosing a standard unit   C G

1 Display the boxes and sets of different sorts of cubes. Explain that the children are to find how many cubes fit in each box and that they should use only one sort of cube at a time.

2 Ask each group of children to choose a type of cube and a box. They then estimate how many cubes will fill the box and check by filling the box and counting the cubes. Ask, *Will the number of cubes be the same if we use another type of cube?*

3 Suggest that the children test this by choosing another type of cube, and then estimating and measuring the number needed to fill the same box.

Resources

School
Sets of cubes of different sizes (e.g. building block cubes, cube beads, dice, Multilink, Clicubes, Maths Cubes, Multibase units, Cuisenaire units, Colour Factor units, Centicubes); cuboid-shaped boxes of different sizes (matchbox to cereal box)

4 Discuss the results, encouraging the children to see that:
(a) the amount of space inside the box (its capacity or internal volume) stayed the same because the same box was used; and
(b) the number of cubes used (probably) changed, depending on the size and type used.

5 Encourage the children to recognise that use of a standard unit is sensible, enabling us to compare each other's measurements. Remind them of centimetre cubes.

a centimetre   a centimetre square   a centimetre cube

The volume of the centimetre cube is one cubic centimetre.

You may wish to introduce the notation 'cm³' as the mathematical shorthand for 'cubic centimetre'. However, it is recommended that you use, for example, 'cu cm' until work on indices is introduced, or until children fully understand that volume is linked to three dimensions.

6 Show examples of centimetre cubes (Centicubes, or loose metric units from Cuisenaire or Multibase sets), allowing children to measure them if desired.

7 Ask individual children to use centimetre cubes to estimate, measure and record the approximate space in identical boxes. The results should be almost, if not exactly, the same. Remind the children of the approximate nature of all measurement.

C How many will fit inside?

1 Get each pair or small group to construct the same open cube (or cuboid) with interlocking tiles such as Polydron or Clixi.

2 The children now decide for themselves how to fit as many Centicubes as they can inside the box so that none show above the rim. (Check: if a sheet of paper is laid on the box it should lie flat on the rim.)

3 Afterwards, compare results. *Who fitted the most cubes inside? How did you manage to fit the most cubes inside? Did you have any space left over inside … or did the cubes fit the space exactly?*

4 Encourage the children to see the need to be systematic and to tightly pack or tessellate the Centicubes.

Resources
School
Polydron or Clixi square tiles; interlocking 1 cm cubes (e.g. Centicubes)

D Making trays

1 Demonstrate the way to make a simple tray (open box) containing a single layer by drawing a rectangle (or square) on squared paper with a second rectangle inside it, as shown.

2 Show that by cutting off the corner squares, folding along the marked lines and sticking the corners a simple open tray can be made. *How many Centicubes will fit inside the tray? What is its capacity (internal volume)?*

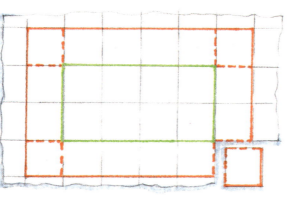

Resources
School
Centicubes; scissors; sticky tape

Scheme
Resource Master 72, 73, and A (1 cm squared grid)

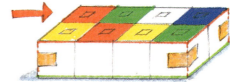

STEPS 4a

3 Ask the children to work in pairs to make one-layer open trays with dimensions of their own choice. They then estimate each tray's capacity, and check by filling them with interlocked Centicubes.

4 The children can then move on to making and checking simple trays with more than one layer.

Use the nets and ideas on RMs 72 and 73 to structure the activities if you wish.

E Making and describing cuboids G P I

Resources

School
Centicubes

Scheme
Book 4a, page 48;
Resource Master A (1 cm squared grid)

1 Ask each child to make a cuboid using twelve Centicubes.

2 Display all the cuboids and let the children make sets for any which are of identical dimensions. Ask, *How many centimetre cubes were used for each shape? What is the volume of each shape?*

3 Explain how to describe a cuboid in terms of height, length and width (in centimetres), and volume (by counting the cubes).

4 Ask the children to work in pairs to explore numbers of Centicubes which can be interlocked to make small cuboids. They should then describe the cuboids made orally, or in writing.

5 Ask the children to draw a two by two rectangle on the squared paper.

6 Ask them to use twelve Centicubes to build a cuboid (or tower, or wall) on the two by two rectangle. Ask, *How many layers are there in the cuboid?*

7 Challenge the children to draw another rectangle on the squared paper on which they can build a cuboid using exactly twelve cubes.

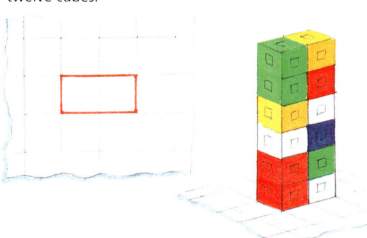

How many layers are there in the cuboid?

How can you describe the cuboid so that other people could build it?

Use Book 4a, page 48 for further practice in building and describing cuboids.

EXTENSION

■ Working in pairs, one child describes a cuboid orally, and the other builds it from the instructions.

F Making and describing prisms   G P

1 Ask the children to draw this shape on the squared grid.

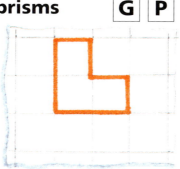

2 Ask the children to use twelve Centicubes to build a tower (prism) on the shape. Ask, *How many cubes are in the bottom layer? How many layers are there? What is the volume of the tower (prism)?*

3 Get the children to increase the height of the tower, recording the cumulative number of cubes used as each layer is added, then the total volume.

4 Working in pairs, the children investigate tower building on other patterns of squares, and describe the tower in terms of number of layers, the number in each layer and total volume.

Resources

School
Centicubes

Scheme
Book 4a, page **49**;
Resource Master A (1 cm squared grid)

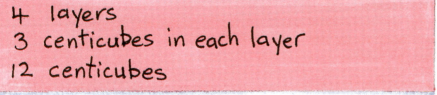

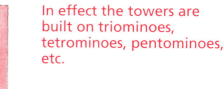

In effect the towers are built on triominoes, tetrominoes, pentominoes, etc.

Use Book 4a, page 49 for further practice in building and describing simple prisms.

EXTENSION

■ Children work in pairs. One child describes a tower orally, and the other builds the model from the instructions.

G Assessment activity   I

1 Ask the child to make a model using Centicubes and to tell you its volume.

2 Now the child selects a small cuboid and copies it as accurately as possible using more Centicubes, describing its characteristics.

3 Invite the child to place the two models in order of size.

4 Ask the child to:
(a) estimate and then measure the approximate capacity (internal volume) of a selected small open box using Centicubes;
(b) tell you whether it is larger or smaller than another box.

Resources

School
Selection of small closed cuboids and open boxes; Centicubes

STEPS 4a

Assessment notes

Oral response	✔
Practical response	✔
Pictorial response	
Written response	

The child has:
correctly used the terms capacity, volume, internal volume, cubic centimetres, length, width and height;
AND
estimated and measured the volumes of some small shapes (including cuboids) by counting centimetre cubes;
AND
estimated and measured the approximate capacities of some small open boxes by counting centimetre cubes.

STRENGTHENING ACTIVITIES

Finding equivalent volumes

Ask the child to find how many white Cuisenaire cubes match different Cuisenaire Rods.

Copying

Make a shape using Centicubes. Ask the child to estimate the number of cubes before copying the shape and counting the cubes used. Ask him/her to make other shapes using the same number of Centicubes.

Cuboids

With the child, make about five cuboids or simple prisms, using Centicubes. Invite the child to arrange them in order of volume, counting aloud the number of cubes. Encourage the child to describe the sequence of shapes systematically.

CHALLENGING ACTIVITIES

Other shapes

Children investigate ways to find the approximate capacities of non-cuboid containers using Centicubes. *What problems are there? Is there anything better than cubes?*

Boxes holding cuboids

The children make a cuboid with interlocking cubes. They then design and make a paper or card box which is as near the size of the cuboid as possible. They decide for themselves which materials and methods to use.

House Brick

Challenge the children to find the volume of a house brick. *What different methods can you think of?*

IDEAS BOARD

■ Typical projects
Shape and Size; Growth; Packaging; Shopping

■ Making cubes
The children can construct their own cube with a volume of 1 cu cm on 1 cm squared grid paper.

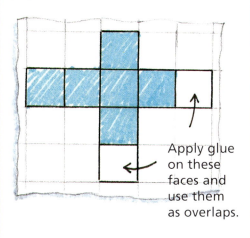

Apply glue on these faces and use them as overlaps.

■ Cubes and cuboids
Use interlocking cubes. Build and investigate the volumes of cubes with sides of 2 cm, 3 cm, etc. Can any cuboids be made from the same numbers of Centicubes used to make a cube?

■ Lorry loads
The children estimate and then check how many interlocking cubes will fit into the storage compartments of model vans or lorries. Can they design model lorries with construction materials which will transport at least fifty interlocking cubes?

■ Cuisenaire or Colour Factor Rods
Investigate different cuboids which can be made using a mixture of rods. (The spaces can be filled using shorter rods.) *What is the total number value of the cuboid of rods? What is the length, width and height of the cuboid made? Is there a link between these three numbers and the total volume?*

■ Cubic decimetres
If you have enough, use 'metric' base 10 blocks (ten centimetre cubes) to find the capacities (internal volumes) of large boxes. Use the notation 'cu dm'.

■ Linking the cubic decimetre and cubic centimetre
Use base 10 materials to introduce the numerical link between cubic centimetres (base 10 units or ones), and cubic decimetres (base 10 blocks). There are 1000 cubic centimetres in a cubic decimetre.

HOME/SCHOOL PROJECTS

The children bring to school a pebble or stone which they estimate to have a volume of between 50 cu cm and 100 cu cm. These can be ordered by volume by estimation, then perhaps by water displacement using measuring cylinders calibrated in cubic centimetres.

SUPPORT MATERIALS

Teaching aids
Multilink (NES Arnold)
Clicubes (Hope Education)
Maths Cubes (ABCeta Playthings)
Multibase System (Hope Education)
Cuisenaire Rods (NES Arnold)
Colour Factor Rods (Hope Education)
Centicubes (Osmiroid)

Teachers' reference materials
Children Learn to Measure, John Glenn (Ed.) (Holt)
Maths Plus: Volume and Capacity 1 and 2, Paul Harling (Ward Lock Educational)

Children's books
Ways to store it, Henry Pluckrose (Franklin Watts)

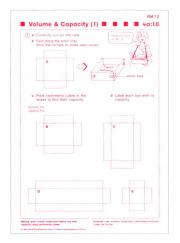 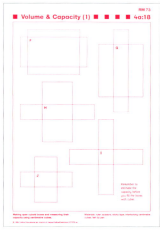

19. MULTIPLICATION PATTERNS (2)

LEARNING CONTEXT

Contribution made by this Step

The children learn the remaining 'new' facts in the x 6 and 6 x tables and the x 9 and 9 x tables and go on to explore the relationships between the x 3, x 6 and x 9 tables.

Objectives

To enable children to:
a Know and apply facts in the x 6 or 6 x tables.
b Know and apply facts in the x 9 or 9 x tables.
c Understand simple relationships between multiples of 3, 6 and 9.
d Test simple related statements or make generalisations.

Background

In previous Steps, the children had opportunities to memorise the facts shown in this diagram in green. The 'new' facts to be learned are shown in red.

Most recently, in Step 3, the children explored the relationships between the x 2, x 4 and x 8 tables. The study of tables in 'families', such as the x 3, x 6 and x 9 families, can assist long-term memorisation of the facts as well as being of interest in their own right because of the patterns and relationships.

10	10	20	30	40	50	60	70	80	90	100
9	9	18	27	36	45	54	63	72	81	90
8	8	16	24	32	40	48	56	64	72	80
7	7	14	21	28	35	42	49	56	63	70
6	6	12	18	24	30	36	42	48	54	60
5	5	10	15	20	25	30	35	40	45	50
4	4	8	12	16	20	24	28	32	36	40
3	3	6	9	12	15	18	21	24	27	30
2	2	4	6	8	10	12	14	16	18	20
1	1	2	3	4	5	6	7	8	9	10
X	1	2	3	4	5	6	7	8	9	10

Mathematics in the National Curriculum

Programme of Study: KS2
Pupils should be taught to:
- explore number sequences, *e.g. counting in different sizes of step, doubling and halving, using a multiplication square,* explaining patterns and using simple relationships. (N 3.a)
- know the multiplication facts to 10 x 10; develop a range of mental methods for finding quickly from known facts those that they cannot recall; use some properties of numbers, including multiples, factors and squares, extending to primes, cubes and square roots. (N 3.c)
- develop their own mathematical strategies and look for ways to overcome difficulties. (UA 2.c)
- understand and use the language of: number; the properties and movements of shapes; measures; simple probability; relationships, including 'multiple of', 'factor of' and 'symmetrical to'. (UA 3.a)

THINKING AND TALKING MATHEMATICALLY

Starting points for discussion

Doubling from *Videomaths* (ITV for Schools).

How are 6 x 8 and 8 x 6 the same (different)?

Revision: number the children, using card badges, and play, *I spy numbers in the x 2 and x 4 ... x 4 and x 8 ... x 2, x 4 and x 8 tables,* etc.

Key language

multiple, common, product, multiplied by, groups, pattern, link, relationship

STEPS 4a

ACTIVITIES IN DETAIL

A x 6 and 6 x tables

Resources

School
Cuisenaire Rods; metre rules calibrated in centimetres; calculators; good supply of small blank cards

Scheme
Resource Master 74

Part 1: The table of sixes (6 x)

1 Working in pairs or small groups, get the children to build up the table of sixes with rods and metre rules, asking them to predict each time where the next rod will reach.

Six four times makes twenty-four. Six five times will make …?

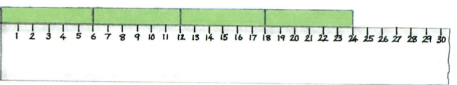

Although the emphasis here is on mental recall of facts, the practical activity will remind children of the distinction between, in this case, x 6 and 6 x.

2 Record the table as the model develops:

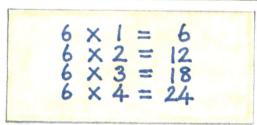

$6 \times 1 = 6$
$6 \times 2 = 12$
$6 \times 3 = 18$
$6 \times 4 = 24$

3 Get each pair or group to make a set of cards marked 6 x 1 and so on up to 6 x 10.

4 They place the cards face down in random order, and, by choosing one at a time, predict, then check, where that number of 6-rods will reach on the rule.

Part 2: The six times table (x 6)

1 Compare the 6 x table with the pattern made by modelling the x 6 table.

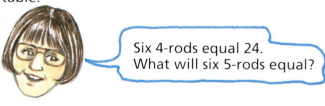
Six 4-rods equal 24. What will six 5-rods equal?

6 x 2 = 12 should be read as 'six two times makes twelve' or 'six multiplied by two equals twelve'. 2 x 6 should be read as 'two six times makes twelve' or 'two multiplied by six equals twelve'.

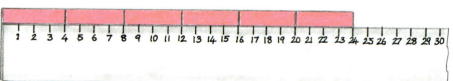

2 Record the table as the pattern develops.

$1 \times 6 = 6$
$2 \times 6 = 12$
$3 \times 6 = 18$
$4 \times 6 = 24$

3 Again using sets of cards marked 1 × 6 up to 10 × 6, pairs of children can predict then check where that set of six rods will reach on the rule.

RM 74 provides individual practice.

B   × 9 and 9 × tables   C G P I

Resources

School
Cuisenaire Rods; metre rules calibrated in centimetres; calculators; good supply of small blank cards

Scheme
Resource Masters 75 and 76

Part 1: Patterns in the table

1 Repeat Parts 1 and 2 of Activity A, now using the 9-rods to construct:
- the table of nines (9 ×);
- the nine times table (× 9).

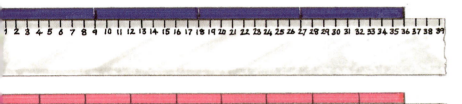

2 Afterwards, ask, *Can you see any patterns in the table which will help you work out the answers in your head?*

9 times table
1 × 9 = 9
2 × 9 = 18
3 × 9 = 27
4 × 9 = 36
5 × 9 = 45

Table of 9s
9 × 1 = 9
9 × 2 = 18
9 × 3 = 27
9 × 4 = 36
9 × 5 = 45

3 Patterns to discuss in the answers to the tables are:
- the digits add up to nine;
- there is an ascending sequence of numbers in the tens digit and a descending sequence of numbers in the units digit.

Part 2: The finger method

1 Demonstrate this method for finding or checking multiples of nine in the 9 × and × 9 tables.

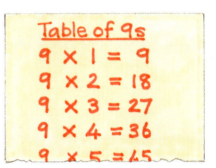

The 9 × table can be shown on your fingers.

2 Allow time for the children to practise this method.

RM 75 provides individual practice. RM 76 provides a game for two players to practise mental recall of facts in the × 6 and × 9 tables.

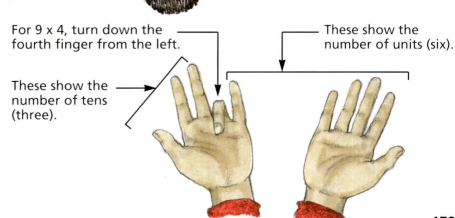

For 9 × 4, turn down the fourth finger from the left.

These show the number of tens (three).

These show the number of units (six).

EXTENSION

- Using mental and/or pencil and paper methods only, the children can continue the 9 x (or x 9) table beyond 9 x 10. (This could be an opportunity to revise the 'easy' way to add nine, i.e. add ten and subtract one.)

C Common multiples in pairs of tables

C G P

Part 1: Choosing how to find common multiples

1 Ask the children to choose numbers up to 50 which are multiples of two and five and record these in order.

2 Revise that these are 'common multiples' of the x 2 and x 5 tables.

3 Introduce the tasks on Book 4a, page 50.

Part 2: Visual check

1 Afterwards, compare results.

2 Provide pairs or small groups with a metre rule and Cuisenaire Rods.

3 Show how the common multiples can be confirmed with the use of Cuisenaire Rods by placing ten 3- and 6-rods (then ten 6- and 9-rods) along the edge.

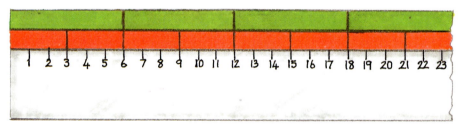

EXTENSION

- After attempting the challenge on Book 4a, page 50, the children can try to find, by testing examples, other multiplication operations which are equivalent, e.g. x 3 followed by x 3 is the same as x 9.

Resources

School
Cuisenaire Rods; metre rules calibrated in centimetres; calculators

Scheme
Book 4a, page 50

What is special about all these multiples?

Book 4a, page 50 encourages the children to select the materials and mathematics for the task, to plan work methodically and to choose how to record and present findings. In the challenge, they also need to test examples. (See Ma 1/4a, b, c).

Why is there a 'crack' through both sets of rods at eighteen?

D Common multiples to 100

Part 1: Revising common multiples within table facts

1 Using RM 16 and cubes, ask the children to put a cube of the same colour on the first ten multiples of three.

2 Using cubes of a second colour to represent multiples of six, ask the children to predict then check which of the numbers (up to 30) will have two cubes on them.

3 Repeat for a third colour of cubes for multiples of nine.

4 Ask, *Why do some squares have no (one, two, three) cubes on them? What patterns can you see?*

Resources

School
Multilink cubes (or similar)

Scheme
Resource Master 16 (100-square: 2 cm squares); Book 4a, page 51

Some children may find it helpful to extend the multiple cube towers to 100 before marking the squares, as asked on Book 4a, page 51, since these make a highly visual 3-D pattern.

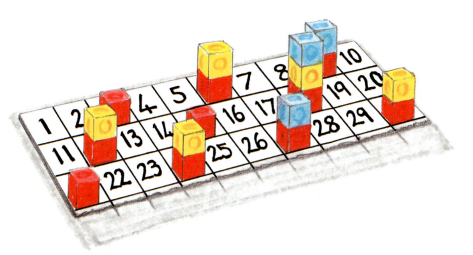

Part 2: Common multiples beyond tables facts

1 Introduce the task on Book 4a, page 51.

2 Afterwards, useful points to discuss are:

a The pattern of the tables continues infinitely but it is convenient to know the facts up to x 10 to help us with mental calculations.

b Every second multiple of three is a multiple of six.

c Every third multiple of three is a multiple of nine.

EXTENSION

■ Make up more examples like this:

36 is the fourth multiple of nine, the sixth multiple of six and the twelfth multiple of three.

E Multiples of three, six and nine

*Read RM 77 to determine photocopying requirements which will depend on how you group the children.

1 Organise the children to work in pairs or small groups.

2 Introduce the collaborative activity on RM 77

3 Afterwards, compare results.

Resources

School
Large sheets of plain paper; scissors; glue pens

Scheme
Resource Master 77*; Resource Master 16 (100-square: 2 cm squares)

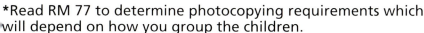

STEPS 4a

4 If a visual check is required, the children might position ten 3-, 6- and 9-rods simultaneously along the edge of a metre rule to confirm the common multiples (see stage 3 of Activity **C**).

EXTENSION

■ Work methodically to find and record numbers up to, say, 50 which are not multiples of three, six or nine. These might be glued in the outermost region of the sorting diagram made for RM 77 or listed in order.

F Assessment activity   I

*In advance, make cards like these:

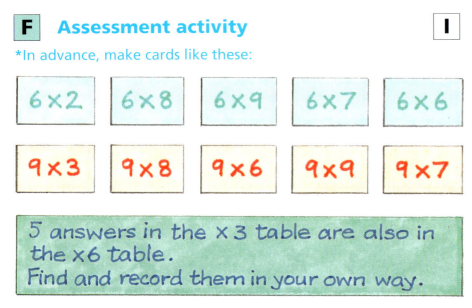

> 5 answers in the × 3 table are also in the × 6 table.
> Find and record them in your own way.

Resources

School
Tables and statement cards*

1 Place the cards face downwards and ask the child to turn them over one at a time and to tell you the answer. (In advance, decide on a reasonable time limit for each response, e.g. ten seconds.)

2 Provide the statement card, give help with reading it if required, and leave the child to record his or her findings.

3 Afterwards, ask the child to explain her or his results to justify her or his conclusions.

Assessment notes

Oral response	✔
Practical response	
Pictorial response	
Written response	✔

(will depend on strategy chosen for stage 3)

The child has:
given correctly at least eight correct answers out of ten to facts from the 6 × and 9 × tables;
AND
used examples to comment on a statement relating the × 3 and × 6 tables
AND
justified his or her conclusion.

STRENGTHENING ACTIVITIES

Finger rule

If the child masters this rule for multiplying by nine (see Part 2 of Activity B), this is a useful strategy for checking products within table facts.

Memorising table facts

Make a set of cards for each table (sixes and nines) with the answers written on the back. The child gives the answer to each one and the cards can be sorted into two sets for known and unknown facts. (Often it is products >5 and <10 which cause most problems.) The child can then concentrate on learning these facts with the help of apparatus if necessary.

Patterns and relationships

If a child needs more practice in exploring the relationships between, say, the x 3 and x 6 tables, a 100 number track might assist. On this, the child places a cube of one colour, say, yellow on all the multiples of three and red cubes on all the multiples of six. The red ones are positioned on top of the yellow ones to create 'towers' so that the repeating pattern of cubes is clearly visible.

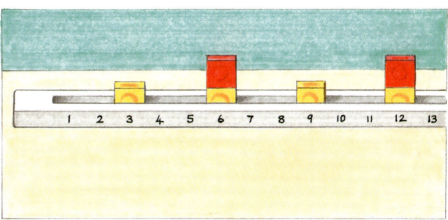

A similar development is suitable for exploring links between x 3 and x 9 or x 6 and x 9.

CHALLENGING ACTIVITIES

Number puzzles

The child can explore statements like:
- If you multiply a number by nine, the digital root is always nine. *True or false? Find out with the help of a calculator.* Remember:
- The digital root of 32 is 5 because 3 + 2 = 5.
- The digital root of 147 is 3 because 1 + 4 + 7 = 12 and 1 + 2 = 3.

HOME/SCHOOL PROJECTS

Having played *Points Capture* at school (RM 76), the children take the game to play at home with others.

IDEAS BOARD

■ Multiplication bingo
Adapt the instructions in Part 2 of Activity **A** of Step 3 to provide further practice in mental recall of the x 6, 6 x, x 9 and 9 x tables or to revise other tables.

■ Number badges
Each child wears a card displaying a number from, say, 1 to 31. Give commands like, *Multiples of three, put your hands in the air*, or *Multiples of three and six form a ring*, or *Those of you who are not multiples of three, line up at the front in order*. After several goes, cards are swapped.

■ Beat the calculator
Make cards for the tables facts being practised. Playing in pairs, the children see who is the quicker at working out the answer, the one with the calculator or the one recording the answer after using mental recall. Whoever has more cards at the end wins, then roles are reversed.

■ Table rings
Display a large ring of numbers 0 to 10 in random order with the number they are to be multiplied by in the centre.

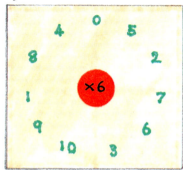

Groups or the whole class can call out the product for the number you point to. Vary the speed with which you move from number to number to suit the ability of the children.

■ Calculator problems
Calculators such as the Galaxy 9 X can be programmed to provide missing number problems such as 6 x ? = 54 and to respond to the numbers keyed in.

SUPPORT MATERIALS

Teaching aids
Cuisenaire Rods (NES Arnold)
Texas 1103, 1104 and *Galaxy 9 X calculators* (Texas Instruments)
Multilink Number Track 1–100 and *Cubes* (NES Arnold)

Teachers' reference materials
Primary Mathematics Today, 3rd edn, chapter 15, Elizabeth Williams and Hilary Shuard (Longman)

Software
Dots and Patterns 1 from *Mathematical Investigations*, Anita Straker (ILECC)
Multiple from *MicroSMILE 1* (ILECC)
Gusinter from *Number Games*, Anita Straker (ILECC)

Radio and TV
Doubling from *Videomaths* (ITV Schools)

Games
Table Tops, Multiplication Games, Multiplication Bingo, Multiplication Puzzles, Cateno (NES Arnold)

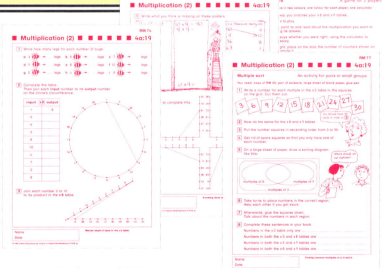

20. ROTATION

LEARNING CONTEXT

Contribution made by this Step

Children use different techniques involving the systematic rotation of shapes, create and describe patterns with rotational symmetry and compare shapes before and after a given amount of turn. They also start to classify shapes by their order of symmetry.

Objectives

To enable children to:
a Create patterns with rotational symmetry or rotate shapes systematically from given information.
b Choose the materials and mathematics to test polygons for rotational symmetry.
c Use or interpret language related to rotation.

Background

In Step 3a:26 the children continued and created simple patterns by rotating shapes and interpreting instructions using the language of rotation.

This Step extends this work but now places more responsibility on the children to select the materials and mathematics for the task as well as to work systematically.

Although the emphasis is on creating patterns involving rotation, the work complements the work on translation, reflection, angles and direction to be found in other Steps in this book. Rotation is concerned with turning, i.e. a shape turning around a fixed point like a roundabout. The amount of rotation can be measured in angles – the roundabout rotates through 360° in a complete turn – so the two topics are closely linked.

Many natural forms have both rotational and reflective symmetry. Also, systematic rotation of shapes has frequently been used as a decorative feature in artefacts throughout the ages and by many cultures so environmental examples are easy to find.

> **Mathematics in the National Curriculum**
>
> **Programme of Study: KS2**
> Pupils should be taught to:
> ■ make 2-D and 3-D shapes and patterns with increasing accuracy, recognise their geometrical features and properties, and use these to classify shapes and solve problems. (SSM 2.b)
> ■ recognise ... rotational symmetries of 2-D shapes. (SSM 2.c)
> ■ transform 2-D shapes by translation, reflection and rotation, and visualise movements and simple transformations to create and describe patterns. (SSM 3.a)
> ■ use right angles, fractions of a turn and, later, degrees, to measure rotation, and use the associated language. (SSM 3.c)

THINKING AND TALKING MATHEMATICALLY

Starting points for discussion

Turning from *Videomaths* (ITV Schools)

Examples of trademarks, artefacts and textile designs which have rotational symmetry, or patterns created by rotation.

Picture cards from a pack of playing cards. *What can you tell me about the design of the picture cards? What is the same about all of them?*

> **Key language**
>
> two-dimensional (2-D), regular polygons, names for 2-D shapes, rotational symmetry, matching, rotate, identical, motif, clockwise, anticlockwise

ACTIVITIES IN DETAIL

A Rotational symmetry

Resources

School
Pattern Block Pieces; regular polygon stamps or plastic shapes; stencils and templates of letters or shapes in assorted sizes; assorted rubber stamp pads and inkpads; large sheets of paper

Scheme
Book 4a, page 52

Part 1: Pattern Block Pieces and rotational symmetry

1 Working in pairs (or small groups), let the children build up Pattern Block Pieces systematically around a central block to create patterns with turning (rotational) symmetry. (A sheet of paper underneath allows the patterns to be rotated freely.)

2 Although examples such as (**a**) are correct, encourage the creation of 'swirling' or 'twisting' patterns like example (**b**).

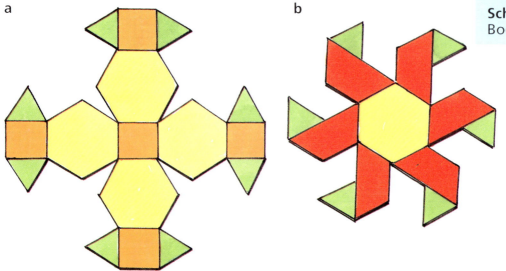

a   b

3 Afterwards, compare patterns and results. *How are they the same/different? In what ways might you sort them?*

Part 2: Creating patterns with rotational symmetry

1 Introduce the tasks on Book 4a, page 52 in which the children have to choose the materials and the mathematics for a task and work systematically. (See Ma 1/4a.)

2 Encourage the children not to copy the examples given but to create their own patterns which can be as simple or complex as they wish.

3 Afterwards, patterns might be displayed so that those with a common attribute are grouped together, e.g. all those built up around a regular pentagon.

B Geometric shapes

Resources

School
2-D shape templates and/or set of 2-D geometric shapes; blank card for set labels; set hoops

Part 1: Testing for rotational symmetry

1 Provide each group with a supply of geometric shape templates and/or geometric shapes. Which shapes can the children name?

2 Get the children, working individually or in pairs, to draw shapes on paper. Ask them to predict in how many positions a matching shape would fit on top and cover the drawn shape completely.

3 The children should record each prediction.

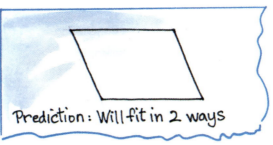

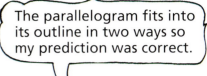

The parallelogram fits into its outline in two ways so my prediction was correct.

4 Ask, *How can you check your predictions?* If the children do not suggest it, demonstrate this way, at least:

Draw a matching (congruent) shape on paper and mark a corresponding vertex on this and the original shape drawn. Cut out the second shape and see how many times it fits the outline of its 'twin'.

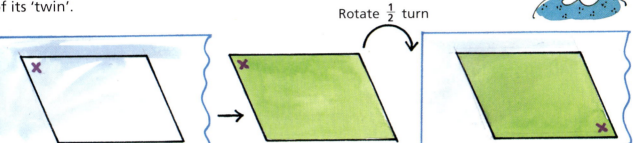

5 The children can continue to predict and test different 2-D shapes.

Part 2: Sorting

1 Arrange set hoops and make set labels so that the children can all contribute cut-out shapes which fit their outlines in one, two, three … ways.

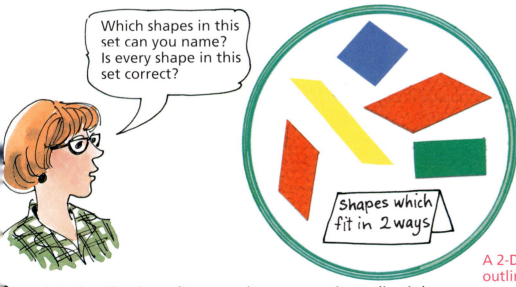

Which shapes in this set can you name? Is every shape in this set correct?

Explain that if a shape fits more than once on its outline it has turning or rotational symmetry.

A 2-D shape which fits its outline twice in a whole turn, e.g. a parallelogram, has rotational symmetry of order two. You may wish to introduce this term informally. Shapes which fit their outline once only in a complete turn do not have rotational symmetry.

EXTENSION

The children order, say, the shapes in Pattern Block Pieces by the number of ways a shape will fit its outline, first by prediction then by checking. They decide the best way to record results.

C Regular polygons

1 Revise the meaning of regular 2-D shapes by asking, say, *What is special about a square? How is a regular pentagon different from a non-regular one? What is the special name for a regular triangle?*

2 Introduce the tasks on RM 78, demonstrating an alternative procedure for finding out about the rotational symmetry of a shape, using tracing paper. (Don't use a regular polygon for the demonstration.) The pin goes through the centre of both matching shapes and you rotate the traced shape on top of the other one, counting how many times it fits in a complete turn.

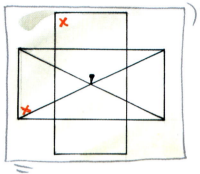

Why isn't an oblong a regular polygon?

3 Afterwards, discuss results. Can the children predict for regular polygons not tested? Can they generalise about the order of rotational symmetry for any regular polygon?

Follow-up

RM 79 requires the children to use and apply the knowledge and skills introduced so far and to work systematically to overcome possible difficulties.

The examples of rotational symmetry on Book 4a, page 53 can be used for group or class discussion.

EXTENSION

- Children can find different shapes with at least one curved side. They can predict then check how many times each will fit into its outline. *What is special about the circle?*

Resources

School
Paper; scissors; tracing paper; Blu-Tack; paperclips

Scheme
Resource Masters 78 and 79; Book 4a, page 53

When tracing shapes, the children may find it helpful to secure the tracing paper with tiny blobs of Blu-Tack or with paperclips.

A regular polygon is a 2-D shape bounded by straight lines with all sides and angles equal. Here the children rotate regular polygons about a central point until the shape again fits its outline. The shape is said to have 'rotational symmetry' about that point and the point is the 'centre of rotation'.

D Clockwise and anticlockwise

1 Ask the children to explain and/or demonstrate the meaning of clockwise and anticlockwise.

2 Extend this by relating the terms to quarters of a turn, perhaps using drawings like this:

Draw what you think this shape would look like if you rotated it a quarter turn clockwise. Compare your drawings with each other.

Resources

School
Polydron or Clixi square tiles

Scheme
Book 4a, page 54

3 Introduce the tasks on Book 4a, page 54 which revise quarter-turns and direction of turn.

4 Encourage the children to work out the answers in their heads first, before they check with the square tiles.

E LOGO windmills

1 The children can experiment with choosing three digits to represent three different lengths, *x*, *y* and *z*, and investigating what happens when these lengths are drawn four times in order with a right-angled turn after each length.

2 In essence, the program is:

repeat 4 [fd *x* rt 90 fd *y* rt 90 fd *z* rt 90]

where *x*, *y* and *z* are different lengths.

3 The children can investigate ideas such as:

a) Does the same kind of pattern emerge with any three digits?

b) What if the order of the three digits is changed?

Resources

School
LOGO graphics software

The format and instructions used to create a diagram similar to these with rotational symmetry will vary according to the computer. Similar commands can be devised for other programmable robots with pen attachments such as Pip or Roamer.

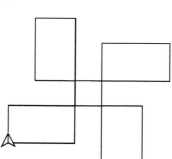

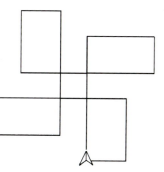

Changing the order of x, y and z creates the same shape but with a different starting point.

c) What if you change each length in some way, e.g. double or halve each one?

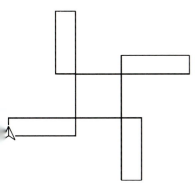

Changing x, y and z to different lengths has a distorting effect on the original 'windmill' whilst still preserving the rotational symmetry of the shape.

4 Children waiting to work on the computer can experiment on squared grid.

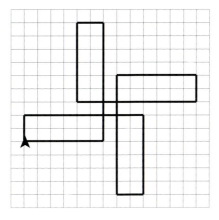

TEPS 4a

F **Assessment activity**

1 Ask the child to make a simple pattern which has rotational symmetry.

2 Afterwards, ask the child to describe how the pattern was created. (Alternatively, ask him/her to show you and describe the method used for creating an original pattern made previously.)

3 Draw the outlines of four polygons (regular and non-regular) on a sheet of paper and ask the child to find a way to check if these have rotational symmetry.

4 Afterwards, ask the child to explain his/her results.

Assessment notes

Oral response	✔
Practical response	✔
Pictorial response	✔
Written response	(will depend on strategy chosen for stage 3)

The child has:
created a simple pattern with rotational symmetry and described it, using some terms associated with rotation;
AND
chosen the materials and mathematics to test four polygons for rotational symmetry;
AND
explained his/her results, using some terms associated with rotation or rotational symmetry.

Resources

School
Access to materials used in this Step, i.e. tracing paper; pin; assorted 2-D shape stencils and templates; scissors

STRENGTHENING ACTIVITIES

Checking

If the child cannot check whether a shape has rotational symmetry, you may need to demonstrate the techniques in Activities **B** and **C** on a one-to-one basis. Emphasise the fact that if a shape fits on its outline more than once in a complete turn, it has rotational symmetry.

CHALLENGING ACTIVITIES

Octagons

Use a template of a regular octagon to create different designs with rotational symmetry of order eight.

10-point circles

Use these to design patterns with rotational symmetry of order 2, 5 and 10.

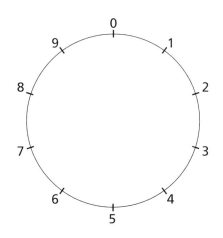

IDEAS BOARD

■ Typical projects
Shape; Movement; Pattern; Advertising

■ Geoboards
Make shapes or patterns with elastic bands on Geoboards to create patterns with rotational symmetry.

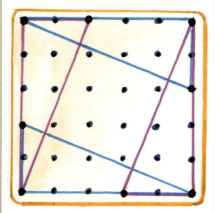

■ History
Find examples of artefacts with rotational symmetry from other times and cultures such as this stamp block from Mexico dating back several hundred years.

■ Car wheels
Compare designs on car hub caps. Do they all have rotational symmetry? Alternatively, collect pictures from car brochures. Sort and display the designs.

■ More letters
Use upper and lower case letter templates to make designs based on a square (i.e. four equally spaced letters) and compare the shapes made at the centre.

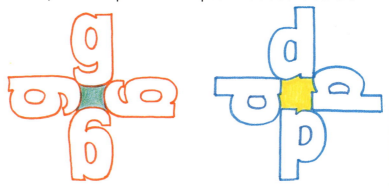

■ Art
Mathematics through Art and Design contains many ideas for creating patterns with rotational symmetry.

■ More ideas
Any of the ideas suggested on the Ideas Board in 3b:26 on page 247 can be reused.

HOME/SCHOOL PROJECTS

Ask the children to collect and bring to school examples of trademarks, advertising logos, etc., showing rotational symmetry. Display according to order of rotational symmetry.

SUPPORT MATERIALS

Teaching aids
Lettering Stencils (NES Arnold)
Drawmee Stencils (Taskmaster)
Polydron Tiles (Taskmaster)
Clixi Tiles (NES Arnold)
Pattern Blocks (NES Arnold)
Tracing Paper (Philip & Tacey)
Geometric Shapes (NES Arnold)
Valiant Roamer and Turtle (Valiant Technology)
Pip (Swallow Systems)

Teachers' reference materials
Mathematics through Art and Design, Anne Woodman and Eric Albany (Collins Educational)
Lettercraft, Tony Hart (Heinemann)
Geometrics File and Symmetry Patterns, Alan Wiltshire (Tarquin)

Software
Mosaic (AUCBE)
Picture Craft (ILECC)
Symmetry Patterns from *Maths with a Story 1*, Peter Smith (ILECC)
Turnflex from *Maths with a Story 2*, Peter Smith (ILECC)

Radio and TV
Turning and *Movement* from *Videomaths* (ITV Schools)

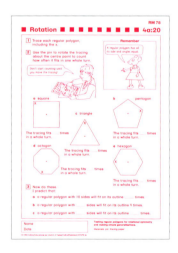
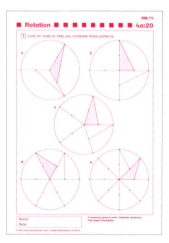

21. PLACE VALUE (2)

LEARNING CONTEXT

Contribution made by this Step

Building on the activities in Step 1, children explore numbers up to 100 000 and just beyond, using apparatus and calculators to develop images of large numbers. They refine their ability to read, write and order such numbers. Knowledge of the positional relationship between digits is refined, partly through studying the effects of multiplying and dividing numbers by ten and 100.

Objectives

To enable children to:
a Read, write and order numbers to 100 000 at least.
b Understand the positional relationship between the digits.
c Relate numbers of this magnitude to some real-life examples.

Background

Correct interpretation of large numbers is an important life skill. To develop this, the children need careful experience and analysis of the structure of multi-digit numbers.

Clear images can be introduced and strengthened by the use of structural apparatus. At this stage, regular oral, written and calculator-based exploration of numbers with up to six digits also greatly enhances the children's ability to make sense of large numbers in a variety of contexts: measurement, money and such things as population statistics, commonly found in geographical topics.

> **Mathematics in the National Curriculum**
>
> **Programme of Study: KS2**
> Pupils should be taught to:
> ■ read, write and order whole numbers, understanding that the position of a digit signifies its value; use their understanding of place value to develop methods of computation, to approximate numbers to the nearest 10 or 100, and to multiply and divide by powers of 10 when there are whole-number answers. (N 2.a)
> ■ understand and use the relationships between the four operations, including inverses. (N 3.f)
> ■ check results by different methods, including repeating the operations in a different order or using inverse operations; gain a sense of the size of a solution, and estimate and approximate solutions to problems. (N 4.c)
> ■ search for patterns in their results. (UA 4.b)
> ■ make general statements of their own, based on evidence they have produced. (UA 4.c)

THINKING AND TALKING MATHEMATICALLY

Starting points for discussion

Display of brochures showing prices of top of the range cars (or homes of different types). *Which is the most expensive? Can you place them in order of cost?*

Atlas data. *What is the height of Mount Everest? ... the distance of a circumnavigation of the world? ... the populations of local (small) towns?*

> **Key language**
>
> digit, value, column, exchange, larger, smaller, greater than, less than, roughly, approximately, round up (down), zero, place-holder, ascending order, descending order, multiple, product

ACTIVITIES IN DETAIL

A Numbers with up to six digits

*Two- or three-spike abaci can be taped together to make five- or-six spike abaci. Alternatively, divide an A4 sheet of paper into colums, label these and use counters or cubes instead of beads.

Resources

School
Five-spike abacus; six-spike abacus*; beads; demonstration place value board

Scheme
Resource Masters 80 – 82; Book 4a, page 55

Part 1: Revising four-digit numbers

1 Show some four-digit numbers on an abacus labelled Th H T U, asking the children to read them aloud. Include some containing zero in various positions. Talk about the value of the digits in each position.

Part 2: Revising five-digit numbers

1 On the board, or a demonstration place value board, show 9999 and ask, *What happens if we add another one?* From previous activities, the children should remember that another column (ten thousands) is added to the left of the thousands column.

Th	H	T	U
9	9	9	9

+1 →

TTh	Th	H	T	U
1	0	0	0	0

nine thousand nine hundred + one → ten thousand
and ninety-nine

It is important to ensure that the activities in Step 1 have been worked through before the activities in this Step are introduced.

Note that in the text 'units' and 'ones' are used interchangeably, but *in abbreviations* in pupils' materials 'U' is used in preference to 'O', to avoid confusion with zero.

Part 3: Six-digit numbers

1 The children practise showing and reading aloud several five-digit numbers and discussing the value of the digits. Then show 99 999. *What happens if another one is added?* Establish the fact that, as before, another column can be added to the left. Label it as shown:

	Thousands				
H	T	U	H	T	U
1	0	0	0	0	0

one hundred thousand

2 The children practise reading several six-digit numbers, using the modified notation of the columns, shown above, to help. Re-introduce the more usual notation for the columns, making sure that the children can read the abbreviations, to help them interpret the value of digits in different positions:

HTh	TTh	T	H	T	U
1	3	2	0	5	4

one hundred and thirty-two thousand and fifty-four

Always try to place such numbers in a real-life context and to ask children to 'round' the numbers to the nearest ten and 100.

3 The children illustrate and write six-digit numbers, which you say aloud, on RMs 80 and 81. Ask them to tell you the value of certain digits.

4 Show the three common ways in which large numbers with five or more digits are written. Discuss the strengths and weaknesses of each, emphasising the need to separate the thousands.

Use RM 82 for practice in converting the word form of large numbers into figures in a cross-number puzzle.

Book 4a, page 55, provides abacus problems, suited to paired work, in which the children have to make choices and think logically.

B Sequencing large numbers   G P

Resources

School
Six-spike abacus (see hint, Activity A); calculators

Scheme
Resource Masters 80 and 81; Book 4a, page 56

Part 1: Using an abacus

1 Write the following sequence on the board. Discuss the changes to the first number to make it into the second, and so on:

2 Ask the children to build the sequence on an abacus, and record it on either or both RMs 80 and 81.

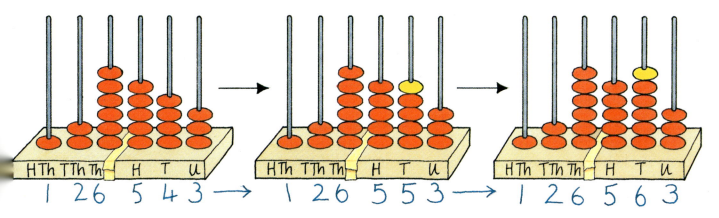

3 Encourage the children to see that, despite each number having six digits, the sequence is simply one of adding ten to the previous number. Ask them to continue the sequence using the abacus and recording the numbers.

Part 2: Sequences of rounded numbers

1 Discuss with the children sequences of counting on and back in thousands, hundreds and tens from various starting points. For example:

6000	7000	8000	9000	10 000 ...
97 000	98 000	99 000	100 000	101 000 ...
54 800	54 900	55 000	55 100	55 200 ...
61 010	61 020	61 030	61 040	61 050 ...

Illustrating these on an abacus shows clearly which column, and therefore which place value, is changing.

2 Show how this can be done on a calculator:

Constant for addition of 100 (7 key presses)

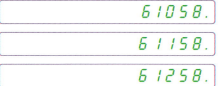

Choose a starting number, e.g.   **61058.**

Press [=] to add on 100   **61158.**

Press [=]   **61258.**

Part 3: Building sequences

1 The children work in pairs to investigate and record sequences of numbers which are built by adding (or subtracting) tens, hundreds and thousands, using an abacus and a calculator. RMs 80 and 81 could be used for recording.

Book 4a, page 56, provides further practice in reading, writing and sequencing large numbers.

EXTENSION

■ Children investigate sequences arising from addition (or subtraction) of tens of thousands, then hundreds of thousands.

C Positional relationships: Multiplying and dividing   G

Part 1: Multiplication by ten

1 Remind the children of their previous activities in Step 1, in which they used base 10 materials, taking ten of a piece and, by exchange, recognising that:
– it is exchanged for one piece of the next larger size;
– the new piece is transferred into the next column on the left;
– the empty place is 'held' with a zero.

Give children chance to practise this if necessary.

Part 2: Multiplication by 100

1 Ask, *What would you have to do if you had one hundred of a piece in a column?*

2 On the board, write several calculations requiring multiplication by 100, of some one-, two-, and three-digit numbers:

```
     3          14         134
  × 100       × 100       × 100
  _____       _____       _____
```

Resources

School
Base 10 materials; place value boards; six-spike abacus (see hint, Activity A); calculators

Scheme
Resource Masters 80, 81 and 83

Show this also on the abacus.

Encourage the use of calculators, at least to check the answers.

Discuss the pattern of the answers:
(a) Each answer has zero in the ones and tens positions.
(b) Each number being multiplied by 100 is moved *two* columns to the left, into a column with a value *100* times larger. This clearly shows how the positions of the digits change.

3 Ask the children to use calculators to explore and record similar examples, using the calculator constant for multiplication by 100:

4 Discuss the pattern of the answers in relation to the starting numbers. Ask the children to suggest a rule for a 'quick way' to multiply whole numbers by 100. Relate the idea to a real-life context such as '100 boxes each holding 12 pencils' and others from work on measurement or money.

Part 3: Divisibility by 100

1 Look back at the calculations. Ask, *How can we tell if a number is exactly divisible by a hundred?* Encourage the children to recognise that any whole number which has zeros in the ones *and* tens columns is exactly divisible by 100. Check using other calculations if required.

Part 4: How many tens?

1 The children, in groups, use base 10 materials to show a round large number such as 3000. They work out, by exchanging pieces, that this is the same as:

3000 ones
300 tens
30 hundreds
3 thousands

Further practice is found on RM 83.

It is a good idea to illustrate the starting and finishing number on, for example, the abacus or place value charts on RMs 80 and/or 81.

As before, it is important to avoid such statements as, 'When we multiply by 100 we write the number and then *add* two zeros at the end'. Stress the *movement* of digits two-places to the left, with zeros filling the empty spaces left by the move.

Relate this also to the recognition of numbers divisible by ten.

EXTENSION

■ Use calculators or other means. Explore and record the results of multiplying any large number by 100.

D Analysing and ordering numbers C G P

*If possible photocopy RMs 84 and 85 onto card in advance. (Or the children can mount them on card.) Run off several sets and cut them up.

Part 1: Expanded form

1 Remind the children that numbers can be written in 'standard form' and in 'expanded form'. Show an example of each type:

Ask them to represent five- and six-digit numbers in both forms. They can check the expanded form by using a calculator to enter each element, adding the parts to make up the original number.

Resources
School
Calculators

Scheme
Resource Masters 84 and 85*

Standard form	Expanded form
61 234	60 000
	+ 1 000
	+ 200
	+ 30
	+ 4

STEPS 4a

197

2 The children can use the cards from RMs 84 and 85 in the same way to build the expanded form of large numbers by overlaying.

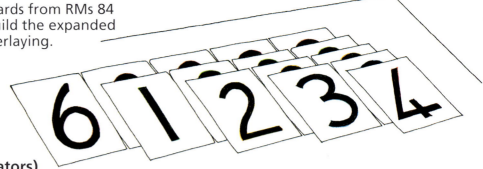

Part 2: Back to zero (calculators)

1 Write a five-digit number (without any zeros) on the board. Discuss how to 'zap the digits' one at a time (five subtractions) on the calculators to gradually reduce the number to zero.

	61234.
− 4 =	61230.
− 3 0 =	61200.
− 2 0 0 =	61000.
− 1 0 0 0 =	60000.
− 6 0 0 0 0 =	0.

2 Get children to work in pairs to investigate ways to reduce similar numbers to zero, using five ... four ... three ... two ... one ... subtractions, e.g.:

	61234.	
− 3 4 =	61200.	3 subtractions
− 1 0 0 0 =	60200.	
− 6 0 2 0 0 =	0.	

Part 3: Making up (calculators)

1 The children use calculators. Write a five-digit number on the board, e.g. 23 145. Ask, *What must I add to change this number to*, say, *23 245?* Continue providing target numbers until every digit has been changed.

2 Write a five-digit number on the board. Ask the children to work in pairs to increase the number to 100 000 by adding in 'place value' steps. For example:

```
67 881  →    + 9      =   67 890
67 890  →    + 10     =   67 900
67 900  →    + 100    =   68 000
68 000  →    + 2000   =   70 000
70 000  →    + 30 000 =   100 000
```

E Ordering large numbers   [C] [I]

Resources
School
Pack of playing cards (picture cards removed)
Scheme
Book 4a, page 57;
Resource Master 86

1 Remind the children of previous experience of ordering whole numbers. Through discussion, establish the following rules:
- A whole number with more digits is always larger than a whole number with fewer digits.
- If numbers have the same number of digits, start at the left and compare the digits in matching columns or 'places' until a difference is seen, the first larger digit indicating a larger number.

2 Display some pairs of numbers. Ask children to order the numbers and to explain how they decide on relative size.

3 Use RM 86 and playing cards. Shuffle the cards and turn them over one at a time, reading out the number. Each child writes that digit in a single space on one of the grids on RM 86. Once it has been written it cannot be repositioned. The purpose of the game is to make a true number statement (inequality) after ten or fifteen cards have been turned, read and recorded.

Use Book 4a, page 57, for further practice in analysing and ordering numbers up to 100 000.

F Assessment activity   [I]

Resources
School
Number cards*

*Prepare about 20 cards, showing random five-digit numbers (including some ending in 0, 00, 5 and 50) and one card showing 100 000.

Part 1: Reading, writing and ordering numbers

1 Ask the child to choose one of the cards and read the number.

2 Ask her/him to choose another card showing a larger (smaller) number, and to explain why it is larger (smaller).

3 Ask the child to write down the two numbers in digits and to put > or < between them to make a true sentence, reading it aloud.

4 Ask the child to pick out the card showing 100 000.

Part 2: Positional values

1 Ask the child to write a two-digit number, then to write and say the number which is ten, then 100, times larger.

2 Show about five of the cards, including one ending in 00. Ask, *Which number can be divided exactly by 100?*

Assessment notes

Oral response	✓
Practical response	✓
Pictorial response	
Written response	✓

The child has:
correctly read and said some five-digit numbers;
AND
correctly interpreted and written some numbers to 100 000;
AND
correctly multiplied a whole number by 10 and 100;
AND
correctly recognised a number exactly divisible by 100.

STEPS 4a

STRENGTHENING ACTIVITIES

Spoken numbers

Say pairs of numbers with up to five digits. *Which is the larger (smaller)?* Stress the need to listen carefully to the early part of a spoken number to indicate its size.

Digit cards

Use six digit cards, including a zero.

Ask the children to make and read aloud as many five-digit numbers as they can. Observe the child's use and interpretation of the zero card. If it is placed at the beginning of a five-digit number, how does the child read it? Discuss as appropriate.

CHALLENGING ACTIVITIES

Telephone directories

Investigate ways to find the number of entries in a telephone directory.

Calculator 100 000

Investigate and record ways to multiply whole numbers to show 100 000 on a calculator display. For example:

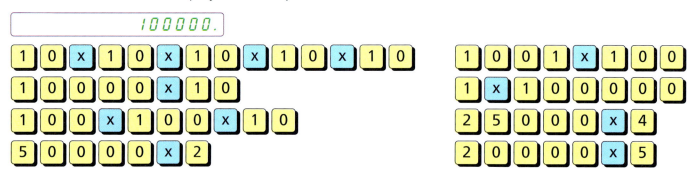

Can they be recorded in a systematic way?

Palindromes

Following on from the Challenging Activities in Step 1, children investigate palindromic five-digit numbers between 10 001 and 99 999. *Can you find how many there are without writing down every example?*

IDEAS BOARD

■ History
Use reference material to explore systems of notation and place value in history: Hindu, Babylonian, Mayan, Egyptian and Roman.

Babylonian

Egyptian

Roman

■ Rounding
Revise and extend Activity **D** in Step 1 (page 31). Use various contexts and lists of numbers and amounts. Constantly ask children to round or approximate to the nearest ten and 100. Some children might explore rounding to the nearest 1000.

■ House numbering
Numbering of houses began in the eighteenth century. Investigate where and when. *How are the houses in your street numbered?*

■ Newspapers
Use a highlighter pen to mark every example of numbers used in a daily newspaper. *Are they written in digits or words or both? Can you find examples of the use of, say, 50K to mean 50 000?*

■ Large numbers file
Groups of children collect over a period of time five-digit numbers from different contexts, including available and relevant reference material, for example, soccer match attendances, salaries of MPs and ministers, populations, car prices, house prices, mileage on staff cars.

■ Money
Use facsimile coins and notes. Practise rounding amounts of money to the nearest £1, £10 and £100. Extend to include mail order catalogues and brochures for new cars. *Why is the use of a price such as £5995 so common in pricing of cars?*

HOME/SCHOOL PROJECTS

Ask the children to collect, and bring to school, examples of five- and six-digit numbers. Sort the examples by source and/or purpose. (Note that some, e.g. telephone numbers, are merely a string of numbers, not designed to be read in relation to place value.)

SUPPORT MATERIALS

Teaching aids
Shape, Pattern and Number Abacus (NES Arnold)
Multibase System (Hope Education)
Four-Spike Abacus (Hope Education)
5-Hooped Abacus (NES Arnold)
5-Row Abacus (NES Arnold)

STEPS 4a

Teachers' reference materials
Lines of Development in Primary Mathematics, Mary Deboys and Eunice Pitt (Blackstaff Press)
Maths Plus: Adding and Subtracting 1 and 2, Paul Harling (Ward Lock Educational)
Calculated To Please: Calculator Activities for the National Curriculum, Paul Harling (Collins Educational)

Software
Boxes from *MicroSMILE 1* (ILECC)
Find Me and *Size Game* (MEP Primary Maths)
Counters from *Micros in the Primary Classroom* (Longman)
Line Up, *Spots* and *Make 37* from *Number Games*, Anita Straker (ESM)
Cranky (ESM)
Ergo (MEP Microprimer)
Monty (ATM)

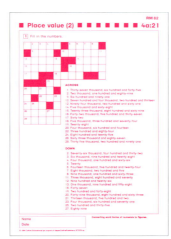

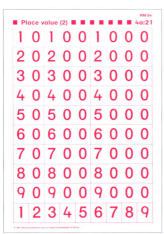
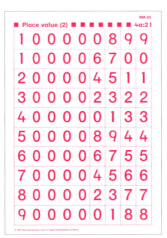
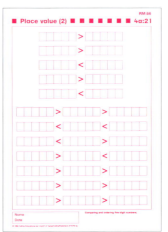

22. PROBABILITY

LEARNING CONTEXT

Contribution made by this Step

Children are introduced to a simple probability scale on which they position events ranging from 0 (impossible to happen) to 1 (certain to happen). The children estimate probability, using both this scale and various games, and justify their decisions.

Objectives

To enable children to:
a Use a probability scale marked 0, $\frac{1}{2}$, 1 to estimate and compare likelihood.
b Make and test predictions or statements related to simple experiments.
c Start to give and justify estimates of probability.

Background

In Step 3b:21, the children compared and ordered events, using terms such as 'very likely', 'quite likely', 'certain', 'impossible' etc., considered when there was an even or equal chance of a particular outcome and distinguished between 'fair' and 'unfair' in contexts such as simple games.

As work progresses, the children should be encouraged to discuss the task they are engaged on, record their results (often in the form of tables or charts) and predict and justify what might happen, based on their own experiences or what has happened so far. An example of this is part way through a game, when they may wish to modify predictions they made at the beginning.

Mathematics in the National Curriculum

Programme of Study: KS2
Pupils should be taught to:
- develop understanding of probability, through experience as well as experiment and theory, and discuss events and simple experiments, using a vocabulary that includes the words 'evens', 'fair', 'unfair', 'certain', 'likely', 'probably', and 'equally likely'. (HD 3.a)
- understand that the probability of any event lies between impossibility and certainty, leading to use of the scale from 0 to 1. (HD 3.b)
- recognise situations where probabilities can be based on equally likely outcomes, and others where estimates must be based on experimental evidence; make or approximate these estimates. (HD 3.c)
- explain their reasoning. (UA 4.d)

THINKING AND TALKING MATHEMATICALLY

Starting points for discussion

Display some words linked with probability, e.g. 'chance', 'very likely', 'certain', etc. Can the children add to the word bank?

Different kinds of dice: make statements about rolling dice which are impossible, unlikely, equally likely, likely and certain.

Key language

chance, likelihood, probability, scale, evens, equal chance, statement, outcome, estimate, predict, replace, withdraw

ACTIVITIES IN DETAIL

A Introducing the probability scale C P I

*In advance, prepare on card or OHP sheets, with the same dimensions:

a probability word line:

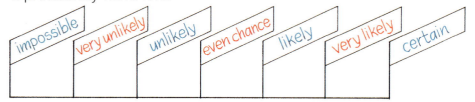

a probability scale, numbered as shown:

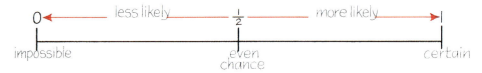

Prepare word cards: 'likelihood', 'chance', 'probability', 'evens'.

Part 1: Revising

1 Display the probability word line and revise the vocabulary. If appropriate, use word cards for 'likelihood', 'chance', 'probability' and 'evens'.

2 Display or dictate some probability statements, using the future tense, since here the children are predicting the likelihood of an event yet to take place. For example:

'June will be the sixth month next year.'
'Three of you will be off sick next Monday.'
'A week today will be Saturday.'
'It will rain within the next week.'
'Nobody will get told off today.'
'In ten years time, it will be the year two-thousand and ninety-four.'
'The next child to come in the room will be a girl.'
'Whoever answers my next question will be a boy.'
'In two years time, (Jim) will be old enough to go to secondary school.'

3 Ask the children to:
– decide in pairs or small groups, then as a class, where these statements should be positioned and why;
– suggest further statements for each category.

4 Remind the children that :
– some events are fixed, e.g. 'Wednesday will follow Tuesday';
– others depend on local conditions, e.g. the time of year: 'It will snow within the next week' is quite likely in January but not in August in Britain;
– others are purely a matter of personal opinion.

Part 2: Probability scale

1 Explain that instead of using a word line, likelihoods or probabilities can be shown on a scale ranging from 0 (impossible) to 1 (certain).

Resources

School
Playing cards; card for probability lines and word cards*

Scheme
Book 4a, page 58;
Resource Master 87

2 Compare and discuss the word line and the scaled line. *How are they the same/different?*

3 Discuss the meaning of 0 and 1 and point out that an even chance is represented as $\frac{1}{2}$ since the probability of that outcome is exactly one chance out of two, i.e. both are equally likely.

4 Which of these do the children think can be mapped to $\frac{1}{2}$ on the scale. Why?

(a) 'You will put your right sock on first tomorrow morning.'
(b) 'When you next toss a coin, it will come up heads.'
(c) 'If you choose a counting number up to 100, it will be odd.'
(d) 'If you roll a standard dice, you will get a four.'

5 Can the children suggest any further statements where there are two possible outcomes (e.g. related to playing cards), both equally likely?

Book 4a, page 58 and RM 87 provide practice for individuals or children, working in pairs, to estimate and place events in order of likelihood on a probability scale.

EXTENSION

■ The children make and position statement cards relating to a standard dice on the probability scale.

B Comparing and ordering probabilities G I

1 Display some coloured spinners and ask the children to comment on the results if these were spun.

1   2   3

Resources
Scheme
Book 4a, page 59;
Resource Master 88

If you spun the second spinner, what would be your chance of spinning blue? Why do you think that? Would you have a good chance of spinning yellow?

2 Use and encourage the children to use sentences like these, in which they have to justify their predictions: *'It is more (less) likely that I would spin ... than ... because ...'* *'There is a good (very poor, etc.) chance that you will spin ... because ...'*

3 If it arises naturally, draw attention to any numerical statements the children make, e.g. 'More than half is coloured blue so ...'

4 Introduce the tasks on Book 4a, page 59, which require the children to compare and order the probability of events, and RM 88 which pairs of children might tackle together.

Book 4a, page 59, and RM 88 extend tasks introduced in Book 3b, page 50, and RMs 3b 83 and 84 by relating similar spinners to the probability scale.

STEPS 4a

C Numerals 1 to 100

Resources
Scheme
Resource Master 89

1 Introduce the tasks on RM 89 and leave the children to estimate and justify the positioning of the statements on these on the probability scale.

2 During and after the activity, ask questions which require the children to justify their decisions, e.g.:

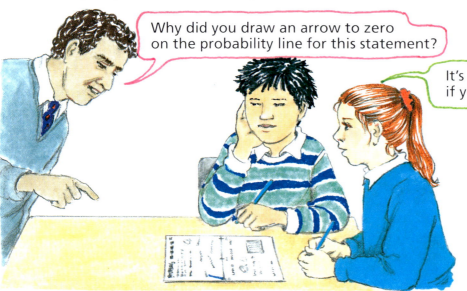

Why did you draw an arrow to zero on the probability line for this statement?

It's impossible to withdraw a zero if you don't have one to start with!

The value in this activity lies in the discussion between children as they consider and justify the best position on the scale for each statement. Some of the statements are deliberately challenging and intended to make the children reason with each other.

EXTENSION

■ The children can design their own probability scale with fractions other than $\frac{1}{2}$ placed between the limits of 0 and 1. Can they write statements which relate to these fractions?

D Testing statements with a 1–6 dice

Resources
School
Standard dice (1–6); board games (e.g. Ludo) requiring a 6 to start*

Scheme
Resource Master 90

*In advance, ask the children if they have a board game (requiring a six to start) which they can bring to school.

Part 1: Throwing a six to start

1 Discuss or display any games requiring a six on the dice to start. *Why do think this is sometimes a rule? Is it a fair rule? How likely are you to roll a six on your first go? What if you had to roll a one to start?*

2 Display this statement:

> 6 is harder to get than any other numbers on a 1–6 dice.
> True or false?

3 Organise the children to work in pairs or small groups to devise a test to check whether this statement is true (or not – depending on opinion!).

206   STEPS 4a

4 Only if necessary, offer advice or guidance on how to start the test by encouraging them to consider:
- how many rolls of the dice to make;
- how to record their results;
- how to come to a conclusion.

5 Recording can take many forms which may include:

Number thrown:	1	2	3	4	5	6
Tally:	|||| |||	||||		||||	|||| ||||	|||| ||	|||| ||

6 Afterwards, discuss the tests and compare results. *What conclusions have you come to? Is six the most difficult number to roll?*

If a more structured approach is preferred, the children can carry out the activity on RM 90.

Part 2: Class survey

1 Collate the results from the different pairs/groups so that everyone's results are included.

	1	2	3	4	5	6
Group A	14	12	7	11	9	11
Group B	11	13	12	15	10	13

2 When the six frequencies are displayed, there is likely to be a fairly even distribution of each number rolled.

EXTENSION

■ Provide biased, 'unfair' dice for the children to test. Can they design and test one of their own?

E More estimating and justifying

1 Introduce the paired game on RM 91.

2 As the games get under way, ask the children to explain their predictions and justify them, e.g. *What do you think will happen? Why?*

3 Afterwards, groups or the whole class might be asked to consider together:
- their responses to the questions for discussion;
- how player A (or player B) can be certain of winning.

Resources

School
16 mm counters; dice 1–6

Scheme
Resource Master 91, one copy between two children

EXTENSION

■ The children devise tests to find out how many rolls of the dice player B is most likely to need to move from start to finish.

STEPS 4a

F Assessment activity I

Resources
School
Glue stick; blue pen
Scheme
Resource Master 88*

*In advance, prepare a probability scale numbered as shown on card, then affix four spinners cut from RM 88, one coloured blue and joined to '1' on the scale.

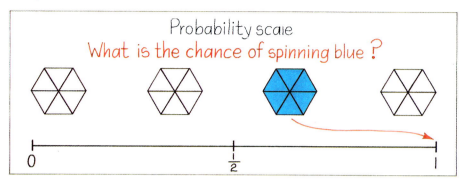

1 Ask the child, *What do 0, $\frac{1}{2}$ and 1 on the probability scale mean?*

2 Indicating the spinner joined to 1, ask, *Why has this been linked to the scale here?*

3 Explain that you want her/him to:
(a) colour the other three spinners in different ways;
(b) draw lines to where he/she thinks they best fit on the scale.

4 Afterwards, ask the child to justify his/her decision for each spinner, e.g. *Why did you join the spinner to this point on the scale?*

5 Ask the child, *If you wanted to check if your estimate for this spinner is correct, what would you do?*

Assessment notes

Oral response	✔
Practical response	
Pictorial response	✔
Written response	

The child has:
used and interpreted a probability scale marked 0, $\frac{1}{2}$ and 1;
AND
estimated the probability of certain outcomes in a simple experiment involving spinners;
AND
justified his/her estimates;
AND
suggested how one of these spinners might be tested to try to justify his/her decision.

STRENGTHENING ACTIVITIES

Probability scale

If the child has problems relating 0, $\frac{1}{2}$ and 1 to statements, etc., he or she may benefit from having a prompt like this to use until more confidence is gained:

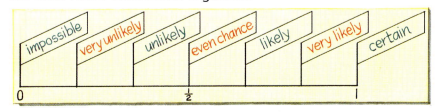

Statements

Children who lack the confidence or knowledge to test statements such as: *Six is the hardest number to roll on an ordinary dice*, may need to be guided as to the method and materials to use or to work within a group of more confident children.

CHALLENGING ACTIVITIES

Sixths

Draw a probability scale divided into sixths. The children make up statements related to ordinary 1–6 dice for each marked point on the scale, e.g: 'The chance of rolling a 0 ...', 'A number less than 6 ... ', 'A square number', etc.

Possible outcomes

Design a method of recording to show all possible outcomes if two 1–6 dice are thrown at the same time. For example:

If you roll a red dice and a green dice 1–6 at the same time, there are 36 different combinations.
True or false?

  is different from

Statements

Provide examples of more complex statements for the child to choose the materials and mathematics to prove or disprove.

IDEAS BOARD

■ Surveys

Relate the probability scale to results of a real-life survey, for example, of local traffic or birds feeding at a bird table. The children can write statements and/or make drawings to place on a probability scale, e.g. *'The probability of seeing a golden eagle is'* ... *'of seeing a car today is ...'*

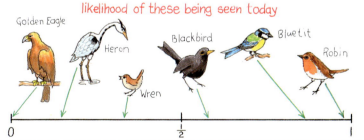

■ Typical projects

Games, chance, environmental surveys: predicting, checking and recording what the results are most likely to be and linking predictions or outcomes to a probability scale.

■ Lucky numbers

Organise the class into six groups of approximately the same number.
❏ Each group is allocated a 'magic number' from one to six, a supply of counters and a dice 1–6.
❏ The players take it in turn to roll the dice and win the number of counters shown by the dice.
❏ When the magic number is rolled, they get that number of counters and six extra.
❏ The winner is the first player to get 25 counters at least.

Afterwards, discuss, What was the hardest number to roll in your group ... in other groups?

■ Science

Design fair tests and predict probable outcomes with the help of a probability scale.

HOME/SCHOOL PROJECTS

The child takes home a probability scale marked 0, $\frac{1}{2}$ and 1 and a sentence starting, 'The chance of ...', and explains what these words mean. The family make up three sentences, using these words and link each sentence to a numbered point on the scale. The sentences could relate to a theme, e.g. food.

SUPPORT MATERIAL

Teaching aids
Loaded dice (NES Arnold)
Assorted blank and spot dice (Taskmaster)
Spinner and overlays (Taskmaster)
1–10 Spinners and *Probability Spinners* (Hope Education)

Teachers' reference materials
Probability (PM649) (The Open University)
Chance Encounters, Challengers D, Tony Fleet (Longman)
P'raps, P'raps Not (Association of Teachers of Mathematics)
Probability Park from *Cross-Curricular Big Book* (Collins Educational)

Children's books
Investigating Chance, Ed Catherall (Wayland)

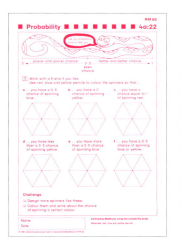

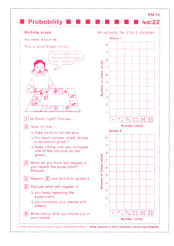

23. DIVISION (1)

LEARNING CONTEXT

Contribution made by this Step

Using division facts related to the multiplication tables, the children work with informal and formal methods of pencil-and-paper calculations and practise mental recall.
   Activities include:
– revising sharing and grouping through practical tasks;
– using the multiplication square to check division facts;
– games to promote mental recall of division facts;
– calculator investigations.

Objectives

To enable children to:
a Solve division problems related to facts within the multiplication tables or suggest a situation from which a division expression might have arisen.
b Know division facts related to the x 6, x 8 or x 9 tables by quick recall.
c Start to interpret remainders shown on the calculator.

Background

In Step 3b:27, the emphasis was on children memorising division facts related to the x 2, x 5 and x 10 tables, on dividing two-digit numbers by one-digit numbers with the help of a calculator where required and on solving division problems. In Step 3b:34, the children explored division facts related to the x 3 and x 4 tables.
   In earlier Steps in this handbook, the children were encouraged to memorise facts in the x 6, x 8 and x 9 tables. Here they explore related division facts.
   Division is the most complex of all operations, representing two completely different procedures, sharing and grouping. Both need to be modelled with materials to distinguish them, even when the emphasis is on mental recall of division facts and developing reliable pencil-and-paper calculations.

> **Mathematics in the National Curriculum**
>
> **Programme of Study: KS2**
> Pupils should be taught to:
> ■ know the multiplication facts to 10 x 10; develop a range of mental methods for finding quickly from known facts those that they cannot recall. (N 3.c)
> ■ develop a variety of mental methods of computation with whole numbers up to 100, and explain patterns used; extend mental methods to develop a range of non-calculator methods of computation that involve addition and subtraction of whole numbers, progressing to methods for multiplication and division of up to three-digit by two-digit whole numbers. (N 3.d)
> ■ understand multiplication as repeated addition, and division as sharing and repeated subtraction; use associated language and recognise situations to which the operations apply. (N 3.e)
> ■ understand and use the features of a basic calculator, interpreting the display in the context of the problem, including rounding and remainders. (N 3.h)

THINKING AND TALKING MATHEMATICALLY

Starting points for discussion

What does 48 ÷ 8 mean? Tell me a sharing story to show what it means. What about a grouping story?

Each child divides a sheet into nine equal regions and writes numerals from 2 to 10 inside these. What divisions can the children write in the regions which give the answer indicated by the numeral?

> **Key language**
> divide, divided by, sets of, equal groups, multiple, share, group, remainder

ACTIVITIES IN DETAIL

A Revision of grouping and sharing

Resources

School
31 counters or other counting objects for each group

Part 1: Grouping as one aspect of division

1 Taking the number of children in the class, say 31, ask the children to work out what will happen if they are grouped in different ways, using pencil-and-paper methods of their choice.

2 Afterwards, compare results and methods of recording and calculation.

3 Answers can be checked by the children physically grouping themselves.

4 If necessary, revise the links between repeated subtraction and the familiar streamlined notation.

31 children
Groups of 3, 4, 5, 6, 7, 8, 9, 10

If I put you in groups of these sizes, what will happen? How many groups will there be? Will anyone be left over?

The same number has been chosen as the starting point for grouping (partition) in Part 1 and sharing (quotition) in Part 2 so that the common form of recording, i.e. as a division, can be revised.

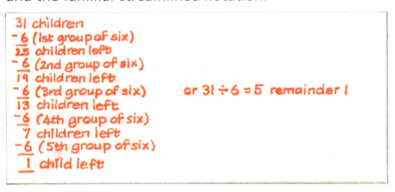

Part 2: Sharing as one aspect of division

1 Arrange the children in groups of different sizes, ranging from, say, groups of three up to groups of ten, and identify each group with a letter written on paper.

2 Ask the children to work out and record how many whole biscuits each person would get if you had 31 biscuits to share between the children in each group.

3 Afterwards, compare results and strategies for calculation.

4 Provide each group with 31 counting objects to revise the sharing (*one for you, one for you …*) procedure and to confirm the accuracy of the answers.

5 Revise the relationship between the sharing operation and repeated subtraction.

That's seven each and three left over – not enough for another one each.

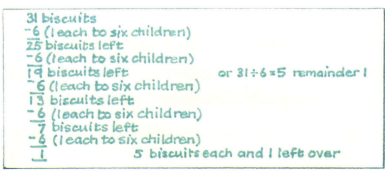

6 Remind the children that, say, 31 ÷ 6 can represent two operations.

EXTENSION

■ The children can try to calculate mentally how many groups and children left over there would be if the class is grouped in 11s, 12s, 13s ....

Thirty-one divided by six equals five remainder one.

Thirty-one children grouped in sixes and thirty-one biscuits shared between six children can both be recorded as 31 ÷ 6 = 5 remainder 1.

31 ÷ 6 = 5 remainder 1

B 100-multiplication square   C I

1 Introduce the tasks on RM 92.

2 Afterwards, ask the children to explain the link between multiplication and division on the completed multiplication grid.

3 If necessary, demonstrate that if you want to find or check the answer to 42 ÷ 6 (or x 6 = 42), you scan the sixth row until 42 is found. Forty-two is also in the seventh column of the answers.

sixth row →

6	6	12	18	24	30	36	42
5	5	10	15	20	25	30	35
4	4	8	12	16	20	24	28
3	3	6	9	12	15	18	21
2	2	4	6	8	10	12	14
1	1	2	3	4	5	6	7
X	1	2	3	4	5	6	7

What number multiplied by six equals forty-two? Forty-two divided by six equals … ?

← seventh column

RM 93 provides further practice and revision of input/output tables. (The multiplication square on RM 92 can be used afterwards to confirm answers.)

Resources

Scheme
Resource Masters 92 and 93

As far as possible, encourage the children to work out the multiplication facts on RM 92 by mental methods. However, practical apparatus such as 10 x 10 pegboards should be available for those wishing to check answers.

Knowing and understanding multiplication facts and the relationship between multiplication and division are very important. Later on, the children will use both multiplication and division facts to record calculations within division sentences.

C Division facts related to the x 6,   C P
   x 8 and x 9 tables

Part 1: The ÷ 6 table

1 Display the x 6 multiplication table, then, alongside, start to write the corresponding ÷ 6 table. Ask, *What comes next?*

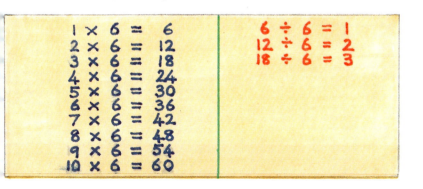

Resources

School
Calculators; 16 mm counters; metre rules; small blank cards; Cuisenaire Rods

Scheme
Book 4a, page 60

2 When the ÷ 6 table is completed, ask, *How are the tables the same and how are they different?*

Part 2: Mental recall

1 Organise some of the following to allow children to practise mental recall of the ÷ 6 table facts:

(a) Display the answers in the × 6 table in random order as centimetre lengths, e.g. 12 cm, 54 cm, 36 cm, etc. Each pair of children has Cuisenaire Rods and a metre rule. They estimate, then check, how many 6 cm rods placed end to end, starting at 0 cm, will be needed to make the given length.

(b) Each pair of children needs a calculator and cards, placed face downwards in a pack, showing the division expressions, e.g. 24 ÷ 6 =, 60 ÷ 6 = . They take it in turns to turn over the top card, then one child writes down the answer on paper while the other uses the calculator to find the answer. Whoever gives the correct answer first wins that card. On the next round, roles are reversed.

(c) Play *Division Bingo*. The children write on a sheet of paper any eight numerals from 1 to 10. You call out the division expressions in random order, e.g. 48 ÷ 6, 6 ÷ 6, etc. and the children loop the answer if it is on their card. Play continues until one child (or more) wins by being first to loop all the numbers.

2 Organise similar activities to practise recall of facts in the ÷ 8 and ÷ 9 tables.

Book 4a, page 60 provides further practice in mental recall of these division facts.

The children have most recently learned facts in the × 6, × 8 and × 9 tables. This activity provides an opportunity to revise the links between multiplication and division facts in these tables and, using Book 4a, page 60, to recall these mentally.

D Conventional notation   C G I

Part 1: Division facts related to tables (no remainders)

1 Each group needs 48 cubes.

2 Use a situation as an example, such as: *If you had a box of 48 oranges and were packing them in sixes, how many packs would you make up?*

Resources

School
Interlocking cubes

Scheme
Book 4a, pages 61 and 62

214   STEPS 4a

3 Show how this can be recorded as a repeated subtraction with the final answer recorded in the units column above the line:

4 The children can model the operation with cubes at each stage, predicting how many will be left after subtraction.

5 Compare this with the shortened form of recording:

We could make eight packs of six oranges, with no oranges left over.

6 Discuss the advantages of using the latter method, e.g.:
(a) When you know your tables, you can work out the answer in fewer stages.
(b) If more subtractions of groups of six were involved, e.g. 96 ÷ 6, the division would be very long – it is not an economical way of working.
(c) Errors are less likely since there are fewer operations – in the example shown, you have to repeatedly subtract six eight times.

7 Repeat for other examples if necessary.

Book 4a, page 61 provides individual practice.

Part 2: Division facts related to tables (with remainders)

1 Book 4a, page 62 provides individual practice in extending the skills introduced in Part 1 to include remainders.

2 Although the emphasis is on pencil-and-paper calculations, less confident children should have access to cubes, etc. to help them model the operation or to check their results afterwards.

Whenever a standard method for a number operation is demonstrated, it is important to stress that this is only one way of finding the answer and other methods of calculation and recording can be used in preference to this.

EXTENSION

■ The children create division expressions and calculate the answers so that these are always >10.

E Calculator division   C P I

Resources

School
Calculators

Scheme
Resource Master 94

1 Ask the children to suggest several division facts they know related to tables up to x 9 and display these. Include some with remainders. *What do you think will happen if you do the same divisions on your calculator?*

2 When testing these examples, then others of their own, the children should be able to generalise that:
(a) when there is no remainder, the calculator displays a whole number answer like this:

Twenty-four is exactly divisible by six. The answer is a whole number.

(b) when there is a remainder, the calculator displays a decimal fraction after the point, like this:

> The answer is between eight and nine times. How many would we have to add to forty-two to make the calculator show an answer of nine?

At this stage, it is not necessary for the children to interpret the decimal fraction which represents the remainder (although tenths will be familiar). It is only necessary to recognise from the answer if the number is exactly divisible or not.

3 Introduce the game on RM 94 which requires the use of several skills:
– using the links between multiplication and division;
– recognising whole numbers on the calculator display;
– mental recall of addition, multiplication and division facts.

F Assessment activity   I

÷6	÷8	÷9
12÷6	32÷8	27÷9
42÷6	48÷8	45÷9
54÷6	80÷8	72÷9

*For each child, make a card like this with three division facts related to the x 6, x 8 and x 9 tables to give answers from 2 to 10.

1 Ask the child to work out the answers mentally and to tell them to you.

2 Afterwards, ask the child to choose one of these division facts and to tell you a 'story' out of which that division might have arisen (or at least explain what this division might mean).

3 Ask the child to explain how he or she knows if the answer to a division problem on the calculator has a remainder or not. (The child might want to use the calculator to demonstrate.)

Resources
School
Division card*; calculator

Assessment notes

Oral response	✓
Practical response	
Pictorial response	
Written response	

The child has:
calculated answers to three division facts related to the x 6, x 8 and x 9 tables by mental recall;
AND
suggested a situation out of which one of these divisions might have arisen;
AND
has explained how to recognise a whole number answer as a result of a division on a calculator.

G Division situations   C I

1 Introduce the problems on Book 4a, page 63, some of which involve multiple operations and/or applying knowledge to unfamiliar situations.

2 Encourage the children to:
– try to overcome any difficulties without asking you for help;
– use any methods of calculation or recording.

Resources
Scheme
Book 4a, page 63

3 Afterwards, discuss and compare results and methods of calculation.

EXTENSION

■ The children can try to write 'story' division problems for each other to solve, perhaps in the format given on Book 4a, page 63.

STRENGTHENING ACTIVITIES

Children who cannot work out division facts by mental recall or pencil and paper methods probably still need to rely on apparatus to model the sharing and grouping operations. It is better that a child can succeed with apparatus than fail without it. Similarly, a completed 100-multiplication square can be used to find or check answers.

Self-correcting games

Self-correcting games such as this will enable the child to practise division facts in private or allow you to diagnose which facts are causing problems. When the child feels confident about recalling the facts mentally, you can retest.

8 ÷ 8	1
16 ÷ 8	2
24 ÷ 8	3
32 ÷ 8	4
40 ÷ 8	5
48 ÷ 8	6
56 ÷ 8	7
64 ÷ 8	8
72 ÷ 8	9
80 ÷ 8	10

Fold here | Cut the fold to make ten flaps.

CHALLENGING ACTIVITIES

Missing numbers

Using a calculator if wished, the children can try to find and list:
(a) all the solutions to a 'missing numbers' division such as 3** ÷ 9 = **, where * stands for a missing digit; or
(b) all the solutions to ☐ ÷ * = 14, remainder 6, where * is a single-digit number.

HOME/SCHOOL PROJECTS

Give each child the same division expression, e.g. 45 ÷ 6. The child and others at home decide on a 'story' out of which this division might have arisen. They write and/or illustrate the story to show what it means and the answer. Stories can be compared at school, and perhaps sorted into 'sharing' and 'grouping' stories.

STEPS 4a

IDEAS BOARD

■ Table challenge
Challenge the children to memorise the division tables suggested in Activity **C**.

■ Calculator remainders
Some calculators such as the Galaxy 9X can be programmed to express remainders in different ways.

■ Number lines and counting back
Table-top and wall number lines can be used to revise counting back in equal groups.

■ Class division frieze
Display a large frieze divided into sections. Each section is headed from 2 to 10. The children contribute division expressions for any number they choose. More confident children might wish to extend the frieze beyond 10. One section might look like this:

■ Division ring
Use a ring like this for whole class activities. The children have to divide the number you are pointing to by the number in the centre and call out the answer.

Vary the speed at which you point to suit the children.

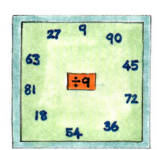

SUPPORT MATERIALS

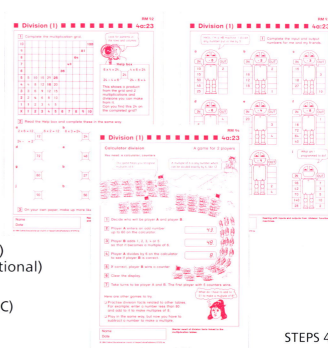

Teaching aids
Cuisenaire Rods (NES Arnold)
Metre Rules (Taskmaster)
Texas 1103, 1104 and *Galaxy 9x Calculators* (Texas Instruments)
Blank Playing Cards (Taskmaster)
Wall and Table-top Number lines 0–100 (Taskmaster)

Teachers' reference materials
Primary Mathematics Today, 3rd edn, chapter 15, Elizabeth Williams and Hilary Shuard (Longman)
Calculated to Please 2, Paul Harling (Collins Educational)

Software
Guzinter from *Number Games*, Anita Straker (ILECC)

24. MONEY

LEARNING CONTEXT

Contribution made by this Step

The children broaden their experience of the notation and handling of money through reading, writing and ordering amounts, and solving simple problems, using their developing computational skills. A calculator is used where appropriate.

Objectives

To enable children to:
a Extend their experience of reading, writing and ordering amounts of money.
b Develop written methods to solve simple problems related to money, using all four operations.
c Use and interpret a calculator in the context of money.

Background

At all stages, the topic of money is both practical and numerical. Where possible, computation should be accompanied by access to coins and notes, and situations developed to use money in cross-curricular and real-life contexts.

The links with the developing skills of arithmetic become clearer at this stage, and understanding of money should be linked to the developing ideas of two-place decimals (see Step 17). Estimation and approximation continue to be important skills, developed partly in discussion.

Although facsimile coins will be used throughout this work, it is advisable to have a set of real coins and notes for discussion purposes.

Mathematics in the National Curriculum

Programme of Study: KS2
Pupils should be taught to:
- extend their understanding of the number system to ... decimals with no more than two decimal places in the context of measurement and money. (N 2.b)
- understand and use the features of a basic calculator, interpreting the display in the context of the problem, including rounding and remainders. (N 3.h)
- develop their use of the four operations to solve problems, including those involving money and measures, using a calculator where appropriate. (N 4.a)
- check results by different methods, including repeating the operations in a different order or using inverse operations; gain a sense of the size of a solution, and estimate and approximate solutions to problems. (N 4.c)

THINKING AND TALKING MATHEMATICALLY

Starting points for discussion

Display of mail order brochures. *What would you buy if you had £50? How would you pay for the items? How would you check the bill?*

£5, £10 and £20 notes. *How can we recognise the different notes?*

Bag of mixed coins. *Can you pick out the £1 coins without looking?*

Key language

price, cost, expense, spending limit, budget, approximately, error, correct change, receipt, bill, value, equivalent, dear, cheap, purchase, buy, sell

ACTIVITIES IN DETAIL

A Notation, equivalents and place value   C G I

Resources

School
Coins and notes; abacus; calculators

Scheme
Book 4a, page 64

Organise some of the following, as revision:

Images of money

1 Show amounts on a place value board, initially with just two columns, then with four. Relate the image of the amount to a labelled abacus. Ask the children to read the amounts shown.

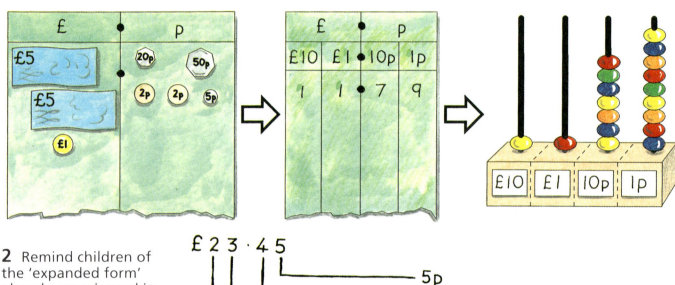

2 Remind children of the 'expanded form' already experienced in number work.

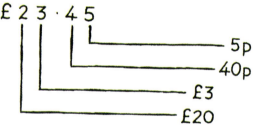

Counting on and back

1 Ask the children to count forwards and backwards in steps of, say, 20p, 50p and £1, starting at amounts above £1.

> one pound thirty, one pound fifty, one pound seventy...

> Three pounds seventy, three pounds twenty, two pounds seventy...

> Thirteen pounds ten, fourteen pounds ten, fifteen pounds ten...

Converting and ordering amounts

1 Ask the children to write and say numbers of pennies in pounds and pence. Then reverse the process.

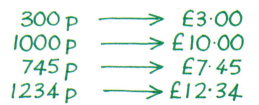

> Three hundred pennies equal three pounds.

2 Write various amounts of money in different ways. Ask, *Which is the largest (smallest) amount? Can you place all the amounts in ascending order?*

£0·03

480p

27p

6p

£4·78

£5·00

£6

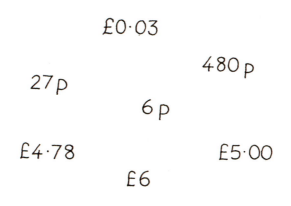

Calculator notation

1 Ask the children to key, say, £5.80 into a calculator, then press [=]. The display shows: `5.8`

Discuss the fact that these are different forms of the same amount.

2 Next key in £1.00 and press [=]. The display shows: `1.`

Discuss the equivalence of the two forms.

Further practice can be found on Book 4a, page 64.

B Addition   G P I

*In advance, put price labels on four or five items such as toys or games, collected from around the school, or on pictures of these. Price so that pairs of these can be 'purchased' for amounts up to £20.

Resources

School
Coins and notes to £20; calculators; price-labelled items*; place value baseboards and abaci (optional)

Scheme
Book 4a, page 65;
Resource Master 95

Using the prices shown, only eight purchases of two items are possible, ranging from £7.72 to £17.10.

Part 1: Practical information

1 Make sure each group has a supply of coins, notes and calculators.

2 Ask the children, preferably working in pairs, to choose two items at a time and to work out what these would cost. Rule: They can only spend up to £20 each time.

3 Encourage the children to estimate first, using coins and notes to help if they want, and to record the addition in their own way, using the calculator to check.

4 Afterwards, compare results and methods of recording.

EXTENSION

■ *What sets of three items could you purchase for up to £30 each time?*

Part 2: Formal recording

1 Revise the formal addition of two amounts, initially with totals to £10.

no 'carrying'	'carrying' from 1p to 10p column	'carrying' from 10p to £1 column	'carrying' from 1p to 10p and from 10p to £1 columns
£6.24 + £1.33 ——— £7.57	£6.39 + £2.24 ——— £8.63 1	£6.52 + £2.61 ——— £9.13 1	£7.55 + £1.66 ——— £9.21 1 1

2 Extend to totals greater than £10 if you consider this appropriate, here shown with the maximum of three 'carrying' figures.

3 Encourage the children to:
- estimate totals before the calculation;
- use apparatus to either find or check answers, e.g. coins and notes, baseboards and abaci such as those suggested in Activity **A**;
- ask themselves if the answer is sensible;
- use the calculator if a further check is required.

Book 4a, page 65 provides individual practice.

carrying from 1p to 10p, from 10p to £1 and from £1 to £10 columns

£ 5.65
+ £ 6.76
————
£ 12.41
  1 1 1

EXTENSION

■ The children roll four dice and translate the numbers into an amount of money in decimal form. For example:

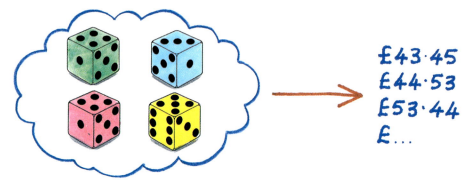

£43.45
£44.53
£53.44
£…

They then investigate ways to make up the amount, using different coins and notes. Ask, *What is the smallest number of notes/coins which can be used to make this amount?*

Part 3: Estimating and approximating

1 Ask, *Why are so many goods advertised with a price ending in 99p?*

2 Introduce the paired activity on RM 95 for practice in:
- rounding to the nearest pound;
- estimating totals;
- adding two-digit numbers;
- using and interpreting a calculator in the context of money.

Many children find it useful to use squared paper to keep the decimal points aligned.

This activity is deliberately challenging and intended to encourage the children to find ways to overcome potential difficulties.

C Subtraction

G P I

Resources

School
Coins and notes to £20; calculators; price-labelled items*; place value baseboards and abaci (optional)

Scheme
Book 4a, page 66; Resource Master 96

*In advance, put price labels on four or five items, collected from around the school, or on pictures of these, so that change from £10 can be calculated.

Part 1: Informal subtraction

1 Make sure each group has a supply of coins, notes and calculators.

2 Ask the children, preferably working in pairs, to choose one item at a time and to find out the change they would get if they paid with a £10 note.

3 Encourage the children to estimate first, record the operation in their own way, then use coins and notes to check.

4 Afterwards, compare results and methods of recording, making sure that the 'shopkeeper's method' of giving change by counting on is discussed.

Estimating and checking the amount of change when using the shopkeeper's method is particularly important since the change can simply be counted out without the total amount being considered.

$$£3·45 \xrightarrow{+5p} £3·50 \xrightarrow{+50p} £4·00 \xrightarrow{+£1·00} £5·00 \xrightarrow{+£5·00} £10·00$$

5 Make sure the children can check calculations using a calculator, and interpret the display. This might be by addition or subtraction, e.g.:

Part 2: Formal recording

1 Revise the formal subtraction of two amounts, initially with amounts of up to £10.

no decomposition

```
  £7·76
- £3·43
———————
  £4·33
```

decomposition of 10p into 1p amounts

```
   5 1
  £9·6̸4̸
- £3·36
———————
  £6·28
```

decomposition of £1 into 10p amounts

```
   4 1
  £5̸·4̸8
- £2·72
———————
  £2·76
```

decomposition of £1 into 10p and 10p into 1p amounts

```
   7 13 1
  £8̸·4̸5̸
- £3·79
———————
  £4·66
```

STEPS 4a   223

2 Extend this to subtraction using amounts greater than £10 if appropriate:

£17.38
− £ 5.64
───────
£11.74

> The opportunity to subtract money practically is important (e.g. through buying and selling items from the class shop, post office, etc.), even when the child is able to calculate with pencil-and-paper.

3 Encourage the children to:
– estimate answers before the calculation;
– use apparatus to check answers, e.g. coins and notes and/or baseboards such as those suggested in Activity **A**;
– ask themselves if the answer is sensible;
– use the calculator if a further check is required.

Book 4a, page 66 provides individual practice. RM 96 provides reinforcement.

D Multiplication   C I

1 Discuss occasions when people buy two or more of an identical item, for example, stamps, packaged foods, sweets, tickets for a show, train or bus tickets for a family.

2 Choose up to four identical, and identically priced items, but with prices written *only* in pence. Discuss different ways to find the total amount needed to pay for all the items, and how to convert the number of pence to decimal form.

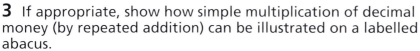

4 cakes each costing 35p
35p + 35p + 35p + 35p = £1·40

       35
   ×   4
   ─────
      140p

Resources

School
Coins and notes; calculators; sets of identical items, priced in pence; abacus

Scheme
Book 4a, page 67

> I bought four cakes, each costing 35p. How much do I need to pay?

3 If appropriate, show how simple multiplication of decimal money (by repeated addition) can be illustrated on a labelled abacus.

4 If you have a class shop, the children can find total prices of multiples of cheap items, recording the calculations and checking, using a calculator.

5 Discuss the importance of rounding and approximation. For example, the total cost of four items at £0.99 is (1p × 4) less than four at £2.

Book 4a, page 67 provides further practice.

> With experience, the children will learn when to count on, or add if numbers are small, use multiplication for numbers they can manage, and use a calculator for more complex prices.

E Division

*In advance mount and cut out copies of RM 97.

Part 1: Practical sharing

1 Remind the children that an amount of money is not always linked to a fixed number of coins. Therefore, division often requires exchanges.

Resources

School
Coins and notes; calculators; shopping cards*

Scheme
Resource Master 97; Book 4a, page 68

2 Give groups a small number of mixed coins and ask them to investigate ways to share the amount equally between two, three or more children.

3 Encourage them to talk about the way it is done. *How can we tell if the amount can be shared equally between two children? Are any coins left over?*

4 Give children who would enjoy a greater challenge a small number of notes, and then a mix of coins and notes. Ask them to carry out the same investigation as in stage 2.

Part 2: Shopping

1 Use the shopping cards prepared from RM 97.

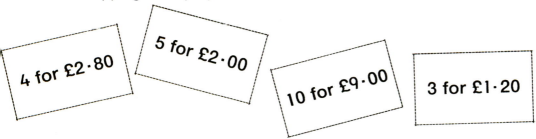

Ask the children to suggest ways to find the cost of one item. *Would fractions or division help? Can they remember a way to record the calculation?*

2 Working in pairs, one child chooses a card, the other finds the cost of one item, firstly using coins, then checking by using written division and/or a calculator.

Book 4a, page 68 provides further practice.

The cards on RM 97 can also be used to play Snap and matching or ordering games.

F Assessment activity

*In advance, prepare price cards for £0.72, £1.60, £6.04 and £10.20.

1 Ask the child to place the price cards in order of amount of money, largest first, and say the amounts aloud.

2 Ask him/her to choose the card for £10.20 and one other card, then calculate (mentally or in writing) the sum of the amounts, check with a calculator and interpret the display.

3 Ask the child to take the other two cards and calculate the difference between the two amounts, checking with a calculator.

4 Ask the child to select a card and work out the cost of three items of that price, checking with a calculator.

5 Ask her/him to choose a price card and work out the amount each would get if the total was shared between four people.

I Resources

School
Calculator; price cards*

Assessment notes

Oral response	✔
Practical response	✔
Pictorial response	
Written response	✔

The child has:
correctly ordered different amounts of money written in decimal form;
AND
correctly carried out different written calculations of money using all operations in decimal form;
AND
used a calculator to check calculations, interpreting the display.

STEPS 4a

STRENGTHENING ACTIVITIES

Class shop

For some children a practical 'counting' context is important. Encourage regular use of the class shop, or involve the child as your helper when money is handled as part of classroom routines.

Place value

Coins and notes are merely tokens for amounts of money. To develop clear images of the values of 'columns' in decimal notation of money, label and use base 10 materials to represent money.

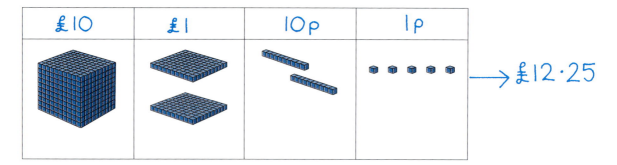

CHALLENGING ACTIVITIES

Sharing

Using a practical and/or written method, investigate the characteristics of amounts of money which are exactly divisible by two, five and ten.

Calculator

Use a calculator to divide an amount of money (in decimal form) by a single-digit number of your choice. Investigate calculator displays which show you immediately that the chosen amount is *not* exactly divisible by the chosen number. Give the child a hint: *How many digits are shown to the right of the decimal point?*

HOME/SCHOOL PROJECTS

Ask the children to accompany their parents or others to a supermarket. Ask them to try to keep a running total of items bought, using a calculator. Is it difficult to keep track? The children could bring discarded check-out slips to school for discussion in class.

IDEAS BOARD

■ Typical projects
Money; Ourselves; The Bank; Shops; The Post Office

■ Bills
Discuss the various bills which families receive through the post, for example, gas, electricity, telephone. What is the difference between a bill and a receipt?

■ Graphs
Make a bar-line graph to show amounts children spend on different items each week.

■ Bank bags
Collect the range of plastic money bags from a local bank. Discuss the number of coins which are placed in each bag. The bank checks the amount by weighing. What is the weight of a 'full' bag of coins?

■ Prices
Ask the children to research some prices paid for items in the early lives of their parents and grandparents. *What would similar items cost today?*

■ Rounding
Practise rounding amounts of money to the nearest 10p and £1. More able children should also try rounding amounts to the nearest 50p, 20p and 5p.

■ Games
Play domino and board games which give practice in interpreting amounts of money. (See *Support Materials* for some suggestions.)

■ Multiple shopping
Ask the children to collect examples of advertisements or packaging, displaying signs such as 'Three for 50p'.

SUPPORT MATERIALS

Teaching aids
Money Bingo (Philip & Tacey)
All Change (Hope Education)
Pound-O and *Money Match* (Taskmaster)
Mr Money (NES Arnold)

Teachers' reference materials

Primary Mathematics Today, 3rd edn, chapter 13, Elizabeth Williams and Hilary Shuard (Longman)

Maths Plus: Money 1 and *Money 2*, Paul Harling (Ward Lock Educational)

The Banking Information Service, 10 Lombard Street, London EC3V 9AT

Bank of England Resource Pack for Primary Schools (The Bank of England, Threadneedle Street, London EC2R 8AH)

The Royal Mint, Llantrisant, Pontycwm, Glamorgan, CF7 8YT

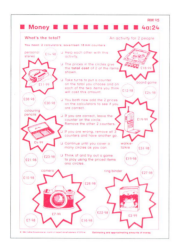

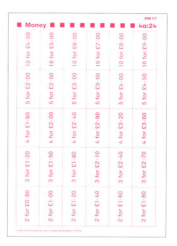

25. TRANSLATION

LEARNING CONTEXT

Contribution made by this Step

Children use different techniques and materials to translate points and shapes. Some of these involve movement of specified distances and directions, e.g. through using co-ordinates and eight points of the compass.

Objectives

To enable children to:
a Translate points or shapes a specified distance or in a given direction.
b Select the materials and mathematics to create simple patterns by translation and plan work methodically.
c Use or interpret language associated with translation.

Background

In Step 3b:13, the children used translation as a technique to generate movement and started to copy, continue and devise patterns created by movement in a straight line. This Step extends this work by including more precise language involving distance and direction, more complex construction techniques and combining translation with work on co-ordinates in the first quadrant.

Translation is part of transformation geometry in which the effect of moving sets of points, lines, 2-D or 3-D shapes in a straight line is investigated.

Mathematics in the National Curriculum

Programme of Study: KS2
Pupils should be taught to:
- visualise and describe shapes and movements, developing precision in using related geometrical language. (SSM 2.a)
- make 2-D and 3-D shapes and patterns with increasing accuracy, recognise their geometrical features and properties, and use these to classify shapes and solve problems. (SSM 2.b)
- transform 2-D shapes by translation, reflection and rotation, and visualise movements and simple transformations to create and describe patterns. (SSM 3.a)
- try different mathematical approaches; identify and obtain information needed to carry out their work. (UA 2.b)

THINKING AND TALKING MATHEMATICALLY

Starting points for discussion

Talk about the directions in which you can slide specific pieces in chess or draughts.

Examples of patterns and designs which could be copied or adapted by moving a printing block in a straight line.

Art project on printing techniques: comparing the movements made to obtain different effects.

Key language

slide, translate, movement in a straight line, translation, distance, direction, parallel, prism, skeleton shape

STEPS 4a

ACTIVITIES IN DETAIL

A Sliding movement

Resources

School
Assorted templates, mathematical and non-mathematical, e.g. transport, animals, etc. with at least one straight edge; A3 sheets of plain paper; A3 sheets of 1 cm squared paper

Part 1: Revising the translating movement

1 Revise movement in a straight line by getting the children to:
- draw lines in different orientations and of different lengths;
- draw arrows to indicate the direction of movement;
- draw, slide in the direction indicated then redraw the outlines of assorted templates.

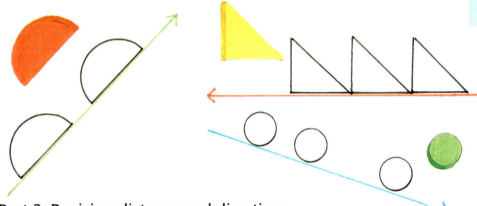

Part 2: Revising distance and direction

1 To revise the eight points of the compass, ask the children to construct a simple compass rose on the corner of a sheet of squared paper.

2 They can now record translations in a given direction.

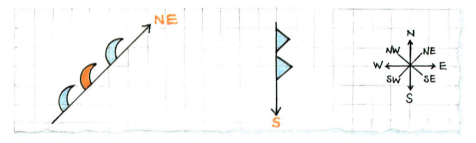

B Co-ordinates and translation

Resources

School
16 mm counters

Scheme
Book 4a, page 69;
Resource Master 98

1 Introduce the tasks on Book 4a, page 69, for which the children each need a copy of RM 98.

2 Afterwards, discuss:
- the patterns in the new co-ordinates for the counter in task 2, i.e. the first number of every co-ordinate has increased by two and the second number by three;
- that an instruction like 'Move three squares West.' involves a sliding movement or movement in a straight line which is called a translation.

EXTENSION

On RM 98, if you are only allowed to move the counter North-East to a new position seven points away, find all the possible co-ordinates on which you can start and finish.

C Translations along specified distances

Resources

School
2-D geometric plastic or wooden shapes; Pattern Blocks; assorted non-mathematical templates

Scheme
Resource Master A (1 cm squared grid); Resource Master F (1 cm squared lattice); Book 4a, page 70

Part 1: Making translations

1 Demonstrate how to draw round the template on squared paper and how to make a repeating pattern by sliding the template along the same number of squares in the same direction each time.

How could you make the outlines overlap?

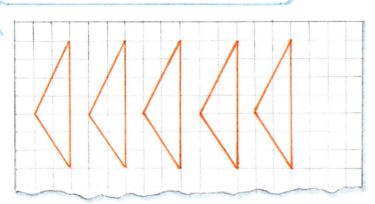

Although geometric shapes are used here as templates, you can use any available templates with at least one straight edge, e.g. letters, numerals, transport shapes, etc. These may also be chosen for task 3 on Book 4a, page 70.

2 The children can practise making translating strip patterns using squared or 'lattice' grids.

3 As work progresses, encourage the children to:

(a) slide the templates in different directions – horizontally, vertically and diagonally;
(b) show the direction of movement and the distance moved for each new pattern;
(c) experiment with overlapping the outlines by different amounts;
(d) devise a systematic method for colouring at least part of each pattern.

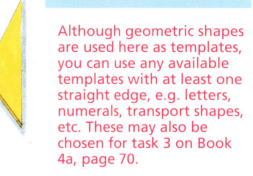

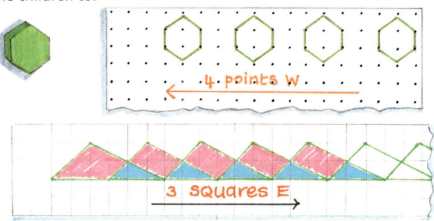

4 Afterwards, compare results and remind the children that these are examples of patterns made by translation – movement in a straight line.

Part 2: Equally-spaced points

1 Introduce the tasks on Book 4a, page 70 in which the children have to measure lengths, and follow instructions involving distance and direction.

2 Afterwards, each child might choose his/her favourite translating pattern created in task 3 on the same page, together with its instruction card and display these as a class or group collection. Can the children match the instruction cards to the patterns?

EXTENSION

■ The children design and use their own templates.

D Constructing skeleton shapes [C] [I]

Part 1: Making skeletal shapes

1 Revise the meaning of prisms.

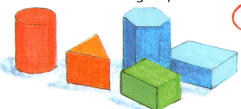

Why are these shapes prisms?

Resources

School
Plastic straws and pipe cleaners; construction kits such as Kugeli; geometric stencils/templates of polygons; several examples of prisms

Scheme
Book 4a, page 71

2 Allow time for the children to make some skeletal prisms from any available materials. (See Step 4a:12, Activity **D** for more detailed information.)

What do you call this shape?

What can you tell me about it? Does it have any parallel lines?

A prism is a 3-D shape with a uniform cross-section and with two end faces of exactly the same shape and size which are parallel to each other and in the same orientation.

3 Afterwards, the children can try to draw observational drawings of these and discuss any related difficulties.

4 Retain the skeleton shapes for Part 2.

Part 2: Drawing prisms using translation

1 Introduce the tasks on Book 4a, page 71.

2 If necessary, demonstrate the construction technique involving translating the outline of the chosen polygon, then joining pairs of corresponding points.

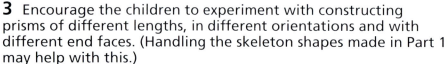

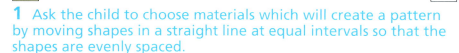

3 Encourage the children to experiment with constructing prisms of different lengths, in different orientations and with different end faces. (Handling the skeleton shapes made in Part 1 may help with this.)

4 As work progresses, draw attention to the parallel lines created by the translation or sliding movement.

E Assessment activity [I]

1 Ask the child to choose materials which will create a pattern by moving shapes in a straight line at equal intervals so that the shapes are evenly spaced.

2 Afterwards, ask the child to explain what she/he has done to create the translating pattern.

Assessment notes

Oral response	✔
Practical response	✔
Pictorial response	✔
Written response	

The child has:
selected the materials and mathematics to create a pattern by translation;
AND
chosen a method to repeat the motif(s) equal distances apart;
AND
described the way the pattern was created using some terms related to distance or direction.

STRENGTHENING ACTIVITIES

Your move

Dictate or write for the child simple instructions (e.g. 5NE or 3N then 4E) to position pegs on a pegboard. Then reverse roles so that the child practises giving you instructions. As work progresses, try to establish any areas of misunderstanding.

Copy and continue

Use simple templates to prepare translations on lined or grid papers for the child to copy and continue.

CHALLENGING ACTIVITIES

Translate and rotate

Use a template or motif to create patterns to show differences between reflection, rotation and translation.

IDEAS BOARD

■ Typical projects

Journeys; Pattern; Movement; Shape and Size; Decorations; Textiles; Printing

■ History

Examine artefacts from different times/ civilisations to find examples of translations; the children could make their own versions.

■ Letter stencils

Design monograms or create overlapping patterns by translating letter stencils the same distance each time.

■ LOGO

Translate a shape using a program similar to this which generates a simple house shape. Move the turtle towards the left-hand side of the screen. Position it heading 0° (facing North), then type:

Repeat 5[fd 100 lt 45 fd 70 lt 90 fd 70 lt 45 fd 100 lt 90 fd 100 pu fd 130 lt 90 pd]

Commands will vary slightly depending on the computer and program used.

■ Technology

The children design things, e.g. book covers, gift wrapping, etc., decorated with a translating motif.

■ Art

- Colour translated motifs with fabric crayons. Transfer the pattern to decorate suitable fabrics, e.g. T-shirts.
- Compare translations created with different kinds of printing blocks.

STEPS 4a

HOME/SCHOOL PROJECT

The children can demonstrate how to translate a motif to someone in their family. They bring that person's work to school to compare with others.

SUPPORT MATERIALS

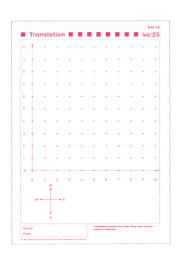

Teaching aids
Assorted rubber stamps (Philip & Tacey)
Drawmee Stencils (Taskmaster)
Pattern Block Pieces (NES Arnold)

Teachers' reference materials
Mathematics through Art and Design, Anne Woodman and Eric Albany (Collins Educational)
The Know How Book of Print and Paint (Usborne)
Primary Mathematics Today, 3rd edn, chapter 11, Elizabeth Williams and Hilary Shuard (Longman)
Ready, Steady, Logo!, Pauline Millward and Eric Albany (Longman)

Software
Picture Craft (BBC Software)
Mosaic (AUCBE)
Picture Builder (Hill McGibbon Software)
Brush (AUCBE)

26. TIME (2)

LEARNING CONTEXT

Contribution made by this Step

Children practise reading and interpreting simple 12- and 24-hour timetables, develop their skills in estimating and measuring duration in seconds and extend their awareness of calendars.

Objectives

To enable children to:
a Read and interpret 12- and 24-hour timetables.
b Estimate and measure duration in seconds.
c Extend awareness of the use and interpretation of calendars.

Background

This Step widens children's experience of time and timing to include information on common types of 12- and 24-hour timetables. It is important to note that the most valuable experiences involve reading and interpreting real timetables which have direct significance to the children, such as local bus times or the opening hours of a nearby sports centre.

Examples of simple timetables are provided in Book 4a, page 74, but you are advised to offer further practice, using timetables from your local area. These can be more complex because they deal with familiar places and situations. In addition, children's awareness of very short periods of time, measured in seconds, is developed, along with longer periods, based on calendars.

> **Mathematics in the National Curriculum**
>
> **Programme of Study: KS2**
> Pupils should be taught to:
> ■ choose appropriate standard units of length, mass, capacity and time, and make sensible estimates with them in everyday situations; extend their understanding of the relationship between units. (SSM 4.a)
> ■ choose and use appropriate measuring instruments; interpret numbers and read scales to an increasing degree of accuracy. (SSM 4.b)
> ■ interpret tables used in everyday life. (HD 2.a)
> ■ try different mathematical approaches; identify and obtain information needed to carry out their work. (UA 2.b)

THINKING AND TALKING MATHEMATICALLY

Starting points for discussion

A selection of timetables and advertisements stating opening hours. *Is the place open every day of the week ... every month of the year? How are the times written? Which times are shown on the 12-hour clock? ... on the 24-hour clock? Why? Are the different types suitable for different purposes?*

> **Key language**
>
> 12- and 24-hour times, am and pm, hour (h, hr, hrs), minute (min, mins), digits, zero, duration, arrive/arrival, depart/departure, destination, stopwatch, accurate/accuracy

STEPS 4a

ACTIVITIES IN DETAIL

A Using calendars C G

1 Revise the names of the days of the week and the months of the year, making sure that children can recite them in order from any starting point and can interpret the various abbreviations used in printed materials. (If necessary refer to Handbook 3a, Step 40.)

2 Use a full-year calendar or planner, or work directly from RM 99. Ask the children to find dates of personal or local interest, e.g. birthdays of friends and relations, major festivals, the start and end of term.

January						Fe
Monday		7	14	21	28	Mon
Tuesday	1	8	15	22	29	Tues
Wednesday	2	9	16	23	30	Wedne
Thursday	3	10	17	24	31	Thurs
Friday	4	11	18	25		Frida
Saturday	5	12	19	26		Satur
Sunday	6	13	20	27		Sund

Resources

School
Old and current calendars, diaries and planners.

Scheme
Book 4a, page 72;
Resource Master 99

3 Ask them to find and list a sequence of days/dates which are one week (then two weeks) apart.

4 Ask, *Why do printed calendars often have gaps at the start and end of each month?* Encourage the children to see that following months start on the next available day space.

5 Discuss ways to find the number of days from one date to another.

One week apart.
4th January
11th January
18th January
25th January
1st February
8th February

How many days are there from the fifteenth of January to the eighteenth of January?

From the fifteenth to the sixteenth is one day. From the sixteenth to the seventeenth is one day, and from the seventeenth to the eighteenth is one day. So that's a total of three days.

I see! You *don't* count both the fifteenth and the eighteenth!

6 Remind the children of the cyclical nature of listing and recording days of the week and months of the year, and the fact that we can count both forwards and backwards. You could illustrate this:

Further practice in interpreting calendars can be found on Book 4a, page 72 and RM 99.

EXTENSION

- Ask the children to find their exact age in years, weeks and days. (Leap years can be ignored except by more able children.)

B 12-hour timetables   C G I

1 Remind the children of the notation of am and pm times.

2 Introduce the idea of a bus timetable by drawing a simple one such as that shown below, using only am or pm.

Bus	Ashtown arr.	dep.	Batton arr.	dep.	Carville arr.	dep.
23	8:00 am	8:10 am	8:30 am	8:35 am	8:50 am	8:55 am
36	8:30 am	8:35 am	9:00 am	9:10 am	9:30 am	9:35 am

Resources

School
Geared analogue clockface

Scheme
Book 4a, page 73

Using local place names helps to make the work more relevant to children's lives.

3 Explain the abbreviations 'arr.' and 'dep.' and discuss the information shown, asking, for example: How long does the Number — bus stay in — ? How long does it take to travel from — to — ? Which bus is fastest between — and — ?

4 Ask a child to move the hands on a geared clock face to illustrate the durations. Encourage children to find durations by counting on rather than attempting to calculate the duration.

Calculation of time will be dealt with in Handbook 4b.

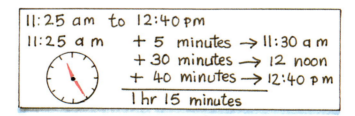

5 Extend the activity to include am and pm times, for example:

PLACE	No. 9 bus	No. 15 bus	No. 18 bus
Carlton Bus Station	11:15 am	11:30 am	11:45 am
Top Lane	11:25 am	11:40 am	11:55 am
Whittle Lakes	11:40 am	12 noon	12:15 pm
Park Gates	12 noon	12:15 pm	12:35 pm
Shopping Centre	12:10 pm	12:30 pm	12:50 pm
Perrys Garage	12:15 pm	12:35 pm	1:00 pm
Leisure Centre	12:30 pm	12:45 pm	1:15 pm
Longton Road	12:40 pm	12:55 pm	1:20 pm
Dreyfuss Cross	1:00 pm	1:15 pm	1:40 pm
Long Row	1:20 pm	1:25 pm	1:55 pm
Henney Bus Station	1:30 pm	1:40 pm	2:10 pm

6 Discuss interpretations of the information. Ask similar questions to those above, but adding also, for example:
How long is the morning (afternoon) part of the journey of the Number 15 bus? Which two places are ____ minutes apart? Jane gets off the Number 9 bus at Park Gates by mistake! How long will she have to wait for the next bus?

Book 4a, page 73 provides practice with 12-hour timetables.

EXTENSION

■ Ask children to investigate possible solutions to the problem:
Sonia was on the Number 18 bus for a total of ____ minutes. Where might she have got on and off the bus?

C 24-hour timetables

*In advance, collect and copy examples of simple local bus timetables. Enlarge them as necessary.

1 Revise and practise writing, reading and interpreting 24-hour clock times, matching them with am and pm times.

2 Provide groups with copies of timetables using the 24-hour clock notation:

PLACE	No.9 bus	No.15 bus	No.18 bus
Carlton Bus Station	11:15	11:30	11:45
Top Lane	11:25	11:40	11:55
Whittle Lakes	11:40	12:00	12:15
Park Gates	12:00	12:15	12:35
Shopping Centre	12:10	12:30	12:50
Perrys Garage	12:15	12:35	13:00
Leisure Centre	12:30	12:45	13:15
Longton Road	12:40	12:55	13:20
Dreyfuss Cross	13:00	13:15	13:40
Long Row	13:20	13:25	13:55
Henney Bus Station	13:30	13:40	14:10

3 Ask the children to use their own methods to work out the duration of journeys.

4 Revise, if necessary, how to find the duration of a journey by counting on from a first to a second given time (see right).

5 Discuss the information which can be derived from the timetable, using similar questions to those in Activity **B**.

Further practice can be found on Book 4a, page 74.

```
11:45  to  13:20

11:45  (+ 1 hour)      ⟶  12:45
12:45  (+ 15 minutes)  ⟶  13:00
13:00  (+ 20 minutes)  ⟶  13:20
                    ─────────────
                     1 hr 35 minutes
```

EXTENSION

■ The children use the timetables to plan, record and time journeys of their own.

Resources

School
Examples of timetables*;
24-hour analogue and digital clockfaces

Scheme
Book 4a, page 74

A 24-hour version of the timetable you used in Activity **B** can be useful to illustrate the links between the two forms.

Ask: *Is it easier to measure duration using twenty-four hour clock notation?*

D To a second

Part 1: Timing in seconds

1 Discuss situations where timing to the second is necessary, e.g. when using a microwave or in a race.

2 Ask, for instance, *Does it take longer to tie a shoe lace than to button up a coat?* Get the children to compare the relative time taken to do three or four simple everyday tasks. Discuss the need for a standard means of comparing short lengths of time.

3 Revise *How long is a minute?* by asking children to put up their hands after one minute has passed from a given signal. Ask, *How did you decide? Did you count? What did you count?*

4 Remind the children that a minute is divided into 60 seconds and that a rough approximation for counting in seconds is *One elephant, two elephants, three elephants ...*

5 Show a range of second timing devices, e.g. tocker timers, clocks and watches with a second hand, digital and analogue stopwatches/clocks. Demonstrate their use.

Resources

School
Stopwatches; stopclocks; tocker timers (5, 10, 15 and 20 second)

Scheme
Resource Master 100

Emphasise the approximate nature of all measurements, even with supposedly accurate instruments.

 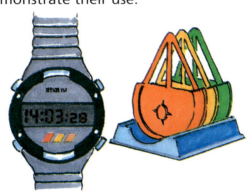 

6 Ask the children to count in seconds while watching the second hand move, or numbers change on a range of instruments, gradually developing a sense of, say, 10 seconds ... 30 seconds. Check the accuracy of the tocker timers.

Part 2: Timing activities

1 Get the children to work in pairs on the following activities, always estimating first, and using a variety of timing devices (always re-started from zero).
- *How much time does it take to ...?*
- *How many ... can you do in, say, 30 seconds?*
- *Which of two tasks takes longer? How much longer?*
- *Who takes the longer time (is slower) to ...?*

2 Remind the children that practice often shortens the amount of time taken to complete a task. Play *Beat the Clock*, asking the children to repeat an identical task, recording the time taken after each go. They should try to reduce the time taken.

Use RM 100 to structure further activities involving estimating, timing and recording in seconds.

EXTENSION

■ Children collect data and make charts of times taken by members of the class to walk to assembly, get changed for PE and so on.

E Assessment activity

1 Successful completion of Book 4a, pages 71 and 72 in activities B and C will indicate attainment of the required simple timetable skills.

2 Show the current calendar. Ask the child to indicate the date of his/her birthday, then to tell you the day and date five days later (and five days earlier).

3 Show the stopwatch. Ask the child to estimate and then measure the time taken to interlock 20 cubes.

Resources
School
Stopwatch; current calendar; interlocking cubes (e.g. Multilink).

Assessment notes

Oral response	✔
Practical response	✔
Pictorial response	
Written response	✔

The child has:
appropriately read and interpreted simple timetables, using 12- and 24-hour notation;
AND
used and interpreted a calendar in relation to personal facts;
AND
estimated and measured duration in seconds with an appropriate degree of accuracy.

STRENGTHENING ACTIVITIES

Nearest to ...

If a child has difficulty recognising 24-hour times show some cards with 24-hour times marked on them. Ask, *Which is the nearest 'o'clock' time?* Gradually move on to using real timetables.

 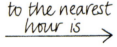 

Spot the time

If a child finds it difficult to link am/pm times, to the 24-hour notation, use two clockfaces, one for 12-hour and one for 24-hour time. Then show times in a digital form. *How can we tell if it is a 'morning' or an 'afternoon' time?*

CHALLENGING ACTIVITIES

Acceleration

Look in car magazines or brochures for information about car acceleration, for example, 0 to 60 mph in 12.3 seconds. Illustrate data for about five different cars. (Avoid explanations of speed and acceleration at this stage.)

Wind-up

Children investigate the duration of operation of wind-up or friction-driven toys. They test each toy three times and think of a way to decide which toy offers the best value.

This activity could provide an informal introduction to averages.

IDEAS BOARD

■ Typical projects
Travel/journeys; Communications; History of Measures.

■ Diaries
Encourage the children to keep a personal diary for a given period of time.

■ Leap year
Find out why we have a leap year.

■ Measuring time
Research ways that time has been measured since ancient times.

■ 12- and 24-hour times
From old catalogues and magazines, cut out pictures of timers on different appliances, and of clockfaces. Display and give the equivalent 12- or 24-hour time.

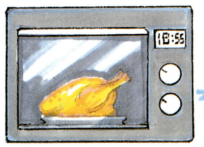 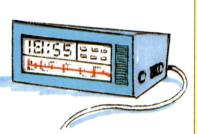

■ Pendulum
Investigate the rate of swing of a pendulum. *What changes the beat of the pendulum? Can the length be adjusted to swing in seconds?*

■ Pulse rates
Pairs of children could take each other's pulses (per minute) before and after exercise. They could research into pulse rates for athletes and for different animals. *What happens to pulse rates in hibernating mammals?*

■ Blinking time
Pairs of children estimate then measure the time each can last without blinking. *Is more than one minute possible?*

■ Names of days and months
Research the origins of the names of the days of the week and the months of the year.

■ Music
Discuss the meaning and importance of time and timing in music. *What is a time 'signature'?*

HOME/SCHOOL PROJECTS

The children list and group the number of timing devices they have at home. Afterwards, ask, *What is the average number of clocks/watches in a house?*

SUPPORT MATERIAL

Teaching aids
Tocker Timers 5, 10, 15 and 20 seconds (Philip and Tacey) (Hope Education)
Seconds Measuring Clock (Philip and Tacey)
Stopwatch (digital) (Hope Education)
Stopwatch (analogue) (NES Arnold)
Card Clock Faces (12- and 24-hour) (NES Arnold)
Digital Clock Face (NES Arnold)
12 Hour Clock Rubber Stamp (NES Arnold)
24 Hour Clock Rubber Stamp (NES Arnold)
Digital Rubber Stamps (NES Arnold)
Time Dominoes – Set 2 (NES Arnold)
Train Journeys (NES Arnold)
It's About Time – Clocks and Calendars Kit (Taskmaster)

Teachers' reference materials
Primary Mathematics Today, 3rd edn, chapter 16, Elizabeth Williams and Hilary Shuard (Longman)
Maths Plus: Time 1 and Time 2, Paul Harling (Ward Lock Educational)

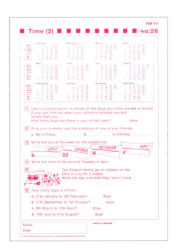

27. MULTIPLICATION

LEARNING CONTEXT

Contribution made by this Step

After activities to memorise the x 7 and the 7 x tables, the children develop pencil-and-paper methods to multiply two-digit numbers by one-digit numbers.

Learning objectives

To enable children to:
a Know facts in the x 7 or 7 x tables.
b Multiply two-digit numbers by a one-digit number with products not exceeding 300.
c Solve multiplication problems without or with a calculator and consider the reasonableness of the answer.

Background

By the end of this Step, the children will have had opportunities to memorise all the table facts up to 10 x 10. The children will already be familiar with most of the facts for the table of seven (7 x) through learning the facts within other tables, and, allowing for commutativity, the only new fact to be memorised is 7 x 7!

This Step draws together several different skills previously introduced – table facts, the effect of multiplying whole numbers by ten and the distributive law.

When multiplying two-digit numbers by one-digit numbers, the children initially use the imagery of apparatus to remind them of the links with repeated addition and the distributive law. This is a standard method for breaking down multiplications into smaller stages which can be tackled mentally or by pencil-and-paper methods. For example, 16 x 9 can be redistributed to become (10 x 9) + (6 x 9) which can then be calculated using multiplication facts.

Some children will continue to need to use apparatus to help them find or check answers to long multiplications for some time. Others will choose to abandon it in favour of pencil-and-paper calculations.

> **Mathematics in the National Curriculum**
>
> **Programme of Study: KS2**
> Pupils should be taught to:
> ■ use their understanding of place value to develop methods of computation ... to multiply and divide by powers of 10 when there are whole-number answers. (N 2.a)
> ■ know the multiplication facts to 10 x 10; develop a range of mental methods for finding quickly from known facts those that they cannot recall. (N 3.c)
> ■ develop a variety of mental methods of computation with whole numbers up to 100, and explain patterns used; extend mental methods to develop a range of non-calculator methods of computation that involve addition and subtraction of whole numbers, progressing to methods for multiplication and division of up to three-digit by two-digit whole numbers. (N 3.d)
> ■ understand multiplication as repeated addition, and division as sharing and repeated subtraction; use associated language and recognise situations to which the operations apply. (N 3.e)
> ■ check results by different methods, including repeating the operations in a different order or using inverse operations; gain a sense of the size of a solution, and estimate and approximate solutions to problems. (N 4.c)

THINKING AND TALKING MATHEMATICALLY

Starting points for discussion

Which multiplication tables are easiest (hardest) to remember? Why?
How can you tell if a number has been multiplied by 2 ... 5 ... 10? Tell me some multiples of ... 2 up to 10 ... 7 up to 70 ..., etc.
Playing Multiplication Bingo to revise table facts. (See Part 2 of Activity A in Step 3.)

> **Key language**
>
> product, multiply, approximate, round up/down, estimate, predict, multiplied by, brackets

ACTIVITIES IN DETAIL

A Table of seven (7x) and the seven-times table (x7)

Resources

School
Cuisenaire Rods; metre rules calibrated in cm; calculators; good supply of small blank cards

Scheme
Resource Master 101

Part 1: The table of seven (7x)

1 Display missing number sentences like these ____ x 7 = ____ and 7 x ____ = ____ . What solutions can the children offer with answers up to 70?

2 Get the children, preferably working in pairs, to build up the 7 x table with rods and metre rules, asking them to predict each time where the next rod will reach.

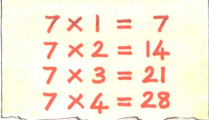

Seven multiplied by four equals twenty-eight.

Seven four times makes twenty-eight.

3 Record the table as the model develops, reading the results as 'seven multiplied by four equals twenty-eight' or 'seven four times makes twenty-eight'.

4 Get each pair to make a set of cards from 7 x 1 to 7 x 10. Place these face down in random order.

5 The children turn these over one by one, and predict then check where that number of 7-rods will reach on the rule.

Although the emphasis here is on mental recall of facts, the use of the rods will help to remind children of the distinction between the 7 x and the x 7 tables.

Part 2: The seven-times table (x 7)

1 Compare the 7 x table with the pattern made by modelling the x 7 table.

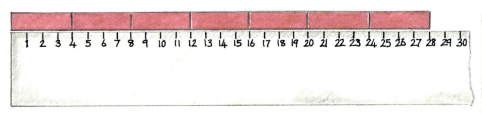

2 Record the pattern.

3 Again using sets of cards marked from 1 x 7 to 10 x 7, pairs of children can predict then check where that set of seven-rods will reach on the rule.

RM 101 provide further practice in the x 7 table and extends also to the x 9 table.

B Revising multiplication facts to 10 x 10   C P

Resources
Scheme
Resource Master 102;
Book 4a, page 75

1 Introduce the tasks on RM 102 which revise multiplication facts up to 10 x 10 through problem-solving on multiplication grids.

2 Allow the children to work with a partner so that they can share their logical thinking and help each other overcome potential difficulties. (Scrap paper is likely to be needed to try out examples!)

A five must go here because five fives make twenty-five.

Any multiplication grid puzzles made by the children could be made available for others in the class to solve when they have finished work early, etc.

The children will be more likely to take more care in their design and presentation if they know they will genuinely be used by others.

3 Stress that when they make up their own multiplication grids, they should be able to do them themselves before trying them out on others!

4 Afterwards, discuss the clues the children used to help them find the answers.

EXTENSION

- Children can attempt to design multiplication grids where the numbers on the axes are all multiples of 10.

Book 4a, page 75, provides practical problems involving multiplication facts.

C The distributive law   C G I

Resources
Scheme
Book 4a, page 76;
Resource Master A (1 cm squared grid)

Part 1: Revising bracket notation

1 Ask, *What can you remember about the use of brackets?*

2 To revise the use of brackets you might:
– ask where to put brackets in examples like this:

$$3 + 5 \times 6 = 33$$

If the answer is thirty-three, where should the brackets go?

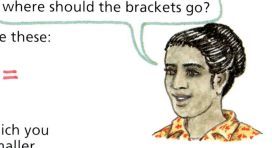

– compare the effect of using brackets in examples like these:

$$(3 + 8) - 6 = \qquad 3 + (8 - 6) =$$

3 Introduce the tasks on Book 4a, page 76.

4 Afterwards, discuss the fact that multiplications which you cannot calculate mentally can be broken down into smaller multiplications which you can calculate mentally, e.g. using table facts.

STEPS 4a

5 Ask, *Why was example 1g more difficult than the others?* Where do the children think it would be most sensible to 'break down' the number? Why?

Part 2: 'Long' multiplications

1 Display some multiplications such as 12 x 8, 15 x 6, 18 x 4 (i.e. with products <100).

2 Ask the children to find the answers in their own way by 'breaking down' the larger number into smaller numbers of their own choice.

3 Afterwards, compare results and methods of recording.

4 Groups might each choose a multiplication and prepare a poster to show different ways of finding the answer.

EXTENSION

■ Using an example such as 24 x 8, the children find the answer in different ways by redistributing the first number in two ways (e.g. 20 + 4), three ways (e.g. 8 + 8 + 8), four ways ...

D Multiplication rectangles

*In advance, draw on the transparency rectangles of these (or similar) dimensions, using RM C:

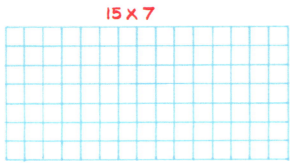

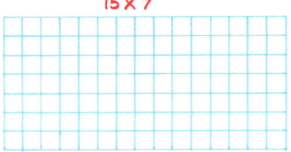

Resources

School
OHP transparency*; OHP; OHP pens

Scheme
Resource Master 103;
Resource Master C
(5 mm squared grid)

Part 1: Multiplying 'teen' numbers by a single-digit number

1 Take a vote about which multiplication table the children find easiest and why. With luck, the answer will be the x 10 table!

2 Draw attention to one rectangle, e.g. 15 x 7. About how many squares are inside? Why do you think that? Are you sure it will be more than 70? Why?

3 Show how by 'splitting' this into two rectangles of 10 x 7 and 5 x 7, the total number of squares can be calculated without too much difficulty.

This activity illustrates the distributive law of multiplication by redistributing the 'teen' number into tens and ones. For example:
15 x 7 = (10 + 5) x 7 =
(10 x 7) + (5 x 7) = 70 + 35 = 105
Most standard long multiplication pencil and paper methods use this law.

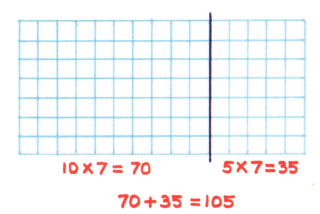

$10 \times 7 = 70$ $5 \times 7 = 35$

$70 + 35 = 105$

4 Partition the other two rectangles similarly and see if the children can calculate the products.

5 Compare results afterwards.

6 Introduce the tasks on RM 103 which provides individual practice in interpreting arrays in this way.

EXTENSION

■ The children can try to draw diagrams to help work out products such as 24 x 6, 35 x 7 ... i.e. where the number to be multiplied is greater than 20.

E Base 10 materials   C I

*Each child will need to make an A3 baseboard like this:

hundreds	tens	ones

Resources

School
Baseboards*; base 10 materials: squares, longs and ones; A3 sheets of plain paper

Scheme
Book 4a, pages 77 and 78

1 Display some multiplications such as these and allow time for the children to try to find the products, using the base 10 materials to find or check the answers, if they wish.

$17 \times 4 =$ $23 \times 5 =$ $18 \times 7 =$

$36 \times 3 =$ $48 \times 5 =$

2 Remind them to estimate the answers first.

3 Afterwards, compare results and methods used.

The use of the imagery created by the apparatus is particularly useful for two reasons:
(a) It revises the links between multiplication and repeated addition.
(b) The related notation evolves out of the practical activity and is more likely to be understood.

STEPS 4a

4 If necessary, demonstrate this procedure, shown here for 23 x 5.

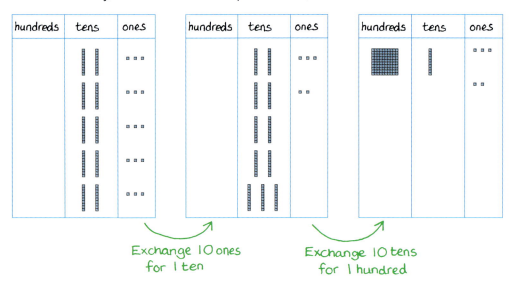

5 Relate this to the following form of notation which again uses brackets.

6 Introduce the tasks on Book 4a, page 77 for which the children can use base 10 materials to find or check their answers.

Book 4a, page 78, provides multiplication problems which the children can solve using the formal method of notation introduced or reliable informal methods.

F Checking strategies C I

Part 1: Estimating and approximating

1 Display some two-digit by one-digit multiplications such as these and, for each one in turn, ask, *What can you tell me about the answers?*

2 Discuss different strategies the children might use:
(a) rounding up or down to approximate an answer, e.g. 18 x 5 = ___ might be rounded up to 20 x 5 = 100 so that answer will be a bit less than 100;
(b) rounding up and down, e.g. 18 is between 10 and 20, so 18 x 5 = ___ is between 10 x 5 = 50 and 20 x 5 = 100;
(c) recognising what the final digit will be, e.g. since 8 x 5 = 40, the answer to 18 x 5 will also end in 0.

RM 104 provides individual practice.

Part 2: Checking, using multiplication or division

1 Ask, *How can you check that the answer to a multiplication such as 25 x 9 = 225 is correct, using:*
– *division; and*
– *another multiplication?*

Resources

School
Calculators

Scheme
Resource Master 104

This activity provides a good opportunity to revise the importance of getting into the habit of estimating/approximating answers in advance, and of reviewing answers to see if they are sensible.

2 Revise how a multiplication can be 'undone' by a division on the calculator, and, in this case, if the answer is 25, the calculation is correct. Use a sequence of key presses like this:

3 Similarly, revise how a multiplication can be checked using the commutative law, i.e. reversing the order of the numbers.

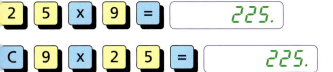

G	**Assessment activity**

*In advance, make cards like these:

I	**Resources**

School
Multiplication cards*

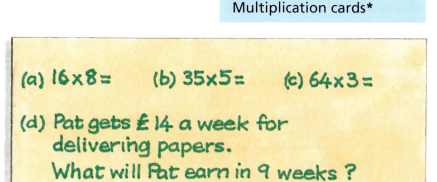

1 Place the ×7 cards face downwards in random order and ask the child to turn over one at a time and to give you the answer.

2 Ask the child to find the answers to the problems on the second card in his or her own time. (The child can choose materials to help with these if wished, but do not allow the calculator in this instance.)

3 Afterwards, discuss the results and how these were calculated. Ask, *Do you think your answers are sensible? Why?* (If necessary, ask direct questions such as, *Why is the answer to the first problem more than 80?*)

In advance, decide on a reasonable time limit for the child to respond to stage 1, e.g. five seconds for each response.

Assessment notes

Oral response	✓
Practical response	
Pictorial response	
Written response	✓

The child has:
given at least nine correct responses out of eleven to facts in the ×7 table;
AND
multiplied, without a calculator, at least three out of four two-digit numbers by one-digit numbers correctly using either a standard or non-standard method;
AND
has commented on the reasonableness of the answers.

STEPS 4a

STRENGTHENING ACTIVITIES

x7 and 7x tables

Establish the facts in the x7 (or 7x) table with which the child has difficulties. You can then design a set of dominoes for these which repeat those facts. Retest when the child is confident about having memorised these.

Long multiplication

If the child cannot multiply two-digit numbers by one-digit numbers without apparatus, check that she or he can use familiar apparatus such as base 10 materials to help find the products as suggested in Activity **D**. Objective **b** does not specify that it should achieved by pencil and paper methods only.

Sensible answers

Commenting on the reasonabless of answers is further developed in later Steps. For the moment, the child, using knowledge of the effect of multiplying by 10 (or multiples of 10 up to 50) can at least comment that a multiplication such as 14 x 7 will have an answer greater than 10 x 7 or 70.

CHALLENGING ACTIVITIES

Using a frame like this and these numeral cards:

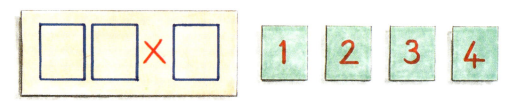

the children have to find the 24 possible products. Which will give the highest total? Lowest total? Predict then check.

IDEAS BOARD

■ Calculator missing numbers
Calculators such as the Galaxy 9 x can be programmed to respond to problems such as 23 x ? = 184 to provide practice in estimating.

■ Cuisenaire Rods
Cuisenaire Rods can be used to demonstrate the distributive law.

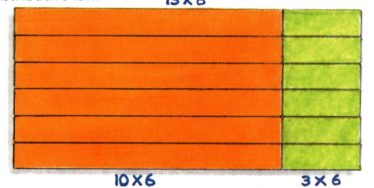

Stretched out along a metre rule, the twelve-rods will match 78cm.

■ Beat the calculator
Using cards for facts in the x 7 and 7 x tables, the children play in pairs and see who can work out the answer more quickly – the one calculating mentally or the one with the calculator.

■ English
The children write, illustrate and compare 'stories' for a given multiplication expression.

■ Card multiplication
Play the game suggested in the Home/School Projects at school first.

HOME/SCHOOL PROJECTS

The picture cards are removed from a pack of playing cards. The remaining cards are placed face down in a pack and each player picks two from the top. The person with the higher product, found by multiplying the value of the cards together, wins all the other player's cards. The person with most cards at the end wins.

SUPPORT MATERIALS

Teaching aids
Multibase System (Hope Education)
Cuisenaire Rods (NES Arnold)
Texas 1103, 1104 and *Galaxy 9x calculators* (Texas Instruments)

Teachers' reference materials
Primary Mathematics Today, 3rd edn, chapter 15, Elizabeth Williams and Hilary Shuard (Longman)

Software

Dots and Patterns 1 from *Mathematical Investigations*, Anita Straker (ILECC)
Multiple from *MicroSMILE 1* (ILECC)
Gusinter from *Number Games*, Anita Straker (ILECC)

Games

Times Table Trio, Multiplication Dominoes, Table Shapes (Taskmaster)
Table Tops, Multiplication Games, Multiplication Bingo, Cateno (NES Arnold)

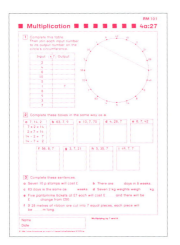
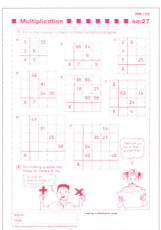

28. 2-D SHAPE (2)

LEARNING CONTEXT

Contribution made by this Step

Using quadrilaterals as the shape under investigation, the children:
- find and construct some with parallel lines;
- investigate diagonals;
- construct pinboard shapes from given information;
- construct and describe Geostrip shapes;
- investigate the interior angles;
- sort in different ways using terms like parallel and perpendicular.

Objectives

To enable children to:
a Know and use properties associated with quadrilaterals.
b Construct quadrilaterals from given information.
c Make simple generalisations or test statements.

Background

In Step 8, the children investigated the properties of triangles in some detail to include classification, using terms like isosceles, the sum of their interior angles, the triangle as a rigid shape and simple construction techniques.
   Now quadrilaterals are explored in more detail. The properties of quadrilaterals are also considered in Steps 31 Reflection and 33 Tessellation. In STEPS 4b, work on the interior angles of quadrilaterals will be extended when measurement in degrees and more complex construction techniques are introduced.

> **Mathematics in the National Curriculum**
>
> **Programme of Study: KS2**
> Pupils should be taught to:
> ■ visualise and describe shapes and movements, developing precision in using related geometrical language. (SSM 2.a)
> ■ make 2-D and 3-D shapes and patterns with increasing accuracy, recognise their geometrical features and properties, and use these to classify shapes and solve problems. (SSM 2.b)
> ■ use right angles, fractions of a turn and, later, degrees, to measure rotation, and use the associated language. (SSM 3.c)
> ■ understand and investigate general statements, *e.g. 'wrist size is half neck size', 'there are four prime numbers less than 10'.* (UA 4.a)
> ■ make general statements of their own, based on evidence they have produced. (UA 4.c)
> ■ explain their reasoning. (UA 4.d)

THINKING AND TALKING MATHEMATICALLY

Starting points for discussion

What can you tell me about … a rhombus, an oblong … etc.?
Name some closed shapes with four straight sides.
Comparing pairs of quadrilaterals for similarities and differences.
Describe a quadrilateral. What shape do the children imagine it is and why?
Set of 3-D shapes: Find shapes whose faces are quadrilaterals.

> **Key language**
>
> angle, acute, obtuse, right, interior, opposite, adjacent, parallel, perpendicular, equal, polygon, perimeter, diagonal, quadrilateral names: square, oblong, rectangle, rhombus/rhombi, parallelogram, kite, trapezium/trapezia

STEPS 4a

ACTIVITIES IN DETAIL

A Revision: parallel sides C G I

*In advance, prepare four flash cards: square, oblong, rhombus, parallelogram (see Part 2, stage 2, below).

Part 1: Constructing parallel lines

1 Provide each group with a selection of rulers (or straight edges) in different widths.

2 Revise the meaning of parallel lines by asking the children to:

(a) draw lines on either side of a ruler and check that they are the same distance apart. (They can do this by sliding the ruler to and fro between the lines or by translating (sliding) a piece of tracing paper, on which two short lines are drawn a ruler width apart, along the constructed lines.)

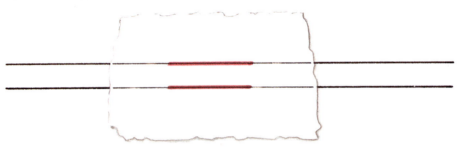

(b) draw by estimation pairs of lines which stay the same distance apart;

(c) draw pairs of parallel lines by taping two pencils together, with their points aligned.

Part 2: Rhombi and parallelograms

1 Provide each group with samples of squares, oblongs, rhombi and parallelograms from 2-D shape sets. *Which do you recognise? Which don't you recognise?*

2 Revise or introduce the spoken and written forms.

Resources

School
Rulers or straight edges in a range of widths; small pieces of tracing paper; card for flash cards*; examples of squares, oblongs, rhombi and parallelograms from 2-D shape sets

Scheme
Resource Master 105

In the Handbook, the Latin form of the plural for rhombus – rhombi, and for trapezium – trapezia have been used. However, the plural forms rhombuses and trapeziums are equally acceptable, according to modern dictionaries. It will make more sense to many children to use the 's' form of the plural.

What can you tell me about parallelograms?

3 Suggest that the children try to design, using the widths of the rulers only, and without any measuring, grid papers with an overall pattern of these shapes.

4 Afterwards, compare results and construction techniques.

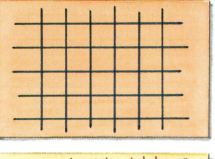 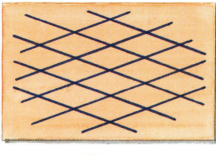

Squares and rhombuses can be made with one ruler.

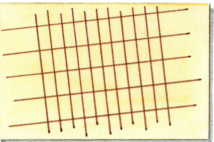 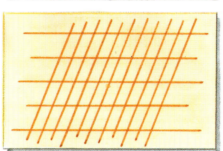

Oblongs and parallelograms need to be made with rulers of two widths.

5 Remind the children that where lines are at right angles to each other, as in the square grid, we can say they are perpendicular to each other.

6 Ask how:
– squares and rhombi are the same/different;
– oblongs and parallelograms are the same/different.

7 By referring to the constructed grids, explain that:
a square is a special rhombus with right-angled corners; and
an oblong is a special parallelogram with right-angled corners.

RM 105 provides individual practice in constructing parallelograms and rhombi.

Isometric pinboards, if available, will support the work on RM 105.

EXTENSION

■ The children can make drawings of objects in and around the classroom which have parallel lines.

B Pinboard quadrilaterals C P I

Part 1: Quadrilaterals

1 Ask the children, working individually or in pairs, to make and record as many different quadrilaterals, i.e. closed shapes with four straight sides, as they can on their pinboards.

2 Encourage them to find unique quadrilaterals, i.e. not reflections or rotations of those already found.

3 As work proceeds, draw particular attention to:
– kites: two pairs of equal adjacent sides
(like two isosceles triangles with a
common base);

Resources

School
6 by 6 pinboards; good supply of elastic bands

Scheme
Book 4a, page 79;
Resource Master F

– parallelograms: both pairs of opposite sides parallel;

– trapezia: one pair of parallel sides only.

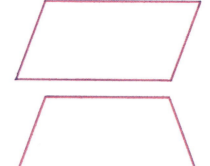

4 Afterwards, compare the different quadrilaterals found (or not found), drawing attention to the angles and parallel sides in particular.

> The only quadrilateral which cannot be made on a square pinboard is the rhombus (apart from a right-angled rhombus, i.e. a square).

Part 2: Comparing kites, parallelograms and trapezia

1 Again using their pinboards, ask the children to construct a kite and show it to you and others in their group. *How are they the same/different?*

2 Repeat for a trapezium and a parallelogram, using terms like 'adjacent' and 'parallel' to describe the relationships between lines.

3 Introduce the tasks on Book 4a, page 79 for which a supply of RM F will be needed.

C Diagonals investigation

*The children may need only half a sheet each of RM A for their drawings.

Part 1: Constructing diagonals

1 Ask each child to draw an identical quadrilateral, then its diagonals.

What can you tell me about the diagonals?

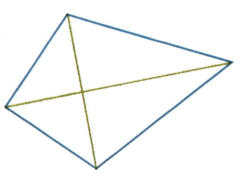

Resources

School
Materials for constructing quadrilaterals: stencils, templates, 1 cm squared grid and lattice papers; geometric 2-D shapes

Scheme
Resource Master 106; Book 4a, pages 80 and 81; Resource Master A and F* (optional) for grid and lattice papers

2 Display terms the children or you use, e.g. 'sides', 'angles', 'equal', 'not equal', 'obtuse', 'acute', 'perpendicular', 'at right angles to'.

3 Get the children, preferably working in pairs, to construct/draw different quadrilaterals using any suitable materials and to add the diagonals.

4 They write on each shape what they are able to find out about the diagonals and the angles around the intersections, using the listed terms and any others they find useful.

5 Afterwards, compare results.

RM 106 provides individual practice.

Part 2: Constructing quadrilaterals

1 Introduce the individual tasks in Book 4a, pages 80 and 81.

2 Encourage the children to decide which quadrilateral can be drawn from each diagonal framework, simply by its shape, *before* constructing it.

3 Points for discussion during and after the tasks might be:
- the need for accurate and careful pencil/ruler constructions;
- that the diagonals of each family of quadrilaterals have their own unique shape;
- that the diagonals of a particular shape, say, kites, have common features.

EXTENSION

■ Without grids to help, the children draw by estimation the diagonals for different kites. Afterwards, they draw the four sides around each diagonal and assess how accurately they constructed the diagonals.

■ *In which quadrilaterals is a diagonal also a line of symmetry?* The children draw round different quadrilaterals, and rule diagonals and lines of symmetry in two colours.

D Sides of quadrilaterals

Resources

School
Geostrips

Geostrips are useful because the colours help children to identify the equality of sides and the position of the sides in relation to each other, i.e. opposite or adjacent.

1 Preferably working in pairs (or small groups), the children find, record in their own way and name different quadrilaterals which can be found by fitting four Geostrips together.

2 You can restrict the set of Geostrips used if preferred, e.g. if supplies are short.

Construct, record and write what you can about the quadrilaterals you can make with these strips.

3 Afterwards, results can be compared and the children reminded that quadrilaterals constructed in this way can be deformed.

We can transform a parallelogram into an oblong by making its corners right-angled.

STEPS 4a

E Interior angles of quadrilaterals

Resources

School
Assorted gummed paper quadrilaterals; shape stencils or templates which include a selection of quadrilaterals; scissors

Scheme
Book 4a, page 82

Part 1: Revising whole turns

1 Get the children to fold two intersecting lines in pieces of paper so that the angles around the intersections can be discussed.

2 After trialling different examples, ask what they found out.

3 Important points to establish are that:
- you can either construct four right angles (**a**) or two acute and two obtuse angles (**b**);
- the four angles combined are equivalent to one whole or full turn.

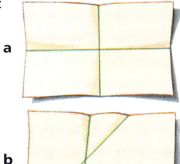

Part 1 will provide an ideal opportunity to revise the terms associated with angles: acute, obtuse and right-angled.

4 Some children may also notice that:
- opposite angles are equal;
- each adjacent acute and obtuse angle forms a straight angle.

Part 2: Interior angles of quadrilaterals

1 Introduce the task on Book 4a, page 82, giving as little help as necessary.

2 Make sure that the children:
- tear rather than cut the corners to ensure a ragged edge, and
- tear as large pieces as possible off the corners to make them easier to fit together.

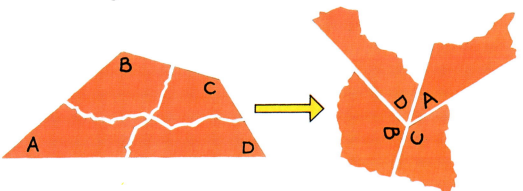

3 Encourage the children to experiment with quadrilaterals they have constructed, as well as provided shapes.

4 Afterwards, compare results and ask, *What can you tell me about the inside or interior angles of quadrilaterals? What if you started with a very large (or very small) quadrilateral? Does it matter if it is a rectangle, kite, rhombus, etc.?*

EXTENSION

■ Test very large or small quadrilaterals. Display your results and what you found out.

By testing quadrilaterals of as many shapes and sizes as possible, the children should be able to generalise/ hypothesise that if the four angles are combined (in this case by being arranged to meet at a common vertex), they form an angle equivalent to a whole turn (see Ma 1/4d).

F Sorting quadrilaterals   G P

*Each group needs a supply of about 12 assorted plastic quadrilaterals or those cut from RM 107.

1 Ask one child in each group to write down any terms the others think useful to describe quadrilaterals.

2 Combine and display the groups' suggestions, drawing attention to any relating to the angles or sides.

Names	Angles	Sides
oblong	obtuse	equal
square	acute	not equal
rectangle	right	perpendicular
trapezium		parallel
rhombus		at right angles
parallelogram		

Resources

School
Plastic shapes, to include squares, oblongs, parallelograms, kites, rhombi, trapezia and asymmetric quadrilaterals, at least*; large backing sheets

Scheme
Resource Master 107 (optional)

3 Provide each group with a selection of quadrilaterals and ask the children to take turns to sort them secretly in different ways and to get the others to predict the criteria.

4 Spend time with each group to discuss the criteria they are using or to sort the shapes secretly for the group to predict your method of sorting.

5 If necessary, provide sorting labels to direct the sorting.

Part 2: Sorting diagrams: parallel and perpendicular

1 The children can compare quadrilaterals sorted onto the regions of the Venn (or related Carroll diagram).

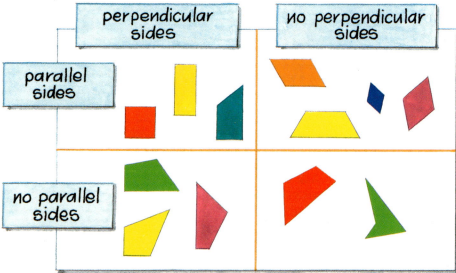

Remind the children that rectangles include both squares and oblongs. A square is a rectangle with opposite *and* adjacent sides equal and with four right angles.

STEPS 4a

2 Afterwards, discuss the names of shapes which have parallel or perpendicular sides, both, or neither.

EXTENSION

■ Use the quadrilateral cards on RM 107 to play *Snap* or pair-matching games. The children must say the correct name for the type of quadrilateral to keep the cards.

G Assessment activity

*In advance, prepare name cards: square, oblong, kite, trapezium, parallelogram, rhombus.

1 Ask the child to construct one each of the shapes on the name cards using Geostrips. (Help with reading these if necessary.)

2 Afterwards, ask the child to tell you about the parallelogram. (If necessary, prompt by asking more direct questions: *What can you tell me about its sides or angles? How do you know it is a parallelogram?*)

3 Repeat stage 2 for the rhombus, trapezium and kite.

4 Afterwards, show, using a quadrilateral drawn with a template or stencil, how you can divide a quadrilateral into two triangles.

5 Ask the child to choose materials to test if you can divide different kinds of quadrilaterals into two triangles.

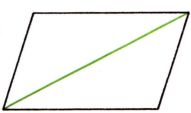

Resources

School
Geostrips; card for name cards*; assorted geometric shape stencils/templates

Whilst the child is carrying out stages 1 and 5, she/he can be left to carry out the tasks in her/his own time and to explain to you afterwards what she/he has done.

Assessment notes

Oral response	✔
Practical response	✔
Pictorial response	✔
Written response	

The child has:
recognised and constructed at least five out of six named quadrilaterals;
AND
described four different quadrilaterals using some terms associated with angles or sides;
AND
tested some examples to find out if different quadrilaterals can be divided into two triangles and justified his/her results.

STRENGTHENING ACTIVITIES

Geostrips

Use geostrips of four lengths only, each length a different colour. Establish the equality of the sides of each colour. Ask the child to make different quadrilaterals with these, to explain to you how these are the same/different and the names for these. This may help you establish areas of misunderstanding.

'I spy …'

The children practise recognition of quadrilaterals and the use of their names, e.g. 'I spy some kites (trapezia, parallelograms or rhombi) …' The child tries to find the relevant shapes from a set and says why the shape is of this type. This may help you diagnose any quadrilateral families whose names are not understood.

CHALLENGING ACTIVITIES

Interior angles

Decide the best way to prove and display your results for this statement: The interior angles of hexagons are equal to eight right angles.

Area

Which quadrilaterals can be drawn, using whole and half squares only on one centimetre squared paper? What is their area?

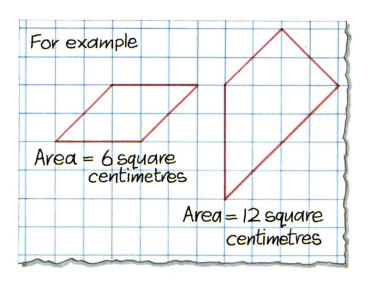

IDEAS BOARD

■ Art

The children can:
– collect and display examples of artefacts, textiles, etc. from other times and cultures in which quadrilaterals feature as a decorative element;
– make 'cut and stretched' paper quadrilaterals. (See also triangles in Art entry in the Ideas Board in Step 8);
– make observational drawings of places in the environment where quadrilaterals can be seen.

■ Technology

The children can measure, mark out and cut out accurately quadrilaterals in different materials, e.g. balsa wood, to make modular structures, etc.

■ 3-D Faces

The children examine 3-D shapes for faces which are quadrilaterals.

■ Programmed shapes

The children try to write programs to create quadrilaterals using LOGO, Pip or Roamer.

TO SQUARE
REPEAT 4 (FD 150 RT 90)
END

How might you change your program to make a larger square? An oblong? A square inside a square?

■ Feelie bag shapes

Place assorted plastic quadrilaterals inside a feelie bag. The children take it in turns to feel one without withdrawing it, predict then check what it is.

■ Shapes in shapes

This is revision of Step 8. The children investigate what kinds of triangles are produced by ruling a diagonal in different quadrilaterals: for example, all kites can be made of two isosceles triangles.

STEPS 4a

HOME/SCHOOL PROJECTS

Ask the children to find examples of quadrilaterals in advertisements, trademarks, logos, etc., and to bring these to school to build up a display.

SUPPORT MATERIALS

Teaching aids
Gummed paper quadrilaterals (Playaway)
6 x 6 Pinboard (Hope Education)
Transparent 6 x 6 Matrix Geoboard (NES Arnold)
Geostrips (NES Arnold)
Geometric Shapes (NES Arnold)
Orbit Material (NES Arnold)
Angle Strips (Philip & Tacey)
Pip (Swallow Systems)
Roamer (Valiant Technology)

Children's books
Shapes and Solids from *Fun with Maths* series (Wayland)
Shape from *Understanding Maths* series (Wayland)

Software
Picture Builder (Hill McGibbon Software)
Picture Craft (ILECC)

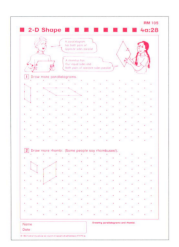
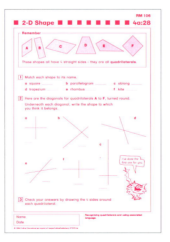
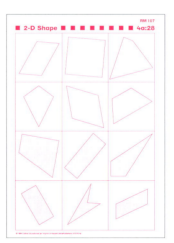

29. FUNCTIONS

LEARNING CONTEXT

Contribution made by this Step

The children:
(a) explore number relationships between inputs and outputs in machines, including those where more than one operation is carried out;
(b) investigate machines which perform equivalent operations;
(c) use function machines to explore the inverse relationship between multiplication and division.

Objectives

To enable children to:
a Interpret function machines with more than one operation.
b Use function machines to investigate multiplication as the inverse of division.
c Explain how function machines operate, using associated terms, or how input and output numbers are related.

Background

Simple function machines were used to support different aspects of number, shape and measure in STEPS 3a and 3b, and to explore addition as the inverse of subtraction. The emphasis in this Step is on exploring number relationships, using addition, subtraction, multiplication and division, and on using mental calculation.

Function machines form part of algebra where we need to encourage the children to look for and generalise about (initially in words): (a) patterns; (b) relationships between the input and output numbers or (c) between functions. For instance, a machine which multiplies, then divides by five has a 'do nothing' effect on the output numbers.

You will find function machines being used at various times to support work in other Steps.

> **Mathematics in the National Curriculum**
>
> **Programme of Study: KS2**
> Pupils should be taught to:
> ■ understand and use the relationships between the four operations, including inverses. (N 3.f)
> ■ understand and use the features of a basic calculator, interpreting the display in the context of the problem, including rounding and remainders. (N 3.h)
> ■ choose sequences of methods of computation appropriate to a problem, adapt them and apply them accurately. (N 4.b)
> ■ use diagrams, graphs and simple algebraic symbols. (UA 3.b)
> ■ explain their reasoning. (UA 4.d)

THINKING AND TALKING MATHEMATICALLY

Starting points for discussion

Display some of the terms in the key language box. Can the children show and/or explain what these mean?

Collect examples (drawings, actual objects, photographs, etc.) of machines which are programmed to perform a repetitive task, e.g. vending machines (coin in, drink out); change machines (£1 coin in, 10 x 10p coins out).

> **Key language**
> function, program, machine, input/output number, operation, start, finish, undo, inverse

ACTIVITIES IN DETAIL

A Revision

C P I

1 Display some simple input/output machines of this type, where the children have to calculate input or output numbers:

Resources
Scheme
Resource Master 108

2 Similarly, revise examples of function machines where the children have to determine the function.

3 Points to revise are:
(a) if you know any two of these: input, output or operation, you can calculate the third;
(b) if you want to calculate the operation, you need to trial more than the first example of an given input/output.

4 Introduce RM 108, which provides revision of interpreting one-operation machines and mental calculations.

5 Afterwards, discuss strategies the children used to calculate the input when the operation and output was known. For example, did they use inverse operations to find or check their results, i.e. convert a division to a multiplication or a subtraction to an addition?

This activity provides a good opportunity to revise terms such as 'input', 'output', 'operation' and 'function machine'.

EXTENSION

■ The children can design puzzles like those on RM 108 for others to try out.

B Combined operations machines

C P I

Resources
Scheme
Book 4a, pages 83 and 84;
Resource Master 109

Part 1: Breaking down an operation

1 Display a simple addition such as 5 + 15 = 20.

2 Working in pairs or small groups, ask the children to find:
– pairs of numbers to add to 5 to total 20;
– sets of three numbers to add to 5 to total 20;

264

STEPS 4a

$5 + 3 + 10 + 2$
$5 + 5 + 5 + 5$
$5 + 4 + 5 + 6$

Can you think of any other three operations to add fifteen to five to make twenty?

– sets of four numbers (and beyond if the children wish) to add to 5 to total 20.

2 Using examples provided by the children, show how the single operation, '+15' can be broken down into two or more smaller operations which carry out the same task, e.g.:

1 operation	+15
2 operations	+15+10; +12+3;
3 operations	+3+10+2; +4+5+6;

3 Repeat for an example such as 16 – 9 to show that the operation '– 9' can be broken down into several equivalent operations.

Book 4a, page 83 provides practice in interpreting and devising function machines with related input/output tables which perform equivalent operations. RM 109 includes equivalent function machines which operate using addition and subtraction.

Part 2: Recording operations

1 Introduce the tasks on Book 4a, page 84, in which the children are introduced to a more formal method for recording function machines.

2 Afterwards, discuss how answers to the first task and the Challenge on this page were found.

can be written as → in → (+3) → (+7) → out

C Calculators as function machines   C   I

Resources

School
Calculators

Scheme
Resource Master 110

1 Provide each child with a calculator and revise how it can be programmed to repeat an operation again and again.
For example: Press [C]

Press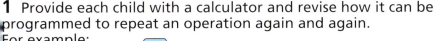

Then press any numbers followed by =, such as:

[1][0][=]
[3][8][=]
[2][9][5][=] etc.

Remind the children not to press C between operations as this undoes the program. If they press C in error, they have to reset the machine.

Ask, *What task or operation is the calculator carrying out? What will the next output number on the display be when you press = after each number chosen?*

2 Can the children suggest how to program the calculator to, say,

subtract 10:   multiply by eight: or divide by three:

STEPS 4a

3 Explain that when you program a calculator to repeat the same operation, this changes it into a function machine.

RM 110 provides individual practice in programming the calculator to divide by six, nine and eight, as well as practising mental recall of division facts.

EXTENSION

■ Provide some examples which are unlikely to be calculated mentally and need to be found by iteration, i.e. trial and improve. For example, press the following keys:

Find out what input numbers you have to key in before you press 'equals' to make the calculator display these numbers: 426, 738, 576, 894.

D Inverse operations   C I

1 Revise addition and subtraction as inverse operations by displaying examples such as these:

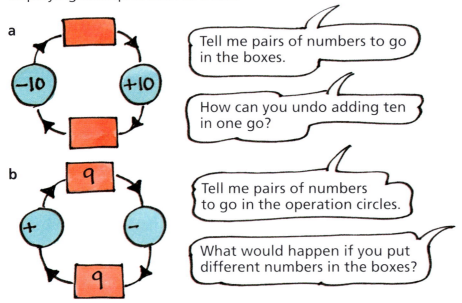

Tell me pairs of numbers to go in the boxes.

How can you undo adding ten in one go?

Tell me pairs of numbers to go in the operation circles.

What would happen if you put different numbers in the boxes?

Resources
School
Calculators

Scheme
Book 4a, page 85

An inverse operation is an operation which 'undoes' a previous operation. For example, ÷ 3 and x 3 are inverse operations because together they have a 'do nothing' effect, i.e. the input and output numbers are identical. For example, 27 → ÷ 3 → 9 → x 3 → 27.

2 Introduce the tasks on Book 4a, page 85, in which the children have to investigate function machines using multiplication and division as inverse operations.

3 Afterwards, see if the children can generalise, after trialling examples, that a multiplication can be 'undone' by a related division, i.e. recognise multiplication and division as inverse operations.

E Scrambled codes   G P

Part 1: Making codes

1 Organise the children to work in twos or threes.

2 Ask, *What can you tell me about coded messages? Who used them? Why? How did the receiver know how to unscramble a coded message?*

Resources
Scheme
Book 4a, page 86;
Resource Master 111

3 Display two sets of operations like these:

4 Demonstrate how, by taking one operation from each set, in any order, you can convert the alphabet into a scrambled code.

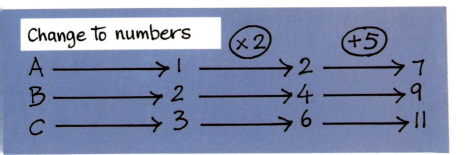

5 In secret, each group can work out a scrambled code for the alphabet using any two operations (after converting the letters to numbers).

6 Note that there are 16 different combinations, each with its own set of output numbers.

Part 2: Breaking codes

1 Once they have worked out their code, for which calculators should be available, they might:
(a) swap their scrambled (output) alphabets with others who try to work out which two combined operations, from the sets displayed in Part 1, stage 3, produced this. (In this way, they will become code-breakers).
(b) write words, names of familiar people, short messages, etc. in their code for other groups to unscramble, using a provided operations key such as this:

2 As the work develops, ask, *What are you doing to try to break the code?* or *If you have a coded message and you know the operations used, what are you doing to decode it?*

3 Afterwards, discuss the patterns and relationships the children found within the tables they created. For example:
(a) If ×2, ×3, ×4 or ×5 has been chosen as one of the operations, the output pattern will grow in increments of two, three four or five.
(b) A series of consecutive numbers operated on in these ways:
→ ×2 → +3 → gives a different set of output numbers from → +3 → ×2 →, but both sets of output numbers increase by two each time.
(c) To undo the operations, you have to work in reverse order and use inverses.

This teacher-led activity is deliberately challenging and intended to make children find strategies to overcome difficulties. It leads the children into recognising the need to use inverse operations, e.g. working backwards so that an alphabet coded using
→ +2 → ×2 →
would have be decoded using → ÷2 → −2 →.

STEPS 4a

Variation

1 Less confident children might scramble the alphabet using a single operation only, e.g. by adding or subtracting any number up to ten.

2 Book 4a, page 86, can be used with RM 111 to provide a more structured approach.

F Assessment activity

I Resources

School
*Function machines

*In advance, prepare machines and tables like these:

Yellow card: In → ×10 → Middle → ×2 → Out

In	Middle	Out
3		
5		
8		

Blue card:
- In → ×2 → +5 → out
- In → ÷2 → −1 → out
- In → ÷6 → ×6 → out
- In → +5 → ×5 → out

In	Out
3	3
6	6
8	8
2	2
10	10

1 Ask the child to explain what the machine (shown in yellow) does.

2 Allow time for the child to complete the table, explaining that where no input number is given, he/she has to choose them.

3 Afterwards, show the child the second (blue) card, and ask, *Which of these machines would give a set of matching input/output numbers like these? Why?*

Assessment notes

Oral response	✔
Practical response	
Pictorial response	✔
Written response	

The child has:
explained how a two-operation machine operates using associated terms;
AND
completed systematically a related input/output table;
AND
recognised multiplication as the inverse of division by matching a function machine to a input/output table.

STRENGTHENING ACTIVITIES

Two-operation machines

If the child can operate one-operation machines but not those with two or more operations, get the child to list, say, pairs of numbers which total five. Show how these can be used as an alternative to adding five in one operation.

Pink card: In → +5 → Out

In	Out
6	11
5	10
2	7
10	15

Green card: In → ○ → Middle → ○ → Out

In	Middle	Out
6	10	11
5	9	10
2	6	7
10	14	15

STEPS 4a

× and ÷ as inverse operations

The child might benefit from writing extended tables like these which relate closely to multiplication tables:

Input numbers beyond 10 might be trialled and recorded with the help of a calculator.

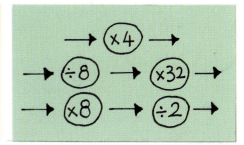

CHALLENGING ACTIVITIES

The child designs equivalent machines which use only the operations of multiplication and division, then feeds in numbers to test them. For example:

IDEAS BOARD

■ Typical projects

Change; Machines; Patterns; Codes; Opposites; Magic

■ History

Find out about famous codes and code-breakers.

■ Wall function machine

With the help of the children, design a giant function machine similar to this.

Affix the circular operations cards with Blu-Tack. The children feed numbers through the machine and record their results on a related table. Can they explain any relationships between the input and output numbers? Can they design machines which do the same in fewer/more operations?
Alter the order of the operations cards to compare what happens.

STEPS 4a   269

HOME/SCHOOL PROJECTS

The child can teach others in the family how to set the constants for addition, subtraction, multiplication or division on the calculator, and how to operate on numbers using these.

SUPPORT MATERIALS

Teaching aids
Texas 1103, 1104 and *Galaxy 9x calculators* (Texas Instruments)

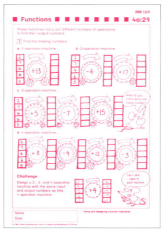

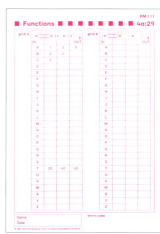

30. DIVISION

Contribution made by this Step

After exploring division facts related to the x 7 table, the children use their knowledge of all multiplication tables to solve division problems, with and without remainders. They also use their knowledge of the effect of multiplying by ten to explore division problems with answers >10.

Objectives

To enable children to:
a Know and apply division facts related to the x 7 table.
b Use pencil-and-paper methods to solve division problems related to tables facts, without and with remainders.
c Develop pencil-and-paper methods to divide two-digit numbers by one-digit numbers with answers > 10.
d Estimate or consider the reasonableness of answers, calculated without or with a calculator.

Background

In Step 23, the children used numbers related to facts in the multiplication tables to practise the skills of division so that answers (quotients) did not exceed ten.

The standard layout for short division was introduced in Step 23 and provides the foundation skills for the long division method introduced here.

Although the children are introduced to standard pencil-and-paper methods for long division, they should not be discouraged from developing informal notation to solve division problems. When solving problems, the children are likely to move between standard and non-standard pencil-and-paper methods, depending on the context or the numbers involved.

Mathematics in the National Curriculum

Programme of Study: KS2
Pupils should be taught to:
■ develop a variety of mental methods of computation with whole numbers up to 100, and explain patterns used; extend mental methods to develop a range of non-calculator methods of computation that involve addition and subtraction of whole numbers, progressing to methods for multiplication and division of up to three-digit by two-digit whole numbers. (N 3.d)
■ understand and use the relationships between the four operations, including inverses. (N 3.f)
■ understand and use the features of a basic calculator, interpreting the display in the context of the problem, including rounding and remainders. (N 3.h)
■ develop their use of the four operations to solve problems, including those involving money and measures, using a calculator where appropriate. (N 4.a)
■ develop their own mathematical strategies and look for ways to overcome difficulties. (UA 2.c)
■ check their results and consider whether they are reasonable. (UA 2.d)

THINKING AND TALKING MATHEMATICALLY

Starting points for discussion

What might 42 ÷ 6 = 7 mean? Tell me a grouping story to show what it means. What about a sharing story?

Investigate grouping arrangements, using the classroom. *If I ask you to sit in twos ... (threes ... eights ... twelves ...), how many groups will there be? Predict, then check. What sizes of equal groups could we have so that there would be no children left over?*

Write different solutions to this: ___ ÷ ___ = 4.

What is the largest remainder you can have if you are dividing by two (...eight ... ten...)? Why?

Key language

divide, groups, share, remainder (rem, r), divisor, count back

STEPS 4a

ACTIVITIES IN DETAIL

A Division facts related to the ×7 table

C P I

Resources

School
Cuisenaire Rods; metre rules; calculators; small blank cards

Scheme
Book 4a, page 87

Part 1: The ÷7 table

1 Display the ×7 table, then, alongside, start to write the corresponding ÷7 table. Ask, *What comes next? Why?*

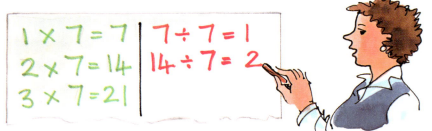

2 When the table is complete, ask, *How are the tables the same (different)?*

Part 2: Mental recall of facts in the ÷7 table

1 Organise some of the following to enable children to practise mental recall:

(a) Display the answers in the ×7 table in random order as centimetre lengths, e.g. 14 cm, 56 cm, 70 cm, etc. Each pair of children has Cuisenaire Rods and a metre rule. They estimate, then check, how many 7 cm rods placed end to end, starting at 0 cm, will be needed to make the given length.

I think we'll need nine to equal sixty-three centimetres.

(b) Each pair of children needs a calculator and cards, placed face downwards in a pack, showing the division expressions for the ÷7 table, e.g. 42 ÷ 7 = , 28 ÷ 7 = (or where the answer is 7, e.g. 35 ÷ 5 =) . They take it in turns to turn over the top card, then one child writes down the answer on paper, while the other uses the calculator to find the answer. Whoever gives the correct answer first, wins that card. On the next round, roles are reversed.

(c) Play *Division bingo*. The children write on a sheet of paper any eight numerals from 1 to 10. You call out division expressions in random order, e.g. 14 ÷ 7, 63 ÷ 7, etc. and the children loop the answer if it is on their card. Play continues until a child (or children) wins by being first to loop all the numbers.

Book 4a, page 87 provides individual practice in problems in which either the divisor or the quotient (answer) is seven.

In Step 27 the children concentrated on facts in the ×7 and 7× tables. This activity provides an opportunity to revise the links between multiplication and division facts in these tables and, using Book 4a, page 87, to recall these mentally.

B Revision of division facts [C] [I]

Resources

School
Counting objects; calculators

Scheme
Book 4a, page 88;
Resource Master 112

1 Using a division expression such as 67 ÷ 9, ask the children to suggest sharing and grouping stories out of which this expression might have arisen. *What do you think the answer will be? How do you know?*

2 Ask the children to work out the answer on paper, using any preferred method, and to compare results and methods with each other.

3 Display some of the informal methods e.g. (a) and include the formal notation also (b):

a $9 \xrightarrow{\times 7} 63 \xrightarrow{+4} 67$
    $\rightarrow 7 \text{ and } 4 \text{ left over}$

b $9 \overline{)67} \quad 7 \, r \, 4$
    $-63 \quad (7 \text{ groups of } 9)$
    4 remainder

4 Remind the children that both the sharing and the grouping stories can be solved using division.

5 Ask the children to work out the same division on the calculator. Do they realise that the displayed answer (7.4444444) means that the answer is 'seven and a bit', i.e. between seven and eight?

6 Introduce the tasks on Book 4a, page 88 which revise division with and without remainders within table facts.

Resource Master 112 provides practice in formal recording.

EXTENSION

■ Suggest a task such as this:
Invent divisions with answers greater than ten with the biggest remainder you can have.

Although formal division notation is revised on page 88, task 5, this method is not imposed on the children and they might prefer informal pencil-and-paper methods to solve the other problems. However, it does provide a reliable method which, if based on understanding, will benefit some children as well as laying the foundations for formal long division notation.

C 'Breaking down' divisions [C] [P] [I]

Resources

Scheme
Resource Masters 113 and 114

Part 1: Revising the grouping aspect of division

1 Through stories, revise the links between repeated subtraction and the grouping aspect of division. *If I share 46 sheets of paper between the six children in this group, how many will each get? How many will be left over?*

2 Relate this to the 'long' division method (a) and the familiar 'short' method (b), using multiplication facts.

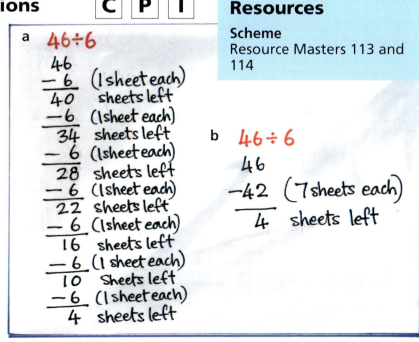

STEPS 4a

3 Ask, *Which way do you prefer? Why?*

4 Display several divisions in which the answer will be between 10 and 20 (initially without remainders) and ask the children, perhaps working in pairs, to try to find the answer using any method they like.

5 Afterwards, discuss results and methods used, and any difficulties encountered.

6 If not suggested, show how a division might be 'broken down' into smaller divisions.

$68 \div 4 \quad 65 \div 5$
$84 \div 6 \quad 133 \div 7$

$68 \div 4$

```
  68
− 20  (5 groups of 4)
  48  left
− 20  (5 groups of 4)  →  17 groups of 4
  28  left
− 28  (7 groups of 4)
   0  left
```

7 Ask, *Can you think of a different way which uses just two subtractions instead of three?*

8 The children can practise 'breaking down' the division in different ways, knowing that the answer should be the same each time.

9 Afterwards, discuss the 'breaking down' they found most convenient and why.

RM 113 provides practice in 'breaking down' the same starting numbers to make them easier to divide.

Part 2: Sharing and 'long' division notation

1 Introduce the tasks on RM 114 which lead the children towards the standard method for long division.

2 Afterwards, discuss the advantages of this method, e.g.:
– multiplying by ten is easier than multiplying by other tables;
– subtracting a multiple of ten is comparatively easy since the units digit remains unchanged;
– splitting a number into tens and units is easier than other splits.

Hopefully, they will recognise that, for these examples, using the ×10 table is most convenient.

RM 113 and 114 highlight the fact that both sharing and grouping problems can be solved using this repeated subtraction method of 'long' division, in two (or sometimes more) manageable stages, using table facts. This is also a useful strategy in mental or informal pencil-and-paper methods, as well as extending knowledge of how numbers work.

EXTENSION

■ Provide simple workcards such as these. The children to try to find all the solutions.

$\square\square \div \square = 8$ remainder 5

$\square\square \div 7 = \square$ remainder 4

■ Display, for the children to solve in their own way, examples of two-digit numbers to be divided by one-digit numbers where the answer will exceed 20, e.g. 456 ÷ 6.

D Solving problems   C I

Resources

School
Counting objects

Scheme
Book 4a, pages 89, 90 and 91

1 Introduce the problems on Book 4a, page 89.

2 Encourage the children to:
– estimate answers first;
– work out the answers using pencil-and-paper methods.

3 Afterwards, compare answers and methods used to find these.

Book 4a, pages 90 and 91, provides practice in mixed operation problems.

EXTENSION

■ The children can write similar division story problems, with answers > 10, for others to try to solve. They should be able to do them themselves first!

E Conventional long division   C I

Resources

Scheme
Book 4a, page 92

1 Display a rectangle of squares in which rows are hidden by, say, a sheet of card, with some related questions:

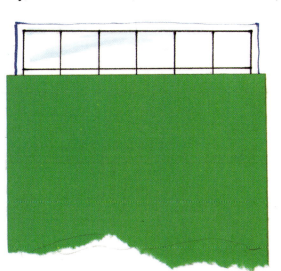

How many rows if there are:
a) 84 squares
b) 78 squares
c) 102 squares
d) 90 squares
e) 114 squares

The method below builds on the standard long multiplication method introduced in Step 4a:27, Activity D, in which the number of elements in rectangular arrays were calculated using the distributive law, e.g. 13 x 4 = (10 x 4) + (3 x 4) = 40 + 12 = 52. But now repeated subtraction is used instead of repeated addition.

2 Ask the children to work out the answers in their own way and to compare these, and methods used, afterwards.

3 If not suggested as one method, extend the notation introduced in Activity C to include the conventional long division notation.

4 The children can then attempt the problems on Book 4a, page 92.

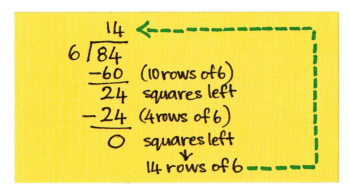

EXTENSION

■ Ask the children to write further divisions without remainders whose answers will be about 10, 20, 30, 40, ... etc.

STEPS 4a

F Checking strategies   C I

Resources
Scheme
Resource Master 115

1 Revise multiplying multiples of ten up to 50 by single-digit numbers and ten, through activities such as:

– getting the children to suggest how tables like these will continue:

– making 'crosses' like these:

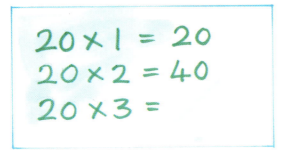

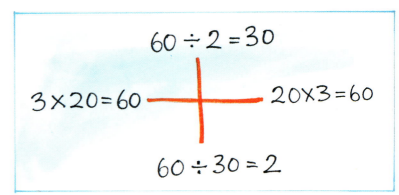

2 Introduce the tasks on RM 115.

G Assessment activity   I

Resources
School
Division cards*

*In advance, make cards like these:

| 7÷7 | 14÷7 | 21÷7 | 28÷7 | 35÷7 |
| 42÷7 | 49÷7 | 56÷7 | 63÷7 | 70÷7 |

What will happen if you share:
a) 45 plums between 7 children?
b) 95 sweets between 5 children?

What will happen if you pack:
a) 63 plums in packs of 7?
b) 64 oranges in packs of 4?

1 Place the ÷ 7 cards face down in random order and ask the child to turn them over one at a time and to tell you the answer.

2 Make sure the child can read the problems on the second card and for each one ask, *Do you think the answer will be greater or less than ten? Why?*

3 Ask the child to find the answers on the second card in his/her own time and in his/her own way, without using a calculator.

4 Afterwards, discuss results and how these were calculated.

Assessment notes

Oral response	✔
Practical response	
Pictorial response	✔ (depending on the strategy chosen for 3)
Written response	✔

The child has:
given at least eight correct answers out of ten to facts in the ÷ 7 table;
AND
given reasonable estimates of expected answers to four division problems;

AND
used pencil and paper methods to solve two problems requiring division by seven within the tables facts;
AND
used pencil and paper methods to solve two division problems with answers > 10.

STRENGTHENING ACTIVITIES

÷ 7 table facts

If the child knows the x 7 table, she/he may benefit from making a display like this for each multiple of seven so that the multiplication facts are closely linked to the division facts:

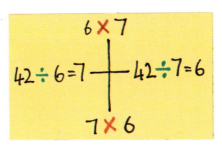

'Long' division

If the child cannot achieve objective **c** (division with answers greater than 10 using pencil and paper methods), she/he may be able to achieve this with the help of apparatus. Cuisenaire Rods, with which the children will be familiar, might help. For example, 98 ÷ 7 can be solved by placing 7-rods along a metre rule until 98 cm is reached and counting how many rods are needed.

Checking answers

For the moment, less confident children should at least be able to say whether an answer will be greater or less than ten, using their knowledge of the x 10 table. The calculator can also be used as a checking device provided you know that the child can interpret the display.

CHALLENGING ACTIVITIES

Provide some missing number cards like these:

Find all the possible ways of putting numbers in these.

a. ☐ ÷ 8 = 14 remainder ☐

b. ☐ ÷ 11 = 21 remainder ☐

There will be eight solutions for example **a** and eleven for **b**, if a 0 remainder is included.

HOME/SCHOOL PROJECTS

Give everyone the same division expression, e.g. 56 ÷ 7. The child and others at home decide on a 'story' for this, write or draw it to show what it means and find the answer.

STEPS 4a

IDEAS BOARD

■ Sharing and grouping

The children contribute stories out of which a given division expression might have arisen, such as 56 ÷ 7 (see *Home/School Projects*). Then these are sorted into two sets, and displayed in book form, or as a sorting diagram (see right).

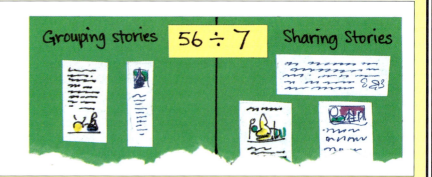

■ Number trios

The children make cards like these from 2 cm squares with the product of the two outer numbers in the middle. They take it in turn to cover any one of these numbers and the second child has to calculate the missing number.

SUPPORT MATERIALS

Teaching aids
Cuisenaire Rods (NES Arnold)
Metre Rules (Taskmaster)
Texas 1103, 1104 and *Galaxy 9x calculators* (Texas Instruments)

Teachers' reference materials
Primary Mathematics Today, 3rd edn, chapter 15, Elizabeth Williams and Hilary Shuard

Software
Guzinter from *Number Games*, Anita Straker (ILECC)

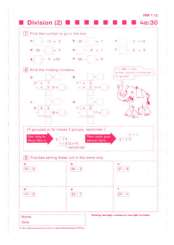   

31. REFLECTION

LEARNING CONTEXT

Contribution made by this Step

The children extend and enrich their understanding of reflective symmetry through the creation and analysis of symmetrical designs, and use symmetrical properties as part of the classification of 2-D shapes, seeking simple generalisations about their characteristics.

Objectives

To enable children to:
a Create and analyse shapes and patterns with two (or more) axes of reflective symmetry.
b Use axes of symmetry as an aid to classification of 2-D shapes.

Background

Reflective symmetry is a characteristic of certain shapes and designs.
   Symmetrical shapes are aesthetically pleasing and worthy of study in their own right. However, reflection, along with translation and rotation, also has a dynamic aspect. Children should be able to manipulate and design reflections. They should develop a range of techniques for making increasingly complex symmetrical designs before combining symmetry with angle and length in the analysis of the characteristics of 2-D and 3-D shapes.
   The overall purpose of this Step is to begin making valid generalisations about the features of 'mathematical' and 'environmental' shapes.

> **Mathematics in the National Curriculum**
>
> **Programme of Study: KS2**
> Pupils should be taught to:
> - visualise and describe shapes and movements, developing precision in using related geometrical language. (SSM 2.a)
> - make 2-D and 3-D shapes and patterns with increasing accuracy, recognise their geometrical features and properties, and use these to classify shapes and solve problems. (SSM 2.b)
> - recognise reflective symmetries of 2-D and 3-D shapes. (SSM 2.c)
> - transform 2-D shapes by translation, reflection and rotation, and visualise movements and simple transformations to create and describe patterns. (SSM 3.a)

THINKING AND TALKING MATHEMATICALLY

Starting points for discussion

Display *Magic Puzzle Book* and *Magic Mirror Books* (see Support Materials).

Wallpaper and fabric designs: *Can you find a motif or a section of the design which shows reflection?*

A drawing of a large (isosceles) triangle: *How could you describe this shape so that everyone would know exactly what it looks like?*

> **Key language**
>
> symmetry, symmetrical, pattern, balance, reflect(ion), reflective, axis, axes, fold, whole, complete, halve, match, 'flip', image, triangle, quadrilateral, regular

ACTIVITIES IN DETAIL

A Folding and cutting

Resources

School
Paper shapes (squares and circles, at least – gummed, on plain, squared or tracing paper); carbon paper; scissors; pins; glue; safe mirrors or Miras

Scheme
Book 4a, page 93

1 Briefly remind the children of previous activities creating shapes with one axis of symmetry.

2 Ask the children to use paper squares or circles and carefully and accurately to fold the paper into four.

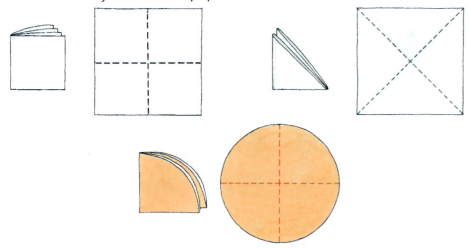

3 Ask them to open out the paper. Encourage them to recognise that the fold lines are axes of symmetry of the paper shape.

4 Revise and extend the ways of creating designs which have two axes of symmetry, beginning with marking, drawing and cutting only around the fold lines.

Tracing paper is useful because designs drawn can be seen from both sides and through several sheets so that copying and cutting out a shape can be exact.

Mirrors or Miras should be available to check the symmetry of developing and completed designs.

Pin pricking

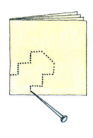 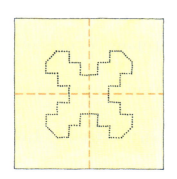

Carbon paper

  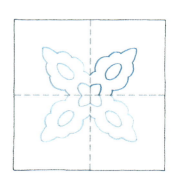

Drawing and cutting

cutout

frame

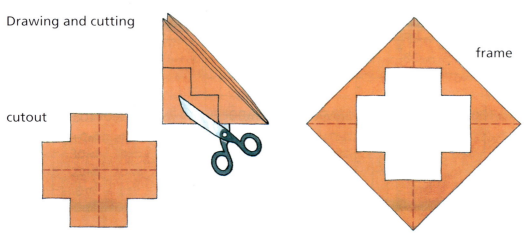

280

STEPS 4a

5 Encourage the children to develop the ideas to include marking and cutting the outer edges of the paper, including 'exploding' paper shapes.

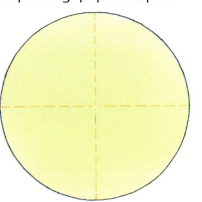
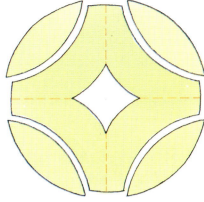

6 Remind the children that, by carefully saving the pieces which have been cut out, or cut off, a 'shadow' symmetrical design can be made.

Use Book 4a, page 93 for further practice.

EXTENSION

■ The children use the folding and cutting technique to create 'snowflakes' which show one, two, three, four or eight axes of symmetry.

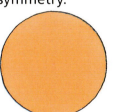

To achieve three or six axes of symmetry, careful estimation of a third of a shape is needed.

B Grid symmetry   G P I

Resources

School
Grid designs*; pegboards and coloured pegs; pin boards and rubber bands; binca squares; tapestry needles; embroidery thread/wool in several colours

Scheme
Selection from Resource Masters A, C, D, F, G and H (grid and lattice papers); Resource Master 116; Book 4a, pages 94 and 95

*In advance, prepare some simple examples of grid designs showing two (or more) axes of symmetry, based upon various available grids.

Part 1: Grid papers

1 Show some of the prepared grid designs. Ask, *What do you notice about these designs? How many axes of symmetry can you see? How can you check for reflective symmetry?*

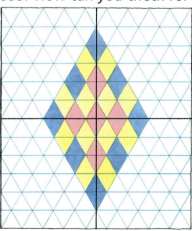
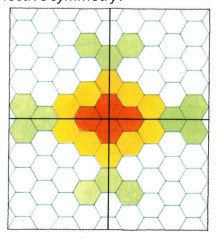

2 Explain that the whole pattern in these designs is built up from a pattern in just one sector. The pattern of lines, marks or colours is first reflected in one axis, and then the two completed sectors are reflected in the second axis.

3 Ask the children to work in pairs. They choose a grid or dot lattice design and draw two axes of reflective symmetry. Then one child draws a pattern of lines, colours or shapes in one sector (not always the top left-hand side!).

4 Ask the second child to construct the reflection of the pattern in an adjacent sector. They then take turns to complete the other sectors of the design.

5 Encourage the children to try designs based on diagonal axes as well as horizontal and vertical axes. *Does this depend on the design of the grid that is being used?*

Encourage the use of a pegboard or pinboard to experiment with possible solutions before committing the work to paper!

Check carefully that the position of the axes does in fact allow a design with two valid axes to be constructed.

Part 2: Binca and cross-stitch patterns

1 Using 5 mm squared paper or RM C, ask the children to mark the horizontal and vertical axes of symmetry and lightly to mark up to 50 crosses in pencil in one quadrant, one to a square, so that the marked squares form a continuous block.

2 Ask them to choose two colours and 'go over' the crosses.

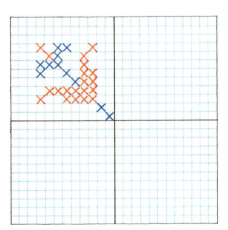 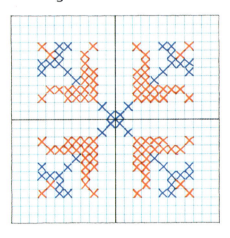

3 The children then reflect this pattern across the axes as before.

4 Use the binca squares. The children mark the horizontal and vertical axes, using running stitch, then transfer the design from the squared paper, one quadrant at a time, using cross stitch.

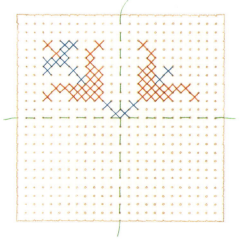

Each hole on the binca is matched to the position of the intersection of a horizontal and a vertical line on the paper.

Further activities which develop the idea of two axes can be found on RM 116 and Book 4a, pages 94 and 95.

C Symmetry and polygons

Part 1: Triangles

1 Give groups a selection of triangles of different types and sizes. Ask the children to find, by using a mirror and then by folding, the axes of symmetry. The axes should be clearly marked using a felt-tipped pen and ruler.

Resources

School
Gummed paper shapes (including several of each with different angles and/or dimensions); safe mirrors or Miras; felt-tipped pens

Scheme
Resource Masters 117–121

isosceles

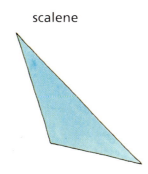
scalene

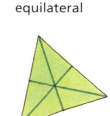
equilateral

2 Use, for example, the isosceles triangle. If it is folded along the (single) axis of symmetry, the children can be encouraged to see that the axis of symmetry:
– divides the 'base' into two equal parts;
– bisects the 'top' angle;
– is perpendicular to the base;
– divides the area of the triangle into two equal amounts.
Also the fold along the axis of symmetry shows that:
– two of the sides are of equal length;
– two of the angles are of equal size.

3 Ask the children to investigate the other triangles in a similar way. *Does it have axes of symmetry? What can we say about other characteristics of the triangles, by folding* (or being unable to fold in the case of a scalene triangle!) *along axes of symmetry?*

4 Encourage the children to suggest generalisations. For example, *All isosceles triangles have one axis of symmetry, two equal angles, two equal sides …*

Part 2: Quadrilaterals

1 Give the children the opportunity to investigate various quadrilaterals (e.g. square, rectangle (oblong), rhombus, parallelogram, trapezium, kite, 'arrowhead', and irregular quadrilateral) in a similar way.

2 Encourage the children to suggest generalisations about the shapes. For example, 'All squares have four axes of symmetry, four equal angles, four equal sides …'

Part 3: Regular polygons

1 Issue a range of *regular* polygons. Ask the children to find, mark and count all the axes of symmetry. They then fold along the axes and say what they know about angles and lengths of sides. Encourage them to generalise the findings by completing the statement: 'All regular polygons have …'

RMs 117–121 provide reinforcement of this activity.

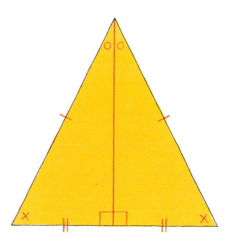

'…the same number of axes of symmetry, sides and angles.'

STEPS 4a

D Assessment activity | I

1 Ask the child to choose a lattice paper and draw a pattern or shape which has two axes of symmetry, clearly showing the axes.

2 Ask the child to choose a paper 2-D shape which has symmetry. Ask him or her to fold it along the axis (or axes), describe the shape as fully as possible, explaining how the folding provides the information.

3 Repeat, using another shape if appropriate.

Resources

School
Paper polygons (triangles, quadrilaterals, regular 2-D shapes)

Scheme
Resource Masters F and G (1 cm squared and 1 cm triangular lattice paper)

Assessment notes

Oral response	✔
Practical response	✔
Pictorial response	✔
Written response	

The child has:
recognised and constructed a simple shape which has two axes of symmetry;
AND
accurately suggested general features of some simple 2-D shapes based on their symmetry.

STRENGTHENING ACTIVITIES

Reflection games

Confusion about matching positions of points in reflection can be helped by use of simple games on a pegboard (or square lattice or grid paper). The children work in pairs, matching positions and colours of pegs placed in four quadrants.

Pairs and fours

If children become confused about reflecting shapes, give practice in constructing symmetrical designs using two, and then four, of a single 2-D shape. For example, combining two parallelograms, then four:

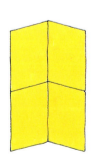 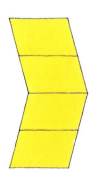 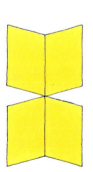

Can you make a pattern with one axis ... two axes of reflective symmetry?

A large-scale example of this uses a trapezium-shaped classroom table.

CHALLENGING ACTIVITIES

Changing reflective symmetry

Using a set of 2-D shapes, the children investigate the construction of patterns of shapes. For example:

What happens if, for example, you:
– add more triangles?
– move the triangles you started with?
– use a different shape as the base shape?
– use a differently shaped piece for 'add-ons'?
– use two or more different shapes as 'add-ons'?

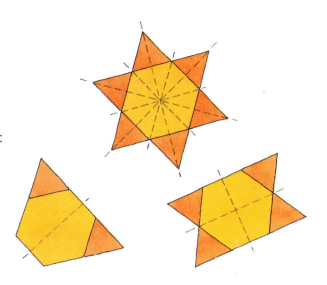

HOME/SCHOOL PROJECTS

The children look for examples of reflective symmetry in the home and garden – windows, chair backs, fireplaces and so on. Ask them to make a sketch of the more interesting designs and bring them into school for display and discussion.

SUPPORT MATERIALS

Teaching aids
Reflecto (Hope Education)
Symmetry in Nature Posters (PCET)
Structuring and Appreciation of Symmetry Activity Kit (Philip and Tacey)
Geometric Gummed Shapes (Playaway)
Safe Mirrors (Taskmaster)
Actipacks: Investigating Mirrors (NES Arnold)
Miras Mirrors and Booklet (NES Arnold)
Roamer (Valiant Technology)
Pip (Swallow Systems)

Teachers' reference materials
Mathematics through Art and Design, Anne Woodman and Eric Albany (Collins Educational)
Maths Plus: Shape 1 and 2, Paul Harling (Ward Lock Educational)

M is for Mirror, Duncan Birmingham (Tarquin Publications)
Magic Mirror Book, Second Magic Mirror Book, Magic Cylinder Book, Magic Puzzle Book, Marion Walter (Tarquin Publications)

Software
Alice and *Mirror* from *MicroSMILE 3 11 More* (ILECC)
Newtiles from *MicroSMILE 2 Next 17* (ILECC)
Tilekit from *SLIMWAM 2* (ATM)
Symmetry Patterns from *Maths With a Story 1* (ILECC)
Mosaic (AUME)
Kaleidoscope (ESM)
Picture Craft (BBC Software)
Paint Pot – Symmetry Pictures (RML)

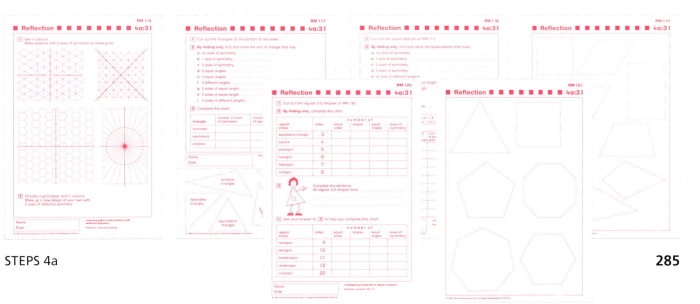

IDEAS BOARD

■ Typical projects
Opposites; Patterns; Reflections; Change; Growth; Shape and Size; Materials

■ Curve stitching
Create examples of curve stitching which show one, then two axes of reflective symmetry. (The children can plan and sketch on paper first.)

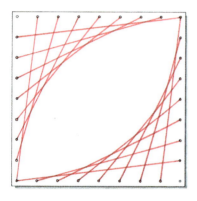

■ Miras
Experiment with symmetry using Miras. These are mirrors which are both transparent and reflecting to allow the position of the image to be clearly seen.

■ PE
In PE ask children to show reflective symmetry:
– with their own bodies;
– in pairs or fours, reflecting body positions when standing still;
– in pairs or fours, developing and performing reflective movements.

■ LOGO, Turtle, Roamer and Pip
Experiment drawing symmetrical shapes on the screen, or symmetrical movements of the Roamer or Pip. Children might work in pairs, one child drawing a path or design, the other completing its reflection across an agreed axis.

■ Folded paper capital letters
Investigate which letters of the alphabet can be created by folding and cutting to use one or two axes or symmetry.

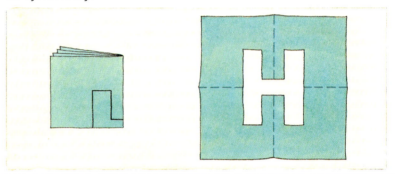

■ Faces
– Collect pictures, drawings or magazine cuttings of faces. Place a mirror so that children can see that they are rarely exactly symmetrical (except by design!).
– Cut pictures of faces in half and get the children to draw the missing halves.

■ Flight
Discuss the fact that birds, butterflies, insects and aeroplanes need to have reflective symmetry in order to be able to fly effectively.

■ Water
Collect and discuss pictures of boats, or coastlines, or river banks, reflected in water. *Is it a true and full reflection? If not, why not?*

■ Wallpaper
Use old pattern books. The children can try to cut out a section which shows reflection in one or two axes.

32. LOGIC

LEARNING CONTEXT

Contribution made by this Step

The children use and interpret sorting diagrams such as Carroll, Venn and decision tree, to sort objects, using three criteria.

Objectives

To enable children to:
a Use decision trees or Venn diagrams to represent the results of classification, using three criteria.
b Identify the attributes of objects within the regions of sorting diagrams.

Background

The children have already had considerable experience of using Venn and Carroll diagrams to represent the result of classification using two different criteria. These are now extended to three criteria. Related tree diagrams, with questions created by the teacher, have also been used on various occasions in group and class activities, e.g. Steps 3b:38, page 334. Here there is more emphasis on the children taking individual responsibility for using and interpreting such diagrams. A decision tree is a simple form of flow diagram, indicating the order in which decisions have to be made. The decisions involve analysing systematically identified attributes of a collection.

In Steps 4b, the children will take more responsibility for creating their own decision trees with questions, and for interpreting other types of simple flow diagram.

You will be able to think of ways to use these diagrams across the curriculum, e.g. in science, to classify natural and manufactured objects, as well as support mathematics itself.

> **Mathematics in the National Curriculum**
>
> **Programme of Study: KS2**
> Pupils should be taught to:
> ■ recognise ... geometrical features and properties, and use these to classify shapes and solve problems. (SSM 2.b)
> ■ collect and represent discrete data appropriately using graphs and diagrams, including block graphs, pictograms and line graphs; interpret a wider range of graphs and diagrams that represent data, including pie charts, using a computer where appropriate. (HD 2.b)
> ■ use diagrams, graphs and simple algebraic symbols. (UA 3.b)

THINKING AND TALKING MATHEMATICALLY

Starting points for discussion

Asking or responding to questions which can have 'yes' or 'no' responses only.

Thinking of opposites such as *It can/cannot, it has/has not, it is/is not*, etc.

Display, say, {2, 4, 6, 8, 10, 12, 14}. *What set of numbers do you think I have put in the brackets? Why do you think the brackets are useful?*

> **Key language**
>
> Venn diagram, Carroll diagram, intersection, decision tree, identify, describe, sort, decide, bracket notation for sets, e.g. {1, 3, 5}; set, yes, no, decision boxes, sorting diagram, curly brackets (braces) for recording sets, e.g. (set of) first three odd numbers = {1, 3, 5}.

STEPS 4a

ACTIVITIES IN DETAIL

A Three-criteria Venn diagram C G I

1 Provide each group with a supply of logic blocks. (If part-sets are given to each group, these should be a random selection.)

2 Revise the attributes of logic blocks by asking the children to describe the four attributes (colour, size, shape, thickness) of a chosen block to each other.

This block is yellow, large, triangular and thin.

3 Agree on two criteria for sorting the blocks and get the children in each group to take turns to place a logic block in a Venn diagram made with hoops and two labels.

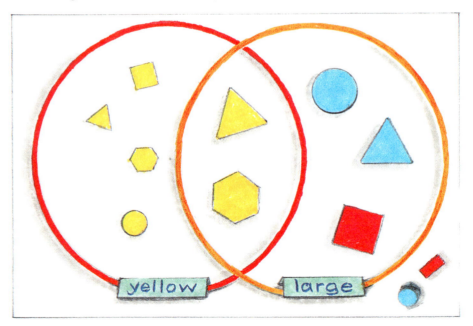

4 Afterwards, ask why blocks have been placed in a certain region (including the region outside the hoops).

5 *What if you wanted to sort the blocks in three ways – red, triangles and large?* Allow time for the children to try to adapt the sorting diagram (with spare hoops and labels readily available).

6 If necessary, introduce the conventional three-criteria Venn diagram and get children to take turns to place a block in the correct region.

Resources

School
Sorting or PE hoops, three for each group; logic blocks (preferably including hexagons); strips of card about 15 cm x 5 cm

Scheme
Book 4a, pages 96 and 97; Resource Master 122

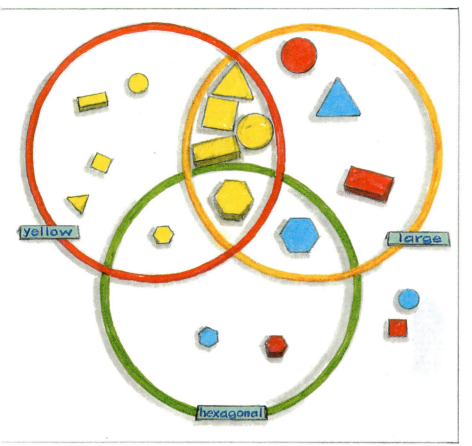

The edges of the table form the boundary of the eighth region, outside the three hoops.

If you have other structured logic sets, use these instead of, or as well as, the logic blocks and modify the sorting labels accordingly. Remind the children that there is no such thing as, say, a 'thick triangle' or 'thin triangle', only blocks which are thick or thin with end faces which are triangular.

7 Ask questions such as:
(a) *How many different regions are there?*
(b) *In which region do shapes which are yellow, hexagonal but not large go?*
(c) *Why do all these shapes belong in this intersection?*

Book 4a, page 96, provides related work for which logic blocks and the hoops may be needed. The task is suited to paired work for children who work well in this way. Page 97 provides similar but more demanding work. RM 122 can be used to sort other collections using three criteria, e.g. using numbers, names, small drawings, etc., at different times.

Variation

The children can compare the eight-region Venn diagram with the eight-region Carroll diagram. (There is a one-to-one correspondence between the eight regions, e.g. the upper left region here corresponds with the intersection of the three sets in the preceding illustration.)

STEPS 4a   289

B Three-criteria decision tree   C I

Resources

School
3-D geometric shapes (familiar and unfamiliar); chalk or masking tape*

*In advance, in a large space, prepare with chalk or masking tape a diagram like this which the children can walk along. (The rhombic question boxes can be made with offset squares.)

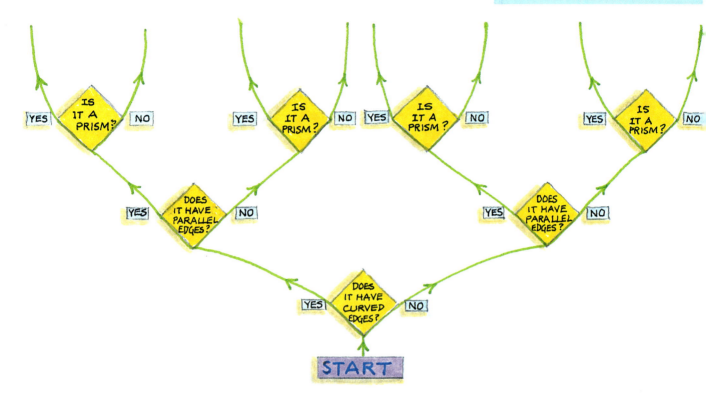

1 Ask for volunteers to negotiate the decision tree by walking up it with a chosen 3-D shape. When a junction is reached, the question is read aloud and the child asked to answer 'yes' or 'no'. Do the spectators agree?

2 As the activity progresses, ask questions such as:
(a) *Why is (Jack) standing at the end of this branch?*
(b) *What shape should (Jasmin) choose to end up in this region?*
(c) *Why are there no shapes at the end of this branch?*
(d) *How is this sorting diagram different from/same as the Venn diagram?* (Some children may, for example, spot that the left-hand region corresponds with the common intersection of the three sorting hoops from the previous activity.)
(e) *What do you think will happen if we alter the order in which the questions are asked?*

3 Try to leave the diagram in position to try some of these variations.

This activity provides a good opportunity to revise some of the properties of 3-D shapes. Even though the names of unfamiliar shapes are not known, they can still be sorted and names introduced informally.

Variations

1 Use questions suggested by and related to the children themselves, e.g. *Do you play a racquet game? Do you have a pet? Do you like yoghurt?*

2 Use questions related to a theme, e.g. Feet. *Are you wearing black shoes? Do your shoes have laces? Are you wearing stripy socks?*

3 Use other structured logic sets.

C Decision tree with questions

1 Provide each group with assorted plane shapes. (One of each shape from the sets of 2-D geometric shapes will suffice.)

2 Revise the names of the shapes in the set.

3 Get the children to suggest words/phrases to describe the properties of shapes and list these.

> tessellates
> has curved sides
>   straight sides
> has acute
>   (right, reflex) angles
> has parallel sides
> has line symmetry
> has some (all) equal sides
> has some (all) equal angles

Resources

School
Geometric 2-D shapes

Scheme
Book 4a, pages 98 and 99;
Resource Master 123

4 Introduce RM 123 and together decide on two questions you might ask to sort the shapes which would give an answer of 'yes' or 'no'. Write these in the rhombus-shaped decision boxes. For example:

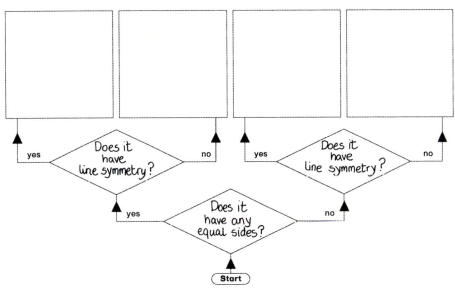

Conventionally, questions in flow diagrams, of which decision trees are a simple example, are enclosed in rhombus-shaped decision boxes from which there are two exit routes, i.e. a 'Yes' or 'No' option (called a binary operation); so questions have to be worded appropriately.

5 The children now slide one shape at a time up the tree until it reaches the end of the correct branch. (Sometimes the choice of questions will result in empty sets at the end of some branches.)

6 If recording is required, the children can draw and colour reduced versions of the shapes or write the names of the shapes.

Book 4a, pages 98 and 99, introduce a third criteria for sorting shapes on a decision tree and related problems. (Some children will benefit from tackling these pages with a partner, since they have to make decisions and justify choices through logical thinking.)

D Number decisions   C G P I

Resources

School
Scissors

Scheme
Resource Master 124*

*Since the children are recommended to work in pairs or threes, you may wish to photocopy one copy of RM 124 only for each team.

1 Introduce the conventional way of writing the members of a set, i.e. using curly brackets (often referred to as braces) and discuss one or two examples, e.g. ask the children to name the first five multiples of seven.

First five multiples of 7 = {7, 14, 21, 28, 35}

An empty set (one with no members) can be represented like this: { }.

2 Organise the children to work in twos or threes and introduce the task on RM 124. (Do not help unless absolutely necessary – the children should try to find ways to overcome difficulties with each other's help.)

3 During and afterwards, ask questions, *Why have you put these numbers at the end of this branch? Where do you think (say) fourteen will go? Why? Can you see any links between the numbers in any subsets?*

EXTENSION

■ Can the children design a decision tree which asks four questions about the same (or another) set of 20 numbers, e.g. *Is it a multiple of two? Is it a multiple of three? Is it a one-digit number? Is it even?*

E Sorting one collection in different ways   C I

Resources

Scheme
Book 4a, page 100;
Resource Master 125

1 Introduce the tasks on Book 4a, page 100 and RM 125 in which the children have to transfer raw data to a related table, decision tree and Venn diagram, i.e. sort the same collection in different ways.

2 Afterwards, ask the children to comment on:
– which method of representing the data they preferred and why;
– links between the three methods of presentation.

EXTENSION

■ The children can choose three criteria, organise a survey similar to that on Book 4a, page 100 and represent the information in different ways.

F Assessment activity   I

Resources

School
Geometric 2-D shapes in assorted colours (including green)

Scheme
Book 4a, page 98

1 Ask the child to explain how the decision tree works.

2 Indicate the shape drawn on one of the end branches and ask, *Why did this shape get positioned here?*

3 Choose a green shape from the geometric 2-D shapes and ask the child to decide where it would go on the decision tree.

4 Ask, *Why does it belong there?*
5 Repeat stages 3 and 4 twice more with two other shapes chosen by the child.

Assessment notes

Oral response	✔
Practical response	✔
Pictorial response	
Written response	

The child has:
used a decision tree diagram representing the results of classification using three criteria;
AND
identified the three attributes of a 2-D shape on a completed decision tree;
AND
identified the regions in which to position at least two 2-D geometric shapes on a three-criteria decision tree and justified his/her decision.

STRENGTHENING ACTIVITIES

Sorting diagrams

Less able children are likely to find the decision tree easier than the Venn diagram since they can make one decision at a time. (On the Venn diagram, you have to consider the three criteria simultaneously.) If the child can interpret the three-decision tree by saying why objects are in a particular region and can manoeuvre objects into the correct region, he/she can still achieve the learning objectives.

Revision

If the child is having difficulties sorting collections using three criteria, he/she may benefit from revision of two-criteria sorting, e.g. Book 3b, page 90, and RM 139.

CHALLENGING ACTIVITIES

Logic blocks

Using logic blocks, can the child decide on three criteria to sort these which do not relate to the standard attributes, i.e. colour, size, shape or thickness. For example, this block has these attributes also:

Having decided on the three criteria, the child designs a suitable sorting diagram to represent the classification.

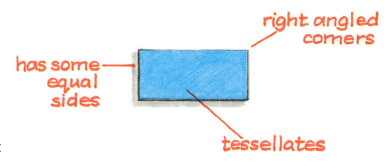

HOME/SCHOOL PROJECTS

Having tried out the activity at school, the child takes home a copy of RM 124 and teaches others in his/her family what to do.
 In advance at school, decide on three criteria for sorting, say, kitchen utensils, which are written on to the set labels on RM 124. The child, with the help of his/her family, tries to draw or write the name of at least one object in each region.

STEPS 4a

IDEAS BOARD

■ Typical projects
Ourselves, Logic, Shape and Size; Opposites; Materials; Animals

■ Across the curriculum
You can adapt the ideas in this Step for use with other current learning. For example, in science, children could decide on questions to sort familiar electrical goods. Or they could sort natural forms, e.g. birds.

■ Punched cards and a three-criteria Venn diagram

The children can revise the use of punched cards by designing sets, one to correspond with each item being sorted on to a three-criteria Venn diagram or decision tree.

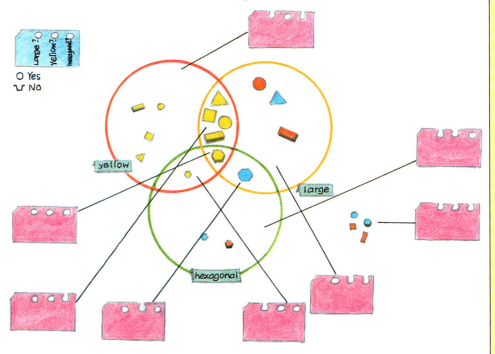

SUPPORT MATERIALS

Teaching aids
Geometric Shapes (NES Arnold)
Logic Blocks (NES Arnold)
Table Top Relations and Functions Cards (NES Arnold)
Attribute Cylinders (NES Arnold)
Table Top Logic Activity Cards (NES Arnold)
Basic Solid Shapes and Solid Shapes Sets (NES Arnold)

Teachers' reference materials
Primary Mathematics Today, 3rd edn, Elizabeth Williams and Hilary Shuard (Longman)
Hands On – Attribute Blocks (Hope Education)
Geometric Plane Shapes (Hope Education)

Software
Branch (MEP)

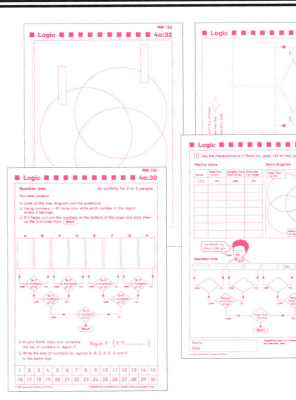

294
STEPS 4a

33. TESSELLATION

LEARNING CONTEXT

Contribution made by this Step

The children:
- construct from given information and choose the materials or mathematics to create tessellations using different techniques;
- investigate the tessellating properties of triangles leading to simple hypotheses or generalisations;
- start to learn about semi-regular tessellations.

Objectives

To enable children to:
a Continue or construct tessellations from given information.
b Test statements, hypothesise or make simple generalisations about the tessellating properties of triangles.
c Select the materials or mathematics to create a tessellation.

Background

In Step 3b:31, the children investigated the properties of familiar 2-D and 3-D shapes to find out if they tessellated. They also experimented to see what happened if two matching shapes, known to tessellate individually, were joined along a full edge or part of an edge.

The study of tessellation is closely linked with the geometry of movement – tiles have to be translated, rotated and/or reflected to make them link with other shapes without gaps or overlaps.

In later handbooks, more complex construction techniques will be used to construct tessellations and the links with angular measure more closely examined as the children start to measure angles in degrees.

> **Mathematics in the National Curriculum**
>
> **Programme of Study: KS2**
> Pupils should be taught to:
> ■ make 2-D and 3-D shapes and patterns with increasing accuracy, recognise their geometrical features and properties, and use these to classify shapes and solve problems. (SSM 2.b)
> ■ select and use the appropriate mathematics and materials. (UA 2.a)
> ■ understand and investigate general statements. (UA 4.a)
> ■ search for patterns in their results. (UA 4.b)
> ■ make general statements of their own, based on evidence they have produced. (UA 4.c)
> ■ explain their reasoning. (UA 4.d)

THINKING AND TALKING MATHEMATICALLY

Starting points for discussion

Brochures advertising wall, floor tiles, etc.; examples of unusual tiles.

Examples of artefacts decorated with tessellating units.

Altair design pads or unusual grid papers.

Examples of Islamic art.

> **Key language**
>
> tessellate, gap, overlap, arrangement, pattern, slide/translate, reflect/flip over, regular, semi-regular, motif

STEPS 4a

ACTIVITIES IN DETAIL

A Revision

Organise at least one of the following activities as revision.

Will it or will it not tessellate?

1 Provide groups of children with sets of matching 2-D shapes.

2 Get the children to predict then check which shapes will tessellate, i.e. fit together without gaps or overlaps in a systematic and predictable way, so that the pattern can continue indefinitely.

3 Results can be displayed on a sorting diagram. (Shapes can be affixed temporarily with Blu-Tack if necessary.)

G Resources

School
Sets of 2-D geometric shapes with matching sets of shapes, e.g. Pattern Block pieces, Logic Blocks, Geometric Shapes; scrap card; large sheets of paper; Blu-Tack (optional); sticky tape

Scheme
Resource Master 126

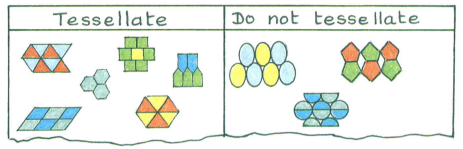

Composite tessellations

1 Using shapes known to tessellate, the children can experiment with combining pairs of these by taping them together along either fully- or partially-touching sides.

2 They now try to make these tessellate by fitting together several matching tiles or by drawing the outlines repeatedly so that they create a tessellation.

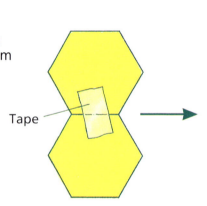

Creating a tessellation

1 Starting with a card rectangle, the children slide to the opposite side pieces cut from two adjacent sides and tape these in position.

2 They now use this as a template to create an individualised tessellation. (They may need to try several designs before they get one they like.)

RM 126 provides further practice in continuing and creating simple tessellations from given information.

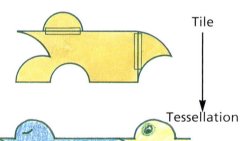

EXTENSION

■ Provided with assorted grid papers, the children can experiment with designing tessellations, simple or complex.

B   Tessellating triangles

`C` `I`

Resources

School
Plastic, card and/or gummed paper triangles to include equilateral, isosceles, scalene, and right-angled; large sheets of plain paper; shape stencils

Scheme
Book 4a, page 101; Resource Master 127

1 Ask questions like, *What kinds of triangles can you name? What is special about a scalene (isosceles, equilateral) triangle?*

2 Introduce the task on Book 4a, page 101 in which the children explore possibilities for tessellating identical triangles.

3 Make sure the children are familiar with any resources available for them to choose for help.

4 As work progresses,
(a) point out any errors, for example, arrangements which create gaps or overlaps or where the positioning of the triangles is random rather than predictable;
(b) ask the children to predict if triangle families not yet tested will tessellate;
(c) encourage the children to persevere if the tessellation does not work out straightaway.

5 If necessary, demonstrate this method which uses paper scalene triangles.

(a) Mark the vertices **a**, **b** and **c**. (This helps to keep track of the process and to avoid flipping over the triangles.)
(b) Secure one triangle on the paper (shown with an asterisk on the following illustrations).

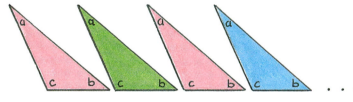

(c) Fit another triangle on top and then rotate the second triangle so that two identical sides are aligned. (Vertices **a** and **b** will now be at opposite ends of the joining line.)
(d) Repeat the previous stage for each of the two remaining sides.
(e) Continue in this way, building outwards from these four triangles.

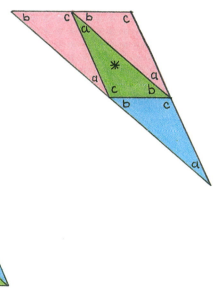

6 Afterwards, ask the children to look for straight angles in the tessellations they have created. (If they have trialled the method explained in stage 5, each straight angle will consist of an **a**, **b** and **c** angle.)

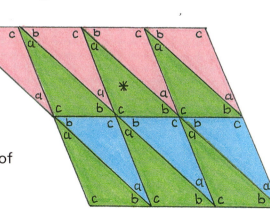

7 Ask, Do you think *all* matching triangles can be made to tessellate?

RM 127 provides a more structured approach in which the children create tessellations from triangles from given information.

EXTENSION

■ The children can try to adapt this technique to try to make different quadrilaterals tessellate.

C Semi-regular tessellations   C I

*If commercial sets of stencils or templates are not available, photocopy directly on to strong card (or mount afterwards on card) RM 128 which provides suitable sets in two sizes.

1 Revise by asking, *What is the meaning of 'regular 2-D shapes'? Which ones tessellate? Can you think of any which don't? What do you think a regular tessellation is? Why?*

2 Introduce, by referring to Book 4a, page 102, the term 'semi-regular' to describe a tessellation made from more than one regular shape, for example:

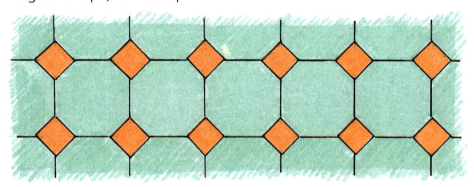

3 Encourage the children to persevere with the tasks and to try to overcome difficulties, particularly in task 3 where more than one attempt may be needed to achieve the tessellation.

4 Afterwards, discuss which shape they found best to start off each tessellation in task 2 and why. (Generally, it is the polygon with the greatest number of sides.)

EXTENSION

■ Using the small and large square from RM 128, can the children design a semi-regular tessellation? This is one possibility:

What about the two sizes of equilateral triangle? This is also possible!

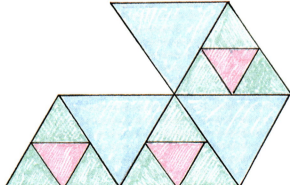

■ *What would happen if you started with a regular pentagon? What other shape(s) would you need to create a tessellation?*

Resources

School
Stencils or templates of regular shapes of uniform length of side (equilateral triangles), squares, hexagons, octagons

Scheme
Book 4a, page 102;
Resource Master 128*

For this activity, the children ideally should have access to a set of templates such as those in Shape Tracer Set 1 in which the regular shapes have a common edge length. Encourage the children to keep trials which *don't* work as expected as evidence to show how they persevered with a difficult task.

D Individualised tessellations ⟦I⟧

1 If available, show and discuss examples of tessellations created by artists such as Maurits Escher. Can the children recognise where the motifs have been translated, reflected or rotated?

2 Introduce the task on Book 4a, page 103, in which the children have to translate and reflect 2-D shapes both to create a tile and to tessellate it. The tessellation will have properties similar to this:

EXTENSION

- Try making a similar tessellation starting with a different shape, e.g. a regular hexagon.

Resources

School
Tessellations by artists such as Maurits Escher (optional); supply of card rectangles (about postcard-size); scissors; large sheets of plain paper

Scheme
Book 4a, page 103

If the children's tiles do not fit together exactly but are reasonably accurate, black felt-pen lines drawn around the outlines can often hide minor flaws.

E Tessellating simple polyominoes ⟦C⟧ ⟦G⟧ ⟦P⟧ ⟦I⟧

1 Join together two cubes of the same colour to form one colour 'dominoes'. Ask the children to find ways of fitting these dominoes together to make different tessellations.

2 If wished, the children can record findings on a squared grid:

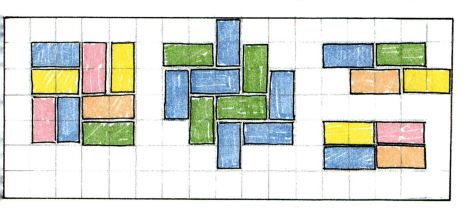

3 Extend to find one-layer shapes made with three or four interlocking cubes, called triominoes and tetrominoes.

4 Organise pairs or small groups to find as many different arrangements as possible, using one colour only for each separate shape.

Resources

School
Interlocking cubes (e.g. Multilink)

Scheme
Resource Master I (2 cm squared grid)

Polyominoes is the name given to sets of interlocking squares. Sets of three squares are called 'triominoes' and of four squares 'tetrominoes'. To make these, use only flat arrangements of cubes, i.e. a single layer, since we are only concerned with the shape of the upper face in this activity.

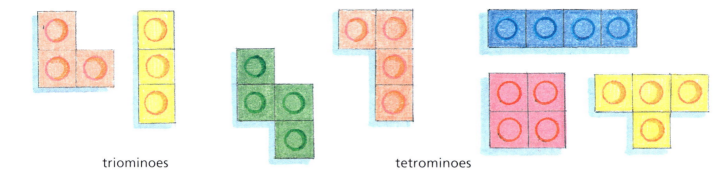

triominoes   tetrominoes

5 Afterwards, ask the groups to try to prove or disprove these statements:

| Matching triominoes tessellate | | Matching tetrominoes tessellate |

All dominoes, triominoes and tetrominoes can tessellate, some in more than one way.

6 The tessellating patterns can be recorded on squared paper. For example:

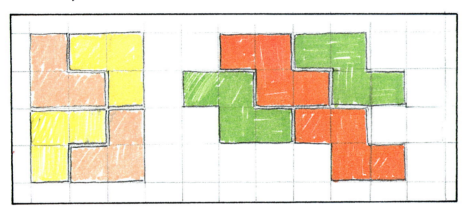

EXTENSION

- *Try to make two different triominoes or tetrominoes tessellate.*

F Assessment activity   I

*On a squared grid or lattice (RMs A, F or I), start off two simple tessellations similar to these:

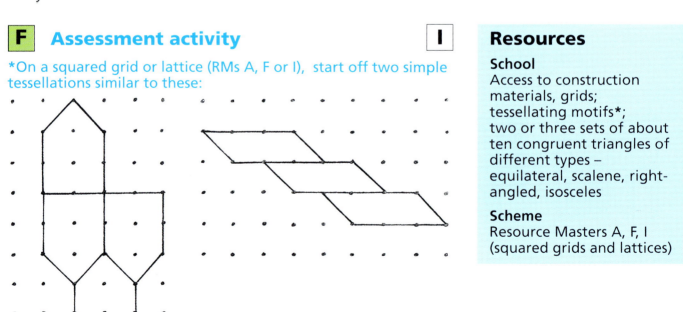

1 Ask the child to continue the shapes so that each motif is repeated several times, forming a tessellation.

Resources

School
Access to construction materials, grids; tessellating motifs*; two or three sets of about ten congruent triangles of different types – equilateral, scalene, right-angled, isosceles

Scheme
Resource Masters A, F, I (squared grids and lattices)

2 Help the child to construct a tessellation with one set of congruent triangles and say, *You can create tessellations with the other sets of matching triangles. Can you show me how you might do this?*

3 Afterwards, discuss the child's results by asking, say, *Why is each set of triangles a tessellation?*

Assessment notes

Oral response	✔
Practical response	✔
Pictorial response	✔
Written response	

The child has:
continued tessellations from given information;
AND
tested a simple statement about the tessellating properties of triangles;
AND
chosen appropriate mathematical techniques to make at least two sets of congruent triangles tessellate.

STRENGTHENING ACTIVITIES

Pattern blocks

Semi-regular tessellations involving squares, triangles and hexagons can be constructed from Pattern Blocks. Given a start, less able children may be able to continue these.

CHALLENGING ACTIVITIES

Four-shape tessellations

The children can try to design a tessellation which uses four different shapes. Remind them of the rules – no overlaps and the pattern should be able to grow in all directions in a predictable way.

Tiles inside tiles

By taking a basic tessellating shape and marking the mid-points of each side, the mid-points can be joined to create an inner shape. (This procedure can be repeated on the inner shape also if wished.)

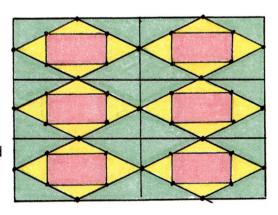

HOME/SCHOOL PROJECTS

Ask the child to bring to school an example of a tessellating design for display, discussion and sorting.

IDEAS BOARD

■ Typical projects
Pattern; Shape and Size; Decoration; Growth

■ History
Find examples of tessellating designs from different times and cultures. Try to recreate some of these.

■ Skeletons
Make skeleton tessellations with materials such as Geostrips, Kugeli, etc.

■ Art
- Printing, mosaics and patchwork, using tessellating motifs.
- See how tessellation is used in examples of Islamic art.

- Study the designs on Altair-type pads. *Are they tessellations? Why (not)?*

■ Activity tiles
These decorated tiles are ideal for experimenting with tessellations.

SUPPORT MATERIALS

Teaching aids
Templates Superpack (NES Arnold)
Shape Tracer Sets 1 and 2 (NES Arnold)
Tessellation Templates (NES Arnold)
Tessellation Shapes (NES Arnold)
Pattern Blocks (NES Arnold)
Tactile Tessellations (NES Arnold)
Gummed paper shapes (Playaway)
Activity Tiles (ATM)
Geostrips (NES Arnold)
Kugeli (NES Arnold)

Teachers' reference materials
Creating Escher-Type Drawings, E. R. Ranucci and J. L. Teeters (Creative Publications)
Tessellations File, Chris de Cordova (Tarquin)
Mathematics through Art and Design, Anne Woodman and Eric Albany (Collins Educational)
The Magic Mirror of M. C. Escher, Bruno Ernst (Tarquin)

Software
Mosaic (AUCBE)
Newtiles from MicroSMILE Next 17 (ILECC)
Picture Maker Plus (ESM)
Tilekit from *SLIMWAM 2* (ATM)
Tile Stretch from *Maths with a Story 2* (ILECC)

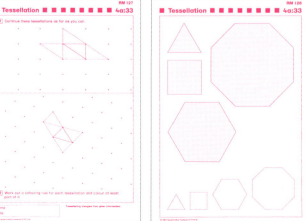

34. SCALE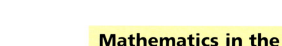

LEARNING CONTEXT

Contribution made by this Step

Through exploring ideas involving simple scales, the children revise and extend previous work on doubling and halving, co-ordinates and length.

Objectives

To enable children to:
a Revise measurement in millimetres and centimetres and co-ordinates in the first quadrant.
b Use halving and doubling to explore scale.
c Make simple hypotheses or generalisations.

Background

In Step 3a:32, the children drew elevations of simple models made with interlocking cubes, enlarged and distorted simple 2-D shapes on grids and started to use simple scales.

In this Step, the emphasis is on investigating the effect on the scale of 2-D shapes and 3-D objects when dimensions are halved or doubled. The children are also encouraged to make simple hypotheses or generalisations about the effect on:
– area when the dimensions of rectangles are doubled;
– volume when the dimensions of simple 3-D objects are doubled;
– a 2-D shape when the numbers of its co-ordinates are doubled.

> **Mathematics in the National Curriculum**
>
> **Programme of Study: KS2**
> No statutory reference to scale. Pupils should be taught to:
> ■ understand and use, in context, fractions and percentages to estimate, describe and compare proportions of a whole. (N 2.c)
> ■ recognise the number relationship between co-ordinates in the first quadrant of related points on a line or in a shape, *e.g. the vertices of a rectangle, a graph of the multiples of 3*. (N 3.b)
> ■ make 2-D and 3-D shapes and patterns with increasing accuracy, recognise their geometrical features and properties, and use these to classify shapes and solve problems. (SSM 2.b)
> ■ find perimeters of simple shapes; find areas and volumes by counting methods, leading to the use of other practical methods, *e.g. dissection*. (SSM 4.c)
> ■ select and use the appropriate mathematics and materials. (UA 2.a)
> ■ make general statements of their own, based on evidence they have produced. (UA 4.c)

THINKING AND TALKING MATHEMATICALLY

Starting points for discussion

Display of illustrations of small objects which have been greatly enlarged in size or large objects which have been greatly reduced.

Read stories in which scale or maps feature, e.g. the *Narnia* books.

Display of scale models or items available in graded sizes.

> **Key language**
>
> Enlarge, reduce, scale, similar, double, halve, half (twice) as big, actual size, half-scale (1 to 2), one-to-one scale (1 to 1), double-scale (2 to 1) co-ordinates, millimetre (mm), centimetre (cm)

STEPS 4a

ACTIVITIES IN DETAIL

A Halving and doubling lengths C I

Resources
Scheme
Book 4a, pages 104 and 105

1 Discuss: *Why are objects sometimes shown larger or smaller in size than they really are? What would you need to know if you wanted to work out their actual size?*

2 Use the terms 'enlargement' and 'reduction' to describe objects treated in this way.

3 Using objects on the children's desks, ask, *What length (width) do you think this (book) would be if it was reduced to half-scale? Why? What if it was enlarged to twice its size?*

4 Use the children themselves to demonstrate scale.

5 Ask, *Why do you think half-scale is sometimes written as 1:2? How do you think double-scale might be written?*

6 Introduce the tasks on Book 4a, pages 104 and 105 which give practice in using scales involving halving and doubling linear measurements.

EXTENSION

■ The children construct a half-scale (or other preferred scale) drawing of themselves or of a friend, making the dimensions as accurate as possible.

B Doubling and halving areas C I

Part 1: Rectangular shapes

Resources
Scheme
Book 4a, pages 106, 107 and 108

1 As revision, ask the children to explain what is meant by 'area' and how it is measured, i.e., by covering a surface in squares (or other convenient units) and counting them.

2 Introduce the tasks on Book 4a, page 106, in which the children investigate the effect of doubling the dimensions of rectangles, leading to the hypothesis that this has the effect of making the area four times as large.

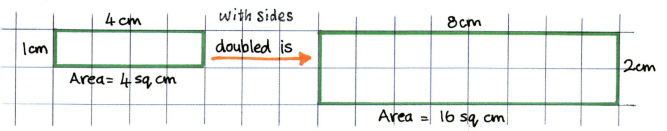

3 Similarly, on page 107, the children investigate the effect of halving the dimensions of rectangles, leading to the hypothesis that the area is reduced to a quarter of what it was each time.

4 As work progresses, and afterwards, ask, *What has stayed the same in each enlarged rectangle? What do you think will happen to the area when you halve the sides of this rectangle?*

5 Introduce informally the term 'similar shapes' to describe each pair of rectangles in which the length of the sides have all been enlarged or reduced by the same scale factor.

Part 2: Non-rectangular shapes

1 Introduce the tasks on Book 4a, page 108, in which the children have to investigate the effect of doubling the length of the sides of letter shapes based on centimetre square units.

2 Encourage the children to persevere if difficulties arise in enlarging the shapes, since more than one attempt may be needed to do this successfully.

EXTENSION

■ Predict then check what would happen if you:
– tried enlarging the rectangles three ... or more ... times;
– tried doubling the sides of isosceles right-angled triangles.

C Co-ordinates and scale C P I

Part 1: Revising describing and plotting co-ordinates

1 Display a numbered grid similar to this, to revise the procedure for describing and plotting co-ordinates.

Resources
School
Resource Masters 129, 130 and A (1 cm squared grid)

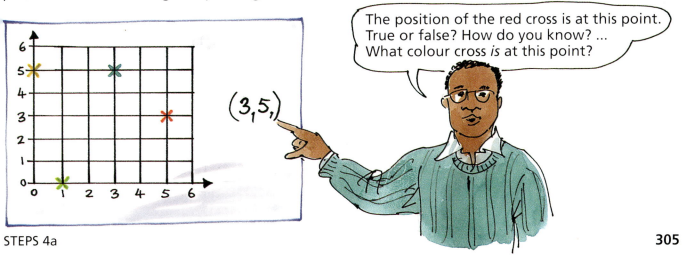

STEPS 4a

2 Working in pairs, the children can:

(a) decide on the co-ordinates for the other crosses, then compare results with others;
(b) volunteer to add further crosses and to write their co-ordinates to see if the others agree;
(c) make statements about the position of the co-ordinates, true or false, for others to comment on.

3 Remind the children of the importance of reading the number on the horizontal axis first.

4 Introduce the task on RM 129, which combines work on co-ordinates with finding out what happens if co-ordinates are doubled.

Part 2: One-way stretches

1 After completing RM129, the children can investigate what happens when the original fish on RM129 is changed:
– by doubling the first number of its co-ordinates only;
– by doubling the second number of its co-ordinates only.

2 Having established the new sets of co-ordinates, they can design suitable grids on RM A to display the transformed fish.

3 If a more structured approach is preferred, use RM 130.

4 Afterwards, discuss:

(a) how the original fish has been stretched or distorted in one direction each time, i.e. become twice as long or twice as wide;
(b) what might happen if you doubled the numbers for the co-ordinates for grids **C** and **D** again.

EXTENSION

■ The children can:

(a) experiment with changing the co-ordinates for the same fish or a new shape in other ways, and plotting the transformed fish to see what happens;
(b) investigate the effect on the area of the enlarged fish compared with the original. (On grid **B**, the area is quadrupled; on grids **C** and **D** the area is doubled.)

> The effect of changing co-ordinates, in ways other than by doubling (i.e. by other scale factors) is extended in later handbooks.

D Interlocking cubes

Introduce some of the following activities:

Growing cubes

1 Working collaboratively within small groups, ask the children to find out how many different-sized cubes can be made from up to 100 smaller cubes each time. (They may be surprised that there are only four with the unit 1 x 1 x 1 cube.)

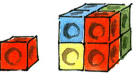

number of cubes: 1   8   27   64

> **Resources**
> **School**
> Good supply of interlocking cubes (Multilink, Centicubes, etc.); base 10 blocks

2 As work progresses, ask how the number of cubes used each time is being calculated.

3 Use one each of the 1 x 1 x 1, 2 x 2 x 2 and 4 x 4 x 4 cubes.

(a) Establish the relationship between these.

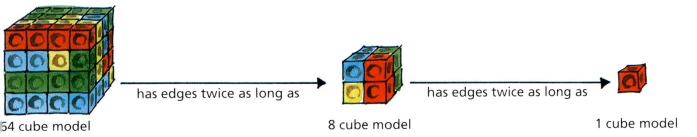

64 cube model   has edges twice as long as   8 cube model   has edges twice as long as   1 cube model

(b) Get the children to try to calculate how many cubes would be needed to make the cube double the length, width and height of the 4 x 4 x 4 model.

(c) Establish that you need eight times as many cubes to make the cube with double the edge length.

Larger cubes

1 Get the class to collaborate in making:
- eight 4 x 4 x 4 cubes. These can be fitted together with sticky tape to form an 8 x 8 x 8 cube. *How many smaller cubes altogether?*
- eight 3 x 3 x 3 cubes. These can be fitted together to make a 6 x 6 x 6 cube. *How many smaller cubes altogether?*

Other shapes

1 Get the children to make some simple flat shapes from four or five cubes.

2 Suggest that the children, perhaps working in pairs, should choose one at a time and try to make a shape where all the edges are doubled in length.

3 Afterwards, compare results. If all three dimensions have been doubled, the children should discover, as with the cubes, that they need eight times as many cubes to make the model.

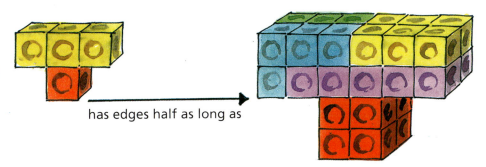

has edges half as long as

STEPS 4a

307

Centicubes

1 Using Centicubes and possible working in pairs, can the children:

– work out by calculation how many cubes they will need to make a cube whose edges are half as long as a metric base 10 block;
– make the cube from Centicubes. (One hundred and twenty-five cubes will be needed to make the 5 x 5 x 5 cube.)

E   Enlarging shapes

1 Demonstrate this method of enlarging shapes, using the outline of a polygon, drawn with stencils or templates (or, if the children prefer, constructed with a ruler and pencil).

(a) Draw a polygon, here shown in blue.
(b) Mark a point near the centre of the shape (shown in red).
(c) Draw pencil lines from this point through the vertices and extending beyond the vertices.
(d) Put a point on the extended lines the same distance as from the central point to the vertices. (The new vertices are now twice the distance from the marked centre.)
(e) Join the outer set of points in order.

Resources

School
Large sheets of blank paper; stencils and templates of geometric shapes

This activity is developed more fully in later handbooks when cubic numbers, etc. will be investigated in more detail. The ideas here are intended to be exploratory and informal.

This activity will provide an opportunity to revise the meaning of parallel lines.

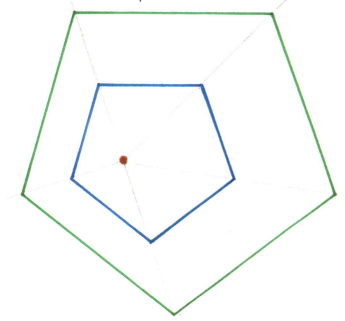

2 Some children will enjoy adding further concentric shapes. Large sheets of paper will be needed.

3 Afterwards, discuss how the enlarged shapes have changed (length of sides) and stayed the same (angles) and use informally the term 'similar' to describe these.

EXTENSION

■ If the children experiment with shapes with curved sides, they will find they have to draw these by estimation.

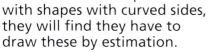

F Assessment activity

*In advance, draw three rectangles on RM A similar to these (with sides an even number of centimetres long.)

1 Ask the child to:
(a) construct rectangles whose sides are half as long and wide as those given;
(b) write the area of each rectangle underneath it. (Give help with one example if required since this is not being assessed here.)

2 Afterwards, ask, *How did you decide what size to draw the smaller rectangles? What can you tell me about the area of each smaller rectangle compared to the larger one?*

I Resources

Scheme
Resource Master A (1 cm squared grid)*

Objective A is not specifically assessed here since it is revision.

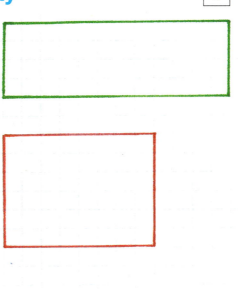

Assessment notes

Oral response	✔
Practical response	
Pictorial response	✔
Written response	

The child has:
constructed three rectangles with half the linear dimensions of given rectangles;
AND
made a hypothesis about the area of the half-scale rectangles being four times less than the area of the originals.

STRENGTHENING ACTIVITIES

Doubling

The child might benefit from making rectangles from four Cuisenaire Rods on top of a sheet of centimetre squared paper then making one with sides twice as long from eight rods.

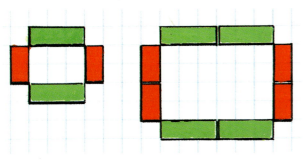

The dimensions of the enclosed rectangles can be measured easily with a ruler and the areas counted in squares and compared.

Half-scale

If the child has difficulty in establishing the links in area between a rectangle and a half-scale version of it, construct four matching rectangles from a grid and a fifth of double the dimensions of one of these. Show how the smaller ones can be arranged on top of, or alongside, the larger one to make an exact match.

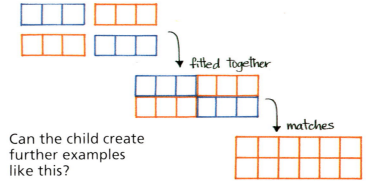

Can the child create further examples like this?

STEPS 4a

CHALLENGING ACTIVITIES

Book covers

Using a book cover from a favourite book, can the child make a half- or double-scale version of it?

HOME/SCHOOL PROJECTS

The children find an object in the kitchen measuring up to 10 cm long. They draw it actual size then half-scale and double-scale to return for a display.

IDEAS BOARD

■ LOGO

The children can experiment with drawing lines and shapes with LOGO then investigate what happens when the sides are halved or doubled.

■ Tile Stretch

Use programs like Tile Stretch to investigate the effect of scale on shapes.

■ A4 paper sizes

Obtain a set of standard sheets, ranging from size A0 to A7 if possible. The children will discover that each size is half the area of the next larger size.

Relationships in area between the different sizes can be described in words or using relationship arrows.

■ Russian dolls

Preferably working in pairs or small groups, the children choose the materials and mathematics to decorate sets of three boxes, e.g. cubes, cuboids or tetrahedra, in which one is half-scale and one double-scale in relation to the third one. Any decoration should be scaled similarly.

SUPPORT MATERIALS

Teaching aids
Multilink Cubes (NES Arnold)
Centicubes and Clicubes (Hope Education)
Maths Cube (Abceta Playthings)

Teachers' reference materials
Primary Mathematics Today, 3rd edn, chapter 34, Elizabeth Williams and Hilary Shuard (Longman)
Will Gulliver's Suit Fit?, Dora Whittaker (Cambridge University Press)

Children's books
The *Narnia* Books (HarperCollins)
Mapstart Series, Simon Catling (Collins Educational)
The Giant Jam Sandwich, J. V. Lord (Pan Books)

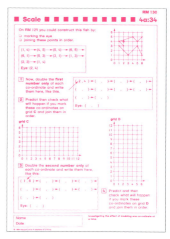

Radio and TV
Size from *Videomaths* (Video Research Unit, Central TV)
The Tile Stretch Game from *Maths with a Story 2*, Peter Smith (ILECC)

135. VOLUME & CAPACITY (2)

LEARNING CONTEXT

Contribution made by this Step

The children reinforce and extend their previous experiences of measuring and estimating capacities of containers. They are encouraged to improve their ability to estimate by filling and emptying containers of various shapes and sizes, describing their work, and developing images of amounts.

Objectives

To enable children to:
a Make sensible estimates in relation to capacity.
b Solve problems related to capacity.
c Record appropriately.

Background

Regular practical work in measuring capacities is important. It develops a child's ability to recognise and therefore estimate amounts held by containers of different sizes and shapes. Appearances can be deceptive. Pourable fillers take the shape of the container so it is important to allow children to experiment with a variety of equipment and devices for measurement, and to understand that all measurements are approximate.

The distinction between volume and capacity is still important, and can be refined slightly by suggesting that volume concerns space used or taken up by something, while capacity concerns available or empty space. Capacity can be referred to as the 'internal volume' of a box or container.

Mathematics in the National Curriculum

Programme of Study: KS2
Pupils should be taught to:
■ choose appropriate standard units of length, mass, capacity and time, and make sensible estimates with them in everyday situations; extend their understanding of the relationship between units. (SSM 4.a)
■ choose and use appropriate measuring instruments; interpret numbers and read scales to an increasing degree of accuracy. (SSM 4.b)
■ try different mathematical approaches; identify and obtain information needed to carry out their work. (UA 2.b)

THINKING AND TALKING MATHEMATICALLY

Starting points for discussion

Why is it important that we have standard measures of amounts of liquid? (Value for money? Accurate doses of medicines?)

Ask, *Could you drink a litre of water in one go? ... 500 ml? ... 100 ml? ... 20 ml?*

Key language

capacity, litre (l), millilitre (ml), fraction, divisions, markings, calibrations, graduations, calibrated/graduated containers, measuring jug/cylinder, scale, level, exact, approximate

ACTIVITIES IN DETAIL

A Capacity scales   G P

Part 1: Making a calibrated container

1 Provide a selection of wide-necked unmarked containers. Ask the children to pour in one unit of water (e.g. 20 ml), mark the level and label the mark.

Resources

School
Squared paper; a range of calibrated/graduated containers; unmarked transparent containers; waterproof pens; funnels

Scheme
Resource Master 131

Remind them to ensure that the eye is horizontal to the water level before marking the position.

2 The children then continue adding units of water, marking each new level, until they reach the top of the container.

3 Encourage the children to mark (and possibly label) mid-points between the unit calibrations and to emphasise and label important calibrations (e.g. 100 ml ... 200 ml) with a longer or bolder line.

4 Ask them to get together in pairs and use their calibrated measures to find the approximate capacities of two or three other containers. *Do the results agree? If not, why not?*

Part 2: Paper scales

1 Ask the children to draw a scale for a capacity measure of their own choice, using squared paper.

2 Discuss their attempts, drawing attention to the need for consistent spacing of the calibrations and sufficient labelling to allow the scale to be read easily.

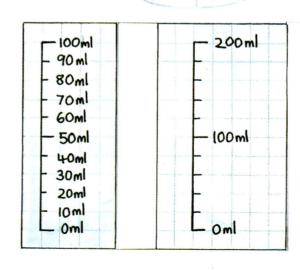
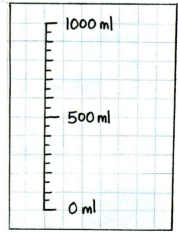

STEPS 4a

Part 3: Commercial calibrated measures

1 Show a range of calibrated measures. Discuss the maximum capacity and the number, spacing and labelling, of the calibrations.

2 Give the children the opportunity to pour different amounts of water into the calibrated containers and read the amount. Emphasise the approximate nature of measurement and the need to estimate 'between-ness' if necessary.

3 Ask them to work in pairs to choose some unmarked containers and find their capacities (to the nearest 10 ml) by filling a container, then pouring the contents into first one and then another calibrated container. *Do the results agree?*

RM 131 provides practice in marking given amounts of liquid on some common scales.

EXTENSION

■ The children investigate ways to find the capacities of unmarked containers. One way to do this is by noting the level on a calibrated container, filling the unmarked container, noting the new lower level on the calibrated container and subtracting one from the other.

B Estimating capacities   G

1 Show a range of unmarked containers. Ask the children to work in pairs to decide on an estimate of the capacity of each container, then check it using the calibrated container. Allow plenty of time for them to discuss the quality of their estimates, encouraging them to learn by practice.

Resources

School
Range of calibrated/graduated containers; unmarked transparent containers; funnels

Scheme
Resource Master 132, Book 4a, page 109

2 Use RM 132 and provide up to ten different containers. Explain to the children that they must *estimate* the capacities of all the containers first. Encourage them to make good estimates if they can, and record them before measuring.

3 Discuss the reason for the difference column. *What information does it give us?*

4 Show a container to the group. Ask each child to estimate its capacity and secretly write his or her estimate. Discuss the range of estimates. Ask one or two children to find the actual capacity. *Who was nearest? What did he or she do, or think of, to help make the estimate?*

Good estimates are based on the ability to recall mentally certain numbered amounts and carry out a visual comparison.

5 Show another container. Suggest about three possible capacities. *Which one is most likely? How did you decide?*

Ask the children to work through the activities on Book 4a, page 109.

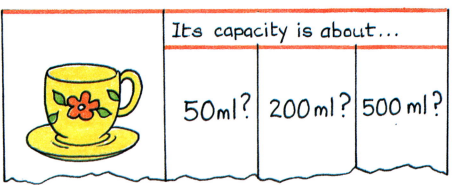

C Calculating capacities

C I

Resources

School
Calculator (optional)

Scheme
Book 4a, page 110

1 Discuss the fact that calculations which use the notation of capacity follow the same rules as other number activities, but require a unit to be attached to amounts, which are measures of capacity.

2 Check that the children are familiar with bar-line graphs (Step 6) and, if desired, the use of a calculator for addition, subtraction and multiplication.

3 Ask the children to try the activities on Book 4a, page 110.

D Assessment activity

I

Resources

School
A range of calibrated/graduated containers; unmarked transparent containers; funnels

1 Ask the child to fill the calibrated container to three (increasingly large) amounts of your choice. Ask him or her to write the amount, checking that the appropriate units are used.

2 Ask the child to choose an unmarked container and suggest an appropriate estimate of its capacity.

3 Ask the child to check the amount practically, using a calibrated container, describing the method to you.
The child has:

Assessment notes

Oral response	✔
Practical response	✔
Pictorial response	
Written response	✔

correctly used a scale on a calibrated container to show a specified amount of liquid;
AND
estimated the capacity of a container with an appropriate degree of accuracy;
AND
appropriately measured and recorded the capacity of an unmarked container.

STEPS 4a

STRENGTHENING ACTIVITIES

Litre shapes

To help children develop estimation skills they need experience of several key fixed amounts. Ask them to select and label containers holding about one litre. Ask, *How many different shapes have you found?* Repeat as appropriate for other important amounts.

These hold about one litre.

Mental arithmetic

To help children to read scales, encourage counting on and counting back in tens, twenties, twenty-fives, fifties, hundreds and two hundreds, to a thousand.

CHALLENGING ACTIVITIES

Weigh a litre

Find the weight of a litre of water. Ask the children to select the equipment and the method. Ask them to write about the way the task was carried out.

Dripping tap

How much water is lost from a dripping tap in one minute? One hour? One day? *What method could you use to find out?*

HOME/SCHOOL PROJECTS

- The children seek out and list containers in the home which are used to hold liquids (or other pourable materials). Examples are basins, sinks, baths, watering cans and buckets, flasks and bottles, and so on. *Do they all have a specified capacity in litres or millilitres?*

- The children can keep a record of the number of litres of fuel bought for the family car in a week or month.

IDEAS BOARD

■ Typical projects
Materials; Food; Water; Weather; Cars; Shops and Shopping; Packaging

■ Same answer?
A pair of children use a small measure such as an eggcup to fill a bottle, gradually. Ask them to record the number of fills and repeat the process. *Do you use the same number of fills each time? If not, why not?*

■ Drinks
Small bottles, cans and cartons of soft drinks often contain either 200 ml, 250 ml or 330 ml. *Why have these amounts been chosen by the manufacturers?* The children can use water to measure the capacity of empty drinks containers. *Is it the same as the amount stated on the label? Is it sometimes more? Is it ever less?*

■ Guess the capacity
Children can work in pairs. One chooses a container. Both estimate how much it holds. They measure its capacity together. *Whose estimate is closest? How do you decide which is closest?*

■ Match the label
Use small unmarked containers of known capacity. Write labels showing various amounts, to the nearest 10 ml. Ask the children to match the labels and containers, then check.

■ How much do you drink?
Children investigate the approximate amount of liquid they drink in a day ... or a week ... or a year. *How long can a person survive without a drink? How long can a camel survive without a drink?*

■ Random containers
Pick up to ten containers of similar capacities and different shapes. *Can they be placed in order of capacity: by sight? By filling and emptying from one to another? By measuring each one?*

SUPPORT MATERIALS

Teaching aids
Litre Set (Hope Education)
Large Displacement Can (Hope Education)
Graduated Cylinders (Taskmaster)
Graduated Beakers (Taskmaster)
Funnels (NES Arnold)

Teachers' reference materials
Children Learn to Measure, John Glenn (Ed.) (Holt)
Maths Plus: Volume and Capacity 1 and 2, Paul Harling (Ward Lock Educational)

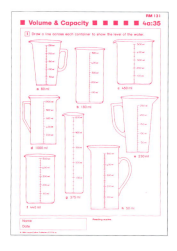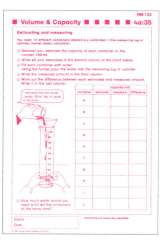

36. COMMON FRACTIONS

LEARNING CONTEXT

Contribution made by this Step

The activities in this Step enrich and extend children's understanding of simple fractions to include simple equivalents. Practical or visual situations are used to show different ways in which fractions can be represented to illustrate and interpret relationships.

Objectives

To enable children to:
a Explore practically the ordering and equivalence of fractions.
b Estimate and calculate simple fractions.
c Add and subtract simple fractions related to practical situations.

Background

Fractions are an important element of our everyday use of mathematics. They are fundamental to the ideas of sharing, estimation and approximation. However, the concepts associated with fractions and their arithmetical manipulation are difficult to understand. This problem is compounded if attempts are made to move too quickly towards formal calculations. Therefore the emphasis should be on a practical (or at least visual) approach, with plenty of revision of the fundamental ideas and terms, making use of contexts such as measurement and shape.

> **Mathematics in the National Curriculum**
>
> **Programme of Study: KS2**
> Pupils should be taught to:
> ■ understand and use, in context, fractions and percentages to estimate, describe and compare proportions of a whole. (N 2.c)
> ■ extend methods of computation to include ... calculating fractions and percentages of quantities, using a calculator where appropriate. (N 3.g)
> ■ present information and results clearly, and explain the reasons for their choice of presentation. (UA 3.c)

THINKING AND TALKING MATHEMATICALLY

Starting points for discussion

Can you walk to a spot about a quarter of the way across the room? How do you decide where to stand? What about one third of the way across? Two thirds?

How many different ways can you fold a square of paper to show quarters? If you folded each quarter into two equal parts, can you still see quarters? Can you show me half of the paper? What other fractions does the folded paper show?

> **Key language**
> fraction, part, unit, equal, equivalent, symbols and words for common fractions, share, divide, numerator, denominator, estimate, estimation, order

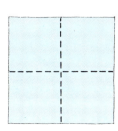

STEPS 4a

ACTIVITIES IN DETAIL

A Ordering simple fractions [C] [G] [P]

1 Give a copy of RM 133 to each child.

2 Ask the children to label the top strip 'one whole' and the others, in word or symbol form, according to the number of divisions shown.

3 Ask them to cut out each whole strip and jumble the order.

4 Revise the ordering of unitary fractions, i.e. fractions with a numerator of one, such as $\frac{1}{3}$ or $\frac{1}{5}$, by placing strips next to each other. *Is a quarter larger than a sixth?*

Resources

School
Card or commercial fraction chart, showing whole, halves, thirds, quarters, fifths, sixths, eighths and tenths, for demonstration

Scheme
Resources Master 133; Book 4a, page 111

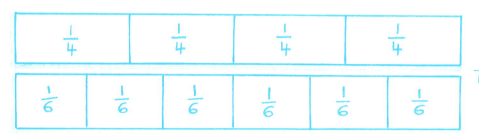

$\frac{1}{4} > \frac{1}{6}$

Emphasise that all the strips are of equal length.

5 Choose pairs of strips, e.g. fifths and sixths. Ask the children to fold the first strip to show, say, three fifths ($\frac{3}{5}$), and the second strip to show, say, four sixths ($\frac{4}{6}$). *Which strip is longer? Which fraction of the whole is larger?*

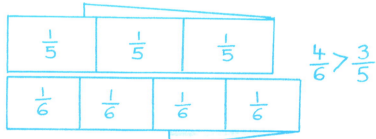

$\frac{4}{6} > \frac{3}{5}$

6 Ask the children to work in pairs. They choose other pairs of strips, fold them, then visually compare the fractions. The compared fractions can be recorded using > and <.

Book 4a, page 111, tasks 1 and 2, provide further practice in ordering fractions.

EXTENSION

■ The children colour and order different fractions of identical shapes drawn on squared paper.

B Introducing equivalent fractions [C] [G] [P]

1 The children use the labelled strips from Activity **A** (RM133).

2 Begin with a clear example of equivalent fractions from recent experience, e.g. division of a whole into halves, quarters and eighths. Show this on a fraction board or display.

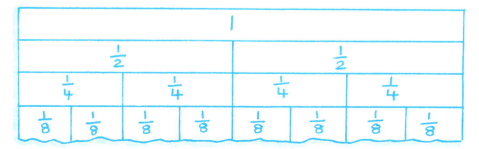

Resources

School
Card or commercial fraction chart (see Activity A); Cuisenaire or Colour Factor Rods

Scheme
Book 4a, page 111

Cuisenaire or Colour Factor Rods can be used if children are familiar with the relative value of the colours.

STEPS 4a

3 Ask the children to align or overlay the strips to answer questions and then to record responses:

> How many halves make a whole? Two halves $\frac{2}{2} = 1$
> How many quarters make a whole? Four quarters $\frac{4}{4} = 1$
> How many eighths make a whole? Eight eighths $\frac{8}{8} = 1$
> How many quarters make a half? Two quarters $\frac{2}{4} = \frac{1}{2}$
> How many eighths make a half? Four eighths $\frac{4}{8} = \frac{1}{2}$
> How many eighths make three-quarters? Six eighths $\frac{6}{8} = \frac{3}{4}$

4 Ask the children to work in pairs to explore and record equivalent fractions found by looking at the strips showing thirds, sixths and halves:

$$\frac{1}{3} = \frac{2}{6} \qquad \frac{2}{3} = \frac{4}{6} \qquad \frac{3}{6} = \frac{1}{2}$$

and fifths, tenths and halves:

$$\frac{2}{10} = \frac{1}{5} \qquad \frac{4}{10} = \frac{2}{5} \qquad \frac{6}{10} = \frac{3}{5} \qquad \frac{8}{10} = \frac{4}{5} \qquad \frac{5}{10} = \frac{1}{2}$$

Book 4a, page 111, tasks 3 and 4, give further practice in matching fractions.

EXTENSION

■ The children explore other equivalent fractions, perhaps using ninths and twelfths and relating them to thirds, sixths and halves. *Is there a pattern linking the numerators and denominators of pairs (or sets) of equivalent fractions?*

C Exploring equivalent fractions C G P

1 Revise folding, cutting out and colouring unitary fractions of 2-D shapes drawn on grid papers of various designs, and making 3-D shapes from interlocking cubes (Steps 3a:23 and 3b:12).

2 Begin with numbers of unit shapes which match the denominator of the fraction. For example:

Resources

School
Interlocking cubes (e.g. Multilink)

Scheme
Book 4a, page 112;
Resource Masters A, D, E, H, I (selection of grids)

$\frac{1}{4}$ is white

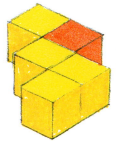

$\frac{1}{5}$ is red.

STEPS 4a

3 List some of the equivalent fractions explored in Activity **B**, showing how they can be represented using interlocking cubes and grid papers. (Select from RMs A, D, E, H, I.)

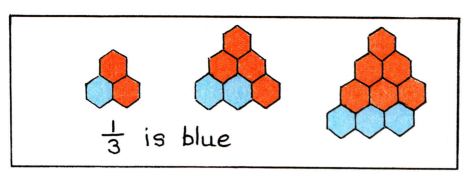

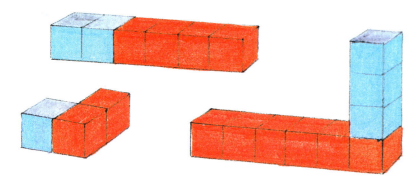

4 Ask the children to work in pairs to show, say, one fifth of the following 2-D and 3-D shapes. Ask, *How many parts of the whole make one fifth of the whole?*

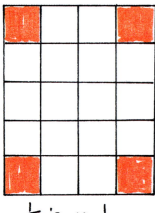

5 Discuss the different ways in which one fifth has been illustrated.

6 Ask the children to explore other unitary fractions of 2-D and 3-D shapes.

Further practice in working with simple equivalent fractions is found on Book 4a, page 112.

EXTENSION

■ The children explore different ways to show non-unitary fractions, such as five eighths, on 2-D grids or with interlocking cubes.

D Fractions of quantities

Part 1: Children in a group

1 Choose a fraction with which to introduce the concept of fractions of quantities, e.g. fifths.

2 Ask, for example, three girls and two boys to stand in a group. Discuss the fact that each child is one fifth of the group.

Resources

School
Mixed colour counters;
Logiblocks

Scheme
Book 4a, page 113

Write both the words and the symbol, and discuss the meaning of the two numbers which form the symbol, that is:

$\frac{1}{5}$ → Numerator (the number of items chosen from the set)
  → Denominator (the number of items in the whole set)

3 *What fraction are girls? ... have dark hair? ... are wearing short socks? ...*

4 Ask, for example, three more girls and two more boys to join the group. *What fraction are girls? Can you think of two ways we can describe the fraction that are girls?*

5 Repeat, with other numbers of children, asking them to establish simple equivalent fractions.

Encourage the children to recognise that three fifths is equivalent to six tenths.

Part 2: Counters

1 Ask the children to work in pairs, using mixed colour counters. They take 24 counters, decide what fraction one counter represents, then explore the fractions which are, say, yellow, red, blue ... and so on. *Is there more than one way to describe the fraction that is, for example, red? How can you write the fractions?*

Part 3: Logiblocks

1 Use sets of Logiblocks. *What fraction is red? ... thin? ... large? ... red triangles? ...*

Further activities are found on Book 4a, page 113.

STEPS 4a

E Estimating fractions G I

1 Ask the children to cut out the strips from RM 133 and label them as follows:

2 Draw straight lines of various lengths on the board. Ask the children to look carefully at their labelled strips. Then ask individual children to mark on one of the lines a point they *estimate* to be, say, one fifth of the line from the left-hand end.

3 Discuss the results and repeat for other simple fractions, e.g. three fifths, of lines of different lengths.

Resource Master 134 provides further practice in estimating amounts.

EXTENSION

■ Ask the children to estimate and mark some fractions of the distance across the hall or playground.

Resources
Scheme
Resource Masters 133 and 134

Include examples such as five fifths ($\frac{5}{5}$), for which the child will mark the right-hand end.

F Linking fractions and division G I

1 Discuss the links between fractions and division, explaining that, for example, the following pairs of statements are equivalent:

$20 \div 4$ is equivalent to $\frac{1}{4}$ of 20.
$15 \div 3$ is equivalent to $\frac{1}{3}$ of 15.

2 Practise simple mental arithmetic of selected 'tables', interchanging the multiplication, division and fractional forms.

3 Introduce the activities on Book 4a, page 114, where the children use the alternative forms and look for patterns.

Resources
School
Calculators

Scheme
Book 4a, page 114

G Adding and subtracting fractions (same denominator) G

Part 1: Tiles

1 Choose a fraction family, for example, eighths.

2 Ask the children to make two strips of eight tiles. One is kept whole to represent one whole.

3 Use the second strip. Ask, *What fraction of the whole is each tile?*

4 Ask the children to break off some tiles. *What fraction have you broken off? What fraction is left?*

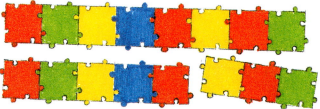

$\frac{3}{8}$ broken off, $\frac{5}{8}$ le[ft]

Resources
School
Polydron or Clixi tiles

Scheme
Resource Masters 135 and 136; Resource Master I (2 cm squared grid)

STEPS 4a

5 Ask them to explore all the possible fractions which can be 'broken off'. *Can two or more fractions be broken off? What fraction is left each time? If you have three eighths and break off two eighths, what is left?*

6 Record and discuss the results.

Bars of the fraction chart on RM 133 can be used to reinforce the tile activity.

Part 2: Grid papers

1 Ask the children to draw different shapes that contain eight unit 'cells' on the grid on RM I (or select from the other RM grids).

2 Repeat the tasks in Part 1, asking the children, for example, to colour three eighths red and one eighth yellow in different ways on the different grids. *How much is coloured altogether? How much is not coloured?*

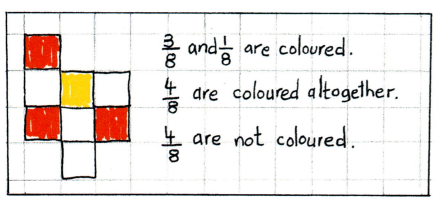

3 Illustrate subtraction by asking the children to colour, for example, five 'cells' or five eighths of the whole shape. Tell them to cross out three of the coloured cells. *What fraction of the coloured cells is left?*

Remember also to use the 'find the difference' form of subtraction during these activities.

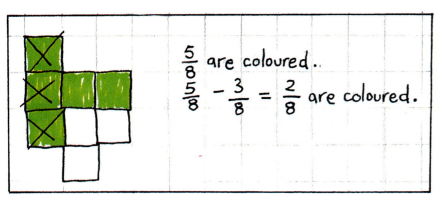

Part 3: Number lines

1 Use RM 135. Show how addition and subtraction of fractions with answers ≤ than one can be illustrated on simple number lines.

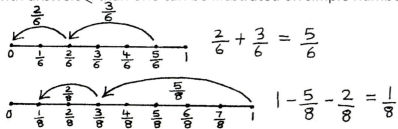

There is further practice in the addition and subtraction of simple fractions on RM 136.

STEPS 4a

H Assessment activity

*In advance, make a card like this.

Colour $\frac{1}{6}$ red.
Colour $\frac{3}{6}$ blue.

I Resources

School
Fraction board; card*

Scheme
Resource Masters 133 (optional) and A

1 Use a fraction board. (if this is not available, use the chart on RM 133.) Ask the child to demonstrate and explain which is larger, one fifth or a quarter, then three quarters or four sixths.

2 Ask him/her to record the inequality using > or <. (Remind the children what these signs mean, if necessary.)

3 Ask the child to indicate two fractions which are equivalent (e.g. five tenths and a half) and to say why.

4 Use squared paper (RM A). Ask the child to draw a rectangle containing 12 squares, and to carry out the instructions on the card. *What fraction is coloured altogether? What fraction is not coloured?*

5 Draw an unlabelled straight line about 20 cm long. Ask the child to mark a point about a quarter of the distance from one end.

Assessment notes

Oral response	✔
Practical response	✔
Pictorial response	✔
Written response	✔

The child has:
ordered some simple fractions;
AND
recognised some simple equivalent fractions;
AND
estimated and illustrated some simple fractions;
AND
added and subtracted simple fractions in a practical context.

STRENGTHENING ACTIVITIES

Games

Use pairing and matching cards and domino games to give practice in recognising the different forms of fractions. (See *Support Materials* for some suggestions.)

Clockface fractions

To practise recognition of fractions, children can use a clockface rubber stamp. They join some or all of the hour marks to the centre and label the fractions they can recognise.

STEPS 4a

CHALLENGING ACTIVITIES

Fraction families

The children investigate equivalent fractions, exploring the patterns of numbers which link the numerators and denominators, for example:

a $\frac{1}{2}, \frac{2}{4}, \frac{3}{6}, \ldots \frac{500}{1000} \ldots$

b $\frac{1}{4}, \frac{2}{8}, \frac{3}{12}, \ldots \frac{250}{1000} \ldots$

HOME/SCHOOL PROJECTS

Investigate the family or a group of friends and neighbours. *What fractions are male/female? ... over 21? ... at school? ...*

IDEAS BOARD

■ Rods

Using a random handful of Cuisenaire or Colour Factor Rods, the children can investigate building fractions (and equivalents) in a range of ways.

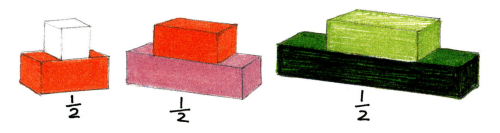

■ Language

Discuss the need to distinguish between, for example, 'third' meaning $\frac{1}{3}$, and 'third' as an ordinal number.

■ Turning

Relate the developing ideas of fractions to amounts of rotation.

■ Puzzles

Make up and solve puzzles such as 'If you find half of me, then add three you get seven. What number am I?'

■ Mental arithmetic

What is $\frac{1}{2}$ of 2, 4, 6, 8, ... ?

What is $\frac{1}{3}$ of 3, 6, 9, 12, ... ?

■ Money

Share out, say, 84p in 1p coins, amongst four children. *How much does each person get? What is $\frac{1}{4}$ of 84p? ... $\frac{1}{2}$ of 84p? ... $\frac{3}{4}$ of 84p? ...*

STEPS 4a

SUPPORT MATERIALS

Teaching aids
Visi-clear Fraction Rubber Stamps (Philip & Tacey)
Aspex Fractions, Set 1 and Set 2 (Philip & Tacey)
Fractions Race Game (Philip & Tacey)
Starting with Fractions (Philip & Tacey)
What Fraction? (Hope Education)
Fraction Squares and Fraction Circles (LDA-Invicta)
Square Parts (Hope Education)
Fraction Game (Hope Education)

Teachers' Reference Materials
Mathematics through Art and Design, Eric Albany and Anne Woodman (Collins Educational)
Primary Mathematics Today, 3rd Edition, chapters 19 and 30, Elizabeth Williams and Hilary Shuard (Longman)
Maths Plus: Fractions 1 and 2, Paul Harling (Ward Lock Educational)

Software
Tower from *MicroSMILE 1* (ILECC)
Wall from *MicroSMILE* Next 17 (ILECC)
Frac 1 and *Frac 2* (MUSE)
Fraction Snap from *Microprimer 1* (MEP)
Bango and *Hunt* from *Mathematics 9-13* (ESM)

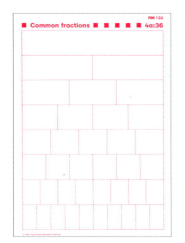
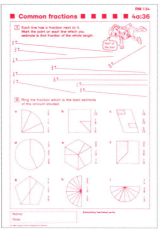

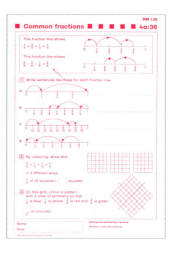

37. LINE GRAPHS

LEARNING CONTEXT

Contribution made by this Step

The children start to interpret and construct simple line graphs.

Objectives

To enable children to:
a Start to construct line graphs.
b Read and interpret line graphs.

Background

In the bar-line graph (a), the type introduced in Step 6, lines are drawn to represent the frequency of an event. A development of this is where the lines are removed and, instead, a point indicates the frequency. The set of points are then joined in order to create a line graph (b). The line graph is often used in preference to the bar-line graph when the named items on the horizontal axis are ordered, say, in a time sequence, so that trends, patterns or relationships can be highlighted or comparisons made.

It does not always make sense to join up points on a line graph since the intermediate points do not always have any meaning, and the children will only learn with experience when this is the case.

Mathematics in the National Curriculum

Programme of Study: KS2
Pupils should be taught to:
■ recognise the number relationship between co-ordinates in the first quadrant of related points on a line or in a shape, e.g. the vertices of a rectangle, a graph of the multiples of 3. (N 3.b)
■ collect and represent discrete data appropriately using graphs and diagrams, including block graphs, pictograms and line graphs; interpret a wider range of graphs and diagrams that represent data, including pie charts, using a computer where appropriate. (HD 2.b)
■ draw conclusions from statistics and graphs, and recognise why some conclusions can be uncertain or misleading. (HD 2.d)
■ use diagrams, graphs and simple algebraic symbols. (UA 3.b)

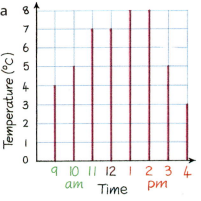 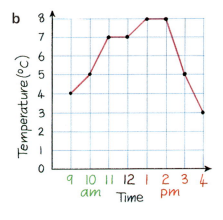

THINKING AND TALKING MATHEMATICALLY

Starting points for discussion

Examples of line graphs collected from newspapers, etc.

What information do they give? What do you have to read to make sense of the information?

How would you immediately recognise these kinds of graphs: block, column, bar-line?

Key language

trend, line graph, 'jagged line' graph, 'saw tooth' graph, experiment, predict, estimate, construct, point, horizontal, vertical, axis, axes, approximately

STEPS 4a

ACTIVITIES IN DETAIL

A 'Jagged line' graph

Part 1: Revising evens chance

1 Organise the children to work in twos or threes, each group sharing one pack of cards.

2 Ask each group to predict, then check, whether these statements, relating to the pack, are true:
- There are 26 red and 26 black cards.
- There are 13 each of Diamonds, Clubs, Hearts and Spades.
- There are four each of Kings, Queens and Jacks.

3 The packs are then shuffled and placed face downwards.

4 Using 5 mm squared grid (RM C) lengthwise, get each group to put a point at the centre left edge, and to obey the following rules, starting at the cross:

(a) Draw a line like this if you turn over a red card.

(b) Draw a line like this if you turn over a black card.

(b) The line should be unbroken (continuous), like a zigzag.

5 Ask each group to predict where the line will end up and why. (They might predict that it will end at about the same level on the opposite edge because there is an evens chance of turning over a red or black card each time.)

6 The start of the line will be similar to this:

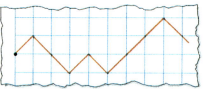

Part 2: Revising less than an evens chance

1 The same experiment can be repeated for these rules with different predictions being made, such as either of these:

| Draw a line like this if you turn over a heart | | Draw a line like this if you don't turn over a heart | |

| Draw a line like this if you turn over an ace | | Draw a line like this if you don't turn over an ace | |

2 Ask, *Can you predict where the line is likely to end up? Why?*

3 If possible, the children should repeat all three experiments on one sheet of squared grid paper, using a different colour for each one so that the pathways and trends for each line can be more easily compared.

Resources

School
Packs of playing cards (jokers not required)

Scheme
Resource Master C (5 mm squared grid)

This activity revises some of the language associated with probability and encourages prediction, reasoning skills and working systematically. It also introduces the idea of a 'jagged line' graph without the need for labelled axes.

4 Points to discuss afterwards are:
(a) that these are sometimes called 'jagged line' or 'saw tooth' graphs;
(b) why the three experiments give such different results, e.g. there is an even chance of a red card, a one-in-four chance of a heart and a one-in-thirteen chance of an ace;
(c) that each graph shows a trend, e.g. in the first experiment the trend is for the line to move up or down about the same number of times, so it will stay close to the horizontal line on which the cross was made.

B Line graph with labelled axes   C G I

Resources
School
Line graph*

Scheme
Resource Master 137

*In advance, prepare for group or class display a simple line graph of this type. (A grid on an OHP transparency is particularly suitable.)

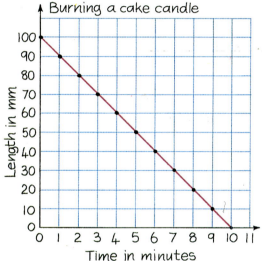

Part 1: Line graph

1 Ask the children to tell you about the graph, if necessary prompting them by asking questions about the horizontal and vertical axes and the meaning of the points. *What 'story' does the unbroken line tell? What information do you think it is meant to give you?*

2 To see if the children can interpret the graph, ask questions like, *What length was the candle after ... minutes? After how many minutes was the candle 40 mm long?*

3 To see if the children can 'read between the points', i.e. interpolate, you might suggest the start of sentences such as:
– During the fifth and sixth minute, the candle reduced in height from ... to ....
– The candle was between 40 mm and 20 mm tall during ....

4 Introduce the term 'line graph' to describe this form of representation.

Since it is reasonable to assume that the height of the candle reduced gradually, it is possible to make sense of the intermediate points (interpolate). For example, between the fifth and sixth minute, the candle reduced in height from 50 mm to 40 mm so after five and a half minutes, the candle would probably measure about 45 mm. Some children will be able to reason in this way.

Part 2: Comparing the bar-line and line graph

1 Introduce the tasks on RM 137 which are intended to highlight the similarities and differences between a bar-line graph and line graph showing the same information.

2 Afterwards, ask, *How are the graphs the same? (Different?) Which do you prefer, the bar-line or line graph? Why?*

3 By covering up the table and the bar-line graph, the children can ask each other questions (to give practice in using and interpreting the graph) like:
– What height was the sunflower after ... weeks?
– After how many weeks was the sunflower ... tall?
– How much did the sunflower grow between week ... and week ...?

4 Ask, *When did the sunflower grow most (least) quickly? How do you know? What does it mean when the line is steeper?*

C Temperature graph C I

1 Ask the children to suggest:
(a) what kind of outdoor temperatures you might get on days such as these and to agree on a suitable temperature (or range):

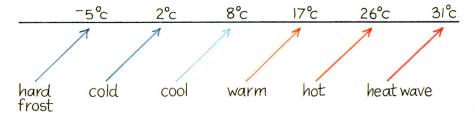

Resources
Scheme
Book 4a, pages 115 and 118

It is assumed that the children will have had experience of taking indoor and outdoor temperatures before tackling the activities on these pages.

(b) how the temperature might vary within a day.

3 Introduce the tasks on Book 4a, pages 115 and 118, which require the children to interpret and construct a simple line graph related to outdoor temperatures over a period of several hours.

4 Afterwards, ask questions like, *What do you think the temperature would have been at 8 am? (at 5 pm?) Why?* to see if they can extrapolate, i.e. estimate measurements outside the range of the plotted points on the axes.

EXTENSION

■ Using the graph drawn for task 2 on Book 4a, page 118, the children write at least five different sentences starting like this:
– The temperature rose ...°C between ... and ....
– The temperature dropped ...°C between ... and ....

D Shadow graph C I

1 Discuss what happens to shadows on sunny days. Ask, *How does your shadow change during the day? When is it at its longest (shortest)? Why? Do they always face in the same direction?*

2 Introduce the tasks on Book 4a, pages 116 and 117 in which the children have to:
(a) interpret a line graph showing the variations in length of the shadow of a stick taken at half-hourly intervals;
(b) make simple estimates about time and length by interpreting between and outside the range of the plotted points.

Resources
Scheme
Book 4a, pages 116 and 117

It is assumed that the children will have had experience of measuring the length of shadows using themselves or sticks.

E Assessment activity   I

1 Mask the text on Book 4a, page 115 so that only the graph can be seen.

2 Ask the child to explain the graph to you.

3 Ask the child to tell you:
- the time when the temperature was 6°C;
- the temperature at noon;
- how much the temperature rose between 9 am and 10 am;
- an estimated temperature at 5 pm.

4 Either ask the child to show you a line graph he or she has constructed and to explain this to you or to provide information on a table like the one on the right and ask the child to construct a line graph on squared paper. (Give help with preparing the axes if required.)

Resources

Scheme
Resource Master A (1cm squared grid); Book 4a, page 115

Time	9am	11am	1pm	3pm	5pm	7pm
Temperature (°C)	11	16	19	18	15	11

Assessment notes

Oral response	✔
Practical response	
Pictorial response	✔
Written response	

The child has:
explained the purpose of a simple line graph;
AND
interpreted it by answering related questions;
AND
constructed a line graph.

STRENGTHENING ACTIVITIES

Extending the bar-line graph

If the child has difficulty interpreting simple line graphs, revise the construction of bar-line graphs but mark the tops of the lines with a cross or point in a contrasting colour. The child copies the axes but now transfers the points only to this graph and joins them in order.

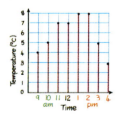 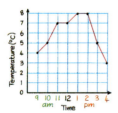

Construction

If the child cannot construct line graphs, he or she may benefit from having the axes drawn and labelled in advance so that he or she need only plot the points. (This requires skills similar to reading co-ordinates.)

CHALLENGING ACTIVITIES

Provide more complicated information such as this for the child to try to design suitables axes so that all the information can be displayed.

Sunflower growth

Age in weeks	1	2	3	4	5	6	7	8	9	10	11	12	13	14
Height in cm	15	33	64	99	133	170	208	231	245	252	254	256	257	257

Afterwards, the child can write down questions to ask about the graph or facts he or she can deduce from it (compare RM 137).

IDEAS BOARD

■ Typical projects

Time; Growth; Hot and Cold; Weather; Water; Candles; Shadows

■ Science

Line graphs can evolve naturally out of experiments involving sequences of time, including some suitable for extended surveys. For example,

(a) Evaporation: record the rate of evaporation of, say, 200 ml of water in different open containers. Make a line graph of each set of results, compare them and make some conclusions.

(b) Cool the same amount of water in containers insulated in different ways and record the temperature every minute. Record as line graphs and compare results.

(c) Record the growth of fast-growing plants at weekly intervals, grown in different conditions and represent the results as line graphs to compare.

(d) Compare the length of shadows measured at regular intervals during a sunny summer's and winter's day and display as line graphs.

(e) Graph monthly the weight of babies from birth to a year. Does the weight increase evenly throughout the year or not?

■ Comparing line graphs

Using, say, eight points each time related to the daily temperature, can the children explain the trends in temperature, recorded hourly from 9 am to 4 pm throughout the day. How much did the temperature rise (fall) between these times?

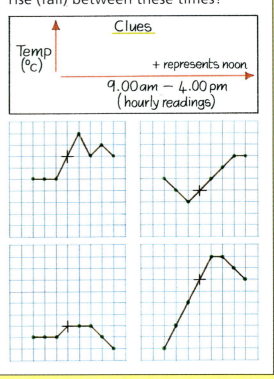

HOME/SCHOOL PROJECTS

Find examples of line graphs in magazines and papers to take to school for discussion, comparison and display. What information do they provide?

SUPPORT MATERIALS

Teachers' reference materials
Maths Plus: Graphs 2, Paul Harling (Ward Lock Educational)
Spectrum Maths: Data Handling (Collins Educational)
Practical Handling Data, Book 4, Glyn Davies (Hodder and Stoughton)

Software
Junior PinPoint (Longman Logotron)
Our Facts (NCET)
Clipboard (BlackCat Software)

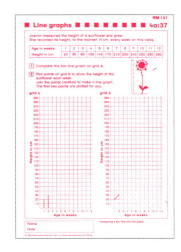

STEPS 4a

38. LOCATION

LEARNING CONTEXT

Contribution made by this Step

These activities bring together the children's experiences of angles, compass directions, length and co-ordinates. The children are introduced to ways of using angle and distance to locate and define position; familiar compass directions are used to specify and illustrate angles.

Objectives

To enable children to:
a Use and interpret instructions related to angle (direction) and distance.

Background

Previous work on co-ordinates (Step 14) has shown how to define position by use of an 'ordered pair' of numbers which specify distances from a vertical and then a horizontal axis. These are sometimes called Cartesian co-ordinates or rectangular co-ordinates.

An alternative way of describing the position of a point is to specify its distance from a fixed point (the origin), and angle (amount of turn) from a fixed direction. At this stage, these ideas should be dealt with informally, using points of the compass to denote direction, giving children the chance to explore the idea without too much concern about the conventions or rules related to the use of polar co-ordinates.

It is important to ensure that the children are familiar with the eight points of the compass before working on this Step.

Formal measurement of angles in degrees is dealt with in later handbooks.

> **Mathematics in the National Curriculum**
>
> **Programme of Study: KS2**
> Pupils should be taught to:
> ■ use co-ordinates to specify location, *e.g. map references, representation of 2-D shapes.* (SSM 3.b)
> ■ use right angles, fractions of a turn and, later, degrees, to measure rotation, and use the associated language. (SSM 3.c)
> ■ select and use the appropriate mathematics and materials. (UA 2.a)

You may later wish to introduce the term 'polar co-ordinates' for this way of representing position.

THINKING AND TALKING MATHEMATICALLY

Starting points for discussion

Place an object on a table. *How can you describe the exact position of the object? Can you think of other ways to describe the exact position?*

Place a directional compass on a table in the centre of the room. *What is North, South, ... North-East ... of that table? How many metres away from the table?*

Display a local map. *What is to the West of the school building? About how far away is it?*

> **Key language**
>
> compass, direction, location, polar grid, distance, route, map, LOGO, (cardinal points of the compass), clockwise, anticlockwise, journey, angle, turn

STEPS 4a

ACTIVITIES IN DETAIL

A Specifying location (distance and direction) C P

Resources

School
Demonstration polar grid*

Scheme
Resource Master 138, one copy between two; Book 4a, pages 119 and 120

*In advance, prepare a demonstration polar grid on the board or on an OHP transparency, using RM 138 as the model.

1 Revise working with Cartesian or rectangular co-ordinates (Steps 3b:14 and 4a:14). Make sure that they understand the conventional notation and can read and plot points.

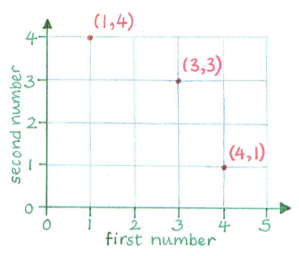

Can you plot the point (0, 2)?

2 Introduce the polar grid, pointing out its main features:
– the eight points of the compass;
– the numbered circles with a common centre, shown at 1cm intervals.

3 Ask, *Can you suggest ways in which the places (points) where lines cross could be identified?*

4 Discuss the suggestions but lead the children towards the convention of noting the distance first, followed by the direction.

5 Invite children, working in pairs, to plot specified points on the grid or on RM 138.

6 Indicate some intersections on the demonstration grid. Invite children to tell you the position by stating the distance and direction.

7 Still working in pairs, ask the children to take turns to describe and plot (or vice versa) points on the grid, using their shared copy of RM 138.

Book 4a, pages 119 and 120, provides additional practice in writing and reading positions identified by distance and direction.

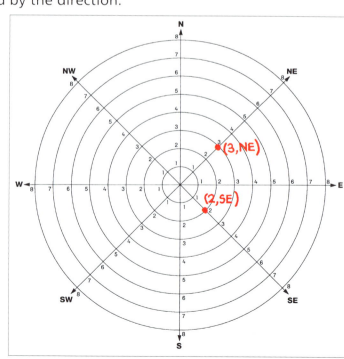

EXTENSION

■ The children work in pairs to invent and play a simple game plotting points on the grid, selecting the materials and the mathematics.

B Relative location

1 The children work in pairs in an open space. Each child has a directional compass. Partner a stands still, then decides how far away, and in which direction (using the eight points of the compass), partner b should stand.

2 Partner b measures out the distance, moving in the specified direction. He/she then stands in the specified position, looking towards partner a.

3 Ask, *What is the position of b in relation to a? What is the position of a in relation to b?*

Resources
School
Directional compass; large recording sheets; trundle wheels or 20 m measuring tape; local, regional and national maps

Scheme
Book 4a, page 121

Morag is six metres South-East of James.

James is six metres North-East of Morag.

Stage 1 provides good practice in estimating distances, since there may not be sufficient space to allow the specified distance!

4 Encourage them to position themselves so that the 'opposite' relationship of every pair of directions has been illustrated: N and S, E and W, SE and NW, SW and NE. Ask, *What happens to the distance between you?* (It stays the same.) *What changes when each of you looks towards the other?* (The directions are reversed.)

5 Show local, regional or national maps. Ask the children to work in pairs, finding places in various compass directions from their home town. *About how far away are they?*

Book 4a, page 121, offers further practice in defining relative location, using distance and direction.

C Moving points

1 Draw a grid of squares on the board and a list of the eight points of the compass (or a compass rose). Ask children in turn to tell you directions and numbers of squares to cross, to draw a sequence of lines on the grid.

2 After each instruction, cross off the specified direction from the list or rose until all have been deleted.

Resources
Scheme
Book 4a, page 122;
Resource Master A (1 cm squared grid)

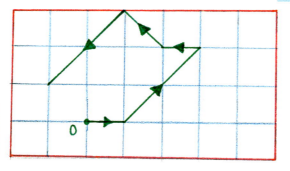

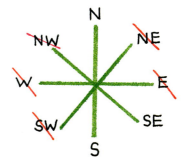

Where should the line go now to use all the points of the compass?

3 Next, mark a point on the grid and ask the children to tell you a sequence of 'numbers of squares to cross' and directions, to draw a triangle. After each instruction, draw the line.

4 List the instructions. Ask, *Can you list the instructions to draw the shape by moving in the opposite direction?*

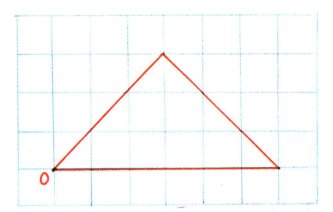

Start at O.
Cross 6 squares E.
Then cross 3 squares NW.
Then cross 3 squares SW.

Start at O.
Cross 3 squares NE.
Then cross 3 squares SE.
Then cross 6 squares W.

Further practice in following distance and direction instructions to draw shapes can be found in Book 4a, page 122.

EXTENSION

■ Ask the children to draw the outline of an island on squared grid paper (RM A or I). They plan and draw a route to reach the treasure chest from the landing position. Ask, *Can you describe the route to return to the landing position? Can you describe a new return route which never crosses the first route?*

D Assessment activity

1 Show a copy of RM 138. Ask the child to plot three or four specified points (intersections).

2 Indicate three or four points. Ask the child to tell you what they are in terms of distance and direction.

3 Ask the child to mark, label and join four points on the grid so that a quadrilateral is drawn.

Resources

Scheme
Resource Master 138

Assessment notes

Oral response	✔
Practical response	✔
Pictorial response	✔
Written response	✔

The child has:
correctly plotted points on a 'distance and direction' grid;
AND
correctly described some intersections, using appropriate terminology and symbols;
AND
chosen, plotted and joined points to draw a simple shape.

STRENGTHENING ACTIVITIES

Missing links

Provide a simple shape drawn on a polar grid, and a list of the polar co-ordinates with some numbers missing. Ask the children to find the missing numbers.

Random points

Use RM 138. Ask the children to stick a pin on the grid, with their eyes closed. *Which is the nearest intersection? What are its (polar) co-ordinates?*

CHALLENGING ACTIVITIES

Between directions

A small group of children use reference material to research into the direction halfway between, say, North and North-West. It is called North-North-West. Why? Ask them to try to create a polar grid which includes the extra directions. Encourage them to describe the method used and present findings to some other children.

Maps

Use atlases to find positions (distance and direction) of other countries in relation to Britain.

IDEAS BOARD

■ Typical projects
Journeys; Maps and Plans; Communications; Routes

■ Globes
Examine a globe, looking at the North or South Pole. Discuss the similarities and differences between the lines (of longitude and latitude) and the polar grid on which they have been working.

■ Art
The children make patterns and pictures on the polar grid. *Can they describe their patterns by referring to distance and direction?*

■ Home to school
Children borrow a simple directional compass. They can (carefully!) travel home in pairs, observing changing directions and distances in paces. Then they can draw simple sketch maps of the route.

■ Half-informed
Use RM 138. Explore the possible positions of intersections if:
– only the distance is specified;
– only the direction is specified;
– the distance is 0 (zero).

■ Turtles
Use *Dart*, *Arrow*, or LOGO to investigate ways to draw geometrical shapes. Encourage the children to find an amount of turn to the left or right which will rotate the turtle half a right angle.

■ Geography
Check for links with the Programme of Study for Key Stage 2 Geography.

HOME/SCHOOL PROJECTS

Ask the children to discuss with people at home the 'directions and distances' to the homes of friends and relations. How many children have friends who live in each direction? Who lives the furthest distance away?

SUPPORT MATERIALS

Teaching aids
Mazes - Photocopiable (LDA)
Directional Compass (NES Arnold)
Mariner's Compass (Hope Education)
Pocket Compass (Hope Education)

Teachers' reference materials
Prism Pack 14: Maps and Mazes (The Mathematical Association)
Maths Plus: Angles and Length, Paul Harling (Ward Lock Educational)
Primary Mathematics Today, 3rd edn, chapters 5, 20 and 34, Elizabeth Williams and Hilary Shuard (Longman)

Software
Maze from *MicroSMILE 1* (ILECC)
Crash from *Microprimer* (MEP)
Goldhunt from *MicroSMILE 1* (ILECC)
Pirates from *Micros in the Primary Classroom* (Longman Logotron)
The Lost Frog (ESM)
Mapping Skills (ESM)

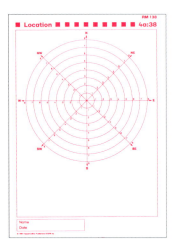

SECTION THREE
SUPPORTING INFORMATION

CALCULATORS

Calculators in the National Curriculum

The National Curriculum Council stated in the Non-Statutory Guidance for Mathematics (1989) that calculators should be available for pupils to use at all four key stages (E5, paragraph 4.1). It suggested that in learning to use calculators children should have the opportunity to:

- become familiar with the number operations to be performed by calculators;
- explore the way a calculator works through a variety of number games and similar activities;
- develop confidence in selecting correct key sequences for various calculations;
- use mental methods to estimate for expected answers, check for reasonableness and interpret results;
- use calculators as a powerful means of exploring numbers and to extend this understanding of the nature of numbers and number relationships.

More recently, the Programmes of Study for Key Stage 1 and Key Stage 2 (1995) also state that children should have the opportunity to use calculators to explore numbers and number structure, and as a tool for calculating with realistic data.

Background

In the belief that children should be introduced to calculators as early as is feasible, a range of calculator activities was introduced and extended in many Steps of Handbooks 1, 2, 3a and 3b. Most children will have already begun to see the calculator as a tool to use alongside other methods in their mathematical activities. Continued experience of the calculator as a positive aid to learning is therefore essential and so suggestions for the use of calculators have been included in many of the Steps in Handbook 4a.

The overall aim is to encourage the children to make independent and sensible use of calculators in the various aspects of their lives.

Key language

calculator, calculate, machine, button, key, operate, press, enter, clear, display, numbers, numerals, add(ition), subtract(ion), multiply, multiplication, divide, division, odd, even, equals, constant, function, estimate, estimation, place value.

A sequence of content and skills objectives

1 Recognising, matching and reading numerals in handwritten, printed, keyboard and display forms.
2 Using the calculator to create and check one- and two-step addition and subtraction bonds.
3 Given an unfinished number sentence, choosing the operation key $\boxed{+}$ or $\boxed{-}$ to create a number display.
4 Using a calculator to illustrate the inverse nature of the processes of addition and subtraction.
5 Entering the constant functions for addition and subtraction.
6 Using the constant functions for addition and subtraction to 'count on' and 'count back' in ones, twos, threes, fives and tens.
7 Using a calculator as an aid to continuing a given sequence of numbers.

8 Recognising multiplication as repeated addition, using a calculator to illustrate the process.

9 Using a calculator to create and check multiplication bonds.

10 Recognising division as repeated subtraction, using a calculator to illustrate the process.

11 Using of a calculator in simple chain calculations involving the four rules of number.

12 Using a calculator to check estimations based on rounded numbers.

13 Using a calculator in money calculations, making use of the decimal point.

14 Using a calculator in simple investigations and puzzles.

15 Using a calculator to create simple number patterns.

16 Using a calculator to generate examples to test predictions.

17 Using a calculator with large numbers.

18 Making appropriate use of a calculator in other aspects of the whole curriculum.

This set of objectives is adapted from *Calculated to Please: Calculator Activities for the National Curriculum*, Books 1, 2 and 3, by Paul Harling (Collins Educational) which includes comprehensive teaching notes and photocopiable resources for the children.

EQUIPMENT SUMMARY

Checklist 1

Resources needed for **Activities in Detail** in Handbook 4a.

NB – *Brand names in italics*

Equipment \ STEPS	1	2	3	4	5	6	7	8	9	10	11	12	13	14	15	16	17	18	19	20	21	22	23	24	25	26	27	28	29	30	31	32	33	34	35	36	37	38
Base 10 materials	•																																					
Abaci (4-, 5-, 6-spike)		•																																				
Calculators			•	•			•				•		•				•		•		•		•	•		•	•											
2-D geometric shapes (regular and non-regular)				•																								•				•				•		
3-D geometric shapes					•														•																			
Geostrips					•				•																													
Clockfaces (12-hour, 24-hour)				•				•																														
Gummed paper geometric shapes																																				•		
Cuisenaire Rods			•																																			
Metre rules (cm divisions)			•																																			
Geared clockface						•																																
Clockface rubber stamps (12-, 24-hour)						•	•																															
Stopwatches or timers						•																																
24-hour digital clockface						•																																
Dice (blank, 1–6)												•																										
Wall number line 0–100									•																													
Pinboards																			•																			
Geometric shape stencils/templates								•																•				•				•						
Counters (assorted sizes)								•																	•			•										
Rulers (mm divisions)																					•																	
Surveyors' tapes																	•	•																				
Trundle wheels																	•	•																				
Place value rubber stamps										•																												
Polydron or Clixi Tiles (square, triangular)										•		•																										
Kugeli																									•													
Osmiroid Magnispectors																•																						
Balance-scales															•	•																						
1g, 5g, 10g, 20g, 50g, 100g, 500g, 1kg weights																•																						
Centicubes																•																						
Spring balances																•																						
Compression scales																•																						
Bathroom scales																•																						
Electronic scales																•																						
Facsimilie coins and notes (all values)																	•							•														
Tape measures																	•	•																				
Interlocking cubes (Multilink or Clicubes)																			•			•										•						
Pattern Blocks																						•																
Playing cards																					•																	
Tocker Timers																										•							•					
Safety Mirrors or Miras																														•	•							
Pegboards and pegs																													•	•								
Logic blocks																																	•					
Calibrated and unmarked transparent containers																																		•				
Funnels																																		•	•			
Equivalent fraction board																																				•	•	
Directional compass																																						•

Checklist 2
Collectable items

Assorted boxes and containers
Colour magazines, catalogues, comics
Graphs from newspapers, magazines, etc.
Margarine tubs
Newspapers
Sand, grain, lentils, peas, etc.

Checklist 3
Everyday items

Assorted shape stencils and templates
Binca, embroidery threads and needles
Blu-Tack
Board games
Calendars, diaries, planners
Carbon paper
Crayons (wax, pastel, etc.)
Elastic bands
Felt-tipped pens – waterproof and water-based
Funnels
Glue (PVA; glue pens)
Large sheets of card/paper
Letter stencils or similar
Maps (national maps; large scale, local; street guide)
Mapping or glass-headed pins
Marker pens
Masking tape
Modelling clay
OHP Transparencies/pens
Paperclips
Plastic bags, assorted sizes
Plastic straws
Polystyrene beakers
Real coins and notes
Rubber bands
Rubber stamps and pads
Scissors
Small adhesive shapes
Small plastic bags
Sorting/storage trays
Sticky tape
String
Tracing paper

Checklist 4

Suppliers which no longer distribute certain resources have been removed. Where possible, alternative distributors are listed.

Suppliers' details

ABCeta Playthings Ltd
16 Torkington Road
Stockport, Cheshire SK7 4RG

Association of Teachers of Mathematics (ATM)
7 Shaftesbury Street
Derby DE3 8YB

Galt Educational
James Galt and Company Ltd
Brookfield Road
Cheadle
Cheshire SK8 2PN
(Galt Educational now distributes some Osmiroid products.)

Hope Education Ltd
Orb Mill
Huddersfield Road
Oldham
Lancs OL4 2ST

Learning Development Aids (LDA)
Duke Street
Wisbech, Cambs PE13 2AE

NES Arnold Ltd
Ludlow Hill Road
West Bridgeford
Nottingham NG2 6HD

Philip & Tacey
North Way
Andover
Hampshire SP10 5BA

Pictorial Charts Educational Trust
27 Kirchen Road
London W13 0UD

Playaway Supplies Ltd
Boundary Road
Shawfield Industrial Estate
Rutherglen
Glasgow G73 1DB

Tarquin Publications
Stradbroke, Diss
Norfolk IP21 4JP

Taskmaster Limited
Morris Road
Leicester LE2 6BR

Transatlantic Plastics
Lulworth Business Centre
Nutwood Way, Totton
Southampton SO40 3WW

Information Technology

ATM
7 Shaftesbury Street
Derby DE23 8YB

AUME
Wheathampstead Education Centre
Butterfield Road
Wheathampstead
Herts AL 4 8PY
(AUME now distributes software formerly available from AUM and AUCBE.)

BlackCat Education Software
3 Beacons View Mount Street
Brecon, Powys LD3 7LY

David Deacon
Felsted School, Dunmow
Essex CM6 3JG
(David Deacon now distributes software formerly available from MUSE.)

ESM
Abbeygate House
East Road, Cambridge CB1 1DB

LETSS
The Lodge, Crown Wood School
Riefield Road, London SE9 0AQ
(LETSS supplies ILECC and Capital Media software.)

Longman Logotron
124 Cambridge Science Park
Milton Road
Cambridge CB4 4ZS
(Longman Logotron supplies BBC Software.)

MAPE Computer Centre
Newman College
Jenners Lane, Bartley Green
Birmingham B32 3NT

NCET
Milburn Hill Road Science Park
Coventry CV4 7JJ
(NCET supplies MESU software.)

SMILE Mathematics
108a Lancaster Road
London W11 1QS

Swallow Systems
134 Cock Lane
High Wycombe, Bucks HP13 7EA

RM
New Mill House
183 Milton Park
Abingdon, Oxon OX 14 4SE

Valiant Technology
Myrtle House, 69 Salcott Road
London SW11 6DQ

Video Research Unit
Central TV, Central House
Broad Street, Birmingham B1 2JB
(Video Research Unit now distributes Central Software.)

STEPS MATHEMATICS

The complete published programme for STEPS MATHEMATICS includes the following components for National Curriculum mathematics for Key Stages 1 and 2.

STEPS 1

STEPS 1 Teacher's Handbook
(A4 loose-leaf file)
0 00 313824 0

STEPS 1 Activity Cards
(boxed set of 120)
0 00 313825 9

STEPS Activity Book 1a
(16 pages, 285 x 210mm)
0 00 312512 2 (pack of 10)

STEPS Activity Book 1b
(24 pages, 285 x 210mm)
0 00 312513 0 (pack of 10)

STEPS Activity Book 1c
(24 pages, 285 x 210mm)
0 00 312514 9 (pack of 10)

STEPS EXTRA Activity Book 1a
0 00 312630 7 (pack of 10)

STEPS EXTRA Activity Book 1b
0 00 312631 5 (pack of 10)

STEPS EXTRA Activity Book 1c
0 00 312632 3 (pack of 10)

STEPS 1 Activity Masters
(60 photocopiable pages)
0 00 312517 3

STEPS 1 Resource Masters
(A4 photocopiable masters)
0 00 312678 1

STEPS 2

STEPS 2 Teacher's Handbook
(A4 loose-leaf file)
0 00 313827 5

STEPS 2 Activity Cards
(Boxed set of 120)
0 00 313828 3

STEPS Activity Book 2a
(32 pages, 285 x 210mm)
0 00 312515 7 (pack of 10)

STEPS Activity Book 2b
(32 pages, 285 x 210mm)
0 00 312516 5 (pack of 10)

STEPS Activity Book 2c
(32 pages, 285 x 210mm)
0 00 312552 1 (pack of 10)

STEPS EXTRA Activity Book 2a
0 00 312633 1 (pack of 10)

STEPS EXTRA Activity Book 2b
0 00 312634 X (pack of 10)

STEPS EXTRA Activity Book 2c
0 00 312635 8 (pack of 10)

STEPS 2 Activity Masters
(86 photocopiable pages)
0 00 312518 1

STEPS 2 Resource Masters
(A4 photocopiable masters)
0 00 312679 X

STEPS 3

3a

STEPS 3a Teacher's Handbook
(A4 loose-leaf file)
0 00 313830 5

STEPS Textbook 3a (1)
(32pp, 245 x 189mm)
0 00 313831 3

STEPS Textbook 3a (2)
(64pp, 245 x 189mm)
0 00 313832 1

STEPS 3a Resource Masters
(A4 photocopiable masters)
0 00 312680 3

STEPS 3a Answer Book
0 00 312575 0 3

3b

STEPS 3b Teacher's Handbook
(A4 loose-leaf file)
0 00 313834 8

STEPS Textbook 3b
(96 pages, 245 x 189mm)
0 00 313835 6

STEPS 3b Resource Masters
(A4 photocopiable masters)
0 00 312681 1

STEPS 3b Answer Book
000 312576 9

STEPS 4

4a

STEPS 4a Teacher's Handbook
(A4 loose-leaf file)
0 00 313837 2

STEPS Textbook 4a
(128 pages, 245 x 189mm)
0 00 313838 0

STEPS 4a Resource Masters
(A4 photocopiable masters)
0 00 312682 X

STEPS 4a Answer Book
000 312577 7

4b

STEPS 4b Teacher's Handbook
(A4 loose-leaf file)
0 00 313840 2

STEPS Textbook 4b
(128 pages, 245 x 189mm)
0 00 313841 0

STEPS 4b Resource Masters
(A4 photocopiable masters)
0 00 312683 8

STEPS 4b Answer Book
000 312578 5

STEPS 5

STEPS 5 Teacher's Handbook
(A4 loose-leaf file)
0 00 313843 7

STEPS Textbook 5 (1)
0 00 313844 5

STEPS Textbook 5 (2)
0 00 312556 4

STEPS 5 Resource Masters
(A4 photocopiable masters)
0 00 313845 3

STEPS 5 Answer Book
000 312579 3

Plus **Evaluation Packs** for all Levels.

STEPS 4a ■ ■ ■ ■ ■ ■ ■ RM 143
Individual Record Sheet — Key Stage 2
Using and Applying Mathematics

Name _____ Date of birth _____

Has had opportunities to:	Y3			Y4			Y5			Y6		
	N	SSM	HD	N	SSM	HD	N	SSM	HD	N	SSM	HD
use and apply mathematics: – in practical tasks												
– in real-life problems												
– within mathematics itself.												
take increasing responsibility for organising and extending tasks.												
devise and refine his/her own ways of recording.												
ask questions and follow alternative suggestions to support the development of reasoning.												

Making and monitoring decisions to solve problems

		Y3			Y4			Y5			Y6		
selects the mathematics for some classroom activities	Ma1/LD2												
tries different approaches and finds ways of overcoming difficulties that arise when solving problems	Ma1/LD3												
is beginning to organise his/her work and check results	Ma1/LD3												
develops own strategies for solving problems and is using these strategies in working within mathematics...	Ma1/LD4												
...and in applying mathematics to practical contexts	Ma1/LD4												
in order to carry through tasks and solve mathematical problems, s/he identifies and obtains necessary information	Ma1/LD5												
checks his/her results, considering whether these are sensible	Ma1/LD5												

Table continues on RM 144

Ma1/LD2 means Attainment Target 1, Level Description 2. Such references may help you decide which level best describes that at which the child is working at the end of the Key Stage.

© 1995 CollinsEducational (an imprint of HarperCollins*Publishers*) STEPS 4a

STEPS 4a ■ ■ ■ ■ ■ ■ ■ ■ RM144

Individual Record Sheet (cont.) Key Stage 2
Using and Applying Mathematics

Name _____ Date of birth _____

Developing mathematical language and communication		Y3			Y4			Y5			Y6		
		N	SSM	HD	N	SSM	HD	N	SSM	HD	N	SSM	HD
discusses his/her work using familiar mathematical language...	Ma1/LD2												
...and is beginning to represent it using symbols and simple diagrams	Ma1/LD2												
discusses his/her mathematical work and is beginning to explain his/her thinking	Ma1/LD3												
uses and interprets mathematical symbols and diagrams	Ma1/LD3												
presents information and results in a clear and organised way, explaining the reasons for his/her presentation	Ma1/LD4												
shows understanding of situations by describing them mathematically using symbols, words and diagrams	Ma1/LD5												

Developing mathematical reasoning

asks and responds appropriately to questions including *'What would happen if...?'*	Ma1/LD2												
shows that s/he understands a general statement by finding particular examples that match it	Ma1/LD3												
searches for a pattern by trying out ideas of his/her own	Ma1/LD4												
makes general statements of his/her own, based on evidence s/he has produced...	Ma1/LD5												
...and gives an explanation of his/her reasoning	Ma1/LD5												

General comments (e.g. personal qualities, attitude to mathematics, etc.)

© 1995 CollinsEducational (an imprint of HarperCollins*Publishers*) STEPS 4a

STEPS 4a
RM 145

Mathematics Forecast Sheet

Teacher _____ Class _____ Period _____

Date	Topic	Main focus	STEPS Handbook
		Other references	3a: 3b: **4a:** 4b: 5:

Date	Topic	Main focus	STEPS Handbook
		Other references	3a: 3b: **4a:** 4b: 5:

Date	Topic	Main focus	STEPS Handbook
		Other references	3a: 3b: **4a:** 4b: 5:

Date	Topic	Main focus	STEPS Handbook
		Other references	3a: 3b: **4a:** 4b: 5:

Notes

© 1994 CollinsEducational (an imprint of HarperCollins*Publishers*) STEPS 4a

STEPS 4a Planning Sheet   RM 146

Class _____ Date _____ Handbook _____
Step number(s) _____ Starting point _____

ACTIVITY: Letter and title	C G P I	Resources

Other references _____
Cross-curricular links _____

STEPS 4a Planning Sheet   RM 146

Class _____ Date _____ Handbook _____
Step number(s) _____ Starting point _____

ACTIVITY: Letter and title	C G P I	Resources

Other references _____
Cross-curricular links _____

© 1994 CollinsEducational (an imprint of HarperCollins*Publishers*) STEPS 4a

STEPS 4a Individual Steps Record   RM 139

Name _____ Date of birth _____

Steps and objectives	Date attained/Comment
1. Place value (1) [Ma2/LD4] a Read, write and order numbers to 10 000 at least b Understand the effect of multiplying whole numbers by ten c Recognise whole numbers > 1000 divisible by ten d Approximate numbers > 1000 to the nearest 10 or 100	
2. Angles a Recognise and make acute, obtuse and reflex angles b Recognise perpendicular lines and planes	
3. Multiplication patterns (1) [Ma2/LD4] a Know and apply facts in the × 8 and 8 × tables b Understand the relationships between multiples of two, four and eight c Test simple related statements or generalisations	
4. Time (1) a Relate times shown on the 24-hour clock to everyday events b Convert 24-hour times to and from 12-hour times	
5. Addition (1) a Add mentally at least three one-digit numbers b Add mentally a one-digit number to a two-digit number c Apply knowledge of these facts to solve problems	
6. Bar-line graphs [Ma4/LD4] a Construct bar-line graphs b Read and interpret bar-line graphs using different scales to represent frequencies	
7. Subtraction (1) a Subtract mentally at least two single-digit numbers from 20 b Subtract mentally a one-digit number from a two-digit number c Solve problems or describe situations from which such subtractions might have arisen	
8. 2-D shape (1) a Know and use properties associated with triangles b Know and use language associated with triangles c Construct triangles from given information d Make generalisations or test statements about triangles	
9. Percentages [Ma2/LD4] a Understand and use simple percentages to describe situations b Know that a half, a quarter, three-quarters and multiples of a tenth can be expressed in different ways	
10. Length [Ma3/LD4] [Ma3/LD5] a Measure in millimetres with reasonable accuracy b Estimate or approximate to the nearest centimetre c Solve problems involving kilometres d Appreciate the relationships between metric units of length and know when it is sensible to use these units e Record lengths using numbers with up to one decimal place	
11. Addition (2) [Ma2/LD4] [Ma2/LD5] a Add a one-, two- or three-digit number to a three-digit number without a calculator or apparatus (totals < 999) b Choose methods to solve problems methodically c Estimate or approximate answers d Start to add numbers with totals > 1000	
12. 3-D shape [Ma3/LD4] a Construct tetrahedra, cuboids or cubes at least from given information or from provided nets b Use or interpret language relating to 3-D shapes c Revise the properties of other familiar 3-D shapes	
13. Subtraction (2) [Ma2/LD4] [Ma2/LD5] a Subtract a one-, two- or three-digit number from a three-digit number without a calculator or apparatus b Choose methods to solve problems methodically c Estimate or approximate answers	
14. Co-ordinates [Ma2/LD4] a Read and interpret co-ordinates in the first quadrant b Join co-ordinates in order to draw simple shapes	
15. Area & Perimeter [Ma3/LD4] a Construct simple 2-D shapes using data related to area or perimeter b Measure, compare and order areas using the square centimetre or other appropriate units of area c Test statements about areas or perimeters d Compare the square millimetre, centimetre, decimetre and metre	
16. Weight [Ma3/LD4] [Ma3/LD5] a Make sensible estimates in relation to weight b Solve practical and written problems involving weight c Record weights appropriately	
17. Decimal fractions [Ma2/LD4] a Understand and use decimal fractions to two decimal places in numbers up to ten b Interpret a calculator display to two decimal places c Start to add or subtract numbers to two places of decimals	

☒ has experienced
☒ has attained
S had strengthening activities
C had challenging activities

Attainment in Steps with a box like this [Ma2/LD4] may help you decide which level best describes that at which the child is working when you make your overall assessment at the end of the Key Stage. [Ma2/LD4] means Attainment Target 2, Level Description 4.

© 1995 Collins Educational (an imprint of HarperCollins*Publishers*) STEPS 4a

RM 140

Steps and objectives	Date attained/ Comment
18. Volume & Capacity (1) Ma3/LD4 a Estimate, measure and record volumes of 3-D shapes by counting centimetre cubes b Estimate, measure and record approximate capacities of small boxes by counting centimetre cubes	
19. Multiplication patterns (2) Ma2/LD4 a Know and apply facts in the x 6 or 6 x tables b Know and apply facts in the x 9 or 9 x tables c Understand simple relationships between multiples of three, six and nine d Test simple related statements or make generalisations	
20. Rotation Ma3/LD4 a Create patterns with rotational symmetry or rotate shapes systematically from given information b Choose the materials and mathematics to test polygons for rotational symmetry c Use or interpret language related to rotation	
21. Place value (2) a Read, write and order numbers to 100 000 at least b Understand the positional relationship between the digits c Relate numbers of this magnitude to some real-life examples	
22. Probability Ma4/LD5 a Use a probability scale marked 0, $\frac{1}{2}$, 1 to estimate and compare likelihood b Make and test predictions or statements related to simple experiments c Start to give and justify estimates of probability	
23. Division (1) a Solve division problems related to facts within the multiplication tables or suggest a situation from which a division expression might have arisen b Know division facts related to the x 6, x 8 or x 9 tables by quick recall c Start to interpret remainders shown on the calculator	
24. Money Ma2/LD4 a Extend experience of reading, writing and ordering amounts of money b Develop written methods to solve simple problems related to money, using all four operations c Use and interpret a calculator in the context of money	
25. Translation a Translate points or shapes a specified distance or in a given direction b Select the materials and mathematics to create simple patterns by translation and plan work methodically c Use or interpret language associated with translation	
26. Time (2) a Read and interpret 12- and 24-hour timetables b Estimate and measure duration in seconds c Extend awareness of the use and interpretation of calendars	
27. Multiplication Ma2/LD4 a Know facts in the x 7 or 7 x tables b Multiply two-digit numbers by a one-digit number with products not exceeding 300 c Solve multiplication problems without or with a calculator and consider the reasonableness of the answer	
28. 2-D shape (2) Ma3/LD4 a Know and use properties associated with quadrilaterals b Construct quadrilaterals from given information c Make simple generalisations or test statements	
29. Functions Ma2/LD4 Ma2/LD5 a Interpret function machines with more than one operation b Use function machines to investigate multiplication as the inverse of division c Explain how function machines operate, using associated terms, or how input and output numbers are related	
30. Division (2) Ma2/LD4 a Know and apply division facts related to the x 7 table b Use pencil-and-paper methods to solve division problems related to tables facts, without and with remainders c Develop pencil-and-paper methods to divide two-digit numbers by one-digit numbers with answers > 10 d Estimate or consider the reasonableness of answers, calculated without or with a calculator	
31. Reflection Ma2/LD4 a Create and analyse shapes and patterns with two (or more) axes of reflective symmetry b Use axes of symmetry as an aid to classification of 2-D shapes	
32. Logic a Use decision trees or Venn diagrams to represent the results of classification, using three criteria b Identify the attributes of objects within the regions of sorting diagrams	
33. Tessellation Ma3/LD4 a Continue or construct tessellations from given information b Test statements, hypothesise or make simple generalisations about the tessellating properties of triangles c Select the materials or mathematics to create a tessellation	
34. Scale Ma2/LD4 Ma3/LD4 a Revise measurement in millimetres and centimetres and co-ordinates in the first quadrant b Use halving and doubling to explore scale c Make simple hypotheses or generalisations	
35. Volume & Capacity (2) Ma3/LD4 a Make sensible estimates in relation to capacity b Solve problems related to capacity c Record appropriately	
36. Common fractions Ma2/LD4 a Explore practically the ordering and equivalence of fractions b Estimate and calculate simple fractions c Add and subtract simple fractions related to practical situations	
37. Line graphs Ma4/LD4 a Start to construct line graphs b Read and interpret line graphs	
38. Location a Use and interpret instructions related to angle (direction) and distance	

© 1995 Collins Educational (an imprint of HarperCollins*Publishers*) STEPS 4a

STEPS 4a Class Record

RM 141

- ◩ has experienced
- ⊠ has attained
- S had strengthening activities
- C had challenging activities

Name:	Place value (1)	Angles	Multiplication patterns (1)	Time (1)	Addition (1)	Bar-line graphs	Subtraction (1)	2-D shape (1)	Percentages	Length	Addition (2)	3-D shape	Subtraction (2)	Co-ordinates	Area & Perimeter	Weight
	1	2	3	4	5	6	7	8	9	10	11	12	13	14	15	16
	Ma2/LD4		Multiplication Ma2/LD4			Ma4/LD4			Ma2/LD4	Ma3/LD4 Ma3/LD5	Ma2/LD4 Ma2/LD5	Ma3/LD4	Ma2/LD4 Ma2/LD5	Ma2/LD4	Ma3/LD4	Ma3/LD4 Ma3/LD5

Attainment in Steps with a box like this Ma2/LD4 may help you decide which level best describes that at which the child is working when you make your overall assessment at the end of the Key Stage. Ma2/LD4 means Attainment Target 2, Level Description 4.

RM 14

	17	18	19	20	21	22	23	24	25	26	27	28	29	30	31	32	33	34	35	36	37	38	Identify and obtain information to solve problems	Interpret situations mathematically, using symbols or diagrams	Justify solutions to problems
	Decimal fractions	Volume & Capacity (1)	Multiplication patterns (2)	Rotation	Place value (2)	Probability	Division (1)	Money	Translation	Time (2)	Multiplication	2-D shape (2)	Functions	Division (2)	Reflection	Logic	Tessellation	Scale	Volume & Capacity (2)	Common fractions	Line graphs	Location			
	Ma2/LD4	Ma3/LD4	Ma2/LD4	Ma3/LD4		Ma4/LD5		Ma2/LD4			Ma2/LD4	Ma3/LD4	Ma2/LD4 Ma2/LD5	Ma2/LD4	Ma2/LD4		Ma3/LD4	Ma2/LD4 Ma3/LD4	Ma3/LD4	Ma2/LD4	Ma4/LD4				

© 1995 Collins Educational (an imprint of HarperCollins*Publishers*) STEPS 4a

Trim and butt to RM141 and stick, or hole punch and file